VMware vSphere 6.7 Clustering Deep Dive

VMware vSphere 6.7 Clustering Deep Dive

International Standard Book Number: ISBN 978-1719827461

 Cover design by DigitalMaterial.nl

Version: 1.0.1

ABOUT THE AUTHORS

Frank Denneman is a Senior Staff Architect working for VMware in the Office of CTO of the Cloud Platform business unit focusing on Resource Management. Frank is a VCDX (029) and co-author of the bestselling "vSphere Host Resources Deep Dive" book and "vSphere Clustering Deep Dive" series. Frank presents on a regular basis at global virtualization events and has been a VMworld Top 10 speaker for six consecutive years. You can find his articles at **www.frankdenneman.nl**. Follow Frank on Twitter @frankdenneman.

Duncan Epping is a Chief Technologist working for VMware in the Office of CTO of the Storage and Availability business unit focusing on hyper-converged infrastructure and data management. Duncan is a VCDX (007) and co-author of 8 books on the topic of VMware including "vSAN Essentials", and the "vSphere Clustering Deep Dive" series. He has 5 patents granted and 1 patent pending on the topic of availability, storage, and resource management. Duncan presents on a regular basis at global virtualization events like VMworld and international VMUGs. You can find his articles on **www.yellow-bricks.com** and you can follow him on twitter @DuncanYB.

Niels Hagoort is a freelance Virtualization Architect with more than 15 years of experience. He has extensive knowledge in the field of designing, building and implementing complex enterprise IT infrastructures. Niels is a VCDX (212) and co-author of the "vSphere Host Resources Deep Dive" book. Niels presents at global virtualization events like VMworld and international VMUGs on a regular basis. You can find his articles at **www.nielshagoort.com**. Follow Niels on Twitter @NHagoort.

INTRODUCTION AND ACKNOWLEDGEMENTS

In December of 2010 we published the very first version of this, now, deep dive series. We had no clue what we were getting ourselves in to. We knew however that we wanted to write a book, which had a different level of depth than most other virtualization related books out there. With over 200 pages on the topic of vSphere HA and DRS we felt we succeeded. Each edition after that added new chapters, use cases, recommended practices, and topics. Needless to say, when we started writing the first version early 2010, we never expected this series to sell over 50,000 copies worldwide.

For this edition of the book we decided to ask Niels Hagoort as the third author. As Niels has a vast experience in enterprise architectures, we felt that it would help aligning our content with you, the reader. On top of that, Niels also brings a deep expertise in networking, which adds a new dimension to this book. It helped he gained massive experience in creating a technical book as he co-authored the Host Deep Dive writing in 2017 with Frank.

At VMworld, in 2012, we met Chris Wahl. Chris was voted as Top vBlogger number 51 that year. We felt a connection with Chris, he understood and shared our passion for the VMware community and love for sharing information and knowledge. (Although the Dutch lion tattooed on his arm may also have helped.) Chris, like us, had a desire to dive deep yet distill to the core. We always appreciated and enjoyed his material, be it in writing or at an event on stage. We are happy he was willing to write the foreword for our book.

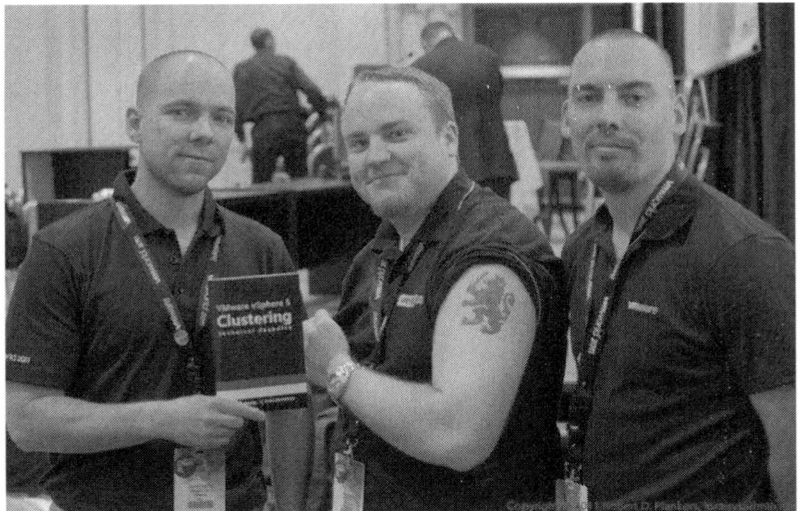

Figure 1: Photo from 2012

Before we start diving deep, there are a couple of things we like to share. First and foremost, the opinions expressed in this book are our personal opinions. Content published was not approved in advance by VMware and does not necessarily reflect the views and opinions of VMware.

We would like to thank our VMware management team (Christos Karamanolis, Charu Chaubal, Kit Colbert) for supporting us on this project. A special thanks goes out to our technical reviewers from VMware R&D: Aalap Desai, Komal Desai, Keith Farkas, Sahan Gamage, Lan Gao, Fei Guo, Sai Inabattini, Adarsh Jagadeeshwaran and Zhelong Pan. Also, a big thank you to community reviewer Marco van Baggum. Thanks for keeping us honest and contributing to this book.

We hope that you will enjoy reading this book as much as we did writing it.

Frank Denneman, Duncan Epping, Niels Hagoort

FOREWORD

The realm of technology is one that has traditionally been constructed on silos. We tend to fragment our skills into very specific areas of expertise, even going so far as to isolate the very people who run data center and cloud operations into little buckets of focus and energy. I'd like to think that this, more than anything, was the root cause for such painfully slow progress towards realizing the dream of a fully software defined data center. I had always felt a bit stifled by this organizational fragmentation and thirsted for a way to put my hands on just about any solution that shows the promise of removing the burden of manual processes. Since you're reading this book, I'll make the assumption that you have had similar thoughts.

The introduction of virtualization into the mainstream technology scene had two great rippling effects on the IT ecosystem: it brutally crushed a number of constraints and assumptions that were choking innovation for delivering applications while also building one of the most positive and influential communities I've yet to witness. Designing and implementing highly efficient vSphere environments required collaboration across technology and team silos and opened the door to many tech professionals who wanted something more from their career. As our grassroots community fought to virtualize anything and everything in our path, we did something incredibly smart by sharing this knowledge on the VMTN forums and across a wide swath of blogs. The VMware community is why I started blogging, sharing, and exploring what could be done to build some truly spectacular solutions for myself and others.

This adventure created a hunger that demanded more in depth and architecture-driven content for future design experts of the world to consume. In 2011, I picked up a copy of the recently released VMware vSphere 4.1 HA and DRS Technical Deepdive book with great anticipation because it focused on the core foundations of vSphere that underpin every virtualization design decision I'd ever need to make. I still have my signed physical copy sitting on the shelf riddled with colored flags and highlighted passages. And, to my delight, I was able to meet the authors - Duncan and Frank - while at VMworld 2011 to snap a photo with my clustering heroes and pick their brains about the book.

Truth be told, this was a bit of a pivot point in my career and stoked my resolve to create content for the community. I thought to myself, "here's two guys writing about their experiences solving real, tangible problems and sharing their knowledge to the betterment of others - I want in!" I can recall countless times where I used their content at my place of work or as part of my consulting engagements, especially when it came to the more obscure topics of co-stop, NUMA locality percentages, and designing around the old Automated Availability Manager architecture - bonus points if you remember AAM!

More than anything, these clustering deepdive books gave me the confidence to tackle larger and more complex design projects. This culminated into preparing for the VMware Certified Design Expert (VCDX) exam, which I took one year after first cracking open the first deepdive book. At the same time, I spent countless hours blogging about my areas of interest, such as using NFS datastores to run virtual machines (which was controversial at the time), and pouring entirely too much money into a home lab to quench my tinkering itch. Later, I was offered the opportunity to submit a book idea to VMware Press, which materialized into Networking for VMware Administrators.

Now days I focus my energy on tearing down technology and operational silos by recording shows for the Datanauts Podcast with fantastic community guests and my partner in crime and network aficionado, Ethan Banks. It is humbling to see tens of thousands of downloads for each episode and hear the success stories of those listening to our shows. I also have the extreme pleasure of running an amazing team of Technical Marketing Engineers at a startup named Rubrik. It really is my dream scenario and I am thankful for the opportunities presented to me at every turn.

Let's focus on your journey. Every adventure starts with a bold first step. For me, it was taking the time to read the delightfully informative clustering deepdive books and absorb all of the lessons there within. You now have that very same tome of knowledge in your hands with everything you need to be wildly successful with vSphere 6.7. What you do with this information is entirely up to you, but know that anything and everything is both possible and within reach with a little grit and some imagination!

Chris Wahl

Chief Technologist

Rubrik

P1

HIGH AVAILABILITY

01

INTRO TO VSPHERE HIGH AVAILABILITY

Availability has traditionally been one of the most important aspects when providing services. When providing services on a shared platform like VMware vSphere, the impact of downtime exponentially grows as many services run on a single physical machine. As such VMware engineered a feature called VMware vSphere *High Availability* (HA). VMware vSphere High Availability, hereafter simply referred to as HA, provides a simple and cost effective solution to increase availability for any application running in a *Virtual Machine* (VM) regardless of its operating system. It is configured using a couple of simple steps through *vCenter Server* (vCenter) and as such provides a uniform and simple interface. HA enables you to create a cluster out of multiple ESXi hosts. This will allow you to protect VMs and their workloads. In the event of a failure of one of the hosts in the cluster, impacted VMs are automatically restarted on other ESXi hosts within that same VMware vSphere Cluster.

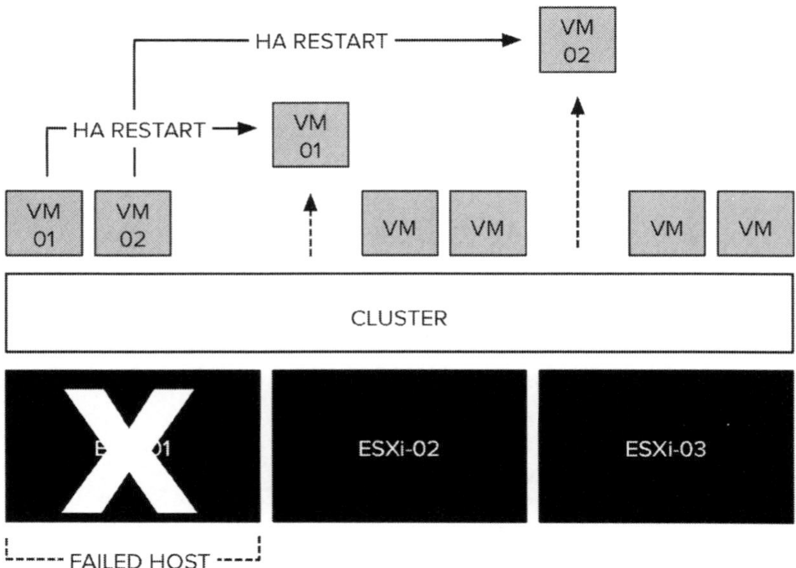

Figure 2: vSphere HA Concept

On top of that, in the case of a guest OS level failure, HA can restart the failed guest OS. This feature is called VM Monitoring, but is sometimes also referred to as VM-HA. This might sound fairly complex but again can be implemented with a single click.

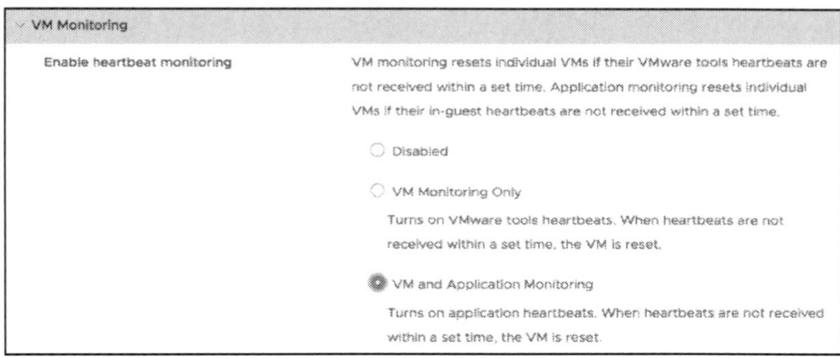

Figure 3: VM and Application Monitoring

Unlike many other clustering solutions, HA is a simple solution to implement and literally enabled within five clicks. On top of that, HA is widely adopted and used in all situations. However, HA is not a 1:1 replacement for solutions like *Microsoft Clustering Services* (MSCS) / *Windows Server Failover Clustering* (WSFC). The main difference between WSFC and HA being that WSFC was designed to protect stateful cluster-aware applications while HA was designed to protect any VM regardless of the type of workload within, but also can be extended to the application layer through the use of VM and Application Monitoring.

In the case of HA, a fail-over incurs downtime as the VM is literally restarted on one of the remaining hosts in the cluster. Whereas MSCS transitions the service to one of the remaining nodes in the cluster when a failure occurs. In contrary to what many believe, WSFC does not guarantee that there is no downtime during a transition. On top of that, your application needs to be cluster-aware and stateful in order to get the most out of this mechanism, which limits the number of workloads that could really benefit from this type of clustering.

One might ask why would you want to use HA when a VM is restarted and service is temporarily lost. The answer is simple; not all VMs (or services) need 99.999% uptime. For many services, the type of availability HA provides is more than sufficient. On top of that, many applications were never designed to run on top of an WSFC cluster. This means that there is no guarantee of availability or data consistency if an application is clustered with WSFC but is not cluster-aware.

In addition, WSFC clustering can be complex and requires special skills and training. One example is managing patches and updates/upgrades in a WSFC environment; this could even lead to more downtime if not operated correctly and definitely complicates operational procedures. HA however reduces complexity, costs (associated with downtime and MSCS), resource overhead and unplanned downtime for minimal additional costs. It is important to note that HA, contrary to WSFC, does not require any changes to the guest as HA is provided on the hypervisor level. Also, VM Monitoring does not require any additional software or OS modifications except for VMware Tools, which should be installed anyway as a best practice. In case even higher availability is required, VMware also provides a level of application awareness through Application Monitoring, which has been leveraged by partners like Symantec to enable application level resiliency and could be used by in-house development teams to increase resiliency for their application.

HA has proven itself over and over again and is widely adopted within the industry; if you are not using it today, hopefully you will be convinced after reading this section of the book.

vSphere 6.7

Before we dive into the main constructs of HA and describe all the choices one has to make when configuring HA, we will first briefly touch on what's new in vSphere 6.0 and describe the basic requirements and steps needed to enable HA. This book covers all the released versions of what is known within VMware as *Fault Domain Manager* (FDM), which was introduced with vSphere 5.0. We will call out the differences in behavior in the different versions where applicable, our baseline however is vSphere 6.7.

What's New?

Compared to vSphere 6.0 the changes introduced with vSphere 6.7 for HA are minor, however there were some significant changes with vSphere 6.5. Some of the new functionality will make the life of many of you much easier. Although the list is relatively short, from an engineering point of view many of these things have been an enormous effort as they required change to the deep fundaments of the HA architecture.

- Admission Control Enhancements
  - Revamped UI, with the default admission control policy now being "percentage based" but defined by the number of "host failures cluster tolerates"
  - The ability to specify the "performance degradation tolerated" by any VM

- Restart Priority Enhancements
    - Increase from 3 to 5 restart priority levels
    - Ability to specify when the next priority level should restart. Not limited to the start of the VMX process as in the past, but now also waiting for an X number of minutes etc.
- HA Orchestrated Restart
    - Ability to specify dependency between VMs using VM to VM rules
- ProActive HA
    - Ability to place a host in maintenance mode (or quarantine mode) when hardware (components) is degraded

This is just a short list and a brief description, in the chapters to follow we will go into detail for every single new and existing feature.

What is Required for HA to Work?

Each feature or product has very specific requirements and HA is no different. Knowing the requirements of HA is part of the basics we have to cover before diving into some of the more complex concepts. For those who are completely new to HA, we will also show you how to configure it.

Prerequisites

Before enabling HA, it is highly recommend validating that the environment meets all the prerequisites. We have also included recommendations from an infrastructure perspective that will enhance resiliency.

Requirements:

- Minimum of two ESXi hosts
- Minimum of 4 GB memory per host
- VMware vCenter Server

- Shared Storage for VMs
- Pingable gateway or other reliable address

Recommendation:

- Redundant Management Network (not a requirement, but highly recommended)
- 8 GB of memory or more per host
- Multiple shared datastores

Firewall Requirements

The following table contains the ports that are used by HA for communication. If your environment contains firewalls external to the host, ensure these ports are opened for HA to function correctly. HA will open the required ports on the ESXi firewall.

PORT	PROTOCOL	DIRECTION
8182	UDP	Inbound
8182	TCP	Inbound
8182	UDP	Outbound
8182	TCP	Outbound

Table 1: Firewall Ports

Configuring vSphere High Availability

HA can be configured with the default settings within a couple of clicks. The following steps will show you how to create a cluster and enable HA, including VM Monitoring, using the vSphere Client (HTML-5). Each of the settings and the design decisions associated with these steps will be described in more depth in the following chapters.

1. Click on the "Hosts & Clusters" view.
2. Right-click the Datacenter in the Inventory tree and click New Cluster.
3. Give the new cluster an appropriate name. We recommend at a minimum including the location of the cluster and a sequence

number ie. ams-hadrs-001.

4. Select Turn On vSphere HA.
5. Ensure "Enable host monitoring" and "Enable admission control" is selected.
6. If required, enable VM Monitoring by selecting VM Monitoring Only or VM and Application Monitoring in the dropdown.
7. Click "OK" to complete the creation of the cluster.

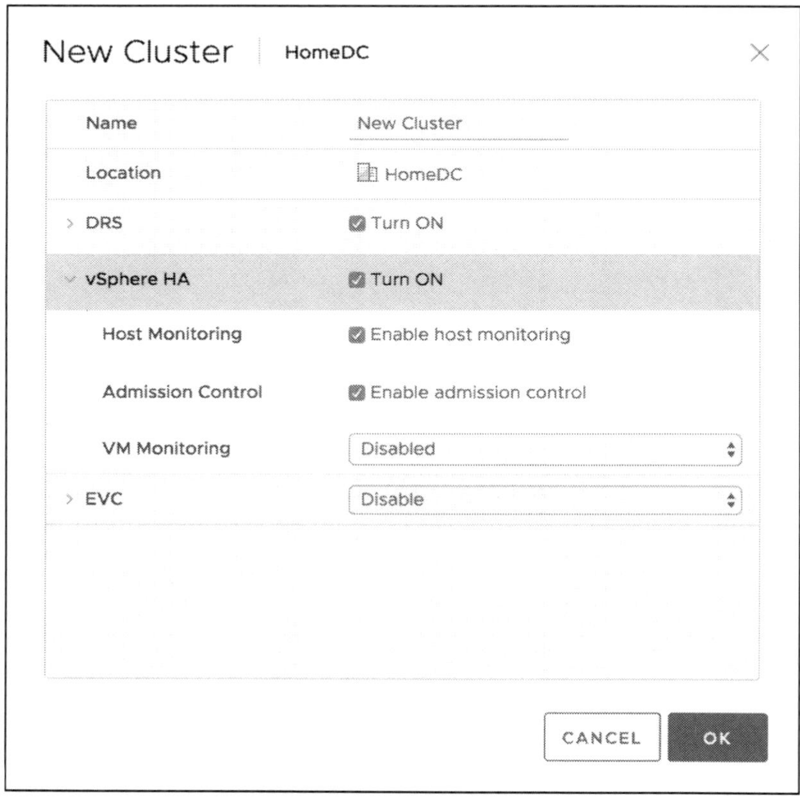

Figure 4: vSphere HA Configuration

When the HA cluster has been created, the ESXi hosts can be added to the cluster simply by right clicking the host and selecting "Move To", if they were already added to vCenter, or by right clicking the cluster and selecting "Add Host".

When an ESXi host is added to the newly-created cluster, the HA agent will be loaded and configured. Once this has completed, HA will enable protection of the workloads running on this ESXi host.

As we have clearly demonstrated, HA is a simple clustering solution that will allow you to protect VMs against host failure and operating system failure in literally minutes. Understanding the architecture of HA will enable you to reach that extra 9 when it comes to availability. The following chapters will discuss the architecture and fundamental concepts of HA. We will also discuss all decision-making moments to ensure you will configure HA in such a way that it meets the requirements of your or your customer's environment.

02

COMPONENTS OF HA

Now that we know what the pre-requisites are and how to configure HA the next steps will be describing which components form HA. Keep in mind that this is still a "high level" overview. There is more under the cover that we will explain in following chapters. The following diagram depicts a two-host cluster and shows the key HA components.

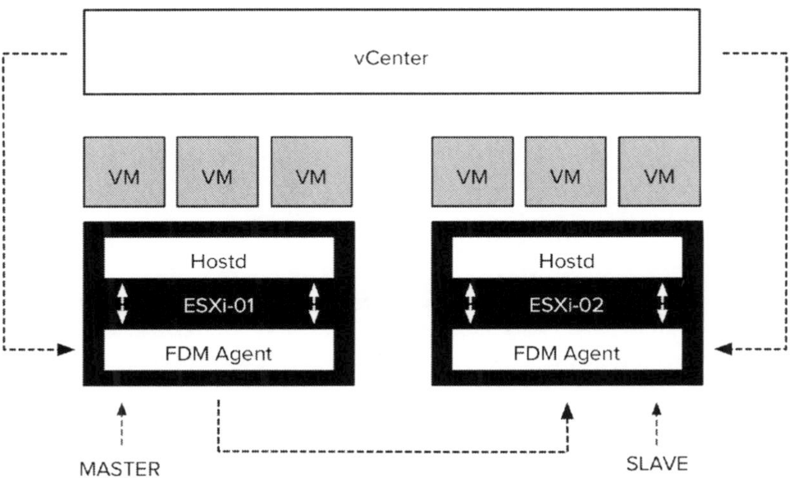

Figure 5: vSphere HA Components

As you can clearly see, there are three major components that form the foundation for HA:

- FDM
- HOSTD
- vCenter

The first and probably the most important component that forms HA is FDM (Fault Domain Manager). This is the HA agent. The FDM Agent is responsible for many tasks such as communicating host resource information, VM states and HA properties to other hosts in the cluster. FDM also handles heartbeat mechanisms, VM placement, VM restarts, logging and much more. We are not going to discuss all of this in-depth separately as we feel that this will complicate things too much.

FDM, in our opinion, is one of the most important agents on an ESXi host, when HA is enabled, of course, and we are assuming this is the case. The engineers recognized this importance and added an extra level of resiliency to HA. FDM uses a single-process agent. However, FDM spawns a watchdog process. In the unlikely event of an agent failure, the watchdog functionality will pick up on this and restart the agent to ensure HA functionality remains without anyone ever noticing it failed. The agent is also resilient to network interruptions and *all paths down* (APD) conditions. Inter-host communication automatically uses another communication path (if the host is configured with redundant management networks) in the case of a network failure.

HA has no dependency on DNS as it works with IP addresses only. This is one of the major improvements that FDM brought. This does not mean that ESXi hosts need to be registered with their IP addresses in vCenter; it is still a best practice to register ESXi hosts by its fully qualified domain name (FQDN) in vCenter.

Although HA does not depend on DNS, remember that other services may depend on it. On top of that, monitoring and troubleshooting will be much easier when hosts are correctly registered within vCenter and have a valid FQDN.

> **Although HA is not dependent on DNS, it is still recommended to**

register the hosts with their FQDN for ease of operations/management.

vSphere HA also has a standardized logging mechanism, where a single log file has been created for all operational log messages; it is called fdm.log. This log file is stored under `/var/log/` as depicted in the screenshot below.

Figure 6: FDM.log

Although typically not needed, we do recommend getting familiar with the fdm.log file as it will enable you to troubleshoot the environment when an issue has occurred. An example when the fdm.log will be very useful is the situation where VMs have been restarted without any apparent reason. The fdm.log file will show when the VMs have been restarted, but more importantly it will also inform you why VMs have been restarted, whether it was the result of a host, network or storage failure for instance.

> **Ensure syslog is correctly configured and log files are offloaded to a safe location to offer the possibility of performing a root cause analysis in case disaster strikes.**

HOSTD Agent

One of the most crucial agents on a host is HOSTD. This agent is responsible for many of the tasks we take for granted like powering on VMs. FDM talks directly to HOSTD and vCenter, so it is not dependent on VPXA, like in previous releases. This is, of course, to avoid any unnecessary overhead and dependencies, making HA more reliable than ever before and enabling HA to respond faster to power-on requests.

That ultimately results in higher VM uptime.

When, for whatever reason, HOSTD is unavailable or not yet running after a restart, the host will not participate in any FDM-related processes. FDM relies on HOSTD for information about the VMs that are registered to the host, and manages the VMs using HOSTD APIs. In short, FDM is dependent on HOSTD and if HOSTD is not operational, FDM halts all functions and waits for HOSTD to become operational.

vCenter

That brings us to our final component, the vCenter Server. vCenter is the core of every vSphere Cluster and is responsible for many tasks these days. For our purposes, the following are the most important and the ones we will discuss in more detail:

- Deploying and configuring HA Agents
- Communication of cluster configuration changes
- Protection of VMs

vCenter is responsible for pushing out the FDM agent to the ESXi hosts when applicable. The push of these agents is done in parallel to allow for faster deployment and configuration of multiple hosts in a cluster. vCenter is also responsible for communicating configuration changes in the cluster to the host which is elected as the master. We will discuss this concept of master and slaves in the following chapter. Examples of configuration changes are modification or addition of an advanced setting or the introduction of a new host into the cluster.

HA leverages vCenter to retrieve information about the status of VMs and, of course, vCenter is used to display the protection status of VMs. (What "VM protection" means will be discussed in later on). On top of that, vCenter is responsible for the protection and unprotection of VMs. This not only applies to user-initiated power-offs or power-ons of VMs, but also in the case where an ESXi host is disconnected from vCenter at which point vCenter will request the master HA agent to unprotect the affected VMs.

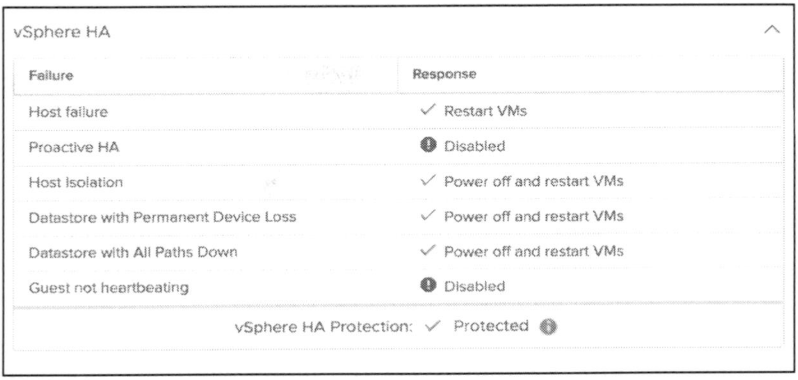

vSphere HA

Failure	Response
Host failure	✓ Restart VMs
Proactive HA	Disabled
Host Isolation	✓ Power off and restart VMs
Datastore with Permanent Device Loss	✓ Power off and restart VMs
Datastore with All Paths Down	✓ Power off and restart VMs
Guest not heartbeating	Disabled

vSphere HA Protection: ✓ Protected

Figure 7: VM Protection Status

Although HA is configured by vCenter and exchanges VM state information with HA, vCenter is not involved when HA responds to failure. It is comforting to know that in case of a host failure containing the virtualized vCenter Server, HA takes care of the failure and restarts the vCenter Server on another host, including all other configured VMs from that failed host.

There is a corner case scenario with regards to vCenter failure: if the ESXi hosts are so called “stateless hosts” and Distributed vSwitches are used for the management network, VM restarts will not be attempted until vCenter is restarted. For stateless environments, vCenter and Auto Deploy availability is key as the ESXi hosts literally depend on them.

If vCenter is unavailable, it will not be possible to make changes to the configuration of the cluster. vCenter is the source of truth for the set of VMs that are protected, the cluster configuration, the VM-to-host compatibility information, and the host membership. So, while HA, by design, will respond to failures without vCenter, HA relies on vCenter to be available to configure or monitor the cluster.

After deploying vCenter Server and configuring your cluster, we recommend setting the correct HA restart priorities for it. Although vCenter Server is not required to restart VMs, there are multiple components that rely on vCenter and, as such, a speedy recovery is desired. When configuring your vCenter VM with the highest priority for restarts, remember to include all services on which your vCenter server depends for a successful restart: DNS, Active Directory and MS SQL (or any other database server you are using).

> **In stateless environments, ensure vCenter and Auto Deploy are highly available as recovery time of your VMs might be dependent on them.**

> **Understand the impact of virtualizing vCenter. Ensure it has the highest priority for restarts and ensure that services which vCenter Server depends on are available: DNS, Active Directory and the potential external database server.**

03

FUNDAMENTAL CONCEPTS

Now that you know about the components of HA, it is time to start talking about some of the fundamental concepts of HA clusters:

- Master / Slave agents
- Heartbeating
- Isolated vs Network partitioned
- VM Protection
- Component Protection

Everyone who has implemented vSphere knows that multiple hosts can be configured into a cluster. A cluster can best be seen as a collection of resources. These resources can be carved up with the use of vSphere Distributed Resource Scheduler (DRS) into separate pools of resources or used to increase availability by enabling HA.

The HA architecture introduces the concept of master and slave HA agents. Except during network partitions, there is only one master HA agent in a cluster. Any agent can serve as a master, and all others are considered its slaves. A master agent is in charge of monitoring the health of VMs for which it is responsible and restarting any that fail. The slaves are responsible for forwarding information to the master agent and restarting any VMs at the direction of the master. The HA agent, regardless of its role as master or slave, also implements the VM/App monitoring feature which allows it to restart VMs in the case of an OS failure or restart services in the case of an application failure.

Master Agent

As stated, one of the primary tasks of the master is to keep track of the state of the VMs it is responsible for and to take action when appropriate. In a normal situation, there is only a single master in a cluster. We will discuss the scenario where multiple masters can exist in a single cluster in one of the following sections, but for now let's talk about a cluster with a single master. A master will claim responsibility for a VM by taking "ownership" of the datastore on which the VM's configuration file is stored.

> **To maximize the chance of restarting VMs after a failure we recommend masking datastores on a cluster basis. Although sharing of datastores across clusters will work, it will increase complexity from an administrative perspective.**

That is not all, of course. The HA master is also responsible for exchanging state information with vCenter. This means that it will not only receive but also send information to vCenter when required. The HA master is also the host that initiates the restart of VMs when a host has failed. You may immediately want to ask what happens when the master is the one that fails, or, more generically, which of the hosts can become the master and when is it elected?

Election

A master is elected by a set of HA agents whenever the agents are not in network contact with a master. A master election thus occurs when HA is first enabled on a cluster and when the host on which the master is running:

- fails
- becomes network partitioned or isolated
- is disconnected from vCenter Server
- is put into maintenance or standby mode
- when HA is reconfigured on the host

The HA master election takes approximately 15 seconds and is conducted using UDP. While HA won't react to failures during the election, once a master is elected, failures detected before and during the election will be handled. The election process is simple but robust. The host that is participating in the election with the greatest number of connected datastores will be elected master. If two or more hosts have the same number of datastores connected, the one with the highest Managed Object Id will be chosen. This however is done lexically; meaning that 99 beats 100 as 9 is larger than 1. For each host, the HA State of the host will be shown on the Summary tab. This includes the role as depicted in screenshot below where the host is a master host.

After a master is elected, each slave that has management network connectivity with it will setup a single secure, encrypted, TCP connection to the master. This secure connection is SSL-based. One thing to stress here though is that slaves do not communicate with each other after the master has been elected unless a re-election of the master needs to take place.

Configuration

Image Profile	(Updated) ESXi-6.7.0-8169922-standard
vSphere HA State	
Status	Running (Master)
Description	• The vSphere HA Agent on the host has been elected as the vSphere HA Master Agent. • This agent is monitoring the vSphere HA protected VMs running on this host and the other vSphere HA operational hosts, and will attempt to restart them after a failure.
Fault Tolerance (Legacy)	Unsupported
Fault Tolerance	Unsupported
EVC Mode	Intel® "Ivy Bridge" Generation

Figure 8: vSphere HA State - Master

As stated earlier, when a master is elected it will try to acquire ownership of all the datastores it can directly access or access by proxying requests to one of the slaves connected to it using the management network. For traditional storage architectures, it does this by locking a file called `protectedlist` that is stored on the datastores in an existing cluster. The master will also attempt to take ownership of any datastores it discovers along the way, and it will periodically retry any it could not take ownership of previously.

The naming format and location of this file is as follows:

```
/<root of datastore>/.vSphere-HA/<cluster-specific-
directory>/protectedlist
```

For those wondering how "cluster-specific-directory" is constructed:

```
<uuid of vCenter Server>-<number part of the MoID of the cluster>-
<random 8 char string>-<name of the host running vCenter Server>
```

The master uses this protectedlist file to store the inventory. It keeps track of which VMs are protected by HA. Calling it an inventory might be slightly overstating: it is a list of protected VMs and it includes information around VM CPU reservation and memory overhead. The master distributes this inventory across all datastores in use by the VMs in the cluster. The next screenshot shows an example of this file on one of the datastores.

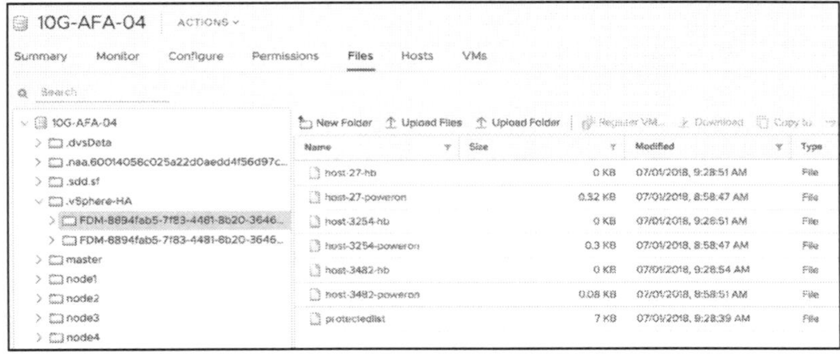

Figure 9: vSphere HA Files

Now that we know the master locks a file on the datastore and that this file stores inventory details, what happens when the master is isolated or fails? If the master fails, the answer is simple: the lock will expire and the new master will relock the file if the datastore is accessible to it.

In the case of isolation, this scenario is slightly different, although the result is similar. The master will release the lock it has on the file on the datastore to ensure that when a new master is elected it can determine the set of VMs that are protected by HA by reading the file. If, by any chance, a master should fail right at the moment that it became isolated, the restart of the VMs will be delayed until a new master has been elected. In a scenario like this, accuracy and the fact that VMs are restarted is more important than a short delay.
Let's assume for a second that your master has just failed. What will happen and how do the slaves know that the master has failed? HA uses a point-to-point network heartbeat mechanism. If the slaves have received no network heartbeats from the master, the slaves will try to elect a new master. This new master will read the required information and will initiate the restart of the VMs within roughly 10 seconds.

Restarting VMs is not the only responsibility of the master. It is also responsible for monitoring the state of the slave hosts and reporting this state to vCenter Server. If a slave fails or becomes isolated from the management network, the master will determine which VMs must be restarted. When VMs need to be restarted, the master is also responsible for determining the placement of those VMs. It uses a placement engine that will try to distribute the VMs to be restarted evenly across all available hosts.

All of these responsibilities are really important, but without a mechanism to detect a slave has failed, the master would be useless. Just like the slaves receive heartbeats from the master, the master receives heartbeats from the slaves so it knows they are alive.

Slaves

A slave has substantially fewer responsibilities than a master: a slave monitors the state of the VMs it is running and informs the master about any changes to this state.

The slave also monitors the health of the master by monitoring heartbeats. If the master becomes unavailable, the slaves initiate and participate in the election process. Last but not least, the slaves send heartbeats to the master so that the master can detect outages. Like the master to slave communication, all slave to master communication is point to point. HA does not use multicast.

Configuration

Image Profile	(Updated) ESXi-6.7.0-8169922-standard
⌄ vSphere HA State	
Status	Connected (Slave)
Description	• The vSphere HA Agent on the host is connected to a vSphere HA Master Agent over the management network. • This state is the normal operating state for agents that are not the vSphere HA Master Agent. • The vSphere HA protected VMs on this host are monitored by one or more vSphere HA Master Agents, and the agents will attempt to restart the VMs after a failure.
› Fault Tolerance (Legacy)	Unsupported
› Fault Tolerance	Unsupported
› EVC Mode	Intel® "Ivy Bridge" Generation

Figure 10: vSphere HA State - Slave

Files for Both Slave and Master

Before explaining the details, it is important to understand that both *Virtual SAN* (vSAN) and *Virtual Volumes* (VVol) have introduced changes to the location and the usage of files. For specifics on these two different storage architectures we like to refer you to those respective sections in the book.

Both the master and slave use files not only to store state, but also as a communication mechanism. We've already seen the protectedlist file used by the master to store the list of protected VMs. We will now discuss the files that are created by both the master and the slaves. Remote files are files stored on a shared datastore and local files are files that are stored in a location only directly accessible to that host.

Remote Files

The set of powered on VMs is stored in a per-host "poweron" file. It should be noted that, because a master also hosts VMs, it also creates a "poweron" file. The naming scheme for this file is as follows: `host-number-poweron`

Tracking VM power-on state is not the only thing the "poweron" file is used for. This file is also used by the slaves to inform the master that it is isolated from the management network: the top line of the file will either contain a 0 or a 1. A 0 (zero) means not-isolated and a 1 (one) means isolated. The master will inform vCenter about the isolation of the host.

Local Files

As mentioned before, when HA is configured on a host, the host will store specific information about its cluster locally.

```
[root@esxi-dell-g:/etc/opt/vmware/fdm] ls -lah
total 28
drwxr-xr-x    1 root     root          512 Jul 25 19:13 .
-r-------T    1 root     root            0 May 17 06:11 .#clusterconfig
-r-------T    1 root     root            0 May 17 06:11 .#hostlist
-r-------T    1 root     root            0 May 17 06:11 .#vmmetadata
drwxr-xr-x    1 root     root          512 Jun 21 13:34 ..
-rw------T    1 root     root         4.4K Jul 24 12:00 clusterconfig
-rw------T    1 root     root         2.3K May 17 06:11 fdm.cfg
-rw------T    1 root     root         2.9K Jul 24 12:00 hostlist
-rw------T    1 root     root         2.3K Jul 25 19:13 vmmetadata
[root@esxi-dell-g:/etc/opt/vmware/fdm]
```

Figure 11: vSphere HA Local Files

Each host, including the master, will store data locally. The data that is locally stored is important state information. Namely, the VM-to-host compatibility matrix, cluster configuration, and host membership list. This information is persisted locally on each host. Updates to this information is sent to the master by vCenter and propagated by the master to the slaves. Although we expect that most of you will never touch these files – and we highly recommend against modifying them – we do want to explain how they are used:

- **clusterconfig** This file is not human-readable. It contains the configuration details of the cluster.
- **vmmetadata** This file is not human-readable. It contains the actual compatibility info matrix for every HA protected VM and lists all the hosts with which it is compatible plus a vm/host dictionary.
- **fdm.cfg** This file contains the configuration settings around logging. For instance, the level of logging and syslog details are stored in here.
- **hostlist** A list of hosts participating in the cluster, including hostname, IP addresses, MAC addresses and heartbeat datastores.

Now although vmmetadata and clusterconfig are not human readable, this does not mean it is impossible to know what information is stored in them. The script prettyPrint.sh allows you to print the information in the above 4 files. For example, the command below prints the clusterconfig information.

```
/opt/vmware/fdm/fdm/prettyPrint.sh clusterconfig
```

If you use this command with "-h" all options will be provided, we feel these speak for itself. When troubleshooting however especially "hostlist" and "vmmetadata" will come in handy. The parameter "hostlist" will give you the host name and host identifier. This will make the fdm.log easier to digest. Below screenshot displays partly the information provided by the "hostlist" parameter.

```
[root@esxi-dell-g:/etc/opt/vmware/fdm] /opt/vmware/fdm/fdm/prettyPrint.sh hostlist
host-78<obj xmlns:xsd="http://www.w3.org/2001/XMLSchema" xmlns:xsi="http://www.w3.org/2001/XMLSchema-instance" xmlns="urn:csi" versionId="1.0" xsi:type="CsiHostList">
   <faultDomainId>ffb4e877-011b-46b6-b5f6-4c9d7e3ea5f7-7-9ac25da-vcsa-06</faultDomainId>
   <version>18</version>
   <host>
      <hostId>host-78</hostId>
      <hostName>esxi-dell-g.rainpole.com</hostName>
      <sslThumbprint>64:E8:64:66:2A:EC:8F:58:09:57:48:1E:37:0C:6E:73:1E:60:12:EA</sslThumbprint>
      <ipAddress>10.10.0.7</ipAddress>
      <mac>2A:6e:96:2f:48:50</mac>
      <mac>24:6e:96:2f:48:52</mac>
      <mac>24:6e:96:2f:48:54</mac>
      <mac>24:6e:96:2f:48:58</mac>
      <mac>a0:36:9f:56:dd:bc</mac>
      <mac>a0:36:9f:56:dd:be</mac>
      <heartbeatDatastore>/vmfs/volumes/5ac08Ab6-81dd612a-a39a-246e962f4918</heartbeatDatastore>
      <heartbeatDatastore>/vmfs/volumes/5a6f1dfb-65376d7c-a4af-246e962f4918</heartbeatDatastore>
      <hostdPort>443</hostdPort>
      <version>6.7.0</version>
      <build>8169922</build>
      <hostInfoState>KNOWN</hostInfoState>
   </host>
```

Figure 12: PrettyPrint.sh Hostlist Example

The “vmmetadata” parameter displays the compatibility list, although we haven’t covered the compatibility list yet it is good to know that this contains information about which VM can be restarted on which host.

Heartbeating

We mentioned it a couple of times already in this chapter, and it is an important mechanism that deserves its own section: heartbeating. Heartbeating is the mechanism used by HA to validate whether a host is alive. HA has two different heartbeating mechanisms. These heartbeat mechanisms allow it to determine what has happened to a host when it is no longer responding. Let’s discuss traditional network heartbeating first.

Network Heartbeating

Network Heartbeating is used by HA to determine if an ESXi host is alive. Each slave will send a heartbeat to its master and the master sends a heartbeat to each of the slaves, this is a point-to-point communication. These heartbeats are sent by default every second.

When a slave isn’t receiving any heartbeats from the master, it will try to determine whether it is Isolated– we will discuss “states” in more detail later on in this chapter.

> **Network heartbeating is key for determining the state of a host. Ensure the management network is highly resilient to enable proper state determination.**

Datastore Heartbeating

Datastore heartbeating adds an extra level of resiliency and prevents unnecessary restart attempts from occurring as it allows vSphere HA to determine whether a host is isolated from the network or is completely unavailable. How does this work?

Datastore heartbeating enables a master to more determine the state of a host that is not reachable via the management network. This datastore heartbeat mechanism is used in case the master has lost network connectivity with one, or multiple, slaves. The datastore heartbeat mechanism is then used to validate whether a host has failed or is merely isolated/network partitioned. Isolation will be validated through the "poweron" file which, as mentioned earlier, will be updated by the host when it is isolated. Without the "poweron" file, there is no way for the master to validate isolation. Let that be clear! Based on the results of checks of both files, the master will determine the appropriate action to take. If the master determines that a host has failed (no datastore heartbeats), the master will restart the failed host's VMs. If the master determines that the slave is Isolated or Partitioned, it will only take action when it is appropriate to take action. With that meaning that the master will only initiate restarts when VMs are down or powered down / shut down by a triggered isolation response.

By default, HA selects 2 heartbeat datastores – it will select datastores that are available on all hosts, or as many as possible. Although it is possible to configure an advanced setting (`das.heartbeatDsPerHost`) to allow for more datastores for datastore heartbeating we do not recommend configuring this option as the default should be sufficient for most scenarios, except for stretched cluster environments where it is recommended to have two in each site manually selected. This is extensively discussed in the Stretched Clusters section of this book. The selection process gives preference to VMFS over NFS datastores, and seeks to choose datastores that are backed by different LUNs or NFS servers when possible. If desired, you can also select the heartbeat datastores yourself. We, however, recommend letting vCenter deal with this operational "burden" as vCenter uses a selection algorithm to select heartbeat datastores that are presented to all hosts. This however is not a guarantee that vCenter can select datastores which are connected to all hosts. It should be noted that vCenter is not site-aware. In scenarios where hosts are geographically dispersed it is recommended to manually select heartbeat datastores to ensure each site has one site-local heartbeat datastore at minimum. More on this topic is covered in the Use Case section of this book, which discusses metro cluster deployments.

> **In a metro-cluster / geographically dispersed cluster we recommend setting the minimum number of heartbeat datastores to four. It is recommended to manually select site local datastores, two for each site.**

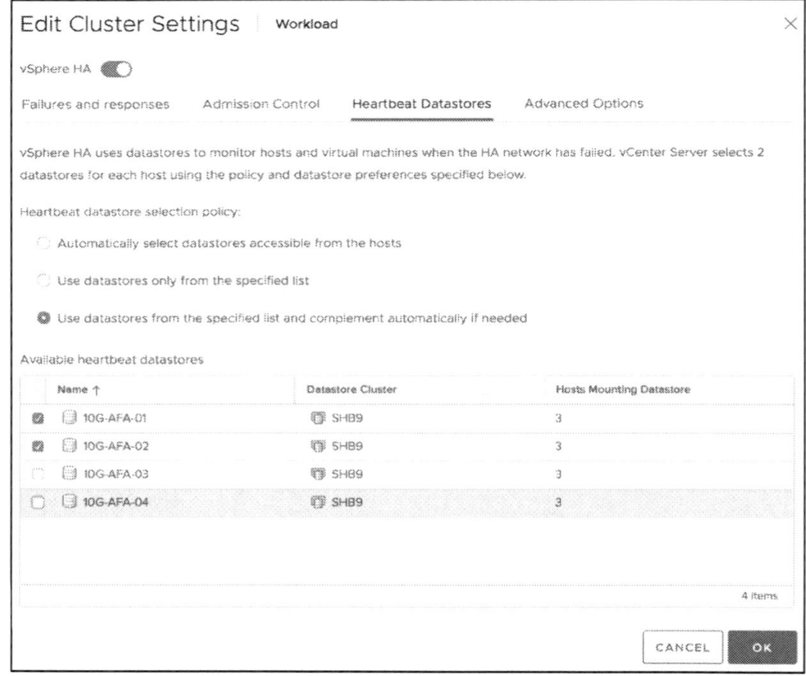

Figure 13: Datastore Heartbeating

The question now arises: what, exactly, is this datastore heartbeating and which datastore is used for this heartbeating? Let's answer which datastore is used for datastore heartbeating first as we can simply show that with a screenshot, see below. vSphere displays extensive details around the "Cluster Status" on the Cluster's Monitor tab. This for instance shows you which datastores are being used for heartbeating currently and which hosts are using which specific datastore(s).

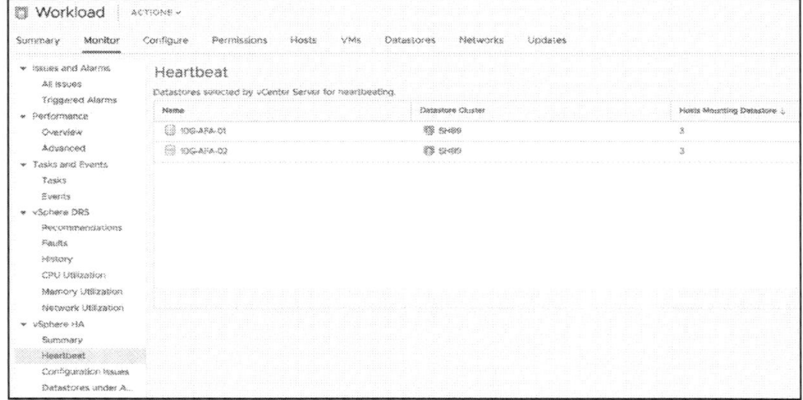

Figure 14: Datastore Heartbeating Selected

In block based storage environments HA leverages an existing VMFS file system mechanism. The datastore heartbeat mechanism uses a so called "heartbeat region" which is updated as long as the file is open. On VMFS datastores, HA will simply check whether the heartbeat region has been updated. In order to update a datastore heartbeat region, a host needs to have at least one open file on the volume. HA ensures there is at least one file open on this volume by creating a file specifically for datastore heartbeating. In other words, a per-host file is created on the designated heartbeating datastores, as shown below. The naming scheme for this file is as follows: `host-number-hb`.

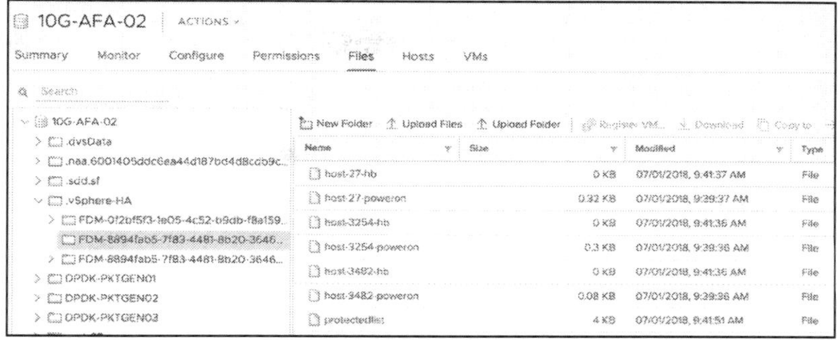

Figure 15: Heartbeat File

On NFS datastores, each host will write to its heartbeat file once every 5 seconds, ensuring that the master will be able to check host state. The master will simply validate this by checking that the time-stamp of the file changed.

Realize that in the case of a converged network environment, the effectiveness of datastore heartbeating will vary depending on the type of failure. For instance, a NIC failure could impact both network and datastore heartbeating. If, for whatever reason, the datastore or NFS share becomes unavailable or is removed from the cluster, HA will detect this and select a new datastore or NFS share to use for the heartbeating mechanism. Unless of course you have selected the option "select only from my preferred datastores" and none of the preferred datastores is available.

> **Datastore heartbeating adds a new level of resiliency but is not the be-all end-all. In converged networking environments, the use of datastore heartbeating adds little value due to the fact that a NIC failure may result in both the network and storage becoming unavailable.**

Isolated versus Partitioned

We've already briefly touched on it and it is time to have a closer look. When it comes to network failures there are two different states that exist. What are these exactly and when is a host Partitioned rather than Isolated? Before we will explain this, we want to point out that there is the state as reported by the master and the state as observed by an administrator and the characteristics these have.

We would recommend everyone to read the following bullet points thoroughly (and multiple times) as the terminology in these situations are often incorrectly used. It sounds like it is just semantics, but there's a big difference in how vSphere HA responds to an Isolation versus how it responds to a Partition.

Let's be very clear and define each state:

- An **isolation event** is the situation where a single host cannot communicate with the rest of the cluster. **Note: single host!**
- A **partition** is the situation where two (or more) hosts can communicate with each other, but no longer can communicate with the remaining two (or more) hosts in the cluster. **Note: two or more!**

Having said that, you can also find yourself in then situation where multiple hosts are isolated simultaneously. Although chances are slim, this can occur when for instance a change is made to the network and various hosts of a single cluster lose access to the management network. Anyway, let's take a look at Partition and Isolation events a bit more in-depth

The diagram below shows possible ways in which an Isolation or a Partition can occur.

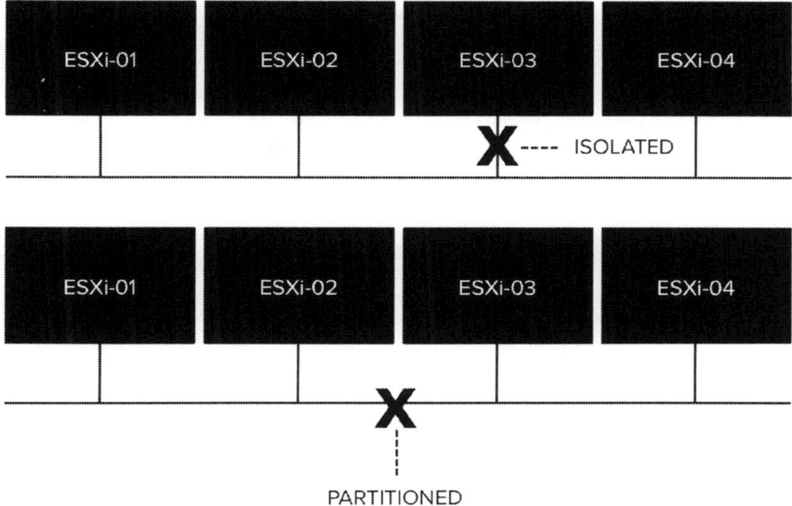

Figure 16: Isolation vs Partition

If a cluster is partitioned in multiple segments, each partition will elect its own master, meaning that if you have 4 partitions your cluster will have 4 masters. When the network partition is corrected, one of the four masters will take over the role and be responsible for the cluster again. This will be done using the election algorithm (most connected datastores, highest lexical number). It should be noted that a master could claim responsibility for a VM that lives in a different partition. If this occurs and the VM happens to fail, the master will be notified through the datastore communication mechanism.

In the HA architecture, whether a host is partitioned is determined by the master reporting the condition. So, in the above example, the master on host ESXi-01 will report ESXi-03 and ESXi-04 partitioned while the master on host ESXi-03 will report ESXi-01 and ESXi-02 partitioned. When a partition occurs, vCenter reports the perspective of one master.

A master reports a host as partitioned or isolated when it can't communicate with the host over the management network, it can observe the host's datastore heartbeats via the heartbeat datastores.

The master cannot alone differentiate between these two states – a host is reported as isolated only if the host informs the master via the datastores that is isolated. This still leaves the question open how the master differentiates between a Failed, Partitioned, or Isolated host.

When the master stops receiving network heartbeats from a slave, it will check for host "liveness" for the next 15 seconds. Before the host is declared failed, the master will validate if it has actually failed or not by doing additional liveness checks. First, the master will validate if the host is still heartbeating to the datastore. Second, the master will ping the management IP address of the host. If both are negative, the host will be declared Failed. This doesn't necessarily mean the host has PSOD'ed; it could be the network is unavailable, including the storage network, which would make this host Isolated from an administrator's perspective but Failed from an HA perspective. As you can imagine, however, there are various combinations possible. The following table depicts these combinations including the "state".

STATE	NETWORK HEARTBEAT	STORAGE HEARTBEAT	HOST LIVENESS PING	ISOLATION CRITERIA MET
Running	Yes	N/A	N/A	N/A
Isolated	No	Yes	No	Yes
Partitioned	No	Yes	No	No
Failed	No	No	No	N/A
FDM Agent Down	N/A	N/A	Yes	N/A

Table 2: HA State

HA will trigger an action based on the state of the host. When the host is marked as Failed, a restart of the VMs will be initiated. When the host is marked as Isolated, the master might initiate the restarts.
The one thing to keep in mind when it comes to isolation response is that a VM will only be shut down or powered off when the isolated host knows there is a master out there that has taken ownership for the VM or when the isolated host loses access to the home datastore of the VM.

For example, if a host is isolated and runs two VMs, stored on separate datastores, the host will validate if it can access each of the home datastores of those VMs. If it can, the host will validate whether a master owns these datastores. If no master owns the datastores, the isolation response will not be triggered and restarts will not be initiated. If the host does not have access to the datastore, for instance, during an "All Paths Down" condition, HA will trigger the isolation response to ensure the "original" VM is powered down and will be safely restarted. This to avoid so-called "split-brain" scenarios.

To reiterate, as this is a very important aspect of HA and how it handles network isolations, the remaining hosts in the cluster will only be requested to restart VMs when the master has detected that either the host has failed or has become isolated and the isolation response was triggered.

VM Protection

VM protection happens on several layers but is ultimately the responsibility of vCenter. We have explained this briefly but want to expand on it a bit more to make sure everyone understands the dependency on vCenter when it comes to protecting VMs. We do want to stress that this only applies to protecting VMs; VM restarts in no way require vCenter to be available at the time.

When the state of a VM changes, vCenter will direct the master to enable or disable HA protection for that VM. Protection, however, is only guaranteed when the master has committed the change of state to disk. The reason for this, of course, is that a failure of the master would result in the loss of any state changes that exist only in memory. As pointed out earlier, this state is distributed across the datastores and stored in the "*protectedlist*" file.

When the power state change of a VM has been committed to disk, the master will inform vCenter Server so that the change in status is visible both for the user in vCenter and for other processes like monitoring tools. Within the vSphere Client you can validate that a VM has been protected on the VM's summary page as displayed in the next screenshot. As shown, the UI also provides information about the types of failures HA can handle for this particular VM.

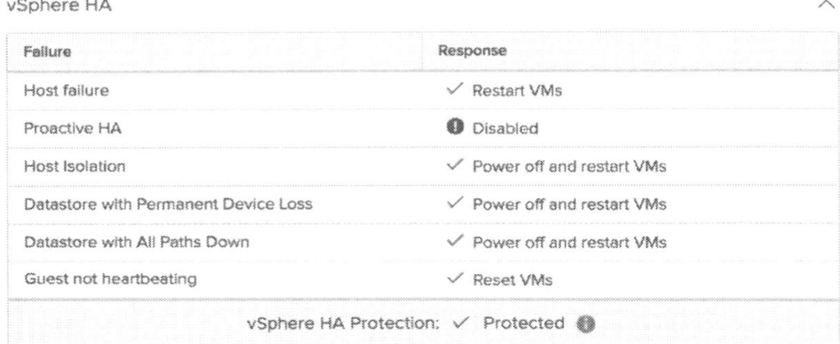

vSphere HA

Failure	Response
Host failure	✓ Restart VMs
Proactive HA	Disabled
Host Isolation	✓ Power off and restart VMs
Datastore with Permanent Device Loss	✓ Power off and restart VMs
Datastore with All Paths Down	✓ Power off and restart VMs
Guest not heartbeating	✓ Reset VMs

vSphere HA Protection: ✓ Protected

Figure 17: VM is Protected

To clarify the process, we have created a workflow diagram of the protection of a VM from the point it is powered on through vCenter:

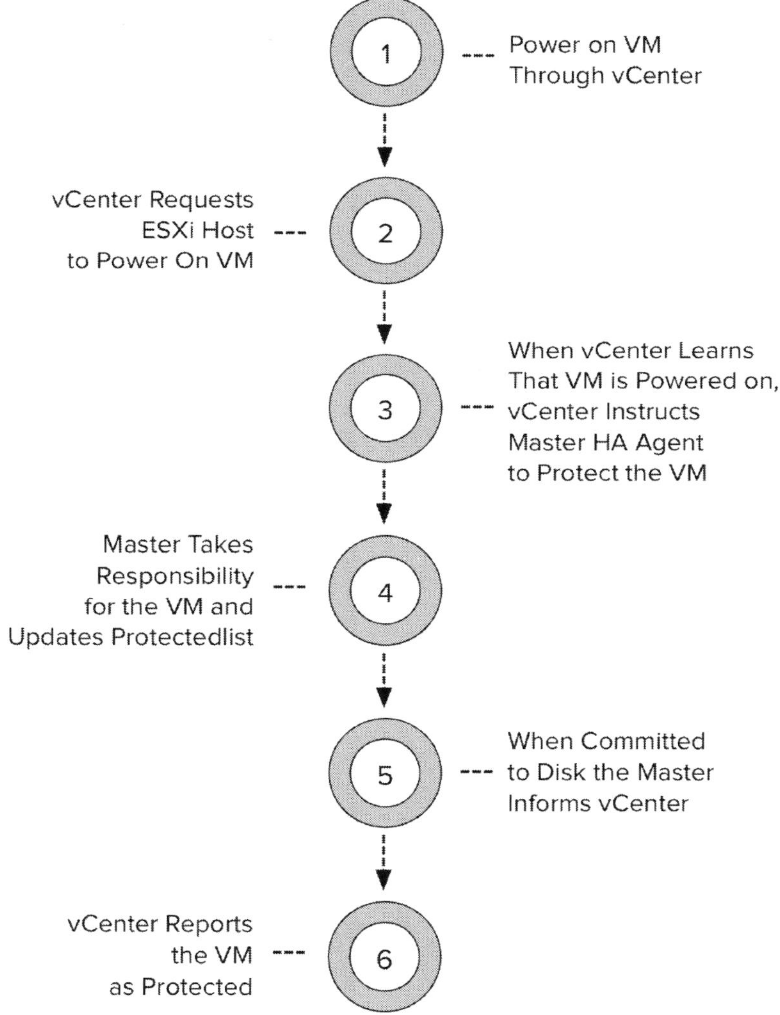

Figure 18: VM Protection Workflow

But what about "unprotection?" When a VM is powered off, it must be removed from the protectedlist. We have documented this workflow in the following diagram for the situation where the power off is invoked from vCenter.

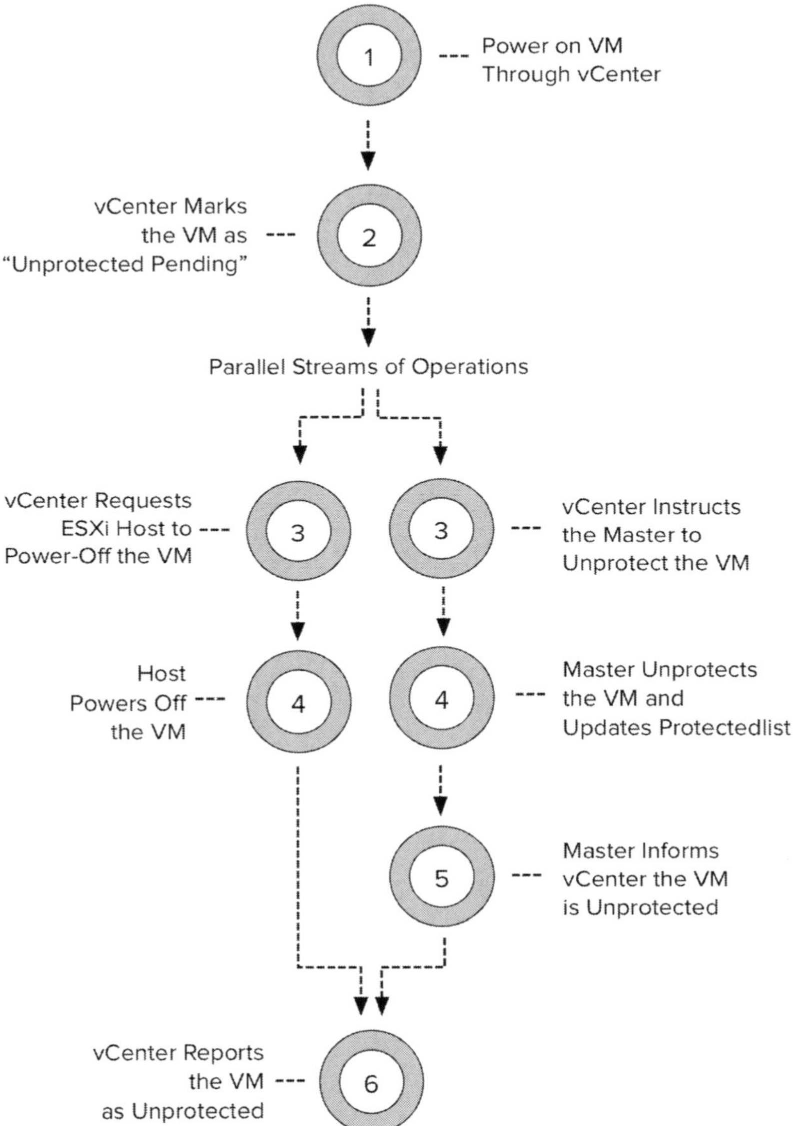

Figure 19: VM Unprotection

We realize a lot of new terminology and concepts have been introduced in this chapter. Understanding these new concepts is critical for availability of your workloads, and in some cases critical for a successful restart of your VMs.

04

RESTARTING VIRTUAL MACHINES

In the previous chapter, we have described most of the lower level fundamental concepts of HA. We have shown you that multiple mechanisms increase resiliency and reliability of HA. Reliability of HA in this case mostly refers to restarting (or resetting) VMs, as that remains HA's primary task.

HA will respond when the state of a host has changed, or, better said, when the state of one or more VMs has changed. There are multiple scenarios in which HA will respond to a VM failure, the most common of which are listed below:

- Failed host
- Isolated host
- Failed guest operating system

Depending on the type of failure, but also depending on the role of the host, the process will differ slightly. Changing the process results in slightly different recovery timelines. There are many different scenarios and there is no point in covering all of them, so we will try to describe the most common scenario and include timelines where possible.

Throughout this chapter we will describe theoretical restart times, please realize that these timings are based on optimal scenarios with maximum availability of resources and no constraints whatsoever. In real life the restart of a VM may take slightly longer, this depends on many variables, some of which we have listed below. Note that this is an example of what may impact restart times, by no means a full list.

- Availability of resources
- Network performance
- Storage performance
- Speed of CPU and available CPUs/Cores
- Speed of memory and available capacity
- Number of VMs impacted
- Number of hosts impacted

Before we dive into the different failure scenarios, we want to explain how restart priority and retries work.

Restart Priority and Order

A feature of HA that has always been a hot discussion is Restart Priority and Order. The main reason for the debate being the lack of proper prioritization or the ability to specify dependency between VMs. This completely changed with the arrival of vSphere 6.5 where the restart mechanism was redesigned and a new functionality was introduced where you have the ability to specify dependency between VMs. Since early days HA can take the configured priority of the VM into account when restarting VMs. However, it is good to know that Agent VMs take precedence during the restart procedure as the "regular" VMs may rely on them. Although Agent VMs are not common, one use case for it would be a virtual storage appliance.

Pre-vSphere 6.5 prioritization was done by each host and not globally. Each host that had been requested to initiate restart attempts would attempt to restart all top priority VMs before attempting to start any other VMs. If the restart of a top priority VM failed, it would be retried after a delay. In the meantime, however, HA would continue powering on the remaining VMs. Keep in mind that some VMs could have been dependent on the agent VMs.

VMs can be dependent on the availability of agent VMs or other VMs. Although HA will do its best to ensure all VMs are started in the correct order, this is not guaranteed. Document the proper recovery process.

Besides agent VMs, HA also prioritizes FT secondary machines. We have listed the full order in which VMs will be restarted below:

- Agent VMs
- FT secondary VMs
- VMs configured with a restart priority of highest
- VMs configured with a restart priority of high
- VMs configured with a restart priority of medium
- VMs configured with a restart priority of low
- VMs configured with a restart priority of lowest

The priority by default is set to medium for the whole cluster and this can be changed in the "VM Overrides" section of the UI.

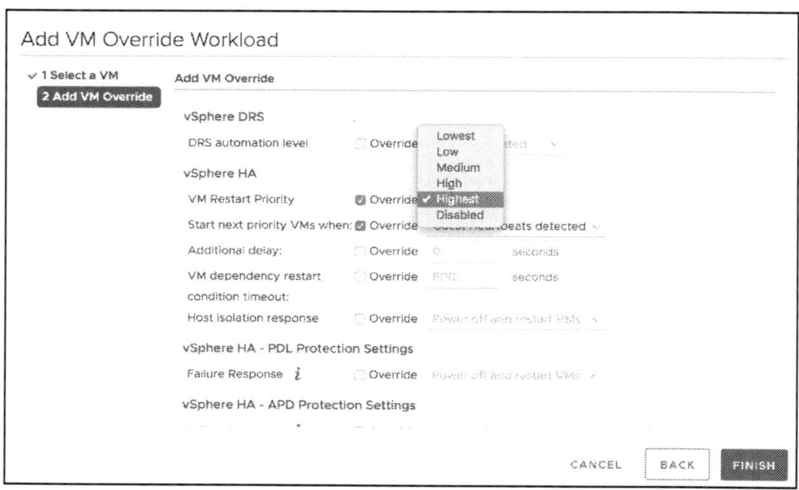

Figure 20: Restart Priority

After you have specified the priority you can also specify if there needs to be an additional delay before the next batch can be started, or you can specify even what triggers the next priority "group", this could for instance be the VMware Tools guest heartbeat as shown in the screenshot below. The other option is "resources allocated" which is purely the scheduling of the batch itself (this is the old behavior), the power-on event completion or the "app heartbeat" detection. That last one is most definitely the most complex as you would need to have App HA enabled and services defined etc. We suspect that if people use this they will mostly set it to "Guest Heartbeats detected" as that is easiest and most reliable.

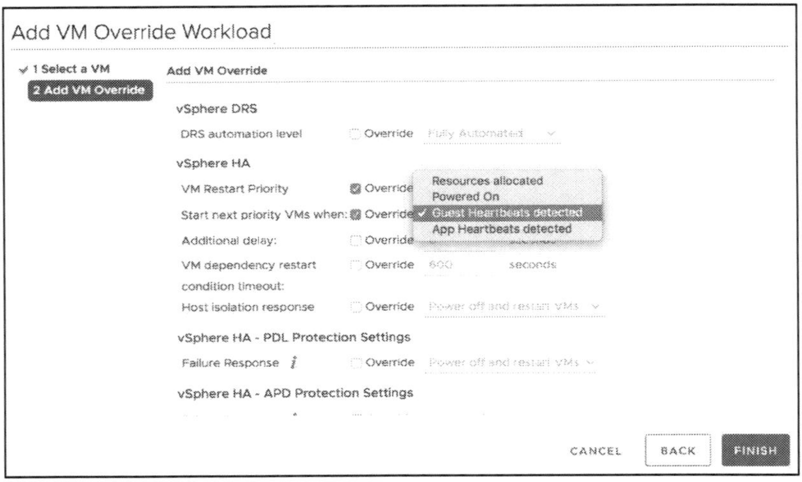

Figure 21: Start Next Priority VMs Batch When ...

If for whatever reason there is no guest heartbeat ever, or it simply takes a long time then there is also a timeout value that can be specified. By default, this is 600 seconds, this can be decreased or increased, depending on what you prefer.

In case you are wondering, yes you can also set a restart priority for vCenter Server. All changes to the restart priority are stored in the cluster configuration. You can examine this if needed through the script we discussed earlier called prettyPrint.sh, simply type the following:

```
/opt/vmware/fdm/fdm/prettyPrint.sh clusterconfig
```

The output which is then presented will look something like below example, we would recommend searching for the word "restartPriority" to find the changes you have made as the output will be more than 100 lines.

```
<dasVmConfig xsi:type="CsiDasVmConfigInfo">
      <key type="VirtualMachine">vm-181</key>
      <dasSettings>
         <restartPriority>highest</restartPriority>
         <restartPriorityTimeout>-1</restartPriorityTimeout>
         <isolationResponse>clusterIsolationResponse</isolationResponse>
         <vmToolsMonitoringSettings>      </vmToolsMonitoringSettings>
      <vmComponentProtectionSettings>   </vmComponentProtectionSettings>
```

Figure 22: Section of PrettPrint.sh Output

The Restart Priority functionality is primarily intended for large groups of VMs, if you have thousands of VMs you can select those ten / twenty VMs and change priority so that they will be powered-on first. However, if you for instance have a 3-tier app and you need the database server to be powered on before the app server then you can also use VM/VM rules as of vSphere 6.5, this functionality is typically referred to as **HA Orchestrated Restart**.

You can configure HA Orchestrated Restarts by simply creating "VM" Groups. In the example below we created a VM Group called App with the application VM in there. We have also created a DB group with the Database VM in there.

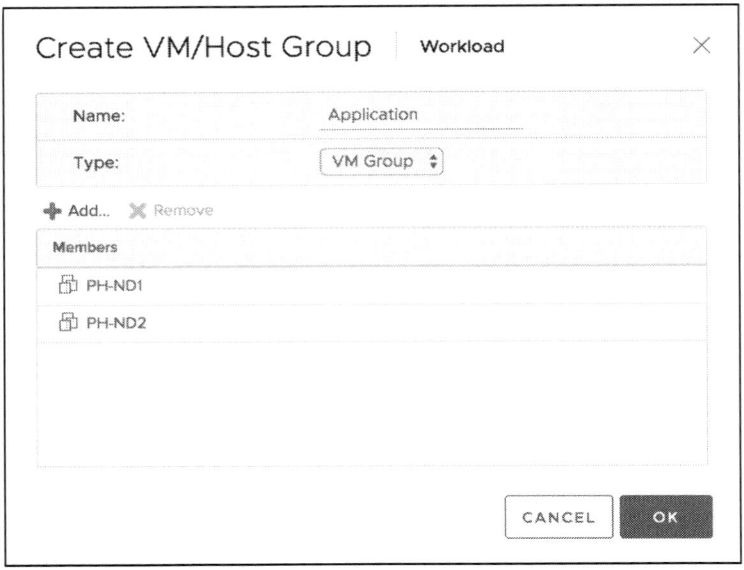

Create VM/Host Group | Workload

Name: Application

Type: VM Group

Add... Remove

Members

PH-ND1

PH-ND2

CANCEL OK

Figure 23: Application Group

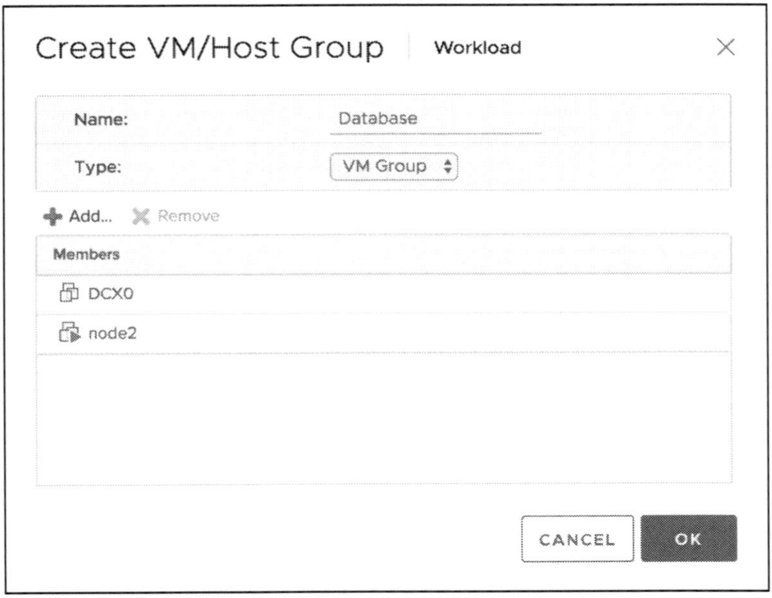

Create VM/Host Group | Workload

Name: Database

Type: VM Group

Add... Remove

Members

DCX0

node2

CANCEL OK

Figure 24: Database Group

This application has a dependency on the Database VM to be fully powered-on, so we specified this in a rule as shown in the below screenshot.

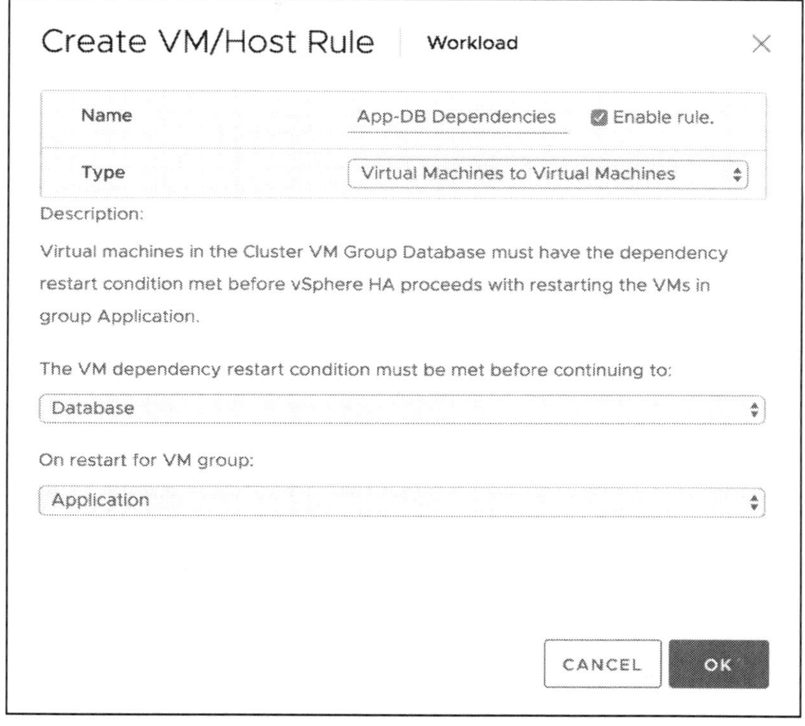

Figure 25: VM to VM Rule Definition

Now one thing to note here is that in terms of dependency, the next group of VMs in the rule will be powered on when the cluster wide set “VM Dependency Restart Condition” is met. This is a mandatory rule, also known as a hard rule. If this is set to “Resources Allocated”, which is the default, then the VMs will be restarted literally a split second later. Think about how to set the “VM Dependency Restart Condition” as otherwise the rule may be useless. Also realize that if the VM Dependency Restart Condition cannot be met, that the next group of VMs are not restarted.

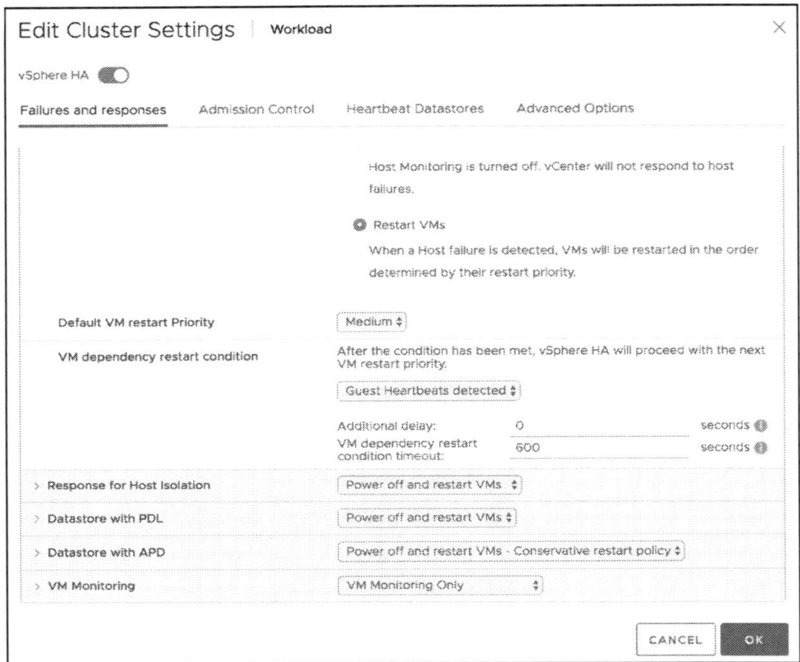

Figure 26: VM Dependency Restart Condition

> **For both restart priority and orchestrated restart, it is important to think about when the next batch should be restarted. vSphere allows you to configure it in various different ways, take advantage of the flexibility offered.**

It should be noted that HA will not place any VMs on a host if the required number of agent VMs are not running on the host at the time placement is done.

Now that we have briefly touched on it, we would also like to address "restart retries" and parallelization of restarts as that more or less dictates how long it could take before all VMs of a failed or isolated host are restarted. Note that the use of Restart Priorities and/or the use of Orchestrated Restart will impact restart timing, but let's take a look at restart retries first before we discuss restarting timing.

Restart Retries

The number of retries is configurable as of vCenter 2.5 U4 with the advanced option `das.maxvmrestartcount`. The default value is 5. Note that the initial restart is included in this number.

HA will try to start the VM on one of your hosts in the affected cluster; if this is unsuccessful on that host, the restart count will be increased by 1. Before we go into the exact timeline, let it be clear that T0 is the point at which the master initiates the first restart attempt. This by itself could be 30 seconds after the VM has failed. The elapsed time between the failure of the VM and the restart, though, will depend on the scenario of the failure, which we will discuss in this chapter.

As said, the default number of restarts is 5. There are specific times associated with each of these attempts. The following bullet list will clarify this concept. The 'm' stands for "minutes" in this list.

- T0 – Initial Restart
- T2m – Restart retry 1
- T6m – Restart retry 2
- T14m – Restart retry 3
- T30m – Restart retry 4

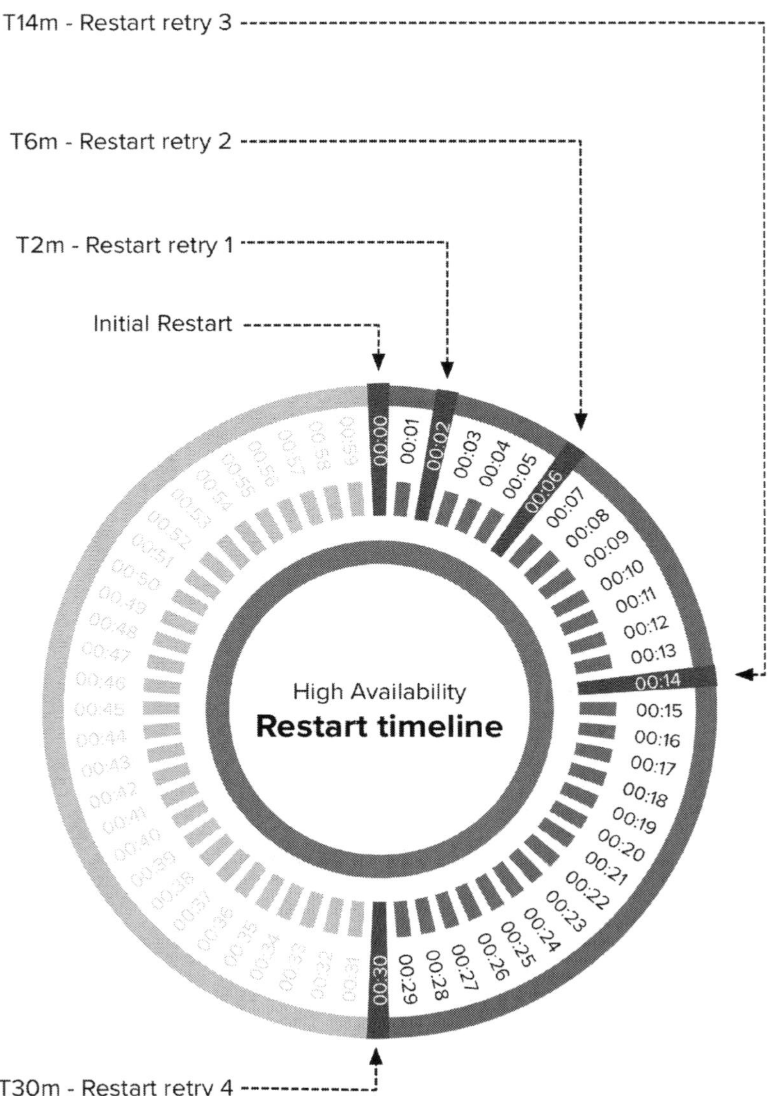

Figure 27: Restart Retry Timeline

As clearly depicted in the diagram above, a successful power-on attempt could take up to ~30 minutes in the case where multiple power-on attempts are unsuccessful. This is, however, not exact science. For instance, there is a 2-minute waiting period between the initial restart and the first restart retry. HA will start the 2-minute wait as soon as it has detected that the initial attempt has failed. So, in reality, T2 could be T2 plus 8 seconds. Another important fact that we want to emphasize is that there is no coordination between masters, and so if multiple masters are involved in trying to restart the VM, each will retain their own sequence. Multiple masters could attempt to restart a VM. Although only one will succeed, it might change some of the timelines.

What about VMs which are "disabled" for HA or VMs that are powered-off? What will happen with those VMs? Before vSphere 6.0 those VMs would be left alone, as of vSphere 6.0 these VMs will be registered on another host after a failure. This will allow you to easily power-on that VMs when needed without needed to manually re-register it yourself. Note, HA will not do a power-on of the VMs, it will just register it for you! (Note that a bug in vSphere 6.0 U2 prevents this from happening, and you need vSphere 6.0 U3 for this functionality to work.)

Let's give an example to clarify the scenario in which a master fails during a restart sequence:

```
Cluster: 4 Host (esxi-01, esxi-02, esxi-03, esxi-04)
Master: esxi-01
```

The host ESXi-02 is running a single VM called VM01 and it fails. The master, ESXi-01, will try to restart it but the attempt fails. It will try restarting VM01 up to 5 times but, unfortunately, on the 4th try, the master also fails. An election occurs and ESXi-03 becomes the new master. It will now initiate the restart of VM01, and if that restart would fail it will retry it up to 4 times again for a total including the initial restart of 5.

Be aware, though, that a successful restart might never occur if the restart count is reached and all five restart attempts (the default value) were unsuccessful.

When it comes to restarts, one thing that is very important to realize is that HA will not issue more than 32 concurrent power-on tasks on a given host. To make that more clear, let's use the example of a two host cluster: if a host fails which contained 33 VMs and all of these had the same restart priority, 32 power on attempts would be initiated. The 33rd power on attempt will only be initiated when one of those 32 attempts has completed regardless of success or failure of one of those attempts.

Note, pre-vSphere 6.5, if there were 31 low-priority VMs to be powered on and a single high-priority VM, the power on attempt for the low-priority VMs would be issued at the same time as the power on attempt for the high priority VM. This has changed with vSphere 6.5 as mentioned earlier, as now you have the ability to specify when the next batch should be restarted. By default however this is "resources allocated", which equals the pre-vSphere 6.5 behavior.

> **Configuring restart priority alone of a VM is not a guarantee that the power on of the VMs will actually be completed in this order. Ensure proper operational procedures are in place for restarting services or VMs in the appropriate order in the event of a failure.**

Now that we know how VM restart priority and restart retries are handled, it is time to look at the different scenarios:

- Failed host
    - Failure of a master
    - Failure of a slave
- Isolated host and response

Failed Host

When discussing a failed host scenario, it is needed to make a distinction between the failure of a master versus the failure of a slave. We want to emphasize this because the time it takes before a restart attempt is initiated differs between these two scenarios. Although the majority of you probably won't notice the time difference, it is important to call out.

Let's start with the most common failure, that of a host failing, but note that failures generally occur infrequently. In most environments, hardware failures are very uncommon to begin with. Just in case it happens, it doesn't hurt to understand the process and its associated timelines.

The Failure of a Slave

The failure of a slave host is a fairly complex scenario. Part of this complexity comes from the introduction of a new heartbeat mechanism. Actually, there are two different scenarios: one where heartbeat datastores are configured and one where heartbeat datastores are not configured. Keeping in mind that this is an actual failure of the host, the timeline is as follows:

- T0 – Slave failure.
- T3s – Master begins monitoring datastore heartbeats for 15 seconds.
- T10s – The host is declared unreachable and the master will ping the management network of the failed host. This is a continuous ping for 5 seconds.
- T15s – If no heartbeat datastores are configured, the host will be declared dead.
- T18s – If heartbeat datastores are configured, the host will be declared dead.

The master monitors the network heartbeats of a slave. When the slave fails, these heartbeats will no longer be received by the master. We have defined this as T0. After 3 seconds (T3s), the master will start monitoring for datastore heartbeats and it will do this for 15 seconds. On the 10th second (T10s), when no network or datastore heartbeats have been detected, the host will be declared as "unreachable". The master will also start pinging the management network of the failed host at the 10th second and it will do so for 5 seconds. If no heartbeat datastores were configured, the host will be declared "dead" at the 15th second (T15s) and VM restarts will be initiated by the master. If heartbeat datastores have been configured, the host will be declared dead at the 18th second

(T18s) and restarts will be initiated. We realize that this can be confusing and hope the timeline depicted in the diagram below makes it easier to digest.

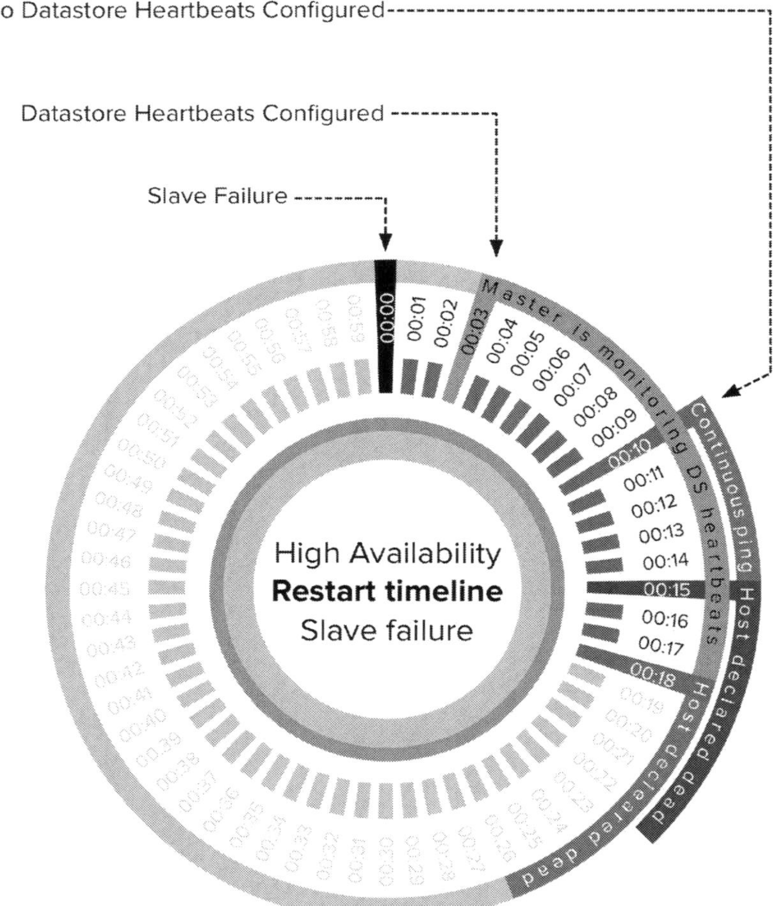

Figure 28: Restart Timeline for Slave Failure

The master filters the VMs it thinks failed before initiating restarts. The master uses the protectedlist for this, on-disk state could be obtained only by one master at a time since it required opening the protectedlist file in exclusive mode. If there is a network partition multiple masters could try to restart the same VM as vCenter Server also provided the necessary details for a restart. As an example, it could happen that a master has locked a VM's home datastore and has access to the protectedlist while the other master is in contact with vCenter Server and as such is aware of the current desired protected state. In this scenario, it could happen that the master which does not own the home datastore of the VM will restart the VM based on the information provided by vCenter Server.

This change in behavior was introduced to avoid the scenario where a restart of a VM would fail due to insufficient resources in the partition which was responsible for the VM. With this change, there is less chance of such a situation occurring as the master in the other partition would be using the information provided by vCenter Server to initiate the restart. That leaves us with the question of what happens in the case of the failure of a master.

The Failure of a Master

In the case of a master failure, the process and the associated timeline are slightly different. The reason being that there needs to be a master before any restart can be initiated. This means that an election will need to take place amongst the slaves. The timeline is as follows:

- T0 – Master failure
- T10s – Master election process initiated
- T25s – New master elected and reads the protectedlist
- T35s – New master initiates restarts for all VMs on the protectedlist which are not running

Slaves receive network heartbeats from their master. If the master fails, let's define this as T0 (T zero), the slaves detect this when the network heartbeats cease to be received. As every cluster needs a master, the slaves will initiate an election at T10s. The election process takes 15s to complete, which brings us to T25s. At T25s, the new master reads the protectedlist. This list contains all the VMs, which are protected by HA. At T35s, the master initiates the restart of all VMs that are protected but not currently running. The timeline depicted in the diagram below hopefully clarifies the process.

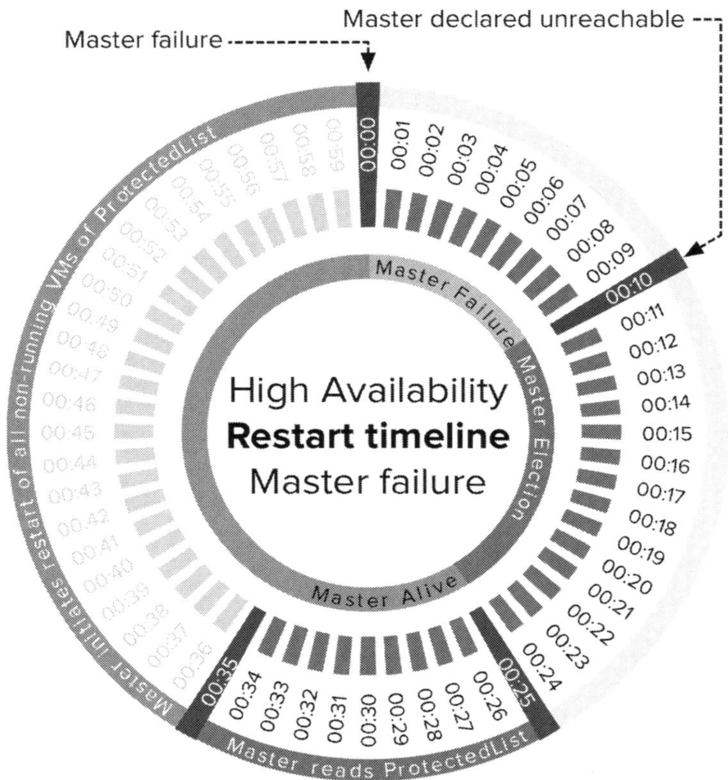

Figure 29: Restart Timeline for Master Failure

Besides the failure of a host, there is another reason for restarting VMs: an isolation event.

Isolation Response and Detection

Before we will discuss the timeline and the process around the restart of VMs after an isolation event, we will discuss Isolation Response and Isolation Detection.

One of the first decisions that will need to be made when configuring HA is the "Isolation Response".

Isolation Response

The Isolation Response (or Host Isolation as it is called in vSphere 6.0) refers to the action that HA takes for its VMs when the host has lost its connection with the network and the remaining nodes in the cluster. This does not necessarily mean that the whole network is down; it could just be the management network ports of this specific host. Today there are three isolation responses: "Disabled", "Power off", and "Shut down". In previous versions (pre vSphere 6.0) there was an isolation response called "leave powered on", this has been renamed to "disabled" as "leave powered on" means that there is no response to an isolation event.

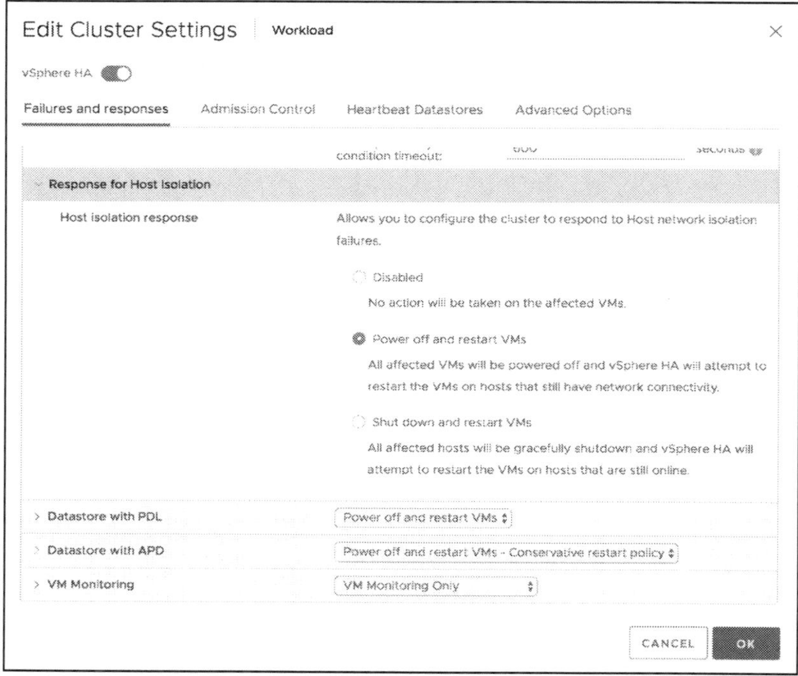

Figure 30: Isolation Response Configuration

The isolation response features answers the question, “what should a host do with the VMs it manages when it detects that it is isolated from the network?” Let’s discuss these three options more in-depth:

- Disabled (default) – When isolation occurs on the host, the state of the VMs remains unchanged.
- Power off and restart VMs– When isolation occurs, all VMs are powered off. It is a hard stop, or to put it bluntly, the “virtual” power cable of the VM will be pulled out!
- Shut down and restart VMs – When isolation occurs, all VMs running on the host will be shut down using a guest-initiated shutdown through VMware Tools. If this is not successful within 5 minutes, a “power off” will be executed. This time out value can be adjusted by setting the advanced option `das.isolationShutdownTimeout`. If VMware Tools is not installed, a “power off” will be initiated immediately.

This setting can be changed on the cluster settings under the option “Response for Host Isolation” in the vSphere Client. Note that this differs from the Web Client, as this used to be located under “VM Options”. It is also possible to override the default or selected behavior on a per VM basis. This can be done in the VM Overrides section of the vSphere Client by selecting the appropriate VMs and then selecting the “Override” option for Host isolation response and selecting the appropriate isolation response.

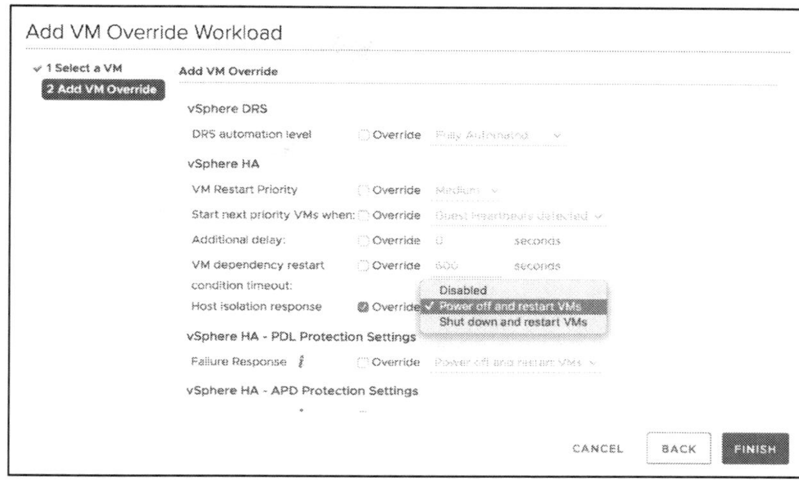

Figure 31: VMs Overrides – Host Isolation Response

The default setting for the isolation response has changed multiple times over the last couple of years and this has caused some confusion. Below you can find the what changed with which version.

- Up to ESXi3.5 U2 / vCenter 2.5 U2 the default isolation response was "Power off"
- With ESXi3.5 U3 / vCenter 2.5 U3 this was changed to "Leave powered on"
- With vSphere 4.0 it was changed to "Shut down"
- With vSphere 5.0 it has been changed to "Leave powered on"
- With vSphere 6.0 the "leave powered on" setting is now renamed to "Disabled"

Keep in mind that these changes are only applicable to newly created clusters. When creating a new cluster, it may be required to change the default isolation response based on the configuration of existing clusters and/or your customer's requirements, constraints and expectations. When upgrading an existing cluster, it might be wise to apply the latest default values. You might wonder why the default has changed once again. There was a lot of feedback from customers that "Disabled" was the desired default value.

> **Before upgrading an environment to later versions, ensure you validate the best practices and default settings. Document them, including justification, to ensure all people involved understand your reasons.**

The question remains, which setting should be used? The obvious answer applies here; it depends. We prefer "Disabled" for traditional environments because it eliminates the chances of having a false positive and its associated down time. One of the problems that people have experienced in the past is that HA triggered its isolation response when the full management network went down. Resulting in the power off (or shutdown) of every single VM and none being restarted. This problem has been mitigated. HA will validate if VMs restarts can be attempted – there is no reason to incur any down time unless absolutely necessary. It does this by validating that a master owns the datastore the VM is stored on. Of course, the isolated host can only validate this if it has access to the datastores. In a converged network environment with iSCSI storage, for instance, it would be impossible to validate this during a full isolation as the validation would fail due to the inaccessible datastore from the perspective of the isolated host.

We feel that changing the isolation response is most useful in environments where a failure of the management network is likely correlated with a failure of the VM network(s). If the failure of the management network won't likely correspond with the failure of the VM networks, isolation response would cause unnecessary downtime as the VMs can continue to run without management network connectivity to the host.

A second use for power off/shutdown is in scenarios where the VM retains access to the VM network but loses access to its storage, leaving the VM powered-on could result in two VMs on the network with the same IP address. An example of when this could happen for instance is with vSAN storage. When vSAN is configured HA leverages the vSAN network for network heartbeating.

This means that if the HA heartbeat does not function properly, it is very unlikely that VMs running on that particular host can access the vSAN datastore. As such for vSAN we always recommend setting the isolation response to "power off".

Realizing that many of you are not designing hyper-converged solutions yet, or are responsible for maintaining a legacy infrastructure let us try to provide some guidance around when to use which isolation policy.

LIKELYHOOD THAT HOST WILL RETAIN ACCESS TO VM DATASTORE	LIKELYHOOD VMS RETAIN ACCESS TO VM NETWORK	RECOMMENDED ISOLATION POLICY	RATIONALE
Likely	Likely	Disabled	VM is running fine, no reason to power it off
Likely	Unlikely	Shutdown	Choose shutdown to allow HA to restart VMs on hosts that are not isolated and hence are likely to have access to storage and network
Unlikely	Likely	Power off	Use Power Off to avoid having two instances of the same VM on the VM network
Unlikely	Unlikely	Power off	VM is unavailable, restart makes most sense. Clean shutdown is not needed as storage is most likely inaccessible

Table 3: Isolation Response Decision Guidance

The question that we haven't answered yet is how HA knows which VMs have been powered-off due to the triggered isolation response and why the isolation response is more reliable than with previous versions of HA. In earlier versions HA did not care and would always try to restart the VMs according to the last known state of the host. That is no longer the case. Before the isolation response is triggered, the isolated host will verify whether a master is responsible for the VM. If, for whatever reason, all hosts in your cluster are isolated from the HA network then HA will not trigger the isolation response. As triggering the isolation response at that time would not lead to an improved situation.

As mentioned earlier, it does this by validating if a master owns the home datastore of the VM. When isolation response is triggered, the isolated host removes the VMs which are powered off or shutdown from the "poweron" file. The master will recognize that the VMs have disappeared and initiate a restart. On top of that, when the isolation response is triggered, it will create a per-VM file under a "poweredoff" directory which indicates for the master that this VM was powered down as a result of a triggered isolation response. This information will be read by the master node when it initiates the restart attempt in order to guarantee that only VMs that were powered off / shut down by HA will be restarted by HA. Of course, this is only possible when the datastores are still accessible during the time of failure.

This is, however, only one part of the increased reliability of HA. Reliability has also been improved with respect to "isolation detection," which will be described in the following section.

Isolation Detection

We have explained what the options are to respond to an isolation event and what happens when the selected response is triggered. However, we have not extensively discussed how isolation is detected. The mechanism is fairly straightforward and works with heartbeats, as earlier explained. There are, however, two scenarios again, and the process and associated timelines differ for each of them:

- Isolation of a slave
- Isolation of a master

Before we explain the differences in process between both scenarios, we want to make sure it is clear that a change in state will result in the isolation response not being triggered in either scenario. Meaning that if a single ping is successful or the host observes election traffic and is elected a master or slave, the isolation response will not be triggered, which is exactly what you want as avoiding down time is at least as important as recovering from down time. When a host has declared itself isolated and observes election traffic it will declare itself no longer isolated.

Isolation of a Slave

HA triggers a master election process before it will declare a host is isolated. In the below timeline, "s" refers to seconds.

- T0 – Isolation of the host (slave)
- T10s – Slave enters "election state"
- T25s – Slave elects itself as master
- T25s – Slave pings "isolation addresses"
- T30s – Slave declares itself isolated
- T60s – Slave "triggers" isolation response

Note that the isolation response gets triggered 30 seconds after the host has been declared isolated. This also means that a restart of the VM will be "delayed" with 30 seconds. Pre vSphere 5.1 this delay did not exist, the delay is configurable however through the advanced setting `das.config.fdm.isolationPolicyDelaySec`. Note though that the minimum value is 30 seconds, if a value lower than 30 seconds is configured HA will still default to 30 seconds.

When the isolation response is triggered HA creates a "power-off" file for any VM HA powers off whose home datastore is accessible. Next it powers off the VM (or shuts down) and updates the host's poweron file.

The power-off file is used to record that HA powered off the VM and so HA should restart it. These power-off files are deleted when a VM is powered back on or HA is disabled, the below screenshot shows such a power-off file, which in this case is stored in a VVol.

```
[root@esxi-hp-06:/vmfs/volumes/vvol:0000000100004001-84590195c951be61/rfc4122.f21565c0-6e5c-4fc5-999d-a64c0d477b1c] ls -lah
total 488464
drwxr-xr-t    1 root     root        3.0K Apr 15 09:58 .
drwxr-xr-x    1 root     root         512 Apr 15 10:56 ..
drwxr-xr-x    1 root     root         420 Apr 15 10:35 .dvsData
-r--------    1 root     root      128.0K Apr 15 09:52 .fbb.sf
-r--------    1 root     root       79.8M Apr 15 09:52 .fdc.sf
-r--------    1 root     root        1.1M Apr 15 09:52 .pb2.sf
-r--------    1 root     root      256.0M Apr 15 09:52 .pbc.sf
-rw-------    1 root     root           0 Apr 15 09:52 .rfc4122.c492c080-6a96-483c-8559-ca45333faecf.lck
-rw-------    1 root     root         423 Apr 15 09:52 .rfc4122.c492c080-6a96-483c-8559-ca45333faecf.meta
-r--------    1 root     root      128.3M Apr 15 09:52 .sbc.sf
drwx------    1 root     root
-rw-------    1 root     root          55 Apr 15 10:56 .vSphereHA-poweroff
-r--------    1 root     root
-rw-r--r--    1 root     root      165.6K Apr 15 10:35 vmware-1.log
-rw-r--r--    1 root     root      166.4K Apr 15 10:56 vmware.log
-rw-r--r--    1 root     root          90 Apr 15 10:35 win-file-srv-01-59643fe5.hlog
-rw-------    1 root     root        8.5K Apr 15 10:56 win-file-srv-01.nvram
-rw-------    1 root     root         563 Apr 15 09:52 win-file-srv-01.vmdk
-rw-r--r--    1 root     root           0 Apr 15 09:52 win-file-srv-01.vmsd
-rwxr-xr-x    1 root     root        2.9K Apr 15 10:56 win-file-srv-01.vmx
[root@esxi-hp-06:/vmfs/volumes/vvol:0000000100004001-84590195c951be61/rfc4122.f21565c0-6e5c-4fc5-999d-a64c0d477b1c]
```

Figure 32: Poweroff File

Of course, the creation of the poweroff file and the fact that the host is declared isolated is also stored in the fdm.log file. Below some example of what that looks like in the fdm.log file. Note that the example has been edited/pruned for readability purposes.

```
2018-03-12T12:08:30.398Z verbose fdm[2111414] Waited 5 seconds for isolation icmp ping reply. Isolated

2018-03-12T12:08:30.398Z info fdm[2111414] Host isolated is true

2018-03-12T12:09:00.399Z verbose fdm[2111421] [LocalIsolationPolicy::GetIsolationResponseInfo] Isolation response for VM
/vmfs/volumes/5981ca3d-a9cb2e29-540a-246e962f4910/Clustering-Deep-Dive-01/Clustering-Deep-Dive-01.vmx is powerOff

2018-03-12T12:09:35.403Z verbose fdm[2111421] [LocalIsolationPolicy::InitiateCreatePowerOffFiles] Creating power-off file for
/vmfs/volumes/5981ca3d-a9cb2e29-540a-246e962f4910/Clustering-Deep-Dive-01/Clustering-Deep-Dive-01.vmx.

2018-03-12T12:09:35.424Z verbose fdm[2111427] [LocalIsolationPolicy::DoVmPowerOff] Powering off /vmfs/volumes/5981ca3d-a9cb2e29-
540a-246e962f4910/Clustering-Deep-Dive-01/Clustering-Deep-Dive-01.vmx
```

Figure 33: Isolation Declared

After the completion of this sequence, the master will learn the slave was isolated through the "poweron" file as mentioned earlier, and will restart VMs based on the information provided by the slave.

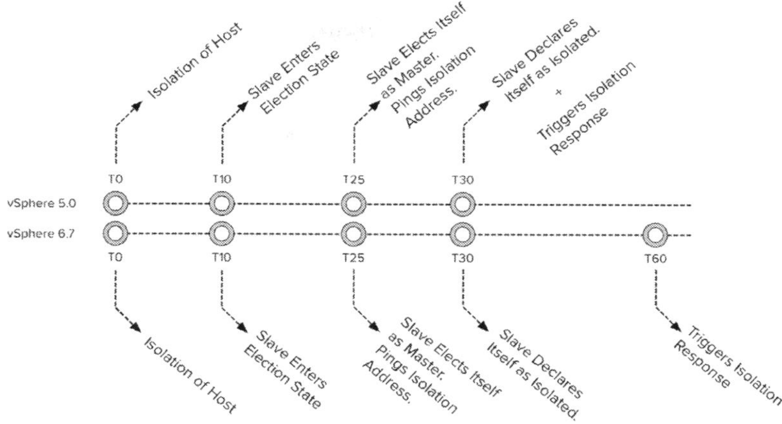

Figure 34: Restart of VM After Isolation

Isolation of a Master

In the case of the isolation of a master, this timeline is a bit less complicated because there is no need to go through an election process. In this timeline, "s" refers to seconds.

- T0 – Isolation of the host (master)
- T0 – Master pings "isolation addresses"
- T5s – Master declares itself isolated
- T35s – Master "triggers" isolation response

Additional Checks

Before a host declares itself isolated, it will ping the default isolation address which is the gateway specified for the management network, and will continue to ping the address until it becomes unisolated. HA gives you the option to define one or multiple additional isolation addresses using an advanced setting. This advanced setting is called `das.isolationaddress` and could be used to reduce the chances of having a false positive. We recommend setting an additional isolation address. If a secondary management network is configured, this additional address should be part of the same network as the secondary management network. If required, you can configure up to 10 additional isolation addresses. A secondary management network will more than likely be on a different subnet and it is recommended to specify an additional isolation address which is part of the subnet.

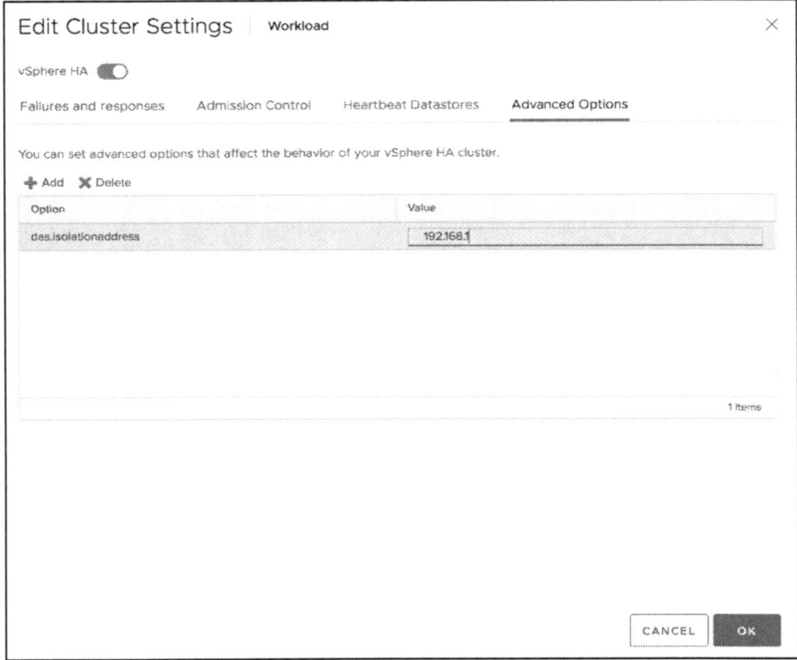

Figure 35: Isolation Address

Selecting an Additional Isolation Address

A question asked by many people is which address should be specified for this additional isolation verification. We generally recommend an isolation address close to the hosts to avoid too many network hops and an address that would correlate with the liveness of the VM network. In many cases, the most logical choice is the physical switch to which the host is directly connected. Basically, use the gateway for whatever subnet your management network is on. Another usual suspect would be a router, a virtual interface on the switch or any other reliable and pingable device on the same subnet. However, when you are using IP-based shared storage like NFS or iSCSI, the IP-address of the storage device can also be a good choice.

> **Select a reliable secondary isolation address. Try to minimize the number of "hops" between the host and this address.**

Isolation Policy Delay

For those who want to increase the time it takes before HA executes the isolation response an advanced setting is available. Thus setting is called `das.config.fdm.isolationPolicyDelaySec` and allows changing the number of seconds to wait before the isolation policy is executed is. The minimum value is 30. If set to a value less than 30, the delay will be 30 seconds. We do not recommend changing this advanced setting unless there is a specific requirement to do so. In almost all scenarios 30 seconds should suffice.

Restarting VMs

The most important procedure has not yet been explained: restarting VMs. We have dedicated a full section to this concept.
We have explained the difference in behavior from a timing perspective for restarting VMs in the case of a both master node and slave node failures. For now, let's assume that a slave node has failed. When the master node declares the slave node as Partitioned or Isolated, it determines which VMs were running on using the information it previously read from the host's "poweron" file. These files are asynchronously read approximately every 30s. If the host was not Partitioned or Isolated before the failure, the master uses cached data to determine the VMs that were last running on the host before the failure occurred.

Before it will initiate the restart attempts, though, the master will first validate that the VM should be restarted. This validation uses the protection information vCenter Server provides to each master, or if the master is not in contact with vCenter Server, the information saved in the protectedlist files. If the master is not in contact with vCenter Server or has not locked the file, the VM is filtered out. At this point, all VMs having a restart priority of "disabled" are also filtered out.

Now that HA knows which VMs it should restart, it is time to decide where the VMs are placed. HA will take multiple things in to account:

- CPU and memory reservation, including the memory overhead of the VM
- Unreserved capacity of the hosts in the cluster
- Restart priority of the VM relative to the other VMs that need to be restarted
- Virtual-machine-to-host compatibility set
- The number of dvPorts required by a VM and the number available on the candidate hosts
- The maximum number of vCPUs and VMs that can be run on a given host
- Restart latency
- Whether the active hosts are running the required number of agent VMs

Restart latency refers to the amount of time it takes to initiate VM restarts. This means that VM restarts will be distributed by the master across multiple hosts to avoid a boot storm, and thus a delay, on a single host.

If a placement is found, the master will send each target host the set of VMs it needs to restart. If this list exceeds 32 VMs, HA will limit the number of concurrent power on attempts to 32 for that particular host. If a VM successfully powers on, the node on which the VM was powered on will inform the master of the change in power state. The master will then remove the VM from the restart list.

If a placement cannot be found, the master will place the VM on a "pending placement list" and will retry placement of the VM when one of the following conditions changes:

- A new virtual-machine-to-host compatibility list is provided by vCenter
- A host reports that its unreserved capacity has increased
- A host (re)joins the cluster (For instance, when a host is taken out of maintenance mode, a host is added to a cluster, etc.)
- A new failure is detected and VMs have to be failed over
- A failure occurred when failing over a VM

But what about DRS? Wouldn't DRS be able to help during the placement of VMs when all else fails? It does. The master node will report to vCenter the set of VMs that were not placed due to insufficient resources, as is the case today. If DRS is enabled, this information will be used in an attempt to have DRS make capacity available.

VM Component Protection

In vSphere 6.0 a new feature, as part of vSphere HA, was introduced called VM Component Protection. *VM Component Protection* (VMCP) allows you to protect VMs against the failure of your storage system, or components of the storage system or storage area network. There are two types of failures VMCP will respond to, those are *Permanent Device Loss* (PDL) and *All Paths Down* (APD). Before we look at some of the details, we want to point out that enabling VMCP is extremely easy. It can be enabled in the Failures and Responses section by simply selecting the response for a PDL and the response for an APD. Note that in the new vSphere Client the term "VM Component Protection" is not used any longer, instead we refer to "Datastore with PDL" and "Datastore with APD" as shown in the below screenshot.

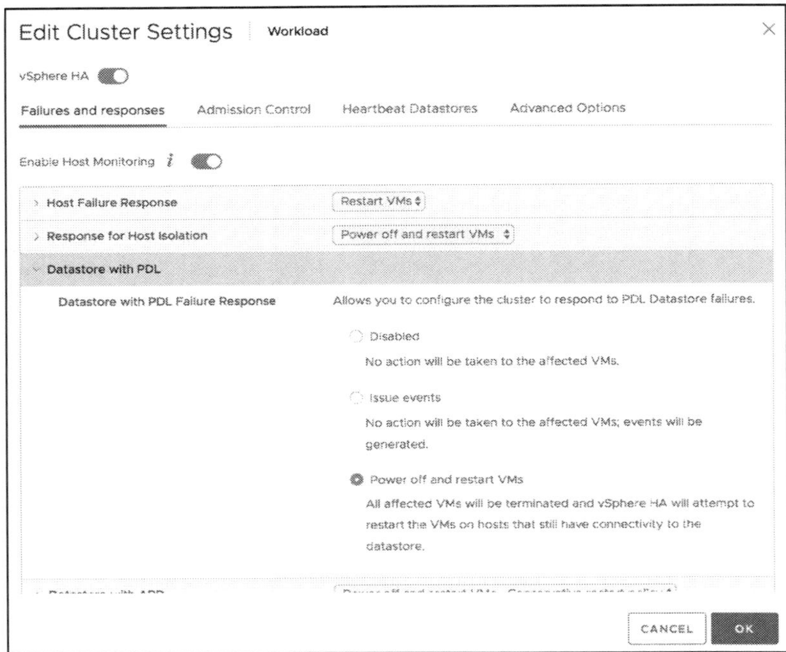

Figure 36: VM Component Protection - PDL

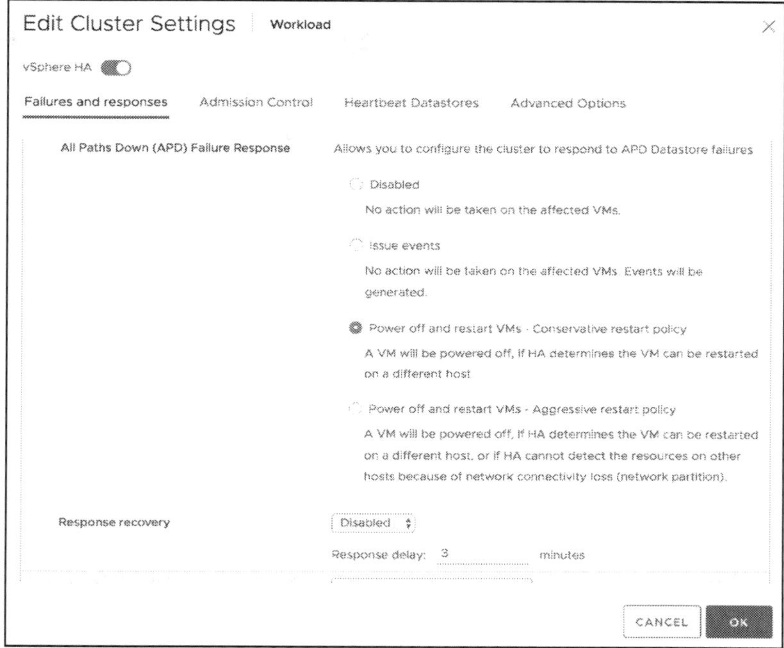

Figure 37: VM Component Protection - APD

As stated there are two scenarios HA can respond to: PDL and APD. Let's look at those two scenarios a bit closer. With vSphere 5.0 a feature was introduced as an advanced option that would allow vSphere HA to restart VMs impacted by a PDL condition.

A PDL condition is a condition that is communicated by the array controller to ESXi via a SCSI sense code. This condition indicates that a device (LUN) has become unavailable and is likely permanently unavailable. An example scenario in which this condition would be communicated by the array would be when a LUN is set offline. This condition is used during a failure scenario to ensure ESXi takes appropriate action when access to a LUN is revoked. It should be noted that when a full storage failure occurs it is impossible to generate a PDL condition as there is no communication possible between the array and the ESXi host. This state will be identified by the ESXi host as an APD condition.

Although the (advanced setting) functionality itself worked as advertised, enabling and managing it was cumbersome and error prone. It was required to set the option "`disk.terminateVMOnPDLDefault`" manually. With vSphere 6.0 a simple option in the Web Client was introduced which allowed you to specify what the response should be to a PDL sense code. This is shown in the screenshot below:

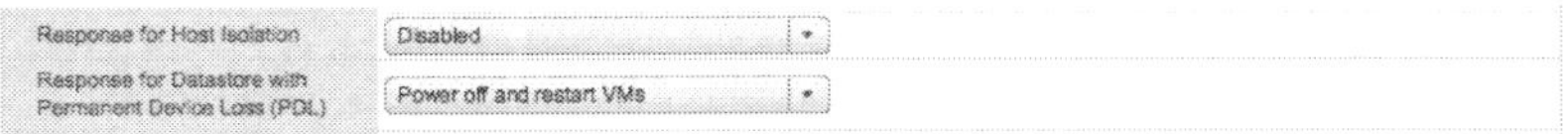

Figure 38: Web Client PDL Response

In the vSphere Client (HTML-5) the experience changed slightly. PDL is no longer spelled out, and the dropdown list has been removed for tick boxes. The options presented however remain the same.

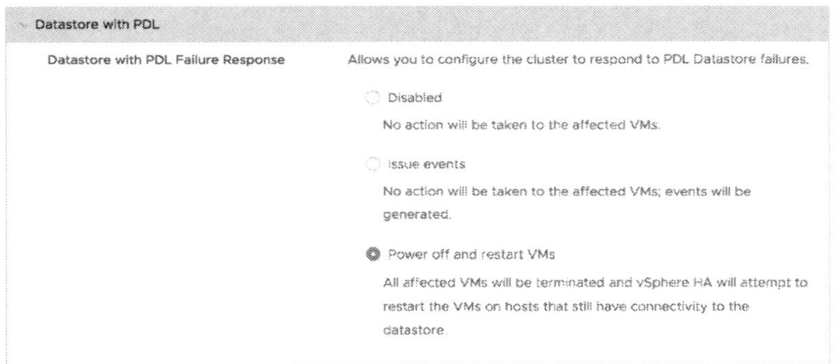

Figure 39: vSphere Client PDL Response

The three options provided are "Disabled, "Issue Events" and "Power off and restart VMs". Note that "Power off and restart VMs" does exactly that, your VM process is killed and the VM is restarted on a host which still has access to the storage device.

Pre-vSphere 6.0 it was not possible for vSphere to respond to an APD scenario. APD is the situation where the storage device has become inaccessible, but the reason is unknown to ESXi. In most cases, it is typically related to a storage network problem when this occurs. With vSphere 5.1 changes were introduced to the way APD scenarios were handled by the hypervisor. This mechanism is leveraged by HA to allow for a response.

As explained earlier, an APD condition is a situation where access to the storage is lost without receiving a SCSI sense code from the array. This for instance can happen when the network between the host and the storage system has failed, hence the name "all paths down." When an APD condition occurs (access to a device is lost) the hypervisor starts a timer. After 140 seconds the APD condition is declared and the device is marked as APD time out. When the 140 seconds has passed, HA will start a timer. The HA time out is 3 minutes by default. When the 3 minutes has passed, HA will take the action defined within the UI. There are four options:

- Disabled
- Issue Events
- Power off and restart VMs – Conservative
- Power off and restart VMs – Aggressive

Note that aggressive and conservative refers to the likelihood of HA being able to restart VMs. When set to "conservative" HA will only restart the VM that is impacted by the APD if it knows another host can restart it. In the case of "aggressive" HA will try to restart the VM even if it doesn't know the state of the other hosts. This could lead to a situation where your VM is not restarted when there is no host that has access to the datastore the VM is located on. Having said that, in a normal situation HA will always know what the state is. The Conservative and Aggressive option really only come in to play when there is a network partition of some kind. It is fair to say that in normal clusters this is fairly unlikely, in a stretched cluster however this is likely to occur.

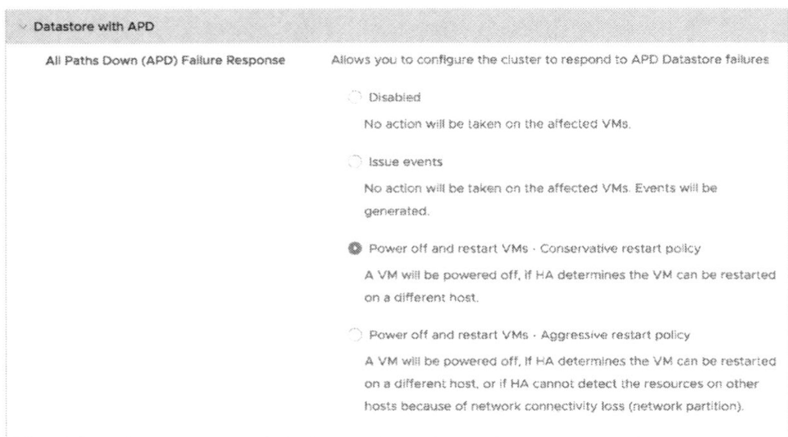

Figure 40: vSphere Client APD Response

It is also good to know that if the APD is lifted and access to the storage is restored during the total of the approximate 5 minutes and 20 seconds it would take before the VM restart is initiated, that HA will not do anything unless you explicitly configure it do so. This is where the "Response recovery" comes in to play as shown in the screenshot above. If there is a desire to do so you can reset the VM even when the host has recovered from the APD scenario, during the 3-minute (default value) grace period. This can be useful in the event where VMs reside in an unrecoverable state after an APD condition has been declared.

Another useful option is the Response Delay. This setting determines when HA response to the declared APD state. By default, as already mentioned, this is set to 3 minutes. Although you can increase or decrease this delay we recommend leaving this unchanged, unless there's a specific reason to change this of course like for instance a recovery time objective of lower than five minutes as defined in a service level agreement.

> **Without access to shared storage a VM becomes useless. It is highly recommended to configure VMCP to act on a PDL and APD scenario. We recommend setting both to "power off and restart VMs" but leave the "response for APD recovery after APD timeout" disabled so that VMs are not rebooted unnecessarily.**

vSphere HA respecting Affinity Rules

Prior to vSphere 5.5, HA did nothing with VM to VM Affinity or Anti Affinity rules. Typically for people using "affinity" rules this was not an issue, but those using "anti-affinity" rules did see this as an issue. They created these rules to ensure specific VMs would never be running on the same host, but vSphere HA would simply ignore the rule when a failure had occurred and just place the VMs "randomly". With vSphere 5.5 this changed vSphere HA is "anti-affinity" aware and in vSphere 6.0 also VM to Host affinity aware. In order to ensure anti-affinity rules were respected you had to set advanced settings or configure in the vSphere Web Client as of vSphere 6.0 as shown below.

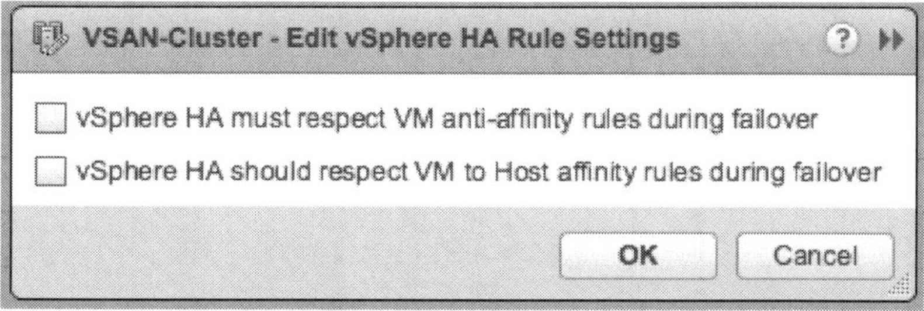

Figure 41: vSphere HA Rule Settings

Now note that this does not mean that when you configure anti-affinity rules or VM to Host affinity rules and have this configured to "true" and somehow there aren't sufficient hosts available to respect these rules that HA would not restart the VM. It would aim to comply to the rules, but availability trumps cluster rules in this case and VMs will be restarted.

In vSphere 6.5 to configure this has disappeared completely. The reason for this is because vSphere HA now tries to respect these rules by default, as it appeared this is the behavior customers wanted.

Note, that if for whatever reason vSphere HA cannot respect the rules, as mentioned before, it will restart the VMs (violating the rule) as these are non-mandatory rules it choses availability over compliancy in this situation.

If you would like to disable this behavior and don't care about these rules during a fail-over event you can set either or both advanced settings:

- `das.respectVmVmAntiAffinityRules` – set to "true" by default, set to "false" if you want to disable it
- `das.respectVmHostSoftAffinityRules` – set to "true" by default, set to "false" if you want to disable it

We recommend against changing the default behavior. vSphere HA will try to conform to the rules, and if needed will violate. We also recommend using a limited number of rules, we will explain the DRS section of the book what the potential impact is of a higher number of rules.

One more thing to note, many people seem to be under the impression that Affinity, Anti-Affinity and VM-to-Host rules are a DRS function. This is mainly the result of the name (DRS Rules) the feature had in the past. However, these are cluster rules and not a DRS function per se. The functionality can also be used with DRS enabled or licensed, although that limits usefulness in our opinion.

05

VSAN AND VVOL SPECIFICS

In the last couple of sections, we have discussed the ins and out of HA. All of it based on VMFS based or NFS based storage. With the introduction of VMware vSAN and Virtual Volumes also comes changes to some of the discussed concepts. We've already seen that the use of vSAN potentially changes the design decision around the isolation response. What else is different for HA when vSAN or VVols are used in the environment? Let's take a look at vSAN first.

HA and vSAN

vSAN is VMware's approach to Software Defined Storage. We are not going to explain the ins and outs of vSAN, but we do want to provide a basic understanding for those who have never done anything with it. vSAN leverages host local storage and creates a shared data store out of it. If you have an interest in learning more about vSAN after reading this section of the book, we can highly recommend reading the freely available vSAN Essentials book by Cormac Hogan and Duncan Epping. The book can be found here: www.vsan-essentials.com.

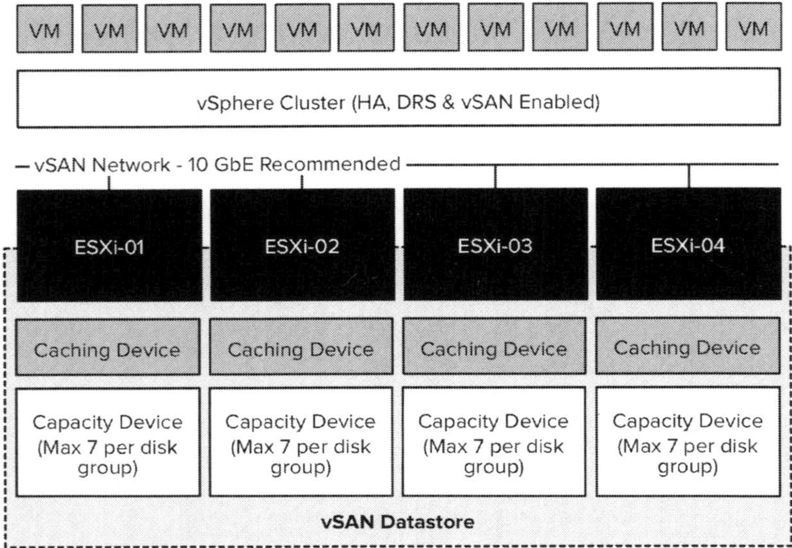

Figure 42: vSAN Datastore

vSAN requires a minimum of 3 hosts and each of those 3 hosts will need to have 1 SSD for caching and 1 capacity device (can be SSD or HDD). Only the capacity devices will contribute to the total available capacity of the datastore. If you have 1 TB worth of capacity devices per host then with three hosts the total size of your datastore will be 3 TB.

Having said that, with vSAN 6.1 VMware introduced a "2-node" option. This 2-node option is actually two regular vSAN nodes with a third "witness" node, where the witness node acts as a quorum and does not run workloads and neither contributes to the capacity of the vSAN Datastore.

The big differentiator between most storage systems and vSAN is that availability of the VM's is defined on a per virtual disk or per VM basis through policy. This is what vSAN calls "Failures To Tolerate", and can be configured to any value between 0 (zero) and 3. When configured to 0 then the VM will have only 1 copy of its virtual disks (objects) that means that if a host fails where the virtual disks (objects) are stored the VM is lost. As such all VMs are deployed by default with *Failures To Tolerate*

(FTT) set to 1. A virtual disk is what vSAN refers to as an object. An object, when FTT is configured as 1 or higher, has multiple components. In the diagram below we demonstrate the FTT=1 scenario, and the virtual disk in this case has 2 "data components" and a "witness components". The witness is used as a "quorum" mechanism. Note that in a two-node configuration, this witness component would be stored on the Witness node, always! Node that the situation below shows the simplest of vSAN policy capabilities. There are also options to increase the stripe size, or use RAID-5 or RAID-6 or even increase the Failures To Tolerate to 2 or 3, which would increase the number of components.

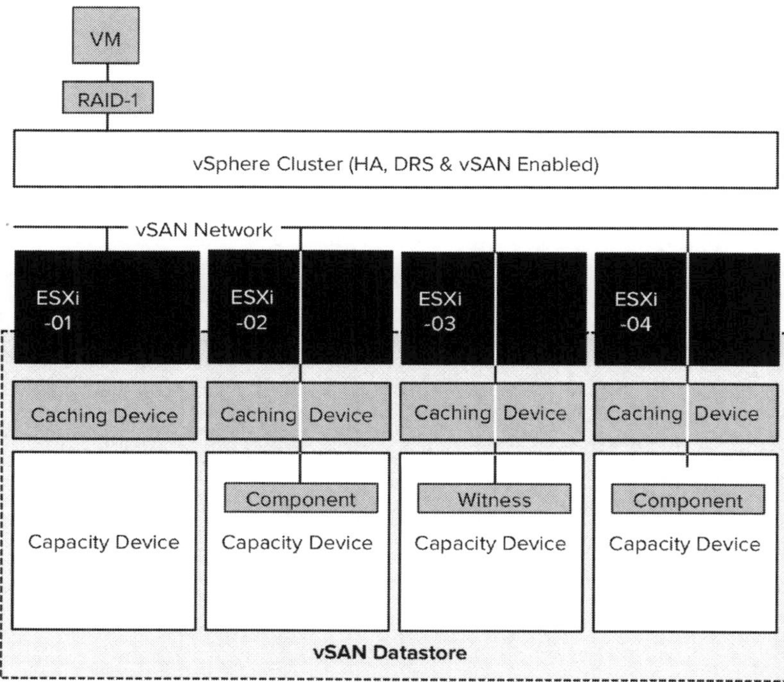

Figure 43: vSAN Network RAID

As the diagram above depicts, a VM can be running on the first host in the cluster while its storage components are on the remaining hosts in the cluster. Note that the above

As you can imagine from an HA point of view this changes things as access to the network is not only critical for HA to function correctly but also for vSAN. When it comes to networking note that when vSAN is configured in a cluster HA will use the same network for its communications (heartbeating etc). On top of that, it is good to know that VMware highly recommends 10GbE to be used for vSAN.

> **10GbE is highly recommend for vSAN, as vSphere HA also leverages the vSAN network and availability of VMs is dependent on network connectivity ensure that at a minimum two 10GbE ports are used and two physical switches for resiliency.**

The reason that HA uses the same network as vSAN is simple, it is too avoid network partition scenarios where HA communications is separated from vSAN and the state of the cluster is unclear. Note that you will need to ensure that there is a pingable isolation address on the vSAN network and this isolation address will need to be configured as such through the use of the advanced setting `das.isolationAddress0`. We also recommend to disable the use of the default isolation address through the advanced setting `das.useDefaultIsolationAddress` (set to false).

If you leave the isolation address set to the default gateway of the management network, then HA will use the management network to verify the isolation. There could be a scenario where only the vSAN network is isolated, in that particular situation VMs will not be powered off (or shutdown) when the isolation address is not part of the vSAN network.

When an isolation does occur the isolation response is triggered as explained in earlier chapters. For vSAN the recommendation is simple, configure the isolation response to "Power Off and restarts VMs". This is the safest option. vSAN can be compared to the "converged network with IP based storage" example we provided earlier. It is very easy to reach a situation where a host is isolated, and all VMs remain running but are restarted on another host because the connection to the vSAN datastore is lost.

> **Configure your Isolation Address and your Isolation Policy accordingly. We recommend selecting "power off" as the Isolation Policy and selecting a reliable pingable device as the isolation address.**

Folder Structure with vSAN for HA

What about things like heartbeat datastores and the folder structure that exists on a VMFS datastore, has any of that changed with vSAN. Yes, it has. First of all, in a "vSAN" only environment the concept of Heartbeat Datastores is not used at all. The reason for this is straight forward, as HA and vSAN share the same network it is safe to assume that when the HA heartbeat is lost because of a network failure so is access to the vSAN datastore. Only in an environment where there is also traditional storage the heartbeat datastores will be configured, leveraging those traditional datastores as a heartbeat datastore. Note that we do not feel there is a reason to introduce traditional storage just to provide HA this functionality, HA and vSAN work perfectly fine without heartbeat datastores. If you however have traditional storage we do recommend implementing heartbeat datastores as it can help HA with identifying the type of issue that has occurred.

Normally HA metadata is stored in the root of the datastore, for vSAN this is different as the metadata is stored in the VM's namespace object. The protectedlist is held in memory and updated automatically when VMs are powered on or off.

Now you may wonder, what happens when there is an isolation? How does HA know where to start the VM that is impacted? Let's take a look at a partition scenario.

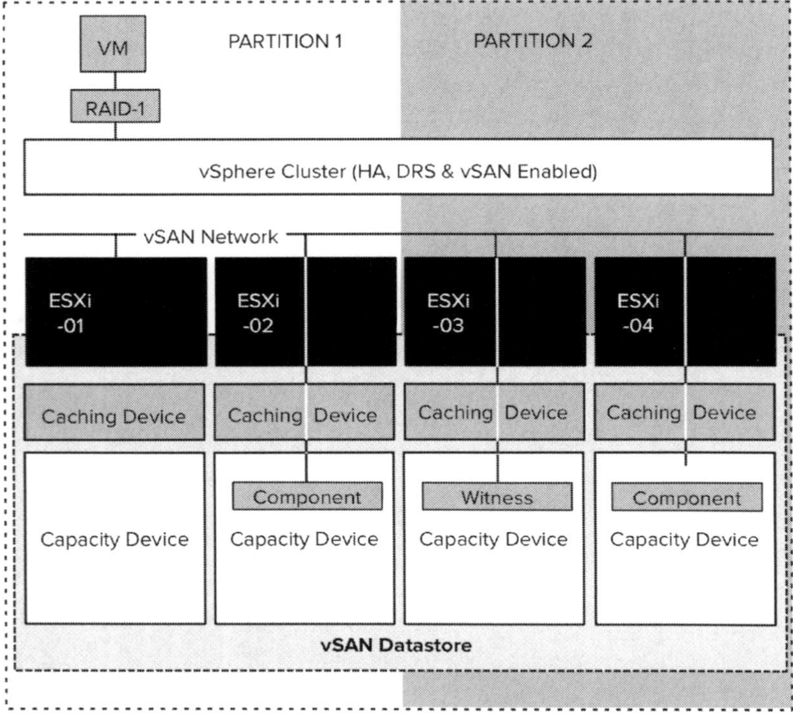

Figure 44: vSAN Partition Scenario

In this scenario, there a network problem has caused a cluster partition. Where a VM is restarted is determined by which partition owns the VM files. Within a vSAN cluster this is fairly straightforward. There are two partitions, one of which is running the VM with its VMDK and the other partition has a VMDK replica and a witness. Guess what happens!? Right, vSAN uses the witness to verify which partition has quorum and based on that result, one of the two partitions will win. In this case, Partition 2 has more than 50% of the components of this object and as such is the winner. This means that the VM will be restarted on either ESXi-03 or ESXi-04 by HA. Note that the VM in Partition 1 may or may not be powered off, this depends on whether ESXi-01 and ESXi-02 can communicate with each other or not. If ESXi-01 and ESXi-02 can communicate then the VM will not be powered off as the isolation response it not triggered. If ESXi-01 and ESXi-02 cannot communicate then the isolation response will be triggered and the VM will be powered off. Note that for the sake of simplicity we simplified the example. For a detailed understanding of how vSAN components, witnesses and the quorum mechanism (votes) work we like to refer to the vSAN Essentials book by Cormac Hogan and Duncan Epping.

One final thing which is different for vSAN is how a partition is handled in a stretched cluster configuration. In a traditional stretched cluster configuration, using VMFS/NFS based storage, VMs impacted by an APD or PDL will be killed by HA through VM Component Protection. With vSAN this is slightly different. HA VMCP in 6.0 and higher is not supported with vSAN.

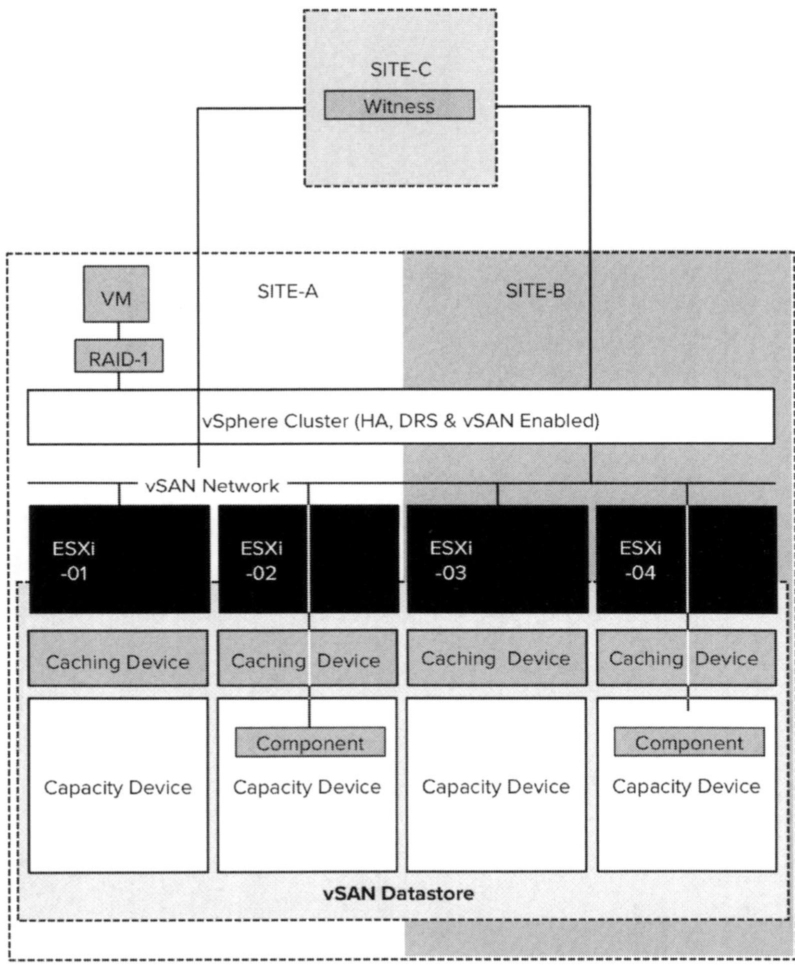

Figure 45: vSAN Stretched Cluster

vSAN has its own mechanism, for now at least. vSAN recognizes when a VM running on a group of hosts, in the diagram above let's say Site B, has no access to any of the components in a stretched cluster. When this is the case vSAN will simply kill the impacted VM. You can disable this behavior, although we do not recommend doing this, by setting the advanced host setting called `VSAN.AutoTerminateGhostVm` to 0.

Heartbeat Datastores, When Can They Help?

We have already briefly discussed this, but we want to reiterate this as it is a topic, which is skipped and overlooked often. Even in a vSAN environment Heartbeat Datastores can be useful. Let us first go over an isolation scenario briefly again and then discuss why the Heartbeat Datastore could be "useful". I used quotes here on purpose, as some might not prefer the behavior when a heartbeat datastore is defined in a vSAN world.
When is an isolation declared? A host declares itself isolated when:

- It is not receiving any communication from the master
- It cannot ping the isolation address
- It is not receiving any election traffic of any other hosts in the cluster

If you have not set any advanced settings then the default gateway of the management network will be the isolation address. Just imagine your vSAN Network to be isolated on a given host, but for whatever reason the Management Network is not. In that scenario isolation is not declared, the host can still ping the isolation address using the management network vmkernel interface. However, vSphere HA will restart the VMs. The VMs have lost access to disk, as such the lock on the VMDK is lost. HA notices the host is gone, which must mean that the VMs are dead as the locks are lost. It will then try to restart the VMs.

That is when you could find yourself in the situation where the VMs are running on the isolated host and also somewhere else in the cluster. Both with the same mac address and the same name / IP address. Not a good situation to be in when those VMs are still accessible over the VM network. Although this is not likely, it still is a risk with a relatively high impact.

This is where the heartbeat datastore could come in handy. If you would have had datastore heartbeats enabled, and accessible during the failure, then this would be prevented. The isolated host would simply inform the master it is isolated through the heartbeat datastore, and it would also inform the master about the state of the VMs, which in this scenario would be powered-on. The master would then decide not to restart the VMs. Do realize that the VMs which are running on the isolated host are more or less useless as they cannot write to disk anymore. Although the heartbeat datastore will prevent the VMs from being restarted, and as such avoid the duplicate mac address and/or IP-address issue, this could still be considered undesirable as the VMs may be unusable as they cannot write to disk.

> **There is no right or wrong in this case. Whether you should or should not use Heartbeat Datastore entirely depends on your preferred outcome. As such we recommend testing with and without heartbeat, and configure based on your preferred outcome.**

HA and Virtual Volumes

Let us start with first describing what Virtual Volumes is and what value it brings to an administrator. Virtual Volumes, or VVols as it is usually referred too, was developed to make your life (vSphere admin) and that of the storage administrator easier. This is done by providing a framework that enables the vSphere administrator to assign policies to VMs or virtual disks, not unlike vSAN. In these policies capabilities of the storage array can be defined. These capabilities can be things like snapshotting, deduplication, raid-level, thin / thick provisioning etc. What is offered to the vSphere administrator is up to the Storage administrator, and of course up to what the storage system can offer to begin with. In the screenshots below, we show an example for instance of some of the capabilities Nimble exposes through policy.

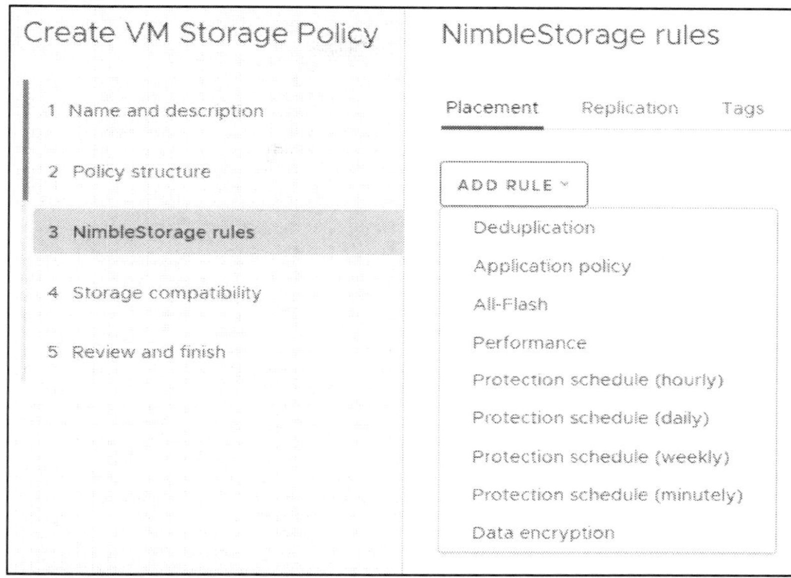

Figure 46: Virtual Volumes Enabling Capabilities

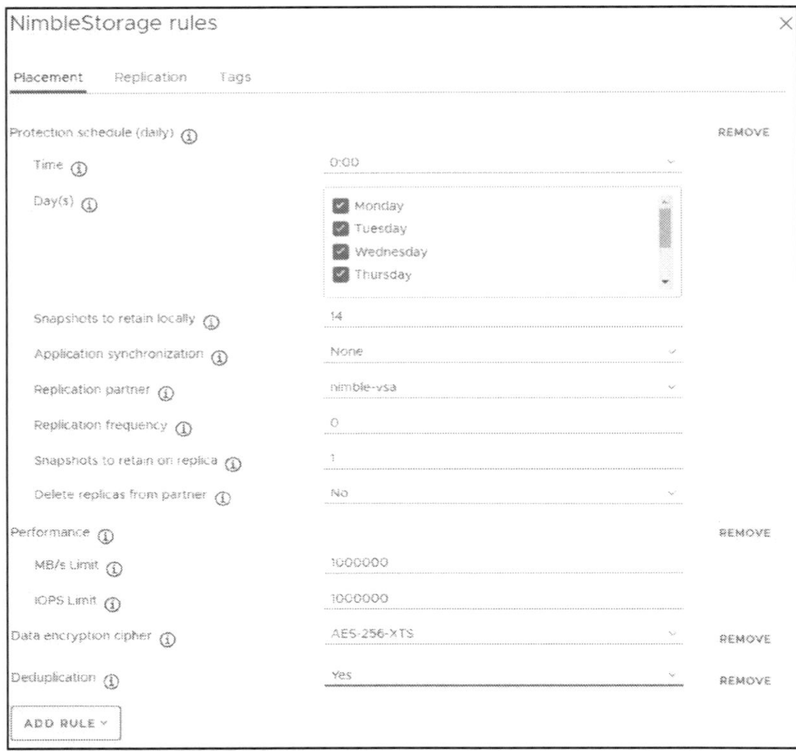

Figure 47: Virtual Volumes Nimble Protection Schedule

When a VM is deployed and a policy is assigned then the storage system will enable certain functionality of the array based on what was specified in the policy. So no longer a need to assign capabilities to a LUN, which holds many VMs, but rather per VM or even per VMDK level control. So how does this work? Let's take a look at an architectural diagram first.

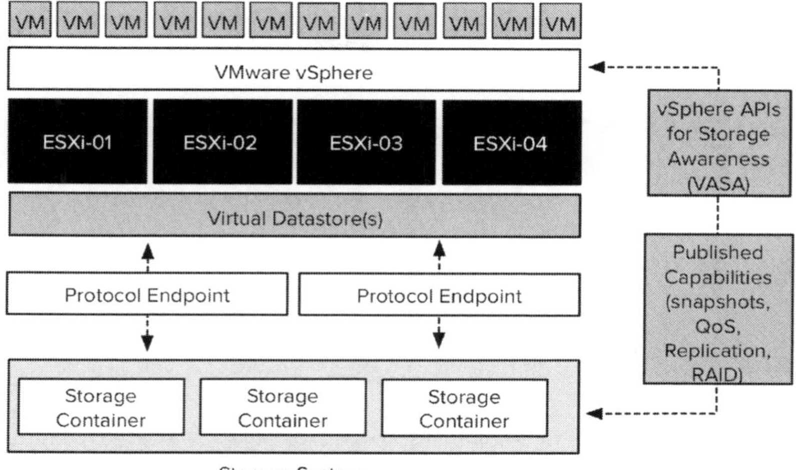

Figure 48: Virtual Volumes Architecture

The diagram shows a couple of components that are important in the VVol architecture. Let's list them out:

- Protocol Endpoints aka PE
- Virtual Datastore and a Storage Container
- Vendor Provider / VASA
- Policies
- Virtual Volumes

Let's take a look at all of these three in the above order.

Protocol Endpoints, what are they? Protocol Endpoints are literally the access point to your storage system. All IO to virtual volumes is proxied through a Protocol Endpoint and you can have 1 or more of these per storage system, if your storage system supports having multiple of course. (Implementations of different vendors will vary.) PEs are compatible with different protocols (FC, FCoE, iSCSI, NFS) and if you ask me that whole discussion with Virtual Volumes will come to an end. You could see a Protocol Endpoint as a "mount point" or a device, and yes, they will count towards your maximum number of devices per host (1024 as of vSphere 6.7). (Virtual Volumes itself won't count towards that!)

Next up is the **Storage Container**. This is the place where you store your VMs, or better said where your virtual volumes end up. The Storage Container is a storage system logical construct and is represented within vSphere as a "virtual datastore". You need 1 per storage system, but you can have many when desired. To this Storage Container you can apply capabilities. If you like your virtual volumes to be able to use array based snapshots then the storage administrator will need to assign that capability to the storage container. Note that a storage administrator can grow a storage container without even informing you. A storage container isn't formatted with VMFS or anything like that, so you don't need to increase the volume in order to use the space.

But how does vSphere know which container is capable of doing what? In order to discover a storage container and its capabilities we need to be able to talk to the storage system first. This is done through the **vSphere APIs for Storage Awareness**. You simply point vSphere to the Vendor Provider and the vendor provider will report to vSphere what's available, this includes both the storage containers as well as the capabilities they possess. Note that a single Vendor Provider can be managing multiple storage systems which in its turn can have multiple storage containers with many capabilities. These vendor providers can also come in different flavors, for some storage systems it is part of their software but for others it will come as a virtual appliance that sits on top of vSphere.

Now that vSphere knows which systems there are, what containers are available with which capabilities you can start creating **policies**. These policies can be a combination of capabilities and will ultimately be assigned to VMs or virtual disks even. You can imagine that in some cases you would like Quality of Service enabled to ensure performance for a VM while in other cases it isn't as relevant, but you need to have a snapshot every hour. All of this is enabled through these policies. No longer will you be maintaining that spreadsheet with all your LUNs and which data service were enabled and what not, no you simply assign a policy. (Yes, a proper naming scheme will be helpful when defining policies.)

When requirements change for a VM you don't move the VM around, no you change the policy and the storage system will do what is required in order to make the VM (and its disks) compliant again with the policy. Not the VM really, but the VVols.

Okay, those are the basics, now what about Virtual Volumes and vSphere HA. What changes when you are running Virtual Volumes, what do you need to keep in mind when running Virtual Volumes when it comes to HA?

First of all, let me mention this, in some cases storage vendors have designed a solution where the "vendor provider" isn't designed in an HA fashion (VMware allows for Active/Active, Active/Standby or just "Active" as in a single instance). Make sure to validate what kind of implementation your storage vendor has, as the Vendor Provider needs to be available when powering on VMs. The following quote explains why:

> *"When a Virtual Volume is created, it is not immediately accessible for IO. To Access Virtual Volumes, vSphere needs to issue a "Bind" operation to a VASA Provider (VP), which creates IO access point for a Virtual Volume on a Protocol Endpoint (PE) chosen by a VP. A single PE can be the IO access point for multiple Virtual Volumes. "Unbind" Operation will remove this IO access point for a given Virtual Volume."*

That is the "Virtual Volumes" implementation aspect, but of course things have also changed from a vSphere HA point of view. No longer do we have VMFS or NFS datastores to store files on or use for heartbeating. What changes from that perspective. First of all a VM is carved up in different VVols:

- VM Configuration
- VM Disk's
- Swap File
- Snapshot (if there are any)

Besides these different types of objects, when vSphere HA is enabled there also is a volume used by vSphere HA and this volume will contain all the metadata which is normally stored under "`/<root of datastore>/.vSphere-HA/<cluster-specific-directory>/`" on regular VMFS. For each HA Cluster a separate folder will be created in this VVol as shown in the screenshot below.

```
[root@esxi-hp-06:/vmfs/volumes/vvol:0000000100004001-84598195c951be61/rfc4122.1afaad68-d4fb-438f-88cb-8a61258a9cb6] ls -lah
total 485384
drwxr-xr-t    1 root     root         1.4K Apr 15 09:36 .
drwxr-xr-x    1 root     root          512 Apr 15 10:04 ..
-r--------    1 root     root       128.0K Apr 15 09:34 .fbb.sf
-r--------    1 root     root        79.8M Apr 15 09:34 .fdc.sf
-r--------    1 root     root         1.1M Apr 15 09:34 .pb2.sf
-r--------    1 root     root       256.0M Apr 15 09:34 .pbc.sf
-r--------    1 root     root       128.3M Apr 15 09:34 .sbc.sf
drwx------    1 root     root          280 Apr 15 09:34 .sdd.sf
-r--------    1 root     root         4.0M Apr 15 09:34 .vh.sf
drwx------    1 root     root         1.5K Apr 15 09:58 FDM-07FCC8A1-D94C-4823-9135-A7ED99140480-26-5913ec2-vcsa-05
[root@esxi-hp-06:/vmfs/volumes/vvol:0000000100004001-84598195c951be61/rfc4122.1afaad68-d4fb-438f-88cb-8a61258a9cb6]
```

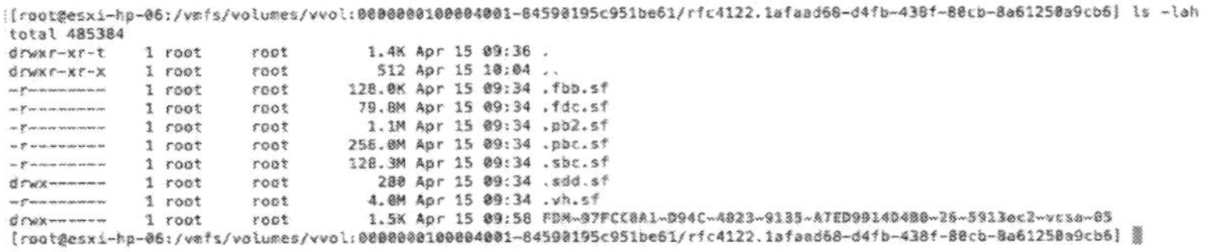

Figure 49: Virtual Volumes Folder Structure

All VM related HA files which normally would be under the VM folder, like for instance the power-on file, heartbeat files and the protectedlist, are now stored in the VM Configuration VVol object. Conceptually speaking similar to regular VMFS, implementation wise however completely different.

```
[root@esxi-hp-05:/vmfs/volumes/vvol:0000000100004001-84598195c951be61/rfc4122.1afaad68-d4fb-438f-88cb-8a61258a9cb6/FDM-07FCC8A1-D94C-4823-9135-A7ED99140480-26-5913ec2-vcsa-05] ls -lah
total 1048
drwx------    1 root     root         1.5K Apr 15 09:38 .
drwxr-xr-t    1 root     root         1.4K Apr 15 09:38 ..
-rw-r--r--    1 root     root            8 Apr 15 10:24 host-63-hb
-rw-r--r--    1 root     root         1.3K Apr 15 09:38 host-63-poweron
-rw-r--r--    1 root     root            8 Apr 15 10:24 host-70-hb
-rw-r--r--    1 root     root          921 Apr 15 09:36 host-70-poweron
-rw-r--r--    1 root     root            8 Apr 15 10:24 host-74-hb
-rw-r--r--    1 root     root          323 Apr 15 09:38 host-74-poweron
-rw-r--r--    1 root     root            8 Apr 15 10:24 host-78-hb
-rw-r--r--    1 root     root          502 Apr 15 09:38 host-78-poweron
-rw-r--r--    1 root     root         2.0K Apr 15 09:59 protectedlist
[root@esxi-hp-05:/vmfs/volumes/vvol:0000000100004001-84598195c951be61/rfc4122.1afaad68-d4fb-438f-88cb-8a61258a9cb6/FDM-07FCC8A1-D94C-4823-9135-A7ED99140480-26-5913ec2-vcsa-05]
```

Figure 50: Virtual Volumes Object for HA Files

The power-off file however, which is used to indicate that a VM has been powered-off due to an isolation event, is not stored under the `.vSphere-HA` folder any longer, but is stored in the VM config VVol (in the UI exposed as the VVol VM folder) as shown in the screenshot below. The same applies for vSAN, where it is now stored in the VM namespace object, and for traditional storage (NFS or VMFS) it is stored in the VM folder. This change was made when Virtual Volumes was introduced and done to keep the experience consistent across storage platforms.

```
[root@esxi-hp-06:/vmfs/volumes/vvol:0000000100004001-84590195c951be61/rfc4122.f21565c0-6e5c-4fc5-999d-a64c0d477b1c] ls -lah
total 488464
drwxr-xr-t    1 root     root        3.0K Apr 15 09:58 .
drwxr-xr-x    1 root     root         512 Apr 15 10:56 ..
drwxr-xr-x    1 root     root         420 Apr 15 10:35 .dvsData
-r--------    1 root     root      128.0K Apr 15 09:52 .fbb.sf
-r--------    1 root     root       79.8M Apr 15 09:52 .fdc.sf
-r--------    1 root     root        1.1M Apr 15 09:52 .pb2.sf
-r--------    1 root     root      256.0M Apr 15 09:52 .pbc.sf
-rw-------    1 root     root           0 Apr 15 09:52 .rfc4122.c492c080-6a96-483c-8559-ca45333faecf.lck
-rw-------    1 root     root         423 Apr 15 09:52 .rfc4122.c492c080-6a96-483c-8559-ca45333faecf.meta
-r--------    1 root     root      128.3M Apr 15 09:52 .sbc.sf
drwx------    1 root     root      [illegible]
-rw-------    1 root     root          55 Apr 15 10:56 .vSphereHA-poweroff
-r--------    1 root     root      [illegible]
-rw-r--r--    1 root     root      165.6K Apr 15 10:35 vmware-1.log
-rw-r--r--    1 root     root      166.4K Apr 15 10:56 vmware.log
-rw-r--r--    1 root     root          90 Apr 15 10:35 win-file-srv-01-59643fe5.hlog
-rw-------    1 root     root        8.5K Apr 15 10:56 win-file-srv-01.nvram
-rw-------    1 root     root         563 Apr 15 09:52 win-file-srv-01.vmdk
-rw-r--r--    1 root     root           0 Apr 15 09:52 win-file-srv-01.vmsd
-rwxr-xr-x    1 root     root        2.9K Apr 15 10:56 win-file-srv-01.vmx
[root@esxi-hp-06:/vmfs/volumes/vvol:0000000100004001-84590195c951be61/rfc4122.f21565c0-6e5c-4fc5-999d-a64c0d477b1c]
```

Figure 51: Virtual Volumes Location of Poweroff File

And that explains the differences between traditional storage systems using VMFS / NFS and new storage systems leveraging Virtual Volumes or even a full vSAN based solution.

06

ADDING RESILIENCY TO HA

In the previous chapter, we extensively covered both Isolation Detection, which triggers the selected Isolation Response and the impact of a false positive. The Isolation Response enables HA to restart VMs when "Power off" or "Shut down" has been selected and the host becomes isolated from the network. However, this also means that it is possible that, without proper redundancy, the Isolation Response may be unnecessarily triggered. This leads to downtime and should be prevented.

To increase resiliency for networking, VMware implemented the concept of NIC teaming in the hypervisor for both VMkernel and VM networking. When discussing HA, this is especially important for the Management Network.

> *"NIC teaming is the process of grouping together several physical NICs into one single logical NIC, which can be used for network fault tolerance and load balancing."*

Using this mechanism, it is possible to add redundancy to the Management Network to decrease the chances of an isolation event. This is, of course, also possible for other "Portgroups" but that is not the topic of this chapter or book. Another option is configuring an additional Management Network by enabling the "management network" tick box on another VMkernel port.

A little understood fact is that if there are multiple VMkernel networks on the same subnet, HA will use all of them for management traffic, even if only one is specified for management traffic!

Although there are many configurations possible and supported, we recommend a simple but highly resilient configuration. We have included the vMotion (VMkernel) network in our example as combining the Management Network and the vMotion network on a single vSwitch is the most commonly used configuration and an industry accepted best practice. Note that we will not go very deep in to the network design aspect at this stage, there are plenty of other resources that can help with this. We will also not discuss the use of a Standard vSwitch versus a Distributed Switch, as that topic does not belong in this book.

Requirements:

- 2 physical NICs
- VLAN trunking

Recommended:

- Minimum of 2 physical switches
- If available, enable "link state tracking" to ensure link failures are reported

The vSwitch should be configured as follows:

- vSwitch0: 2 Physical NICs (vmnic0 and vmnic1)
- 2 Portgroups (Management Network and vMotion VMkernel)
- Management Network active on vmnic0 and standby on vmnic1
- vMotion VMkernel active on vmnic1 and standby on vmnic0
- Failback set to No

Each portgroup has a VLAN ID assigned and runs dedicated on its own physical NIC; only in the case of a failure it is switched over to the standby NIC. We highly recommend setting failback to "No" to avoid chances of an unwanted isolation event, which can occur when a physical switch routes no traffic during boot but the ports are reported as "up". (NIC Teaming Tab)

Pros: Only 2 NICs in total are needed for the Management Network and vMotion VMkernel, especially useful in blade server environments. Easy to configure.

Cons: Just a single active path for heartbeats.

The following diagram depicts this active/standby scenario:

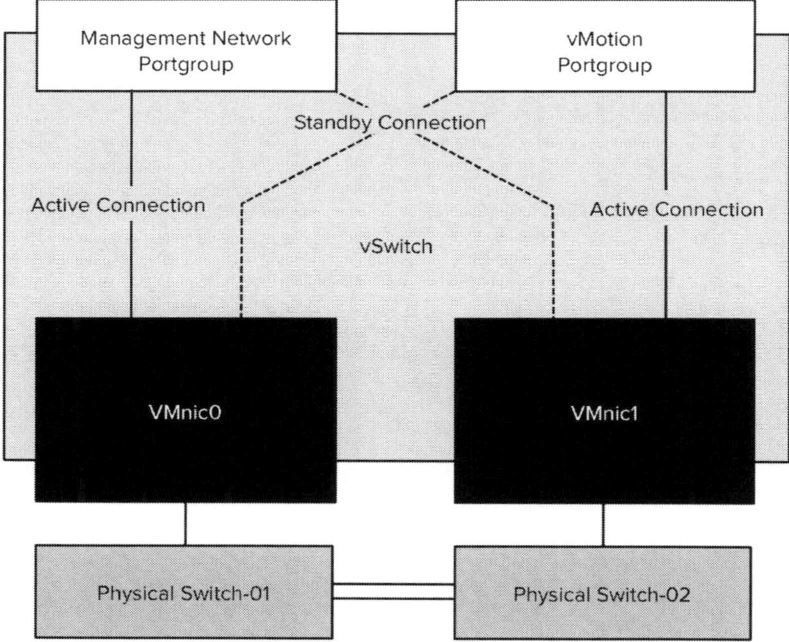

Figure 52: Network Configuration

To increase resiliency, we also recommend implementing the following advanced settings and using NIC ports on different PCI busses – preferably NICs of a different make and model. When using a different make and model, even a driver failure could be mitigated.

Advanced Settings: `das.isolationaddressX = <ip-address>`
The isolation address setting is discussed in more detail in the section titled "Fundamental Concepts". In short; it is the IP address that the HA agent pings to identify if the host is completely isolated from the network or just not receiving any heartbeats. If multiple VMkernel networks on different subnets are used, it is recommended to set an isolation address per network to ensure that each of these will be able to validate isolation of the host.

> **Take advantage of some of the basic features vSphere has to offer like NIC teaming. Combining different physical NICs will increase overall resiliency of your solution.**

Corner Case Scenario: Split-Brain

A split-brain scenario is a scenario where a single VM is powered up multiple times, typically on two different hosts. This is possible in the scenario where the isolation response is set to "Disabled" and network based storage, like NFS / iSCSI and even Virtual SAN, is used. This situation can occur during a full network isolation, which may result in the lock on the VM's VMDK being lost, enabling HA to actually power up the VM. As the VM was not powered off on its original host (isolation response set to "Disabled"), it will exist in memory on the isolated host and in memory with a disk lock on the host that was requested to restart the VM.

Keep in mind that this truly is a corner case scenario which is very unlikely to occur in most environments. In case it does happen, HA relies on the "lost lock detection" mechanism to mitigate this scenario. In short ESXi detects that the lock on the VMDK has been lost and, when the datastore becomes accessible again and the lock cannot be reacquired, issues a question whether the VM should be powered off; HA automatically answers the question with Yes. However, you will only see this question if you directly connect to the ESXi host during the failure. HA will generate an event for this auto-answered question though.
As stated above the question will be auto-answered and the VM will be

powered off to recover from the split-brain scenario. The question still remains: in the case of an isolation with iSCSI or NFS, should you power off VMs or leave them powered on?

As just explained, HA will automatically power off your original VM when it detects a split-brain scenario. This process however is not instantaneous and as such it is recommended to use the isolation response of “Power Off” or “Disabled”. We also recommend increasing heartbeat network resiliency to avoid getting in to this situation. We will discuss the options you have for enhancing Management Network resiliency in the next chapter.

Link State Tracking

This was already briefly mentioned in the list of recommendations, but this feature is something we would like to emphasize. We have noticed that people often forget about this even though many switches offer this capability, especially in blade server environments.

Link state tracking will mirror the state of an upstream link to a downstream link. Let’s clarify that with a diagram.

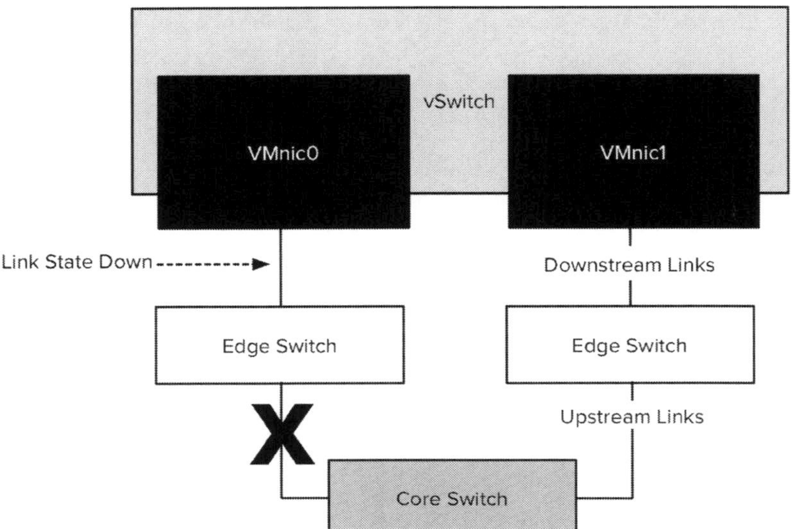

Figure 53: Link State Tracking

The diagram above depicts a scenario where an uplink of a "Core Switch" has failed. Without Link State Tracking, the connection from the "Edge Switch" to vmnic0 will be reported as up. With Link State Tracking enabled, the state of the link on the "Edge Switch" will reflect the state of the link of the "Core Switch" and as such be marked as "down". You might wonder why this is important but think about it for a second. Many features that vSphere offer rely on networking and so do your VMs. In the case where the state is not reflected, some functionality might just fail, for instance network heartbeating could fail if it needs to flow through the core switch. We call this a 'black hole' scenario: the host sends traffic down a path that it believes is up, but the traffic never reaches its destination due to the failed upstream link.

> **Know your network environment, talk to the network administrators and ensure advanced features like Link State Tracking are used when possible to increase resiliency.**

07

ADMISSION CONTROL

Admission Control is more than likely the most misunderstood concept vSphere holds today and because of this it is often disabled. However, Admission Control is a must when availability needs to be guaranteed and isn't that the reason for enabling HA in the first place?

What is HA Admission Control about? Why does HA contain this concept called Admission Control? The "Availability Guide", a.k.a. the HA bible, states the following:

> *"vCenter Server uses admission control to ensure that sufficient resources are available in a cluster to provide failover protection and to ensure that VM resource reservations are respected."*

Please read that quote again and especially the first two words. Indeed, it is vCenter that is responsible for Admission Control, contrary to what many believe. Although this might seem like a trivial fact it is important to understand that this implies that Admission Control will not disallow HA initiated restarts. HA initiated restarts are done on a host level and not through vCenter.

As said, Admission Control guarantees that capacity is available for an HA initiated failover by reserving resources within a cluster. It calculates the capacity required for a failover based on available resources. In other words, if a host is placed into maintenance mode or disconnected, it is taken out of the equation. This also implies that if a host has failed or is not responding but has not been removed from the cluster, it is still included in the equation. "Available Resources" indicates that the virtualization overhead has already been subtracted from the total amount.

To give an example; VMkernel memory is subtracted from the total amount of memory to obtain the memory available memory for VMs. There is one gotcha with Admission Control that we want to bring to your attention before drilling into the different policies. When Admission Control is enabled, HA will in no way violate availability constraints. This means that it will always ensure multiple hosts are up and running and this applies for manual maintenance mode actions and, for instance, to VMware Distributed Power Management. So, if a host is stuck trying to enter Maintenance Mode, remember that it might be HA which is not allowing Maintenance Mode to proceed as it would violate the Admission Control Policy. In this situation, users can manually vMotion VMs off the host or temporarily disable admission control to allow the operation to proceed.

But what if you use something like Distributed Power Management (DPM), would that place all hosts in standby mode to reduce power consumption? No, DPM is smart enough to take hosts out of standby mode to ensure enough resources are available to provide for HA initiated failovers. If by any chance the resources are not available, HA will wait for these resources to be made available by DPM and then attempt the restart of the VMs. In other words, the retry count (5 retries by default) is not wasted in scenarios like these.

Admission Control Policy

The Admission Control Policy dictates the mechanism that HA uses to guarantee enough resources are available for an HA initiated failover. This section gives a general overview of the available Admission Control Policies. The impact of each policy is described in the following section, including our recommendation. Admission Control changed in vSphere 6.5 substantially, or at least the user interface changed, and a new form of admission control was introduced. The user interface used to look like the below screenshot.

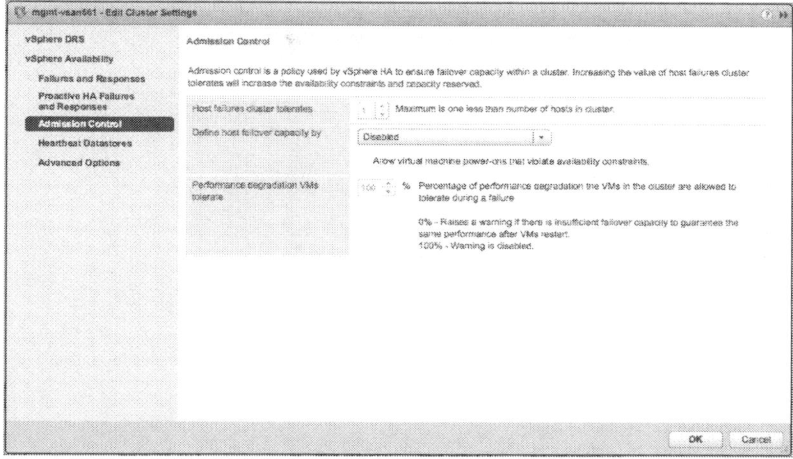

Figure 54: Admission Control

As of vSphere 6.5 the UI has changed, it combines two aspects of the different Admission Control algorithms.

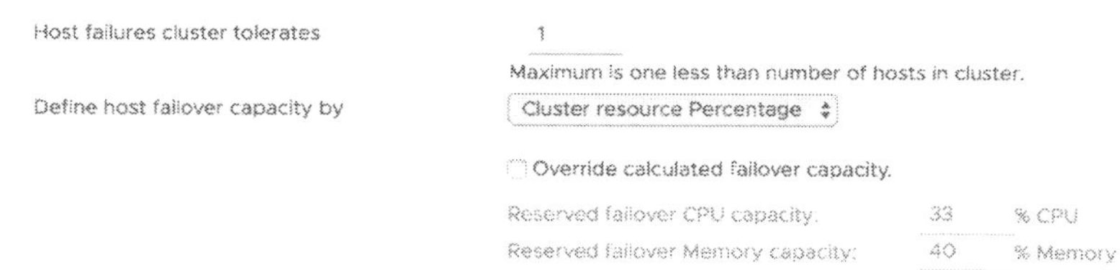

Figure 55: Admission Control Algorithms

Let's look at the different algorithms first, there are three options available. Each option has its caveats but also benefits, we do feel however that for the majority of environments the default Admission Control policy / algorithm is recommend.

Admission Control Algorithms

Each Admission Control Policy has its own Admission Control algorithm. Understanding each of these Admission Control algorithms is important to appreciate the impact each one has on your cluster design. For instance, setting a reservation on a specific VM can have an impact on the achieved consolidation ratio. This section will take you on a journey through the trenches of Admission Control Policies and their respective mechanisms and algorithms.

Cluster Resource Percentage Algorithm

The Cluster Resource Percentage algorithm used to be an admission control policy option and was one of the most used admission control policies. The simple reason for this was that it is the least restrictive and most flexible. It was also very easy to configure as shown in the screenshot below, which is what the UI looked like pre-vSphere 6.5.

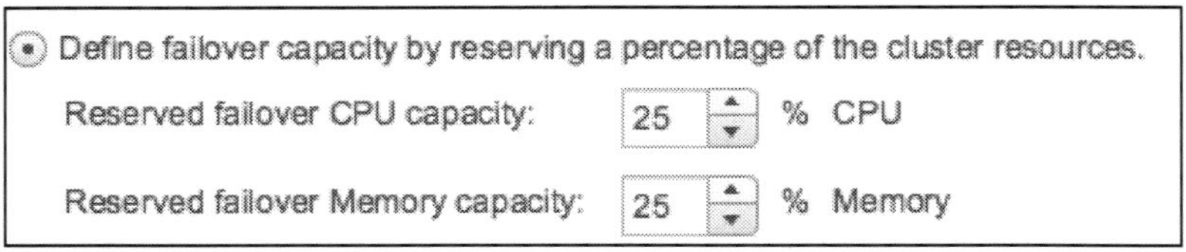

(•) Define failover capacity by reserving a percentage of the cluster resources.

Reserved failover CPU capacity: 25 % CPU

Reserved failover Memory capacity: 25 % Memory

Figure 56: Percentage Based

The main advantage of the cluster resource percentage algorithm is the ease of configuration, and flexibility it offered in terms of how resources were saved for VM restarts. The big change in vSphere 6.5 however is that there no longer is a need to specify a percentage manually, but you can now specify how many Host Failures the Cluster should Tolerate as shows in the below screenshot.

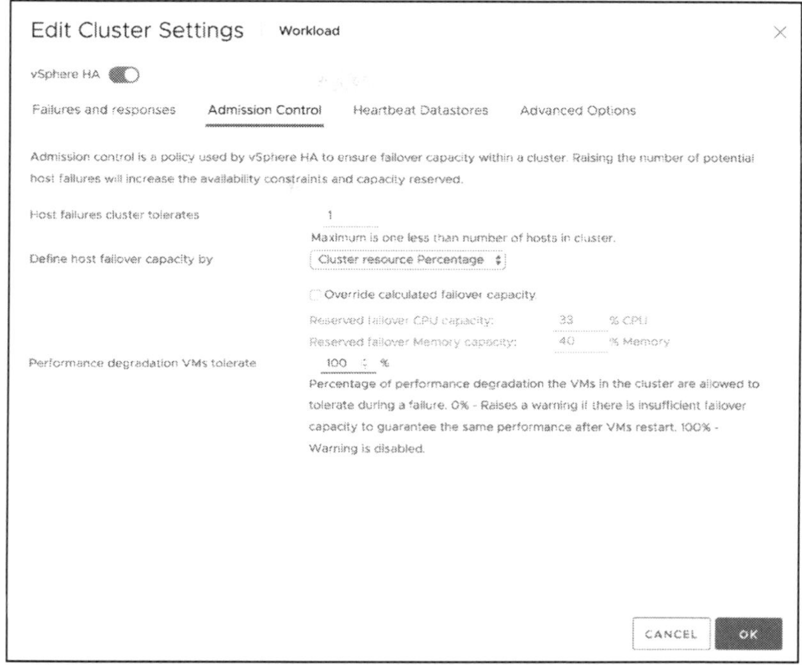

Figure 57: Host Failures Cluster Tolerate

When you specify a number of Host Failures this number is then automatically calculated to a percentage. You can of course override this if you prefer to manually set the percentage, typically customers would keep CPU and memory equal. The big benefit of specifying the Host Failures is that when you add hosts to the cluster the percentage of resources saved for HA restarts is automatically calculated again and applied to the cluster, where in the past customers would need to manually calculate what the new percentage would be and configure this.

If you configure the percentage manually, and it is configured lower than a single host failure, this could result in an error message. This error message will state the following:

> *"Insufficient configured resources to satisfy the desired vSphere HA failover level on the cluster."*

Although this is a warning from vSphere HA Admission Control, it does not stop you from powering on VMs. This warning only indicates that the percentage reserved is less than that of a single host, which potentially could lead to VMs not being restarted due to the lack of available unreserved resources.

So how does the admission control policy work?
First of all, HA will add up all available resources to see how much it has available (virtualization overhead will be subtracted) in total. Then, HA will calculate how much resources are currently reserved by adding up all reservations for memory and for CPU for all powered on VMs.
For those VMs that do not have a reservation, a default of 32 MHz will be used for CPU and a default of 0 MB + memory overhead will be used for Memory. (Amount of overhead per configuration type can be found in the "Understanding Memory Overhead" section of the Resource Management guide.)

In other words:

```
((total amount of available resources - total reserved VM
resources)/total amount of available resources) <= (percentage HA
should reserve as spare capacity)
```

Total reserved VM resources includes the default reservation of 32 MHz and the memory overhead of the VM. Let's use a diagram to make it a bit clearer:

Total cluster resources are 24 GHz (CPU) and 96 GB (MEM). This would lead to the following calculations:

```
((24 GHz - (2 GHz + 1 GHz + 32 MHz + 4 GHz)) / 24 GHz) = 69 %
available
```

```
((96 GB - (1,1 GB + 114 MB + 626 MB + 3,2 GB)/96 GB= 85 % available
```

As you can see, the amount of memory differs from the diagram. Even if a reservation has been set, the amount of memory overhead is added to the reservation. This example also demonstrates how keeping CPU and memory percentage equal could create an imbalance. Ideally, of course, the hosts are provisioned in such a way that there is no CPU/memory imbalance. Experience over the years has proven, unfortunately, that most environments run out of memory resources first and this might need to be factored in when calculating the correct value for the percentage. However, this trend might be changing as memory is getting cheaper every day.

In order to ensure VMs can always be restarted, Admission Control will constantly monitor if the policy has been violated or not. Please note that this Admission Control process is part of vCenter and not of the ESXi host! When one of the thresholds is reached, memory or CPU, Admission Control will disallow powering on any additional VMs as that could potentially impact availability. These thresholds can be monitored on the HA section of the Cluster's summary tab.

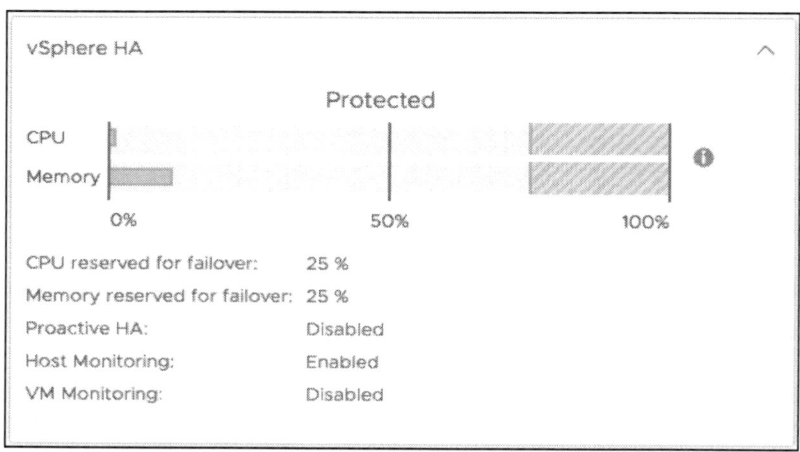

Figure 58: Admission Control Monitoring

If you have an unbalanced cluster (hosts with different sizes of CPU or memory resources), your percentage should set manually and be equal or preferably larger than the percentage of resources provided by the largest host. This way you ensure that all VMs residing on this host can be restarted in case of a host failure. Again, there's a danger to manually configuring percentages as it may lead to a situation where after changes in the cluster no sufficient resources are available to restart VMs. You can also find yourself in a situation where resources might be fragmented throughout the cluster, especially in larger overbooked clusters this can happen. Although DRS is notified to rebalance the cluster, if needed, to accommodate these VMs resource requirements, a guarantee cannot be given. We recommend selecting the highest restart priority for this VM (of course, depending on the SLA) to ensure it will be able to boot.

The following example and diagram will make it more obvious: You have 3 hosts, each with roughly 80% memory usage, and you have configured HA to reserve 20% of resources for both CPU and memory. A host fails and all VMs will need to failover. One of those VMs has a 4 GB memory reservation. As you can imagine, HA will not be able to initiate a power-on attempt, as there are not enough memory resources available to guarantee the reserved capacity. Instead an event will get generated indicating "not enough resources for failover" for this VM.

> **Although HA will utilize DRS to try to accommodate for the resource requirements of this VM a guarantee cannot be given. Do the math; verify that any single host has enough resources to power-on your largest VM. Also take restart priority into account for this/these VM(s).**

Slot Size Algorithm

The Admission Control algorithm that has been around the longest is the slot size algorithm, formerly known as the "Host Failures Cluster Tolerates" policy. It is also historically the least understood Admission Control Policy due to its complex admission control mechanism.

Similar to the Cluster Resource Percentage algorithm you can specify the number of Host Failures the Cluster Tolerates in an N-1 fashion. This means that the number of host failures you can specify in a 64-host cluster is 63. As mentioned before, this "Host failures cluster tolerates" also is available when the percentage-based policy is selected.

Edit Cluster Settings
Workload
vSphere HA
Failures and responses
Admission Control
Heartbeat Datastores
Advanced Options
Admission control is a policy used by vSphere HA to ensure failover capacity within a cluster. Raising the number of potential host failures will increase the availability constraints and capacity reserved.
Host failures cluster tolerates
1
Maximum is one less than number of hosts in cluster.
Define host failover capacity by
Slot Policy (powered-on VMs)
Define slot policy
Cover all powered-on virtual machines
Calculate slot size based on the maximum CPU/Memory reservation and overhead of all powered-on virtual machines.
Fixed slot size
Specify the slot size explicitly.
CPU slot size:
32
MHz
Memory slot size:
100
MB
VMs requiring multiple slots:
VIEW
CALCULATE
Performance degradation VMs tolerate
100
%
CANCEL
OK

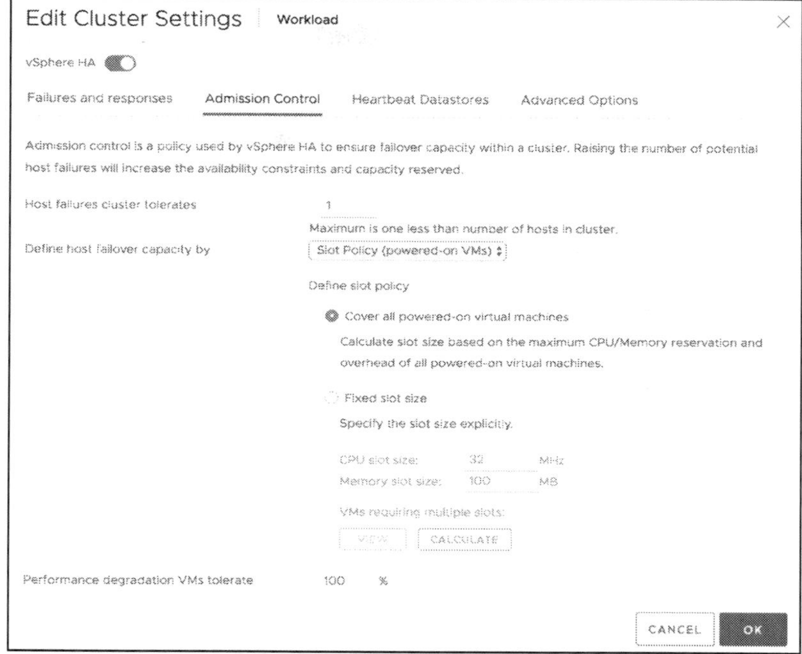

Figure 59: Host Failures Cluster Tolerates

Within the vSphere Client it is possible to specify the slot size algorithm should be used through the dropdown under "Define host failover capacity by".

Define host failover capacity by
Slot Policy (powered-on VMs)
Define slot policy
Cover all powered-on virtual machines
Calculate slot size based on the maximum CPU/Memory reservation and overhead of all powered-on virtual machines.
Fixed slot size
Specify the slot size explicitly.
CPU slot size:
32
MHz
Memory slot size:
100
MB
VMs requiring multiple slots:
VIEW
CALCULATE

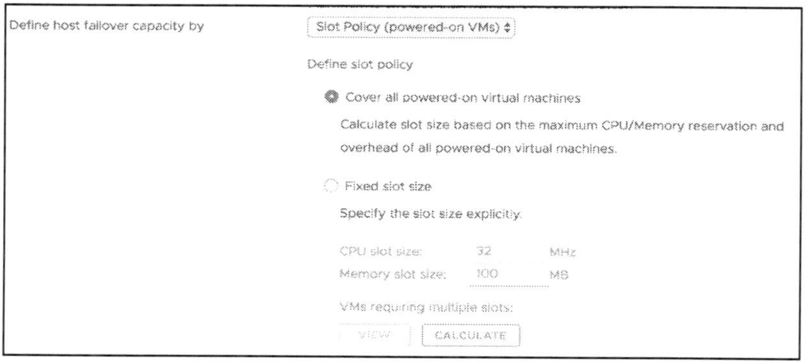

Figure 60: Slot Policy

When "Slot Policy" is selected the "slots" mechanism is used. The details of this mechanism have changed several times in the past and it is one of the most restrictive policies; more than likely, it is also the least understood.

Slots dictate how many VMs can be powered on before vCenter starts yelling "Out Of Resources!" Normally, a slot represents one VM. Admission Control does not limit HA in restarting VMs, it ensures enough unfragmented resources are available to power on all VMs in the cluster by preventing "over-commitment". Technically speaking "over-commitment" is not the correct terminology as Admission Control ensures VM reservations can be satisfied and that all VMs' initial memory overhead requirements are met. Although we have already touched on this, it doesn't hurt repeating it as it is one of those myths that keeps coming back; HA initiated failovers are not prone to the Admission Control Policy. Admission Control is done by vCenter. HA initiated restarts, in a normal scenario, are executed directly on the ESXi host without the use of vCenter. The corner-case is where HA requests DRS (DRS is a vCenter task!) to defragment resources but that is beside the point. Even if resources are low and vCenter would complain, it couldn't stop the restart from happening.

Let's dig in to this concept we have just introduced, slots.

> *"A slot is defined as a logical representation of the memory and CPU resources that satisfy the reservation requirements for any powered-on VM in the cluster."*

In other words, a slot is the worst-case CPU and memory reservation scenario in a cluster. This directly leads to the first "gotcha".

HA uses the highest CPU reservation of any given powered-on VM and the highest memory reservation of any given powered-on VM in the cluster. If no reservation of higher than 32 MHz is set, HA will use a default of 32 MHz for CPU. If no memory reservation is set, HA will use a default of 0 MB + memory overhead for memory. (See the VMware vSphere Resource Management Guide for more details on memory overhead per VM configuration.) The following example will clarify what "worst-case" actually means.

Example: If VM01 has 2 GHz of CPU reserved and 1024 MB of memory reserved and VM02 has 1 GHz of CPU reserved and 2048 MB of memory reserved the slot size for memory will be 2048 MB (+ its memory overhead) and the slot size for CPU will be 2 GHz. It is a combination of the highest reservation of both VMs that leads to the total slot size. Reservations defined at the Resource Pool level however, will not affect HA slot size calculations.

> **Be really careful with reservations, if there's no need to have them on a per VM basis; don't configure them, especially when using host failures cluster tolerates. If reservations are needed, resort to resource pool based reservations.**

Now that we know the worst-case scenario is always taken into account when it comes to slot size calculations, we will describe what dictates the number of available slots per cluster as that ultimately dictates how many VMs can be powered on in your cluster.

First, we will need to know the slot size for memory and CPU, next we will divide the total available CPU resources of a host by the CPU slot size and the total available memory resources of a host by the memory slot size. This leaves us with a total number of slots for both memory and CPU for a host. The most restrictive number (worst-case scenario) is the number of slots for this host. In other words, when you have 25 CPU slots but only 5 memory slots, the number of available slots for this host will be 5 as HA always takes the worst-case scenario into account to "guarantee" all VMs can be powered on in case of a failure or isolation.

The question we receive a lot is how do I know what my slot size is? The details around slot sizes can be monitored on the HA section of the Cluster's Monitor tab by checking the "Advanced Runtime Info" section when the "Host Failures" Admission Control Policy is configured.

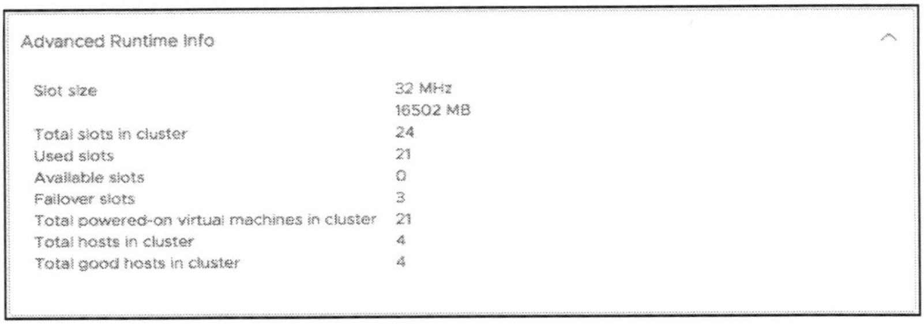

Advanced Runtime Info

Slot size	32 MHz 16502 MB
Total slots in cluster	24
Used slots	21
Available slots	0
Failover slots	3
Total powered-on virtual machines in cluster	21
Total hosts in cluster	4
Total good hosts in cluster	4

Figure 61: Advanced Runtime Info

As you can imagine, using reservations on a per VM basis can lead to very conservative consolidation ratios. However, this is something that is configurable through the vSphere Client. If you have just one VM with a really high reservation, you can set an explicit slot size by going to "Edit Cluster Services" and specifying them under the Admission Control Policy section. In the screenshot above, there is a single VM with a 16 GB reservation; this skews the number of available slots in the cluster as a result. As can be seen, only 24 slots are available.

If one of these advanced settings is used, HA will ensure that the VM that skewed the numbers can be restarted by "assigning" multiple slots to it. However, when you are low on resources, this could mean that you are not able to power on the VM with this reservation because resources may be fragmented throughout the cluster instead of available on a single host. HA will notify DRS that a power-on attempt was unsuccessful and a request will be made to defragment the resources to accommodate the remaining VMs that need to be powered on. In order for this to be successful DRS will need to be enabled and configured to fully automated. When not configured to fully automated user action is required to execute DRS recommendations.

The following diagram depicts a scenario where a VM spans multiple slots:

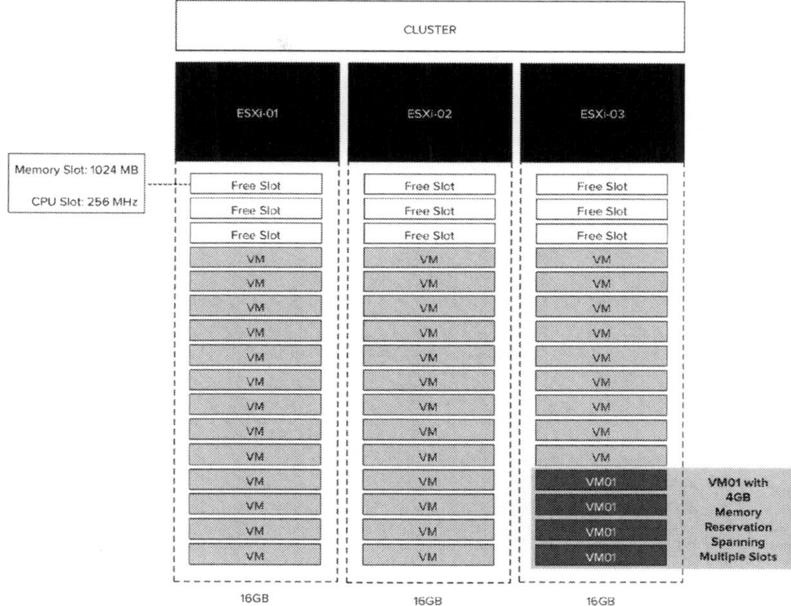

Figure 62: VM Spanning Multiple Slots

Notice that because the memory slot size has been manually set to 1024 MB, one of the VMs (grouped with dotted lines) spans multiple slots due to a 4 GB memory reservation. As you might have noticed, none of the hosts has enough resources available to satisfy the reservation of the VM that needs to failover. Although in total there are enough resources available, they are fragmented and HA will not be able to power-on this particular VM directly but will request DRS to defragment the resources to accommodate this VM's resource requirements.

The great thing about the vSphere Client is that after setting the slot size manually to 1 GB (1024 MB) you can see which VMs require multiple slots when you click "calculate" followed by "view". This is demonstrated in the below screenshots.

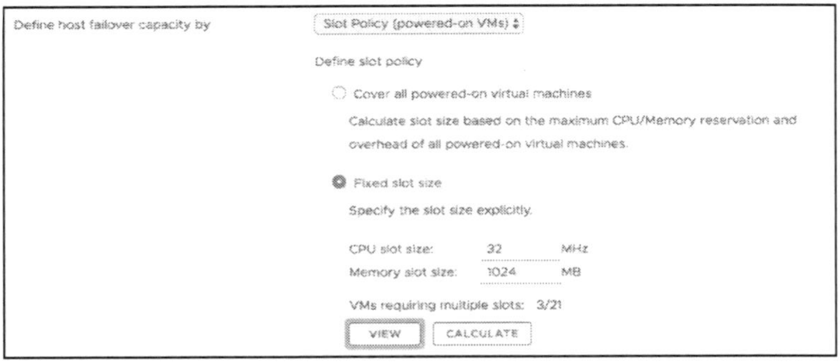

Define host failover capacity by | Slot Policy (powered-on VMs)

Define slot policy

Cover all powered-on virtual machines

Calculate slot size based on the maximum CPU/Memory reservation and overhead of all powered-on virtual machines.

Fixed slot size

Specify the slot size explicitly.

CPU slot size: 32 MHz

Memory slot size: 1024 MB

VMs requiring multiple slots: 3/21

VIEW CALCULATE

Figure 63: Change Memory Slot Size

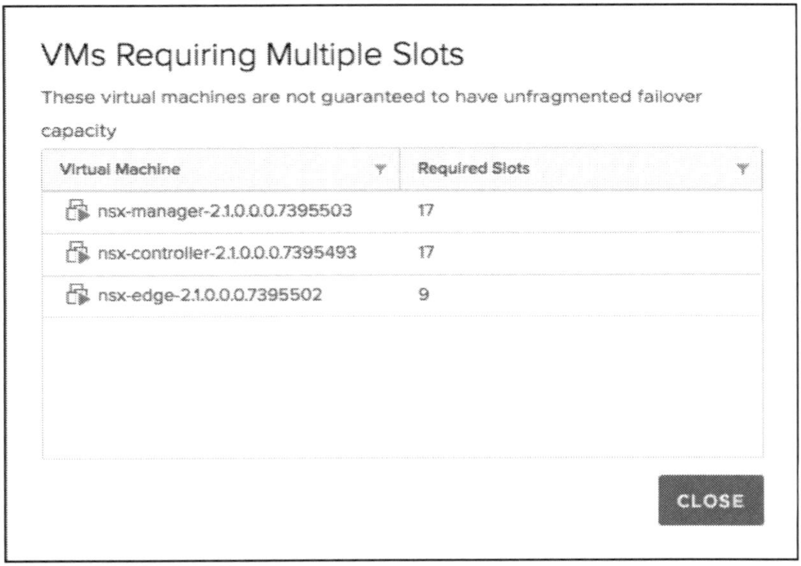

VMs Requiring Multiple Slots

These virtual machines are not guaranteed to have unfragmented failover capacity

Virtual Machine	Required Slots
nsx-manager-2.1.0.0.0.7395503	17
nsx-controller-2.1.0.0.0.7395493	17
nsx-edge-2.1.0.0.0.7395502	9

CLOSE

Figure 64: VMs Requiring Multiple Slots

Admission Control does not take fragmentation of slots into account when slot sizes are manually defined with advanced settings. It will take the number of slots this VM will consume into account by subtracting them from the total number of available slots, but it will not verify the number of available slots per host to ensure failover. As stated earlier, though, HA will request DRS to defragment the resources. This is by no means a guarantee of a successful power-on attempt.

> **Avoid using manually specified slot sizes to increase the total number of slots as it could lead to more down time and adds an extra layer of complexity. If there is a large discrepancy in size and reservations, we recommend using the percentage based admission control policy.**

We highly recommend monitoring this section on a regular basis to get a better understand of your environment and to identify those VMs that might be problematic to restart in case of a host failure. Also, it is possible to identify the VMs with a high reservation in the vSphere Client. You can do this by going to the VM view and adding a column called "Reservations" as shown in the screenshot below.

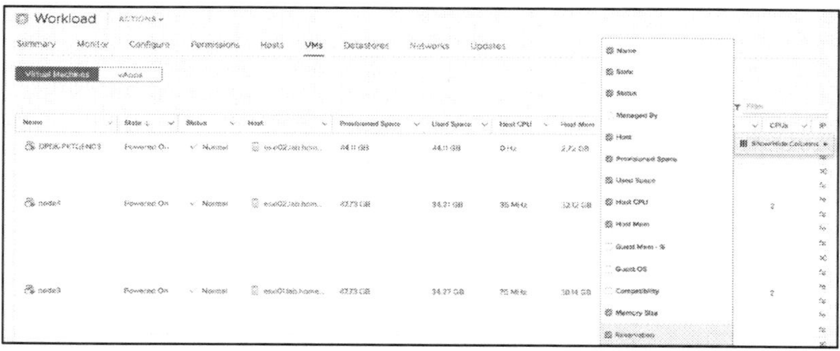

Figure 65: Large Memory Reservation

Using the above view, and the additional column, it is quickly determined that the VMware NSX infrastructure requires reservations, and is potentially skewing the number of slots. However, after manually changing the memory slot size to 1024MB, the number of total slots, used slots and slots available significantly changes as demonstrated in the screenshot below.

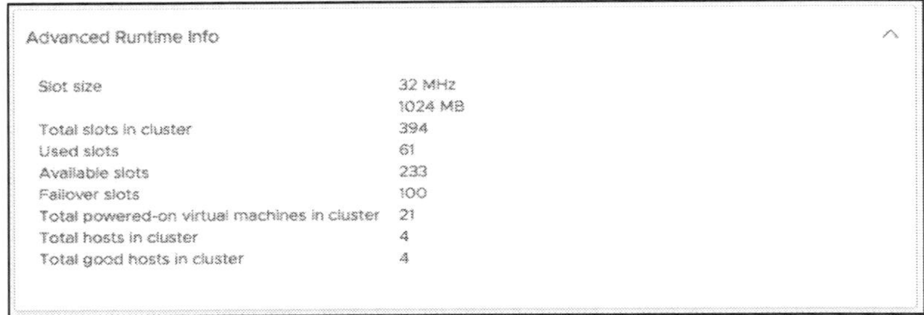

Advanced Runtime Info

Slot size	32 MHz 1024 MB
Total slots in cluster	394
Used slots	61
Available slots	233
Failover slots	100
Total powered-on virtual machines in cluster	21
Total hosts in cluster	4
Total good hosts in cluster	4

Figure 66: Slots Available Changed

Unbalanced Configurations and Impact on Slot Calculation

It is an industry best practice to create clusters with similar hardware configurations. However, many companies started out with a small VMware cluster when virtualization was first introduced. When the time has come to expand, chances are fairly large the same hardware configuration is no longer available. The question is will you add the newly bought hosts to the same cluster or create a new cluster?

From a DRS perspective, large clusters are preferred as it increases the load balancing opportunities. However, there is a caveat for DRS as well, which is described in the DRS section of this book. For HA, there is a big caveat. When you think about it and understand the internal workings of HA, more specifically the slot algorithm, you probably already know what is coming up.

Let's first define the term "unbalanced cluster."

An unbalanced cluster would, for instance, be a cluster with 3 hosts of which one contains substantially more memory than the other hosts in the cluster.

Let's try to clarify that with an example.

Example: What would happen to the total number of slots in a cluster of the following specifications? Yes, we know, the below provided example of host resources is not realistic in this day and age, however it is for illustrative purposes and makes calculations easier.

- Three host cluster
- Two hosts have 16 GB of available memory
- One host has 32 GB of available memory

The third host is a brand-new host that has just been bought and as prices of memory dropped immensely the decision was made to buy 32 GB instead of 16 GB.

The cluster contains a VM that has 1 vCPU and 4 GB of memory. A 1024 MB memory reservation has been defined on this VM. As explained earlier, a reservation will dictate the slot size, which in this case leads to a memory slot size of 1024 MB + memory overhead. For the sake of simplicity, we will calculate with 1024 MB. The following diagram depicts this scenario:

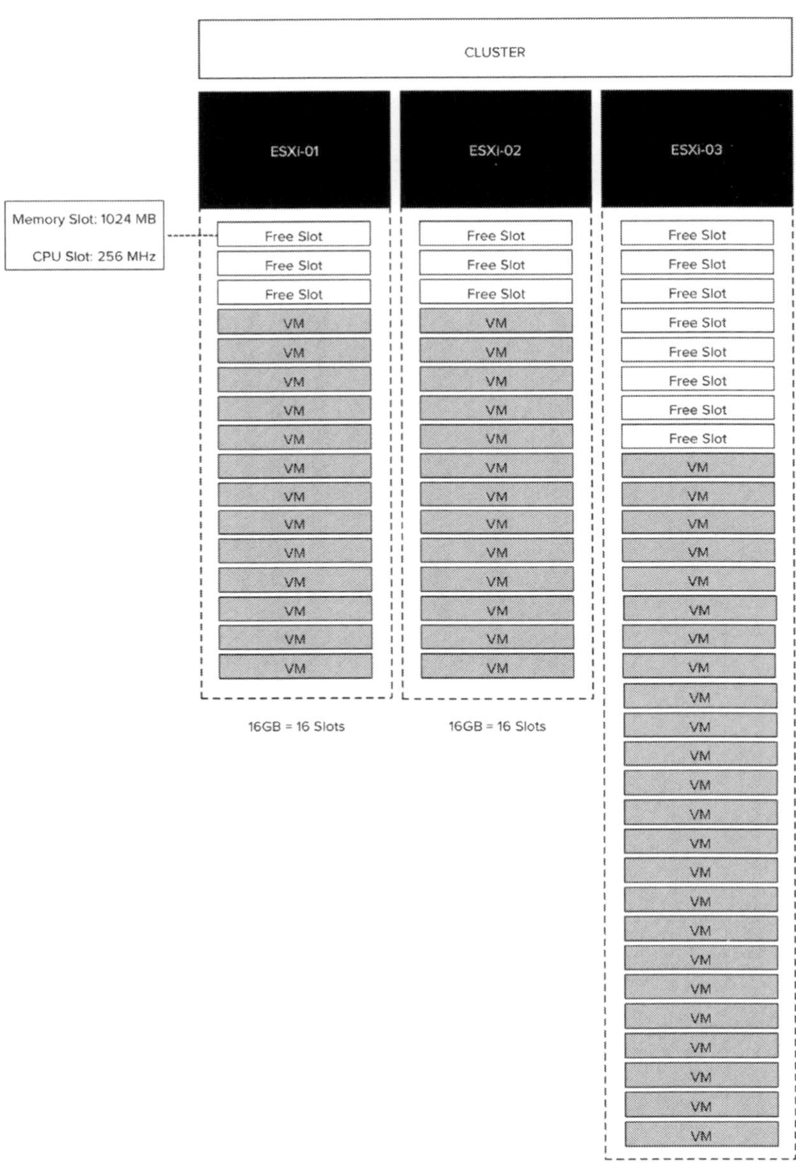

Figure 67: Unbalanced

When Admission Control is enabled and the number of host failures has been selected as the Admission Control Policy, the number of slots will be calculated per host and the cluster in total. This will result in:

HOST	NUMBER OF SLOTS
ESXi-01	16 Slots
ESXi-02	16 Slots
ESXi-03	32 Slots

Table 4: Number of Slots per ESXi Host

As Admission Control is enabled, a worst-case scenario is taken into account. When a single host failure has been specified, this means that the host with the largest number of slots will be taken out of the equation. In other words, for our cluster, this would result in:

```
ESXi-01 + ESXi-02 = 32 slots available
```

Although you have doubled the amount of memory in one of your hosts, you are still stuck with only 32 slots in total. As clearly demonstrated, there is absolutely no point in buying additional memory for a single host when your cluster is designed with Admission Control enabled and the number of host failures has been selected as the Admission Control Policy.

In our example, the memory slot size happened to be the most restrictive; however, the same principle applies when CPU slot size is most restrictive.

> **When using admission control, balance your clusters and be conservative with reservations as it leads to decreased consolidation ratios.**

Now, what would happen in the scenario above when the number of allowed host failures is to 2? In this case ESXi-03 is taken out of the equation and one of any of the remaining hosts in the cluster is also taken out, resulting in 16 slots. This makes sense, doesn't it?

Can you avoid large HA slot sizes due to reservations without resorting to advanced settings? That's the question we get almost daily and the answer is the "Percentage of Cluster Resources Reserved" admission control mechanism.

Failover Hosts

The third option one could choose is to select one or multiple designated Failover hosts. This is commonly referred to as a hot standby.

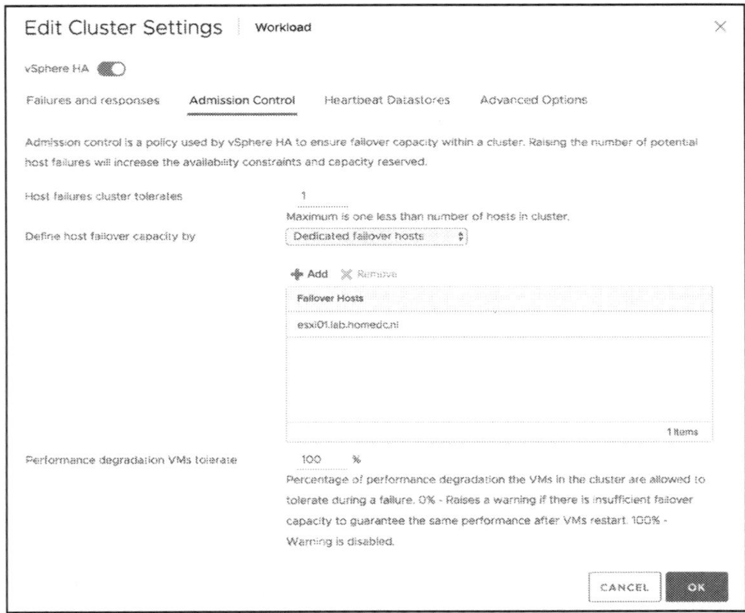

Figure 68: Dedicated Failover Hosts

It is "what you see is what you get". When you designate hosts as failover hosts, they will not participate in DRS and you will not be able to run VMs on these hosts! Not even in a two-host cluster when placing one of the two in maintenance. These hosts are literally reserved for failover situations. HA will attempt to use these hosts first to failover the VMs. If, for whatever reason, this is unsuccessful, it will attempt a failover on any of the other hosts in the cluster. For example, in a when two hosts would fail, including the hosts designated as failover hosts, HA will still try to restart the impacted VMs on the host that is left. Although this host was not a designated failover host, HA will use it to limit downtime.

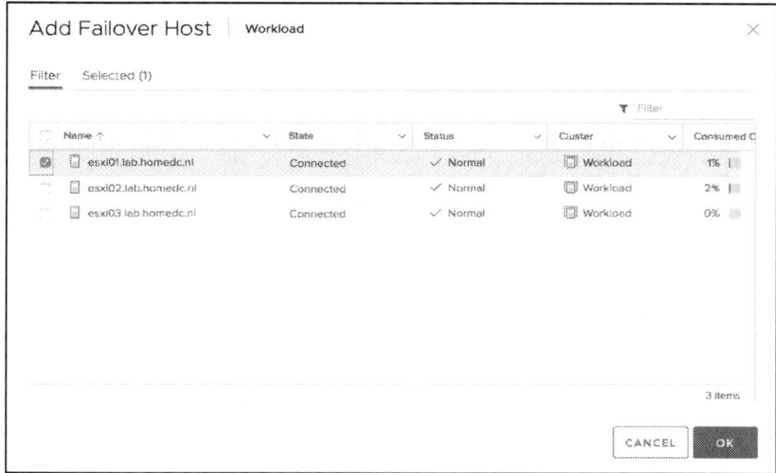

Figure 69: Configure Failover Host Admission Control Policy

Performance Degradation

The question that then rises is if Admission Control is all about ensuring VMs can be restarted, but what about the resources available to the VMs after the restart? Pre-vSphere 6.5 there was no way to guarantee what the availability of resources would be after a restart. Starting with vSphere 6.5 we have the option to specify how much performance degradation can be tolerated as shown in the screenshot below.

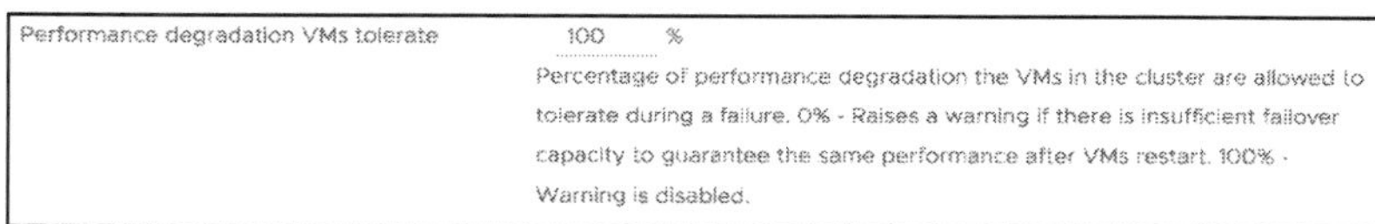

Figure 70: Performance Degradation Tolerated

As said, this feature allows you to specify the performance degradation you are willing to incur if a failure happens. It is set to 100% by default, but it is our recommendation to consider changed the value. You can for instance change this to 25% or 50%.

So how does this work? Well first of all, you need DRS enabled as HA leverages DRS to get the cluster resource usage. But let's look at an example:

- 75 GB of memory available in 3 node cluster
- 1 host failure to tolerate specified
- 60 GB of memory actively used by VMs
- 0% resource reduction tolerated

This results in the following:
75 GB – 25 GB (1 host worth of memory) = 50 GB

We have 60 GB of memory used, with 0% resource reduction to tolerate 60 GB needed, 50 GB available after failure which means that a warning is issued to the vSphere admin. Now the vSphere admin can decide what to do, accept the performance degradation or buy new hosts and add these to the cluster to ensure the performance for all VMs remain the same after an HA initiated restart. Of course, in larger environments it may also be possible to migrate VMs to other clusters in the environment.

Note that the feature at the time of writing does all calculations based on a single host failure and the percentage specified applies to both CPU and memory.

> **To ensure consistent performance behavior even after a failure we recommend considering setting Performance Degradation Tolerated to a different value than 100%. The value should be based on your infrastructure and service level agreement.**

Decision Making Time

As with any decision you make, there is an impact to your environment. This impact could be positive but also, for instance, unexpected. This especially goes for HA Admission Control. Selecting the right Admission Control algorithm can lead to a quicker *Return On Investment* (ROI) and a lower *Total Cost of Ownership* (TCO). In the previous section, we described all the algorithms that form Admission Control and in this section, we will focus more on the design considerations around selecting the appropriate Admission Control Policy for your or your customer's environment.

The first decision that will need to be made is whether Admission Control will be enabled. We generally recommend enabling Admission Control as it is the only way of guaranteeing your VMs will be allowed to restart after a failure. It is important, though, that the policy is carefully selected and fits your or your customer's requirements.

> **Admission control guarantees enough capacity is available for VM failover. As such we recommend enabling it.**

Although we already have explained all the mechanisms that are being used by each of the policies in the previous section, we will give a high-level overview and list all the pros and cons in this section. On top of that, we will expand on what we feel is the most flexible Admission Control Policy and how it should be configured and calculated.

Percentage as Cluster Resources Reserved

The percentage based Admission Control is based on per-reservation calculation. The percentage based Admission Control Policy is less conservative than the "slot based" algorithm and more flexible than "Failover Hosts". It is by far the most used algorithm, and that is for a good reason in our opinion!

Pros:

- Accurate as it considers actual reservation per VM to calculate available failover resources
- Cluster dynamically adjusts when resources are added

Cons:

- Unbalanced clusters can be a potential problem when there's a discrepancy between memory and CPU resources in different hosts

Please note that, although a failover cannot be guaranteed, there are few scenarios where a VM will not be able to restart due to the integration HA offers with DRS and the fact that most clusters have spare capacity available to account for VM demand variance. Although this is a corner-case scenario, it needs to be considered in environments where absolute guarantees must be provided.

Slot Size Algorithm

This algorithm was historically speaking the most used for Admission Control. Most environments are designed with an N+1 redundancy and N+2 is also not uncommon. This Admission Control Policy uses "slots" to ensure enough capacity is reserved for failover, which is a fairly complex mechanism. Slots are based on VM-level reservations and if reservations are not used a default slot size for CPU of 32 MHz is defined and for memory the largest memory overhead of any given VM is used.

Pros:

- Fully automated (When a host is added to a cluster, HA re-calculates how many slots are available)
- Guarantees failover by calculating slot sizes

Cons:

- Can be very conservative and inflexible when reservations are used as the largest reservation dictates slot sizes
- Unbalanced clusters lead to wastage of resources
- Complexity for administrator from calculation perspective

Specify Failover Hosts

With the "Specify Failover Hosts" Admission Control Policy, when one or multiple hosts fail, HA will attempt to restart all VMs on the designated failover hosts. The designated failover hosts are essentially "hot standby" hosts. In other words, DRS will not migrate VMs to these hosts when resources are scarce or the cluster is imbalanced.

Pros:

- What you see is what you get
- No fragmented resources

Cons:

- What you see is what you get
- Dedicated failover hosts not utilized during normal operations

Recommendations

We have been asked many times for our recommendation on Admission Control and it is difficult to answer as each policy has its pros and cons. However, we generally recommend the Percentage based Admission Control Policy. It is the most flexible policy as it uses the actual reservation per VM instead of taking a "worst case" scenario approach like the slot policy does.

However, the slot policy guarantees the failover level under all circumstances. Percentage based is less restrictive, yet offers lower guarantees that in all scenarios HA will be able to restart all VMs. With the added level of integration between HA and DRS we believe the Cluster Resource Percentage Policy will fit most environments.

> **Do the math and take customer requirements into account. We recommend using a "percentage" based admission control policy, as it is the most flexible.**

Now that we have recommended which Admission Control Policy to use, the next step is to provide guidance around selecting the correct percentage. We cannot tell you what the ideal percentage is as that totally depends on the size of your cluster and, of course, on your resiliency model (N+1 vs. N+2). We can, however, provide guidelines around calculating how much of your resources should be set aside and how to prevent wasting resources.

Selecting the Right Percentage

Pre-vSphere 6.5 it was required to manually specify the percentage for both CPU and memory for the Cluster Resource Percentage Policy. It was a common strategy to select a single host as a percentage of resources reserved for failover. We generally recommended selecting a percentage which is the equivalent of a single or multiple hosts. Today the percentage can be manually specified, or can be automatically calculated by leveraging "Host failures cluster tolerates". We highly recommend to not change the percentage manually if there's no reason for it. The big advantage of the automatic calculation is that when new hosts are added to the cluster, or hosts are removed, HA will automatically adjust the percentage value for you. When the percentage value is manually configured then you will need recalculate and re-configure based on the new outcome of the calculations. If you do end up configuring the percentage manually, ensure that it is always set to a value equal to, or larger than, the value of a single host. In other words, in a 4 host cluster, ensure the percentage is set to 25% or higher.

Let's explain why and what the impact and risk is of manual calculations and not using the equivalent of a single or multiple hosts.

Let's start with an example: a cluster exists of 8 ESXi hosts, each containing 70 GB of available RAM. This might sound like an awkward memory configuration but to simplify things we have already subtracted 2 GB as virtualization overhead. Although virtualization overhead is probably less than 2 GB, we have used this number to make calculations easier. This example zooms in on memory but this concept also applies to CPU, of course.

For this cluster, we will define the percentage of resources to reserve for both Memory and CPU to 20%. For memory, this leads to a total cluster memory capacity of 448 GB:

```
(70 GB + 70 GB + 70 GB + 70 GB + 70 GB + 70 GB + 70 GB + 70 GB) *
(1 - 20%)
```

A total of 112 GB of memory is reserved as failover capacity.

Once a percentage is specified, that percentage of resources will be unavailable for VMs, therefore it makes sense to set the percentage as close to the value that equals the resources a single (or multiple) host represents. We will demonstrate why this is important in subsequent examples.

In the example above, 20% was used to be reserved for resources in an 8-host cluster. This configuration reserves more resources than a single host contributes to the cluster. HA's main objective is to provide automatic recovery for VMs after a physical server failure. For this reason, it is recommended to reserve resources equal to a single or multiple hosts. When using the per-host level granularity in an 8-host cluster (homogeneous configured hosts), the resource contribution per host to the cluster is 12.5%. However, the percentage used must be an integer (whole number). It is recommended to round up to the value guaranteeing that the full capacity of one host is protected, in this example, the conservative approach would lead to a percentage of 13%.

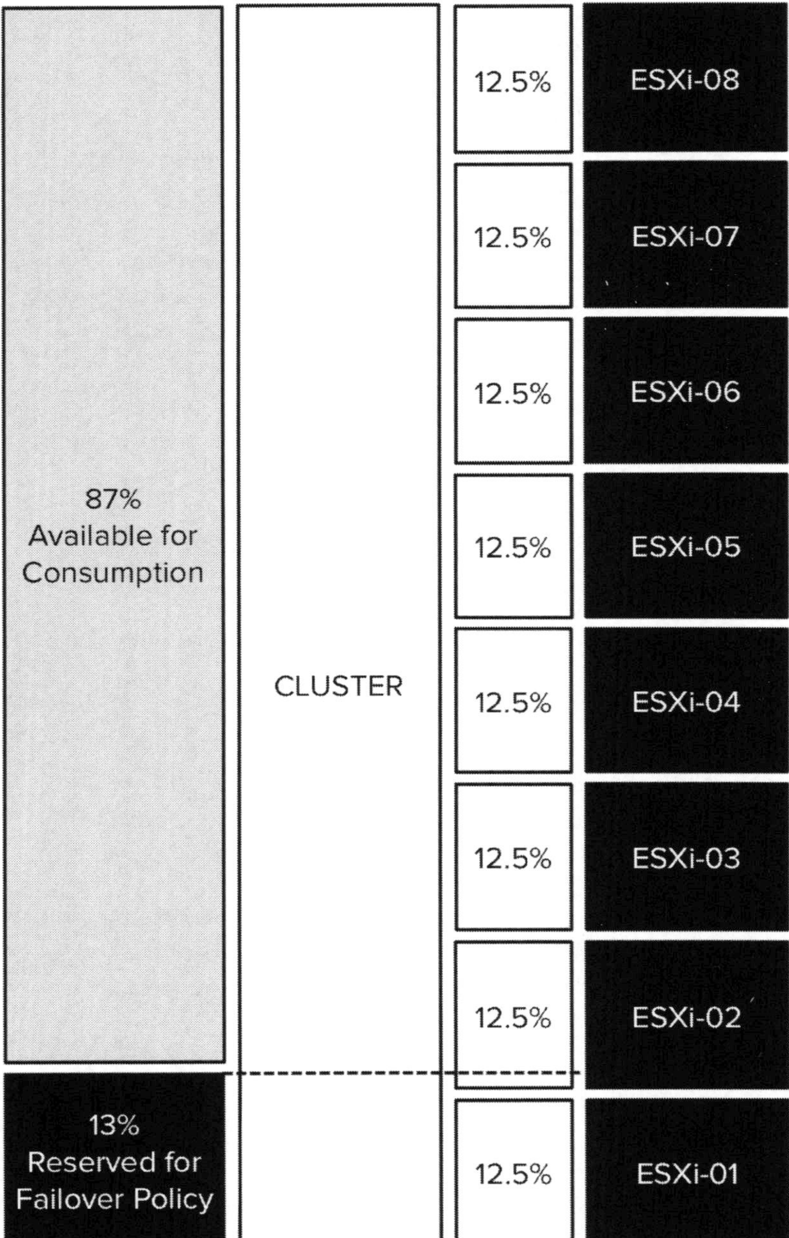

Figure 71: Determining the Percentage

Aggressive Approach

We have seen many environments where the percentage was set to a value that was less than the contribution of a single host to the cluster. Although this approach reduces the amount of resources reserved for accommodating host failures and results in higher consolidation ratios, it also offers a lower guarantee that HA will be able to restart all VMs after a failure. One might argue that this approach will more than likely work as most environments will not be fully utilized. However, it will result, as mentioned earlier, in an error message when configured too low and also does eliminate the guarantee that after a failure all VMs will be recovered. Wasn't that the reason for enabling HA in the first place?

Adding Hosts to Your Cluster

Although the percentage is dynamic and calculates capacity at a cluster-level, changes to your selected percentage might be required when expanding the cluster. The reason being that the amount of reserved resources for a fail-over might not correspond with the contribution per host and as a result lead to resource wastage. For example, adding four hosts to an eight host cluster and continuing to use the previously configured admission control policy value of 13% will result in a failover capacity that is equivalent to 1.5 hosts. The next figure depicts a scenario where an eight-host cluster is expanded to twelve hosts. Each host holds eight 2 GHz cores and 70 GB of memory. The cluster was originally configured with admission control set to 13%, which equals to 109.2 GB and 24.96 GHz. If the requirement is to allow a single host failure 7.68 GHz and 33.6 GB is "wasted" as clearly demonstrated in the diagram below.

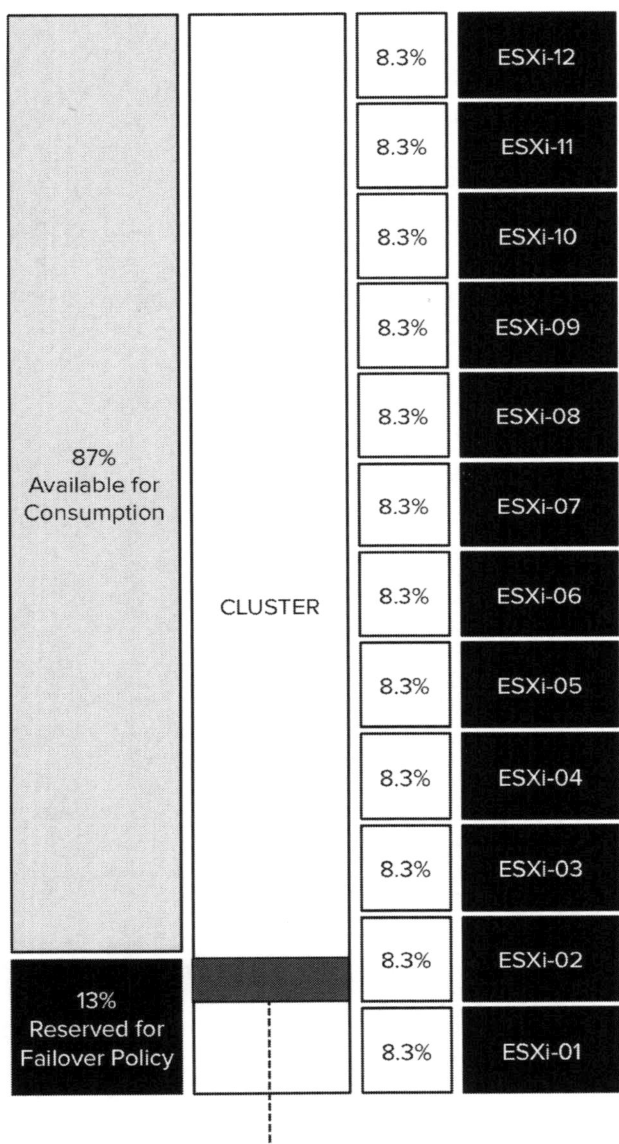

Figure 72: Adding Hosts

Last but not least, we do want to point out the following caveat again when it comes to Admission Control and how CPU and Memory resources are calculated:

> "The total host resources available for virtual machines is calculated by adding the hosts' CPU and memory resources. These amounts are those contained in the host's root resource pool, not the total physical resources of the host. Resources being used for virtualization purposes are not included. Only hosts that are connected, not in maintenance mode, and have no vSphere HA errors are considered."

In other words, vSphere HA Admission Control takes the state of a host in to account when doing its calculations. Be aware that a disconnected host, a host with an HA error, or a host in maintenance mode, will impact the available resources to power-on VMs and subsequently the potentially reserved resources for restarting VMs after a failure.

08

VM AND APPLICATION MONITORING

VM and Application Monitoring is an often overlooked but really powerful feature of HA. The reason for this is most likely that it is disabled by default and relatively new compared to HA. We have tried to gather all the information we could around VM and Application Monitoring, but it is a pretty straightforward product that actually does what you expect it would do.

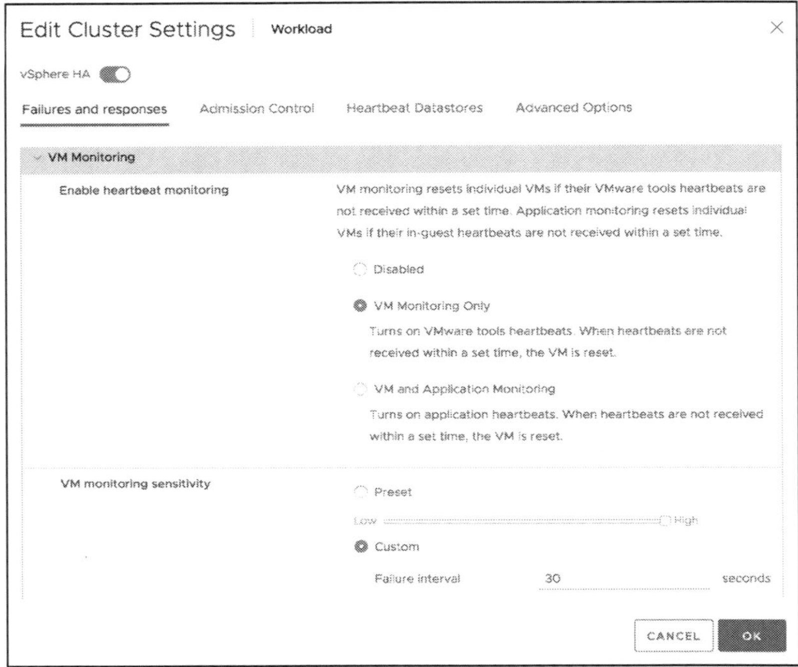

Figure 73: VM and Application Monitoring

Why Do You Need VM/Application Monitoring?

VM and Application Monitoring acts on a different level from HA. VM/App Monitoring responds to a single VM or application failure as opposed to HA which responds to a host failure. An example of a single VM failure would, for instance, be the infamous *blue screen of death* (BSOD). In the case of App Monitoring the type of failure that triggers a response is defined by the application developer or administrator.

How Does VM/App Monitoring Work?

VM Monitoring resets individual VMs when needed. VM/App monitoring uses a heartbeat similar to HA. If heartbeats, and, in this case, VMware Tools heartbeats, are not received for a specific (and configurable) amount of time, the VM will be restarted. These heartbeats are monitored by the HA agent and are not sent over a network, but stay local to the host.

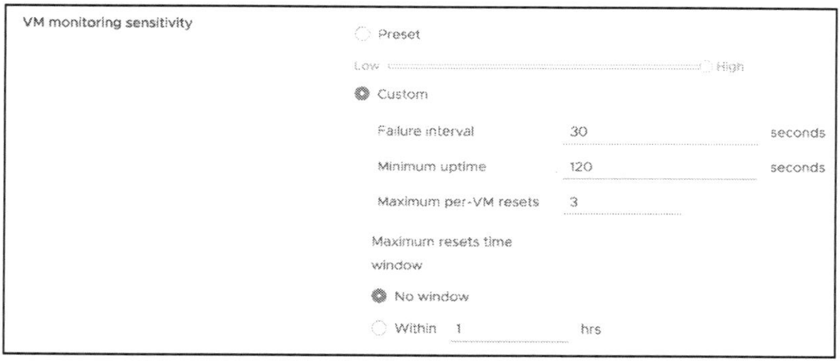

Figure 74: Monitoring Sensitivity

When enabling VM/App Monitoring, the level of sensitivity can be configured. The default setting should fit most situations. Low sensitivity basically means that the number of allowed "missed" heartbeats is higher and the chances of running into a false positive are lower. However, if a failure occurs and the sensitivity level is set to Low, the experienced downtime will be higher. When quick action is required in the event of a failure, "high sensitivity" can be selected. As expected, this is the opposite of "low sensitivity". Of course, within the UI a customer configuration can also be provided, as shown in the screenshot above.

SENSITIVITY	FAILURE INTERVAL	MINIMUM UPTIME	MAX RESETS	MAX RESETS TIME WINDOW
Low	120 Seconds	480 Seconds	3	7 Days
Medium	60 Seconds	240 Seconds	3	24 Hours
High	30 Seconds	120 Seconds	3	1 Hour

Table 5: Level of Sensitivity

It is important to remember that VM Monitoring does not infinitely reboot VMs unless you specify a custom policy with this requirement. This is to avoid a problem from repeating. By default, when a VM has been rebooted three times within an hour, no further attempts will be taken. Unless the specified time has elapsed.

Although the heartbeat produced by VMware Tools is reliable, VMware added a further verification mechanism. To avoid false positives, VM Monitoring also monitors I/O activity of the VM. When heartbeats are not received AND no disk or network activity has occurred over the last 120 seconds, per default, the VM will be reset. Changing the advanced setting `das.iostatsInterval` can modify this 120-second interval.

It is recommended to align the `das.iostatsInterval` with the failure interval selected in the VM Monitoring section of vSphere HA within the Web Client or the vSphere Client.

> **Align das.iostatsInterval with the failure interval.**

Screenshots

One of the most useful features as part of VM Monitoring is the fact that it takes screenshots of the VM's console. The screenshots are taken right before VM Monitoring resets a VM. It is a very useful feature when a

VM "freezes" every once in a while for no apparent reason. This screenshot can be used to debug the VM operating system when needed, and is stored in the VM's working directory as logged in the Events view on the Monitor tab of the VM.

> **VM and Application monitoring can substantially increase availability. It is part of the HA stack and we strongly recommend using it!**

VM Monitoring Implementation Details

VM/App Monitoring is implemented as part of the HA agent itself. The agent uses the "Performance Manager" to monitor disk and network I/O; VM/App Monitoring uses the "usage" counters for both disk and network and it requests these counters once enough heartbeats have been missed that the configured policy is triggered.

As stated before, VM/App Monitoring uses heartbeats just like host-level HA. The heartbeats are monitored by the HA agent, which is responsible for the restarts. Of course, this information is also being rolled up into vCenter, but that is done via the Management Network, not using the VM network. This is crucial to know as this means that when a VM network error occurs, the VM heartbeat will still be received. When an error occurs, HA will trigger a restart of the VM when all three conditions are met:

- No VMware Tools heartbeat received
- No network I/O over the last 120 seconds
- No storage I/O over the last 120 seconds

Just like with host-level HA, the HA agent works independently of vCenter when it comes to VM restarts.

Timing

The VM/App monitoring feature monitors the heartbeat(s) issued by a guest and resets the VM if there is a heartbeat failure that satisfies the configured policy for the VM. HA can monitor just the heartbeats issued by the VMware tools process or can monitor these heartbeats plus those issued by an optional in-guest agent.

If the VM monitoring heartbeats stop at time T-0, the minimum time before HA will declare a heartbeat failure is in the range of 81 seconds to 119 seconds, whereas for heartbeats issued by an in-guest application agent, HA will declare a failure in the range of 61 seconds to 89 seconds. Once a heartbeat failure is declared for application heartbeats, HA will attempt to reset the VM. However, for VMware tools heartbeats, HA will first check whether any IO has been issued by the VM for the last 2 minutes (by default) and only if there has been no IO will it issue a reset. Due to how HOSTD publishes the I/O statistics, this check could delay the reset by approximately 20 seconds for VMs that were issuing I/O within approximately 1 minute of T-0.

Timing details: the range depends on when the heartbeats stop relative to the HOSTD thread that monitors them. For the lower bound of the VMware tools heartbeats, the heartbeats stop a second before the HOSTD thread runs, which means, at T+31, the FDM agent on the host will be notified of a tools yellow state, and then at T+61 of the red state, which HA reacts to. HA then monitors the heartbeat failure for a minimum of 30 seconds, leading to the min of T+91. The 30 seconds monitoring period done by HA can be increased using the `das.failureInterval` policy setting. For the upper bound, the FDM is not notified until T+59s (T=0 the failure occurs, T+29 HOSTD notices it and starts the heartbeat failure timer, and at T+59 HOSTD reports a yellow state, and at T+89 reports a red state).

For the heartbeats issued by an in-guest agent, no yellow state is sent, so the there is no additional 30 seconds period.

Application Monitoring

Application Monitoring is a part of VM Monitoring. Application Monitoring is a feature that partners and / or customers can leverage to increase resiliency, as shown in the screenshot below but from an application point of view rather than from a VM point of view. There is an SDK available to the general public and it is part of the guest SDK.

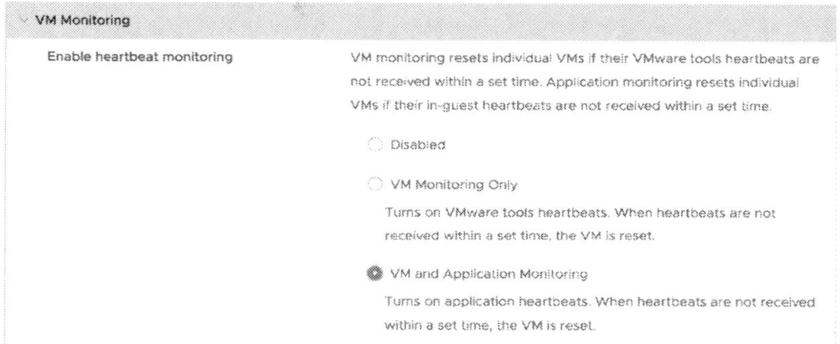

Figure 75: Application Monitoring

The Guest SDK is currently primarily used by application developers from partners like Symantec to develop solutions that increase resilience on a different level than VM Monitoring and HA. In the case of Veritas, a simplified version of Veritas Cluster Server (VCS) is used to enable application availability monitoring, including responding to issues. Note that this is not a multi-node clustering solution like VCS itself, but a single node solution.

Veritas ApplicationHA, as it is called, is triggered to get the application up and running again by restarting it. Veritas ApplicationHA is aware of dependencies and knows in which order services should be started or stopped. If, however, this fails for a certain number (configurable option within ApplicationHA) of times, VMware HA will be requested to take action. This action will be a restart of the VM.

Although Application Monitoring is relatively new and there are only a few partners currently exploring the capabilities, in our opinion, it does add a whole new level of resiliency. Your in-house development team could leverage functionality offered through the API, or you could use a solution developed by one of VMware's partners. We have tested ApplicationHA by Veritas and personally feel it is the missing link. It enables you as System Admin to integrate your virtualization layer with your application layer. It ensures you as a System Admin that services which are protected are restarted in the correct order and it avoids the common pitfalls associated with restarts and maintenance. Note that VMware also introduced an "Application Monitoring" solution which was based on Hyperic technology, this product however has been deprecated and as such will not be discussed in this publication.

Application Awareness API

The Application Awareness API is open for everyone. We feel that this is not the place to do a full deep dive on how to use it, but we do want to discuss it briefly.

The Application Awareness API allows for anyone to talk to it, including scripts, which makes the possibilities endless. Currently there are 6 functions defined:

- `_VMGuestAppMonitor_Enable_()`
    - Enables Monitoring
- `_VMGuestAppMonitor_MarkActive_()`
    - Call every 30 seconds to mark application as active
- `_VMGuestAppMonitor_Disable_()`
    - Disable Monitoring
- `_VMGuestAppMonitor_IsEnabled_()`
    - Returns status of Monitoring
- `_VMGuestAppMonitor_GetAppStatus_()`
    - Returns the current application status recorded for the application
- `_VMGuestAppMonitor_Free(_)`
    - Frees the result of the VMGuestAppMonitor_GetAppStatus() call

These functions can be used by your development team. However, App Monitoring also offers a new executable. This allows you to use the functionality App Monitoring offers without the need to compile a full binary. This new command, vmware-appmonitoring.exe, takes the following arguments, which are not coincidentally similar to the functions:

- Enable
- Disable
- markActive
- isEnabled
- getAppStatus

When running the command vmware-appmonitor.exe, which can be found under "VMware-GuestAppMonitorSDK\bin\win32\" the following output is presented:

```
Usage: vmware-appmonitor.exe {enable | disable | markActive |
isEnabled | getApp Status}
```

As shown there are multiple ways of leveraging Application Monitoring and to enhance resiliency on an application level.

09

VSPHERE HA INTEROPERABILITY

Now that you know how HA works inside out, we want to explain the different integration points between HA, DRS and Storage DRS.

HA and Storage DRS

vSphere HA informs Storage DRS when a failure has occurred. This to prevent the relocation of any HA protected VM, meaning, a VM that was powered on, but which failed, and has not been restarted yet due to their being insufficient capacity available. Further, Storage DRS is not allowed to Storage vMotion a VM that is owned by a master other than the one vCenter Server is talking to. This is because in such a situation, HA would not be able to reprotect the VM until the master to which vCenter Server is talking is able to lock the datastore again.

Storage vMotion and HA

If a VM needs to be restarted by HA and the VM is in the process of being Storage vMotioned and the VM fails, the restart process is not started until vCenter informs the master that the Storage vMotion task has completed or has been rolled back. If the source host fails, however, VM will restart the VM as part of the normal workflow. During a Storage vMotion, the HA agent on the host on which the Storage vMotion was initiated masks the failure state of the VM. If, for whatever reason, vCenter is unavailable, the masking will timeout after 15 minutes to ensure that the VM will be restarted.

Also note that when a Storage vMotion completes, vCenter will report the VM as unprotected until the master reports it protected again under the new path.

HA and DRS

HA integrates on multiple levels with DRS. It is a huge improvement and it is something that we wanted to stress as it has changed both the behavior and the reliability of HA.

HA and Resource Fragmentation

When a failover is initiated, HA will first check whether there are resources available on the destination hosts for the failover. If, for instance, a particular VM has a very large reservation and the Admission Control Policy is based on a percentage, for example, it could happen that resources are fragmented across multiple hosts. (For more details on this scenario, see Chapter 7.) HA will ask DRS to defragment the resources to accommodate for this VM's resource requirements. Although HA will request a defragmentation of resources, a guarantee cannot be given. As such, even with this additional integration, you should still be cautious when it comes to resource fragmentation.

Flattened Shares

When shares have been set custom on a VM an issue can arise when that VM needs to be restarted. When HA fails over a VM, it will power-on the VM in the Root Resource Pool. However, the VM's shares were those configured by a user for it, and not scaled for it being parented under the Root Resource pool. This could cause the VM to receive either too many or too few resources relative to its entitlement.

A scenario where and when this can occur would be the following:

VM01 has a 1000 shares and Resource pool RP-1 has 2000 shares. However, RP-1 has 2 VMs and both VMs will have 50% of those "2000" shares. The following diagram depicts this scenario:

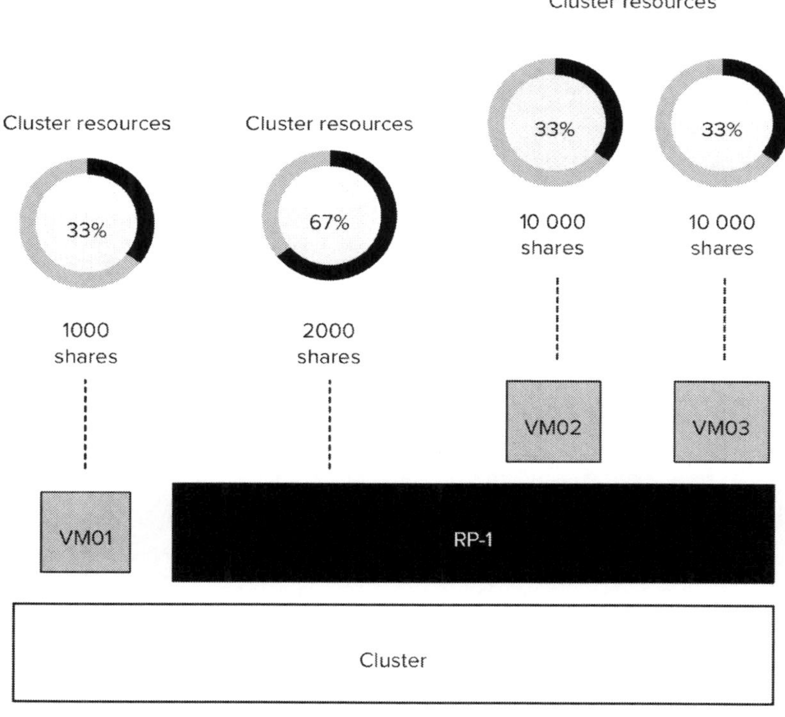

Figure 76: Flatten Shares Starting Point

When the host fails, both VM02 and VM03 will end up on the same level as VM01, the Root Resource Pool. However, as a custom shares value of 10,000 was specified on both VM02 and VM03, they will completely blow away VM01 in times of contention. This is depicted in the following diagram:

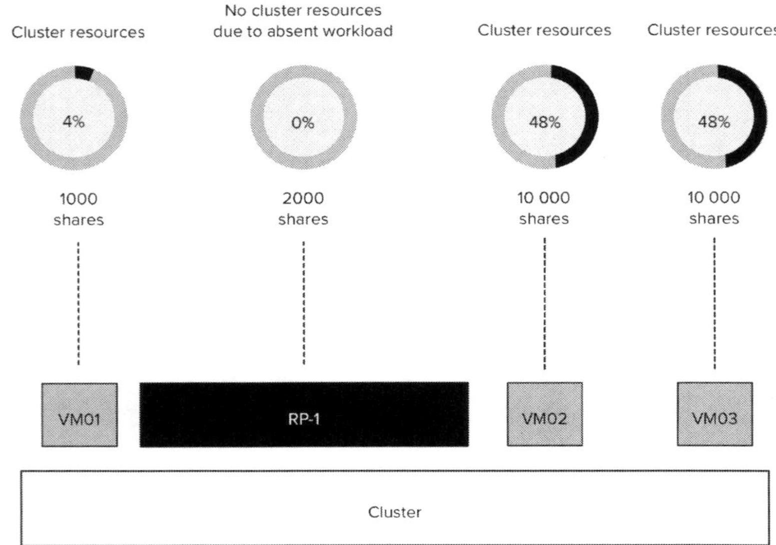

Figure 77: Flattening of Shares

This situation would persist until the next invocation of DRS would re-parent the VMs VM02 and VM03 to their original resource pool. To address this issue HA calculates a flattened share value before the VM's is failed-over. This flattening process ensures that the VM will get the resources it would have received if it had failed over to the correct resource pool.

This scenario is depicted in the following diagram. Note that both VM02 and VM03 are placed under the Root Resource Pool with a shares value of 1000.

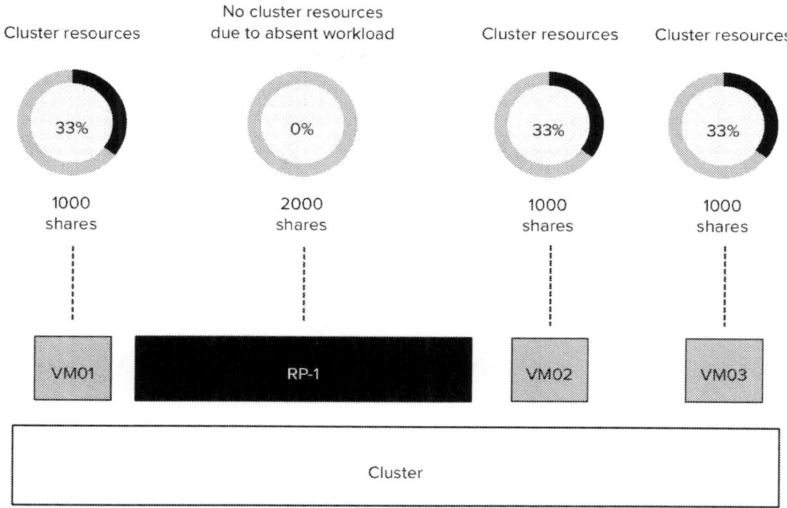

Figure 78: Flattening of Shares

Of course, when DRS is invoked, both VM02 and VM03 will be re-parented under RP-1 and will again receive the number of shares they had been originally assigned.

DPM and HA

If *Distributed Power Management* (DPM) is enabled and resources are scarce during an HA failover, HA will use DRS to try to adjust the cluster (for example, by bringing hosts out of standby mode or migrating VMs to defragment the cluster resources) so that HA can perform the failovers.

If HA strict Admission Control is enabled (default), DPM will maintain the necessary level of powered-on capacity to meet the configured HA failover capacity. HA places a constraint to prevent DPM from powering down too many ESXi hosts if it would violate the Admission Control Policy.

When HA admission control is disabled, HA will prevent DPM from powering off all but one host in the cluster. A minimum of two hosts is kept up regardless of the resource consumption. The reason this behavior has changed is that it is impossible to restart VMs when the only host left in the cluster has just failed.

In a failure scenario, if HA cannot restart some VMs, it asks DRS/DPM to try to defragment resources or bring hosts out of standby to allow HA another opportunity to restart the VMs. Another change is that DRS/DPM will power-on or keep on hosts needed to address cluster constraints, even if those host are lightly utilized. Once again, in order for this to be successful DRS will need to be enabled and configured to fully automated. When not configured to fully automated user action is required to execute DRS recommendations and allow the restart of VMs to occur.

Proactive HA

This is not really an integration point, but it is a function of HA which is not really implemented through HA. Proactive HA was implemented by the DRS team, and requires DRS, but can be found in the vSphere HA configuration section.

What does it do? Well in short, it allows you to configure actions for events that may lead to VM downtime. What does that mean? Well you can imagine that when a power-supply goes down your host is in a so called “degraded state”, when this event occurs an evacuation of the host could be triggered, meaning all VMs will be migrated to any of the remaining healthy hosts in the cluster.

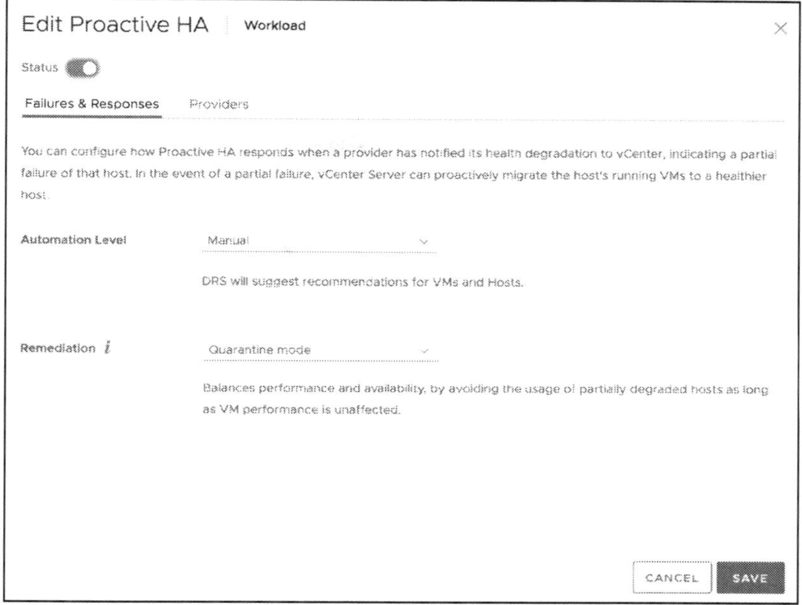

Figure 79: Proactive HA

How do we know the host is in a degraded state? Well that is where the Health Provider comes in to play. The health provider reads all the sensor data and analyze the results and then serve the state of the host up to vCenter Server. These states are "Healthy", "Moderate Degration", "Severe Degradation" and "Unknown". (Green, Yellow, Red) When vCenter is informed DRS can now take action based on the state of the hosts in a cluster, but also when placing new VMs it can take the state of a host in to consideration. The actions DRS can take by the way is placing the host in Maintenance Mode or Quarantine Mode. So, what is this quarantine mode and what is the difference between Quarantine Mode and Maintenance Mode?

Maintenance Mode is very straightforward, all VMs will be migrated off the host. With Quarantine Mode, this is not guaranteed. If for instance the cluster is overcommitted then it could be that some VMs are left on the quarantined host. Also, when you have VM-VM rules or VM/Host rules which would conflict when the VM is migrated then the VM is not migrated either. Note that quarantined hosts are not considered for placement of new VMs. It is up to you to decide how strict you want to be, and this can simply be configured in the UI. Personally I would recommend setting it to Automated with "Quarantine mode for moderate and Maintenance mode for sever failure(Mixed)". This seems to be a good balance between up time and resource availability. Screenshot below shows where this can be configured.

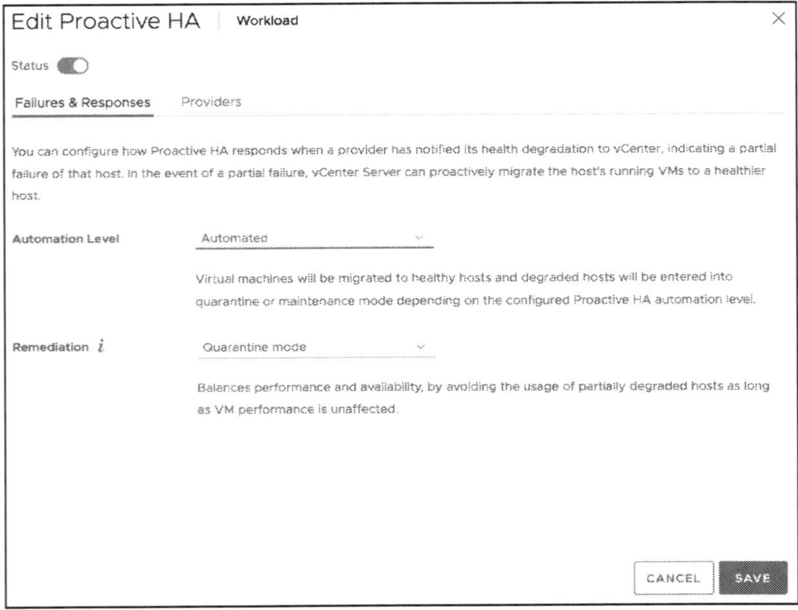

Figure 80: Proactive HA Automated Remediation

Proactive HA can respond to different types of failures, at the start of this section I mentioned power supply, but it can also respond to memory, network, storage and even a fan failure. Which state this results in (severe or moderate) is up to the vendor, this logic is built in to the Health Provider itself. You can imagine that when you have 8 fans in a server that the failure of one or two fans results in "moderate", whereas the failure of for instance 1 out of 2 NICs would result in "severe" as this leaves a "single point of failure". Oh, and when it comes to the Health Provider, this comes with the vendor vCenter Server plugins. This is also the most complicated part of the configuration of Proactive HA. The plugin unfortunately isn't easy to find for all vendors. In some cases even, a vendor may not support Proactive HA. If a provider has been installed it should show up in the configuration section of Proactive HA as shown in the screenshot below.

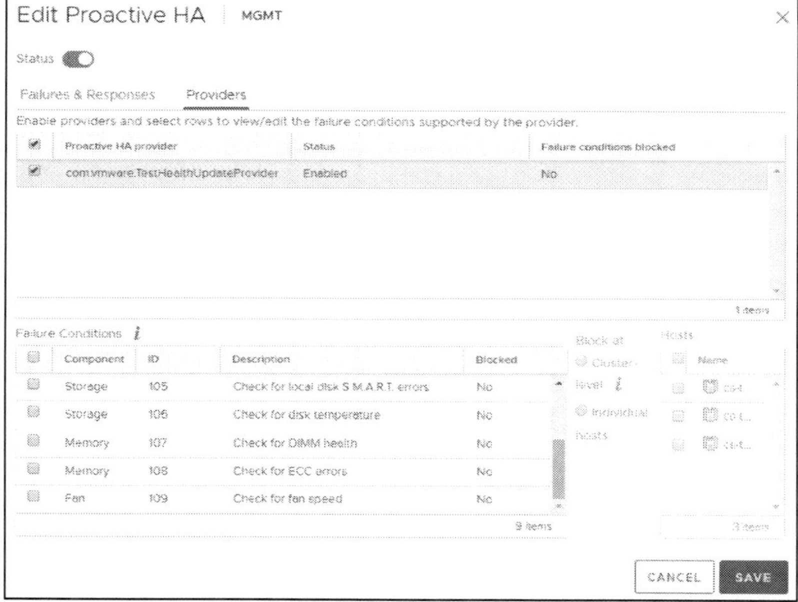

Figure 81: Proactive HA Provider

10

ADVANCED SETTINGS

There are various types of KB articles and this KB article explains it, but let me summarize it and simplify it a bit to make it easier to digest. There are various sorts of advanced settings, but for HA three in particular:

- das.* = Cluster level advanced setting
- fdm.* = FDM host level advanced setting
- vpxd.* = vCenter level advanced setting

How Do You Configure these Advanced Settings?

Configuring these is typically straight forward, and most of you hopefully know this already. If not, let us go over the steps to help configuring your environment as desired.

Cluster Level

In the vSphere Client:

1. Go to "Hosts and Clusters"
2. Click your cluster object
3. Click the "Configure" tab
4. Click "vSphere Availability"

5. Click "Edit" on "vSphere HA"
6. Click the "Advanced Options" button

FDM Host Level

- Open up an SSH session to your host and edit "/etc/opt/vmware/fdm/fdm.cfg"

vCenter Level

In the vSphere Client:

1. Go to "Hosts and Clusters"
2. Click the appropriate vCenter Server
3. Click the "Configure" tab
4. Click "Advanced Settings" under "Settings"

Most Commonly Used

In this section, we will primarily focus on the ones most commonly used, a full detailed list can be found in KB 2033250. Please note that each bullet details the version which supports this advanced setting.

- das.maskCleanShutdownEnabled
    - Whether the clean shutdown flag will default to false for an inaccessible and poweredOff VM. Enabling this option will trigger VM failover if the VM's home datastore isn't accessible when it dies or is intentionally powered off.
- das.ignoreInsufficientHbDatastore
    - Suppress the host config issue that the number of heartbeat datastores is less than das.heartbeatDsPerHost. Default value is "false". Can be configured as "true" or "false".
- das.heartbeatDsPerHost
    - The number of required heartbeat datastores per host.

The default value is 2; value should be between 2 and 5.

- das.isolationaddress[x]
    - IP address the ESXi hosts uses to check on isolation when no heartbeats are received, where [x] = 0 - 9. (see screenshot below for an example) VMware HA will use the default gateway as an isolation address and the provided value as an additional checkpoint. We recommend adding an isolation address when a secondary service console is being used for redundancy purposes.
- das.usedefaultisolationaddress
    - Value can be "true" or "false" and needs to be set to false in case the default gateway, which is the default isolation address, should not or cannot be used for this purpose. In other words, if the default gateway is a non-pingable address, set the "das.isolationaddress0" to a pingable address and disable the usage of the default gateway by setting this to "false".
- das.isolationShutdownTimeout
    - Time in seconds to wait for a VM to become powered off after initiating a guest shutdown, before forcing a power off.
- das.allowNetwork[x]
    - Enables the use of port group names to control the networks used for VMware HA, where [x] = 0 – ?. You can set the value to be "Service Console 2" or "Management Network" to use (only) the networks associated with those port group names in the networking configuration. In 5.5 this option is ignored when VSAN is enabled by the way!
- das.ignoreRedundantNetWarning
    - Remove the error icon/message from your vCenter when you don't have a redundant Service Console connection. Default value is "false", setting it to "true" will disable the warning. HA must be reconfigured after setting the option.

- das.perHostConcurrentFailoversLimit
    - By default, HA will issue up to 32 concurrent VM power-ons per host. This setting controls the maximum number of concurrent restarts on a single host. Setting a larger value will allow more VMs to be restarted concurrently but will also increase the average latency to recover as it adds more stress on the hosts and storage.

We recommend avoiding the use of advanced settings as much as possible. It typically leads to increased complexity, and when unneeded can lead to more down time rather than less down time.

P2

VSPHERE DISTRIBUTED RESOURCE SCHEDULER

11

INTRODUCTION TO VSPHERE DRS

VMware vSphere Distributed Resource Scheduler (DRS) is a resource management solution for vSphere clusters that allows IT organizations to deliver optimized performance of application workloads.

The primary goal of DRS is to ensure that workloads receive the resources they need to run efficiently. DRS determines the current resource demand of workloads and the current resource availability of the ESXi host that are grouped into a single vSphere cluster. DRS provides recommendations throughout the life-cycle of the workload. From the moment, it is powered-on, to the moment it is powered-down.

DRS operations consist of generating initial placements and load balancing recommendations based on resource demand, business policies and energy saving settings. It is able to automatically execute the initial placement and load balancing operations without any human interaction, allowing IT-organizations to focus their attention elsewhere.

DRS provides several additional benefits to IT operations:

- Day-to-day IT operations are simplified as staff members are less affected by localized events and dynamic changes in their environment. Loads on individual virtual machines invariably change, but automatic resource optimization and relocation of virtual machines reduce the need for administrators to respond, allowing them to focus on the broader, higher-level tasks of managing their infrastructure.

- DRS simplifies the job of handling new applications and adding new virtual machines. Starting up new virtual machines to run new applications becomes more of a task of high-level resource planning and determining overall resource requirements, than needing to reconfigure and adjust virtual machines settings on individual ESXi hosts.

- DRS simplifies the task of extracting or removing hardware when it is no longer needed or replacing older host machines with newer and larger capacity hardware.

DRS simplifies separating of VMs for availability requirements or unite virtual machines on the same ESXi host machine for increased performance while maintaining mobility.

> **We recommend enabling DRS to achieve higher consolidation ratios and better load balancing.**

Requirements

In order for DRS to function correctly, the virtual infrastructure must meet the following minimum requirements:

- VMware ESXi grouped in a cluster
- VMware vCenter Server
- VMware Enterprise Plus License
- Meet vMotion requirements (not mandatory, but highly recommended)
    - Shared datastores accessible by all ESXi hosts inside the cluster
    - Private migration network
    - Gigabit ethernet
    - Processor compatibility

For DRS to allow automatic load balancing, vMotion is required. For initial placement though, vMotion is not a requirement.

> **We recommend configuring vMotion to fully benefit from the capabilities of DRS.**

Cluster Level Resource Management

Clusters group the resources of the multiple ESXi hosts and treat them as a pool of resources. DRS presents the aggregated CPU and memory resources as one big host to the virtual machines. Abstracting host resources in a pool structure allows DRS to group, isolate and manage CPU and memory resources beyond the resources of a single host.

It is probably unnecessary to point out, but a virtual machine cannot span hosts even when resources are pooled by using DRS. DRS relies on host-local resource schedulers to allocate physical resources. In addition to resource pools and resource allocation policies, DRS offers the following resource management capabilities:

Initial placement: When a virtual machine is powered on in the cluster, DRS places the virtual machine on a fitting ESXi host or generates a recommendation depending on the automation level.

Load balancing: DRS distributes virtual machine workloads across the ESXi hosts inside the cluster. DRS continuously monitors the workload demand and the cluster resources. DRS compares the results to the ideal resource distribution and performs or recommends virtual machine migrations to ensure workloads receive the resources to which they are entitled, with the goal of maximizing workload performance.

Power management: If *Distributed Power Management* (DPM) is enabled, DRS compares cluster-level and host-level capacity to the demand of the virtual machines, including recent historical demand. It places, or recommends placing ESXi hosts in standby mode if excess capacity is detected or it powers on ESXi hosts if more capacity is required.

Host evacuation: DRS can help move VMs to other hosts to put a host into maintenance mode. Based on the automation level, DRS can perform the vmotion automatically or provide recommendations for user to approve. DRS will also retry moving failed to be moved VMs to accommodate transient vmotion failure or VM misconfiguration.

Cluster maintenance mode: DRS evaluates a set of hosts that can be put into maintenance mode at the same time to speed up the VMware Update Manager remediation process. DRS takes HA, *Fault Tolerance,* (FT) vMotion compatibility and reservations into account when determining the number of ESXi hosts eligible for entering maintenance mode simultaneously. If no constraints are present, cluster maintenance mode aims for 150% consolidation ratio.

Constraint correction: DRS redistributes virtual machines across ESXi hosts in the cluster. It moves virtual machines as needed to adhere to user-defined affinity and anti-affinity rules.

Support for agent virtual machines: Agent virtual machines are virtual machines that are required to be deployed and active on every host and belong to solutions that use ESX Agent Manager. DRS and DPM fully support ESX agents and respect the requirements of the ESX agent virtual machine. DRS and DPM understand that:

- Agent virtual machines do not have to be evacuated for a host to enter maintenance mode or standby.
- Agent virtual machines must be available before virtual machines can complete migration to or be powered up on a host.

DRS Cluster Settings

When enabling DRS on the cluster, you select the automation level and the migration threshold. DRS settings can be modified when the cluster is in use and without disruption of service. The following high-level steps show how to create a cluster and enable DRS:

1. Select Host and Cluster view (Default view)
2. Select Datacenter
3. Right-click on datacenter and select New Cluster

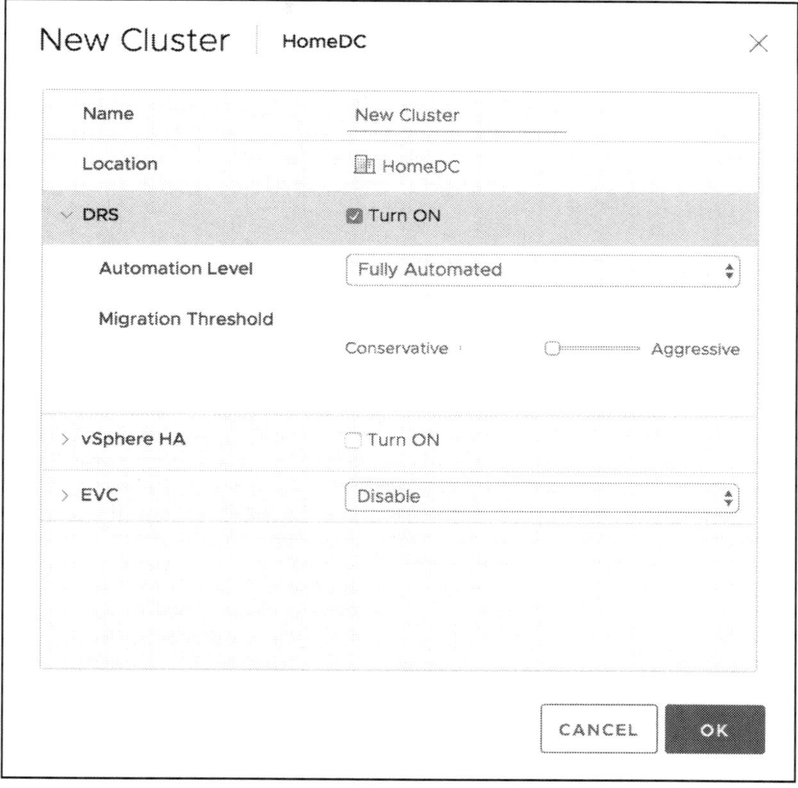

Figure 82: New DRS Cluster

4. Give the new cluster an appropriate name, aligned to your name convention
5. Select Turn ON DRS
6. Select Automation Level
7. Verify Migration Threshold and if necessary adjust slider
8. It's recommended to enable EVC

DRS Automation Levels

Three levels of automation are available, allowing DRS to provide recommendations for initial placement and load balancing operations. DRS can operate in manual mode, partially automated mode and fully automated mode. Allowing the IT operation team to be fully in-control or allow DRS to operate without the requirement of human interaction.

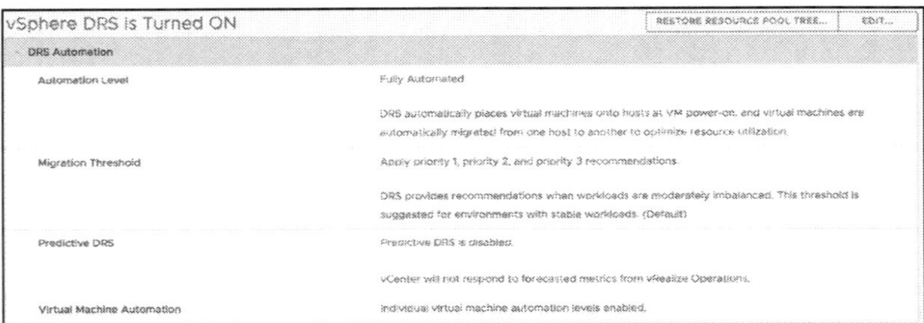

Figure 83: DRS Automation Level

Manual Automation Level

The manual automation level expects the IT operation team to be in complete control. DRS generates initial placement and load balancing recommendations and the IT operation team can choose to ignore the recommendation or to carry out any recommendations.

If a VM is powered-on in a DRS enabled cluster, DRS presents a list of mutually exclusive initial placement recommendations for the virtual machine. If a cluster imbalance is detected during a DRS invocation, DRS presents a list of recommendations of virtual machine migrations to improve the cluster balance. With each subsequent DRS invocation, the state of the cluster is recalculated and a new list of recommendations could be generated.

Partially Automated Level

DRS generates initial placement recommendations and executes them automatically. DRS generates load-balancing operations for the IT operation teams to review and execute. Please note that the introduction of a new VM can impact current active workload, which may result in DRS generating load-balancing recommendations. It is recommended to review the DRS recommendation list after power-on operations if the DRS cluster is configured to operate in partially automated mode.

The vSphere cluster summary screen shows the number of the pending DRS recommendations. This is a click-through function.

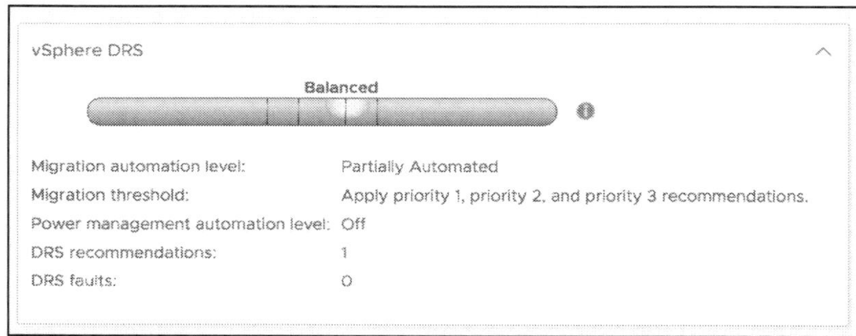

Figure 84: DRS Metrics on Cluster Summary Screen

Click on the number listed and the H5 client automatically takes you to the DRS recommendations screen. These recommendations are refreshed after each load-balancing calculation (5 minutes interval).

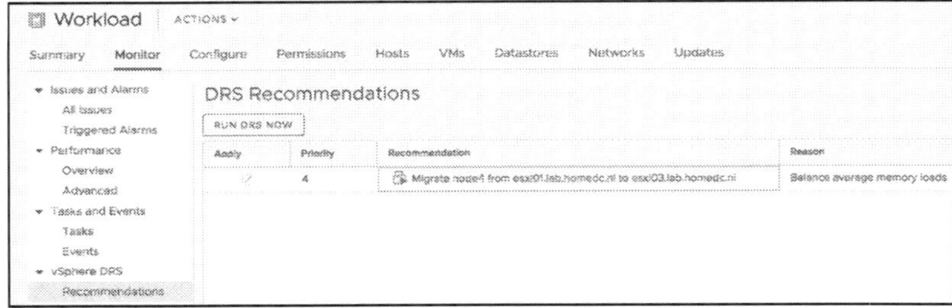

Figure 85: Pending DRS Recommendations

Click on the apply recommendation located on the bottom right side of your screen to start a migration operation.

Fully Automated Level

DRS operates autonomous in fully automated level mode and requires no human interaction. DRS generates initial placement and load balancing recommendations and executes these automatically. Please note that the migration threshold setting configures the aggressiveness of load balancing migrations.

AUTOMATION LEVEL	INITIAL PLACEMENT	LOAD BALANCING
Manual	Recommended host(s) displayed	Migration recommendation is displayed
Partially Automated	Automatic placement	Migration recommendation is displayed
Fully Automated	Automatic placement	Automatic migration

Table 6: DRS Automation Level Operations

Per-VM Automation Level

DRS allow Per-VM automation level to customize the automation level for individual VMs to override the cluster's default automation level. This allows IT operation teams to benefit from DRS at the cluster level while isolating particular VMs. This can be helpful if some virtual machines are not allowed to move due to licensing or strict performance requirement.

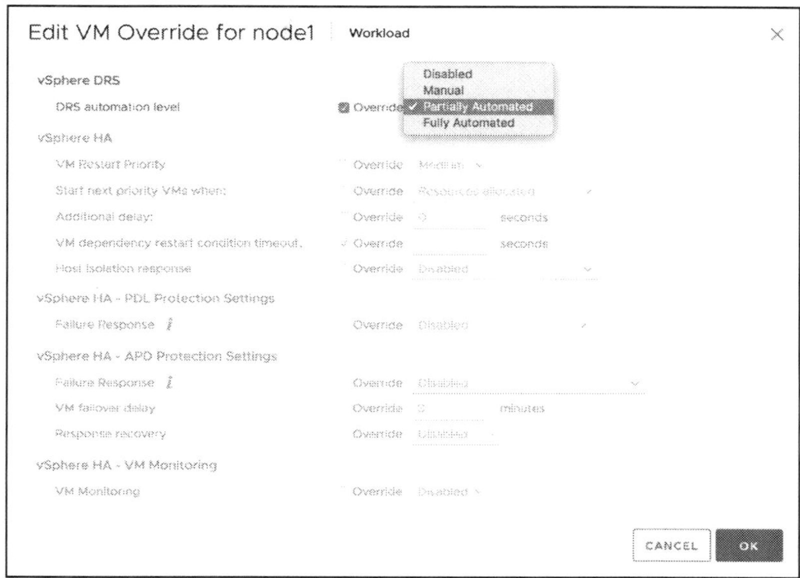

Figure 86: VM Override Options

Please note, that DRS still considers the VM for load balancing operations, it just doesn't automatically move them around anymore.

DRS Recommendations

RUN DRS NOW

Apply	Priority	Recommendation	Reason
✓	5	Migrate node1 from esxi01.lab.homedc.nl to esxi02.lab.homedc.nl	Balance average memory loads

Figure 87: DRS Recommendation of Partially Automated VM

In essence, you create a contract with DRS agreeing that you will be the one to take action if a recommendation is generated for that particular VM. Setting the automation level to manual or partially automated does not exclude it from being considered for load-balancing operations to solve the imbalance of the cluster.

> **Please take this into account when you are configuring highly utilized VMs with a per-VM automation level.**

Impact of Automation Levels on Procedures

When the manual or partially automated automation level is selected, it is expected that the user manually applies the recommendations generated by DRS. Please note that DRS reviews the state of the cluster at an interval of five minutes and publishes recommendations to solve any calculated imbalance of the cluster. Consequently, administrators should check the recommendations after each DRS invocation to resolve the cluster imbalance. Besides inefficiency, it is possible that DRS rules may be violated if the administrators apply the recommendations infrequently. DRS rules are explained in section "Rules" of chapter 15.

The automation level of the cluster can be changed without disrupting virtual machines. It is easy to change, so why not try Fully automated for a while to get comfortable with it?

Initial Placement

Initial placement occurs when a VM is powered on or resumed. The initial placement engine in vSphere 6.7 is renewed and is much more efficient than the previous version.

> **vSphere 6.5 is equipped with the new initial placement engine, similar to one in 6.7. However, it did not support vSphere HA. As a result, only a vSphere cluster with DRS enabled and HA disabled benefitted from the new engine. If HA was enabled in 6.5, DRS would revert to the old initial placement engine. In.6.7 this engine supports HA and is now available for all workloads, and not only clusters who run workloads that ensure availability by leveraging in-app services.**

Old Initial Placement Behavior

DRS took a snapshot of the cluster state to generate a host recommendation for VM initial placement. A snapshot is an overview of all the active ESXi hosts and their current utilization. During a batch power-on operation of multiple VMs, DRS uses the same snapshot for initial placement recommendations. That means that if you want to power-on 64 VMs at once, it will use the same utilization statistics reported in the snapshot. For example, if ESXi host 1 is empty, VM01 is placed on that host. The same logic is applied to VM64 as well, host 1 is empty, thus place VM64 on host 1. As a result, DRS placed most of all VMs on the same host. In reality host 1 is already loaded with 63 other VMs.

Another problem with the old algorithm is the time it takes to power-on a group of VMs. Sometimes it could take more than a minute to power-on the VM. In modern times with containers sharing the infrastructure alongside the VMs, this power-on latency is not desirable. Especially when you design your environment to use instant clones. On average the old algorithm took 4 seconds to 1 minute to complete a VM power-on operation, the new algorithm completes the power-on operations within 10 seconds.

vSphere 6.7 Initial Placement Behavior

In vSphere 6.7, the algorithm completely avoids snapshotting. It keeps the host load up to date when a VM is placed. This result in a far more accurate view for DRS. VMs are placed on an ESXi host that can deliver the resources from the get-go, it does not have to wait for the load-balancing algorithm to run before it can be moved to an ESXi host that can provide the resources the VM demands.

The performance engineering team ran a test comparing the initial placements engines. The test powered on 64 VMs simultaneously on 4 ESXi host cluster. The results are covered in the table below:

	HOST 1	HOST 2	HOST 3	HOST 4
Old Algorithm	11	53	0	0
6.7 Algorithm	16	16	16	16

Table 7: VM Distribution by Initial Placement Algorithm

Virtual Machine Performance Modelling

Due to the lack of historical performance data, DRS will assume that the VM is 100% busy and will select an ESXi host that can run the VM. During initial placement, DRS will take the current demand for the VMs and the capacity of each host into account.
If the cluster is configured with the automation level set to manual, DRS creates a prioritized list of recommended hosts for VM placement. This list is presented to the user to help select an appropriate host.

> **Please note that, due to this performance model the DRS aggressiveness, defined by the DRS migration threshold, has no effect on Initial Placement.**

vCenter Sizing

In previous editions of the book, we recommended to take the impact of the resource utilization by the DRS threads on vCenter Server into account when sizing the vCenter server and designing the cluster environment. It still is important to realize that running DRS is not free, but the DRS redesign reduced the resource utilization dramatically. Comparing the memory consumption of DRS managing large clusters, 6.7 DRS consumes 3 times less memory than 6.0, which already provided a big improvement over 5.5.

Carefully select the appropriate size of your VCSA during deployment , the VCSA deployment process assists you in selecting the size that is suitable for your vSphere environment.

DEPLOYMENT SIZE	NUMBER OF HOSTS	NUMBER OF VMS	CPUS USED BY APPLIANCE	MEMORY USED BY APPLIANCE
Tiny	10	100	2	10 GB
Small	100	1.000	4	16 GB
Medium	400	4.000	8	24 GB
Large	1.000	10.000	16	32 GB
X-Large	2.000	35.000	24	48 GB

Table 8: VCSA Deployment Size

This overview provides you a proper guideline for your deployment size, however it does not take into account how these hosts are grouped within the virtual infrastructure. vCenter creates and runs a single DRS thread per cluster and it can increase the overall memory consumption if you run a high number of vSphere clusters. It is recommended to use the *vSphere Appliance Management Interface* (VAMI) to monitor the CPU and memory consumption of vCenter. Log into vCenter using port 5480. For example: https://vcsa67.lab.homedc.nl:5480/ and go the monitor tab. You can monitor resource utilization on an hourly, daily, weekly, monthly, quarterly, and yearly basis.

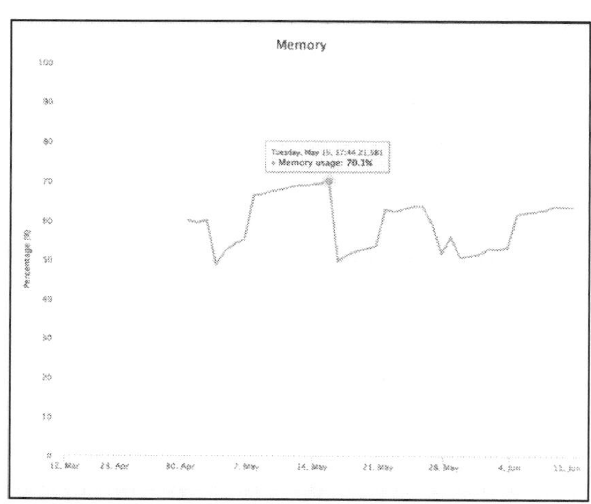

Figure 88: VCSA Last Quarter Memory Utilization View

DRS Thread per Cluster

vCenter creates and runs a single DRS thread per cluster. The DRS thread communicates with the management agent (VPXA) on each ESXi host inside the cluster.

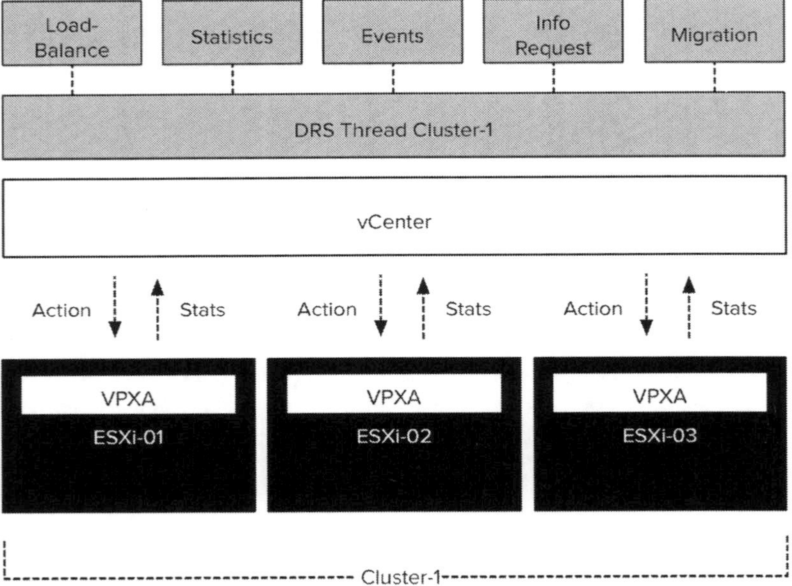

Figure 89: DRS Components

The vCenter agent (VPXA) runs inside each ESXi host in the cluster and enables a two-way communication between the ESXi host and vCenter. VPXA keeps the status of both ESXi and VMs in sync with the status shown in vCenter.

The VPXA sends information when a VM power state changes or when a VM is migrated with vMotion. Periodically, the VPXA sends additional notification and statistics to the vCenter server. DRS sends messages to the ESXi host, such as proposed migrations and information requests.

Prior to 6.7, DRS would process the statistics of all the VPXA's and distribute new resource targets to the VPXAs. The distribution of the new resource targets would happen around the same time as the load-balancing operation, every 5 minutes. In 6.7 the process of dividing host resources amongst the active VMs and the subsequent distribution of resource targets happens every 60 seconds now and runs separately from the load balancing operation. This allows DRS to react much faster to sudden VM demand change.

DRS 6.7 still runs the load-balancing algorithm each 5 minutes. This thread calculates the imbalance of the cluster, applies resource settings and, if needed, generates migration recommendations. If an ESXi host is added or removed (maintenance mode included) a load-balancing operation is triggered.

DRS does not immediately trigger a resource target allocation process (sometimes referred to as resource divvy) when a VM is powered on or off. Similarly when a VM configuration is changed, DRS will take these changes into account during the next periodic Load Balancing or resource target allocation process.

Separate VDI Workloads From VSI Workloads

In large environments, we recommend separating VDI workloads and server workloads and assigning different clusters to each workload to reduce the number of DRS invocations. By isolating server workloads from VDI workloads, only the VDI clusters experience increased DRS invocations, reducing overall overhead, complexity and the number of calculations performed by DRS.

> **Separate VDI workloads and server workloads and assign different clusters to each workload to reduce the DRS invocations.**

Cluster Sizing

The general guideline is that the more hosts you have in the cluster, the more opportunities DRS has to place the virtual machines. The maximum number of hosts supported in vSphere 6.7 for a DRS cluster is 64. Each cluster is able to contain 8000 VMs, with a maximum of 25.000 powered-on VMs per vCenter. It is expected that DRS will not be the limiting factor when designing cluster configurations. However, the following can impact DRS cluster and virtual machine sizing:

Size of host versus the maximum number of virtual machines in a cluster: In vSphere 6.7, the maximum number of VMs inside a cluster is 8000, with the current maximum of 64 hosts per cluster, you can run up to 125 VMs per host on average. Please take the maximums into considerations when researching scale-up versus scale out cluster configurations.

The number of virtual machines versus the number of LUNs required: vSphere 6.7 allows up to 1024 volumes connected to an ESXi host. DRS only considers hosts compatible for virtual machine migration if hosts are connected to the same VMFS datastore. Consistent VMFS datastore connectivity across all hosts in the DRS cluster is regarded as a best practice. If more than 1024 datastores need to be connected, consider using multiple DRS clusters and size them accordingly.

Hardware configuration – Heterogeneous or Homogeneous: Heterogeneous host configurations can impact the effectiveness of DRS. DRS will not migrate VMs if the physical configuration cannot host the VMs. By leveraging EVC, multiple hardware configurations can exist within a DRS cluster and allow older hardware configurations to be mixed with new hardware configurations. Although we recommend enabling EVC, we advise you to refrain from combining hardware configurations that are too different.

For example, vSphere 6.7 and up allows up to 128 vCPUs and 6128 GB of memory to be assigned to a virtual machine, and we expect to see an increase in the number of larger virtual machines within the virtual infrastructure. Larger virtual machines such as 48 or 64 vCPU virtual machines cannot be hosted on a system containing two Octa Core CPUs. Keep your platform in sync with the demands of the applications, but figure out whether you want to have these diverse systems into a single cluster.

Supporting Technology

DRS leverages vMotion to live migrate workloads between hosts, to get the mobility of workloads it is important to review your vMotion configuration and the Enhanced vMotion Compatibilities options of your cluster.

vMotion

vMotion is probably the best example of an industry-changing feature. When virtualization was first introduced, it was all about flexibility and mobility of virtual machines. However, portability and flexibility was somewhat limited based on the power state of the virtual machine. VMware changed the world of IT by introducing vMotion.

The vMotion configuration of your vSphere cluster indirectly impacts the resource allocation of your VMs. DRS calculates how fast it can transfer a VM from the source host to the destination host during the load-balancing process. It calculates how many VMs it can transfer within a single load balancing operation. It adjusts its recommendation based on these numbers. That means that if DRS cannot move VMS fast enough, or cannot move the desired VMs to achieve the best load balance, DRS will reduce the number of recommendations. All based on the fact how many migrations it can fit within the 5-minute window (the time between two load balancing operations). Thus, the bigger and better the pipeline between hosts, the more data can flow, i.e. the more migrations that can occur, the higher the number of movements DRS can generate to get the VMs on hosts that CAN deliver the desired resources.

Multi-NIC vMotion

With this in mind, we recommend multi-nic vMotion almost all of the time. Multi-NIC vMotion uses multiple vmknics that allows ESXi to load balance vMotion migration(s) across the available bandwidth. Even if there is one migration recommended, ESXi will leverage both vmknics, and thus different uplinks to migrate the VM to a new host. Doubling the bandwidth typically cuts the time required to migrate the VMs roughly in half, and thereby allowing DRS to generate more migrations to achieve load utilization balance within the cluster. Regardless of the number of vMotion enabled vmknics or uplinks, the total number of concurrent vMotions is 8 per host.

Although the number of concurrent vMotions hasn't changed for a while, please note that the vMotion performance increases as additional network bandwidth is made available to the vMotion network. While 10GbE is becoming the standard, a lot of organizations are looking at 25 GbE or 40 GbE networks.

10/25/40GbE vMotion Network

vSphere 6.0 introduced the vMotion stream architecture. During the vMotion process, vMotion creates stream channels (TCP/IP connection) between the source and designation host based on the available vmknics. By default a single vMotion stream channel pair is created per vMotion-enabled vmknic. One vMotion stream to prepare the data, one vMotion stream to transmit the data.

A single vMotion stream channel is capable of achieving line rate on 10GbE, to be more precise, running a vMotion worker on an average CPU core allows you to get 18 gigabits per second.

It is recommended to have at least two to three vMotion enabled vmknics on a 25/40GbE vMotion NIC to achieve full line rate.

NUMBER OF VMOTION VMKNICS	NUMBER OF 25 GBE NICS	THROUGHPUT	NUMBER OF 40 GBE NICS
1	1	18 Gb per second	1
2	N/A	28 Gb per second	1
3	N/A	36 Gb per second	1

Table 9: vmknics per Physical NIC Configuration

As you noticed, the increase of throughput is not linear, due to scheduling and other various overheads. Source: VMware KB 2108824

CPU Consumption of vMotion Process

ESXi reserves CPU resources on both the destination and the source host to ensure vMotion can consume the available bandwidth. ESXi only takes the number of vMotion NICs, and their respective speed into account, the number of vMotion operations does not affect the total of CPU resources reserved! 10% of a CPU core for a 1GbE NIC, 100% of a CPU core for a 10 GbE NIC. vMotion is configured with a minimum reservation of 30%. Therefore if you have 1GbE NIC configured for vMotion, it reserves at least 30% of a single core.

vSphere 6.5 introduced encrypted vMotion and encrypts vMotion traffic if the destination and source host are capable of supporting encrypted vMotion, if this is the case, vMotion traffic consumes even more CPU cycles on both the source and destination host.

Encrypted vMotion

As mentioned, vSphere 6.5 introduced encrypted vMotion and by doing so it also introduced a new stream channel architecture. When an encrypted vMotion process is started, three stream channels are created. Prepare, Encrypt and Transmit. The encryption and decryption process consumes CPU cycles and to reduce the overhead as much as possible, the encrypted vMotion process uses the AES-NI Instruction set of the physical CPU. AES-NI stands for *Advanced Encryption Standard- New Instruction* and was introduced in the Intel Westmere-EP generation (2010) and AMD Bulldozer (2011). It's safe to say that most data centers run on AES-NI equipped CPUs. However, if the source or destination host is not equipped with AES-NI, vMotion automatically reverts back to unencrypted if the default setting is selected.

Although the encrypted vMotion leverages special CPU hardware instructions set to offload overhead, it does increase the CPU utilization.

The technical paper *"VMware vSphere Encrypted vMotion Architecture, Performance, and Best Practices"* published by VMware list the overhead on the source and destination host.

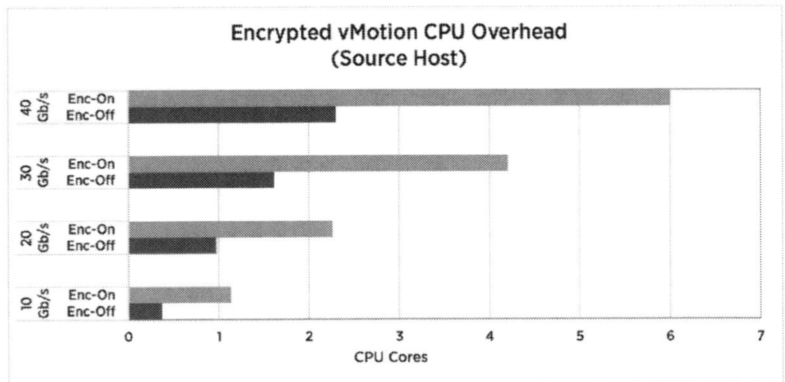

Figure 90: Encrypted vMotion CPU Overhead on the Source Host

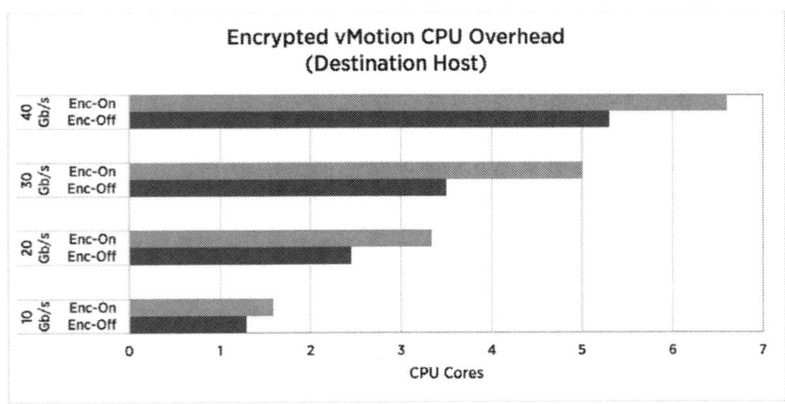

Figure 91: Encrypted vMotion CPU Overhead on the Destination Host

Encrypted vMotion is a per-VM setting, by default every VM is configured with Encrypted vMotion set to Opportunistic. The three settings are:

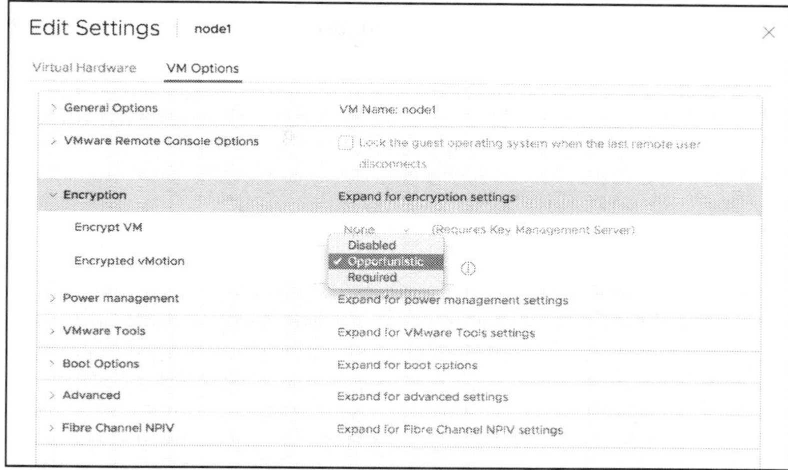

Figure 92: VM Options Encrypted vMotion

SETTING	BEHAVIOR
Disabled	Does not use encrypted vMotion
Opportunistic	Use encrypted vMotion if source and destination host supports it. Only vSphere 6.5 and later use encrypted vMotion
Required	Only allow encrypted vMotion. If the source and destination host does not support encrypted vMotion, migration with vMotion is not allowed

Table 10: Per-VM Encrypted vMotion Settings and Behavior

Please be aware that encrypted vMotion settings are transparent to DRS. DRS generates a load balancing migration and when the vMotion process starts, the vMotion process verifies the requirements. Due to the transparency, DRS does not take encrypted vMotion settings and host compatibility into account when generating a recommendation.

This is important to understand if you are running a heterogeneous cluster with various vSphere versions, or different types of CPU generations. Please make sure the BIOS version supports AES-NI and make sure AES-NI is enabled in the BIOS. Also, verify if the applied *Enhanced vMotion Compatibility* (EVC) baseline exposes AES-NI.

CPU Headroom

It is important to keep some unreserved and unallocated CPU resources of the ESXi host available for the vMotion process, to avoid creating gridlock. DRS needs some resources to run its threads, and vMotion requires resources to move VMs to lesser utilized ESXi host.

Enhanced vMotion Capability

The CPU on the source and destination host must come from the same vendor class to be compatible for vMotion. *Enhanced vMotion Compatibility* (EVC) makes a common CPU feature set between the CPUs available through the use of a baseline. EVC is complementary to the popular building block architecture and allows customers to scale out clusters with various server generations while maintaining a form of standardization. EVC also helps to complete full cluster upgrades with no downtime to any virtual machines. Add the new hosts to the cluster, migrate the VMs and retire the old ones if necessary.

How Does EVC Work?

EVC allows for vMotion between different CPU generations through the use of Intel Flex Migration and AMD-V Extended Migration technologies. EVC leverages a defined baseline that allows all the hosts in the cluster to advertise the same CPU feature set. The EVC baseline does not disable the features within a CPU but indicates to a virtual machine that specific features are not available.

> **Please note that CPU clock speed, cache size, and the number of cores are not included in EVC baselines, they are not masked in any way shape or form! EVC only focuses on CPU features specific to CPU generations, such as SIMD (SSE) or AMD-now instructions. EVC masks these CPU features. This means that the features are still available and active, but they are not visible to the software running inside the VM.**

When enabling EVC, a CPU baseline must be selected. This baseline represents a feature set of the chosen CPU generation and exposes specific CPU generation features. When a VM powers-on within an EVC cluster, this cluster's baseline will be attached to the virtual machine until it powers-off.

AMD EVC MODES	INTEL EVC MODES
AMD Opteron Generation 1 (Rev. E)	Intel "Merom" Generation (Intel Xeon Core 2)
AMD Opteron Generation 2 (Rev. F)	Intel "Penryn" Generation (Intel Xeon 45nm Core2)
AMD Opteron Generation 3 (Greyhound)	Intel "Nehalem" Generation (Intel Xeon Core i7)
AMD Opteron Generation 3 (no 3Dnow!) (Greyhound)	**Intel "Westmere" Generation (Intel Xeon 32nm Core i7) ***
AMD Opteron Generation 4 (Bulldozer) *	Intel "Sandy Bridge" Generation
AMD Opteron "Piledriver" Generation	Intel "Ivy Bridge" Generation
AMD Opteron "Steamroller" Generation	Intel "Haswell" Generation
AMD "Zen" Generation	Intel "Broadwell" Generation
	Intel "Skylake" Generation

Table 11: Supported EVC Modes in ESXi 6.7

* EVC baseline that introduces AES-NI (see encrypted vMotion)

> **The EVC baseline is attached to the virtual machine until it powers off even if it is migrated to another EVC cluster.**

EVC is set at the cluster level, go to the vSphere cluster and select the configure tab. A VMware EVC option is listed inside the configuration tree. One simple but fantastic feature is the EVC Compatibility checker in the UI. If you select a baseline, the compatibility checker immediately lists the ESXi hosts that are not compatible in the cluster.

Change EVC Mode
Workload
Select EVC Mode
Disable EVC
Enable EVC for AMD Hosts
Enable EVC for Intel® Hosts
VMware EVC Mode:
Intel® "Sandy Bridge" Generation
Description
Applies the baseline feature set of Intel® "Sandy Bridge" Generation processors to all hosts in the cluster.
Hosts with the following processor types will be permitted to enter the cluster:
Intel® "Sandy Bridge" Generation
Intel® "Ivy Bridge" Generation
Intel® "Haswell" Generation
Future Intel® processors
Compared to the Intel® "Westmere" Generation EVC mode, this EVC mode exposes additional CPU features including AVX, XSAVE, and ULE.
Note: Some "Sandy Bridge" microarchitecture processors do not provide the full "Sandy Bridge" feature set. Such processors do not support this EVC mode; they will only be admitted to the Intel® "Nehalem" Generation mode or below.
For more information, see Knowledge Base article 1003212.
Compatibility
The host cannot be admitted to the cluster's current Enhanced vMotion Compatibility mode. Powered-on or suspended virtual machines on the host may be using CPU features hidden by that mode.
esxi03.lab.homedc.nl
esxi01.lab.homedc.nl
esxi02.lab.homedc.nl
CANCEL
OK

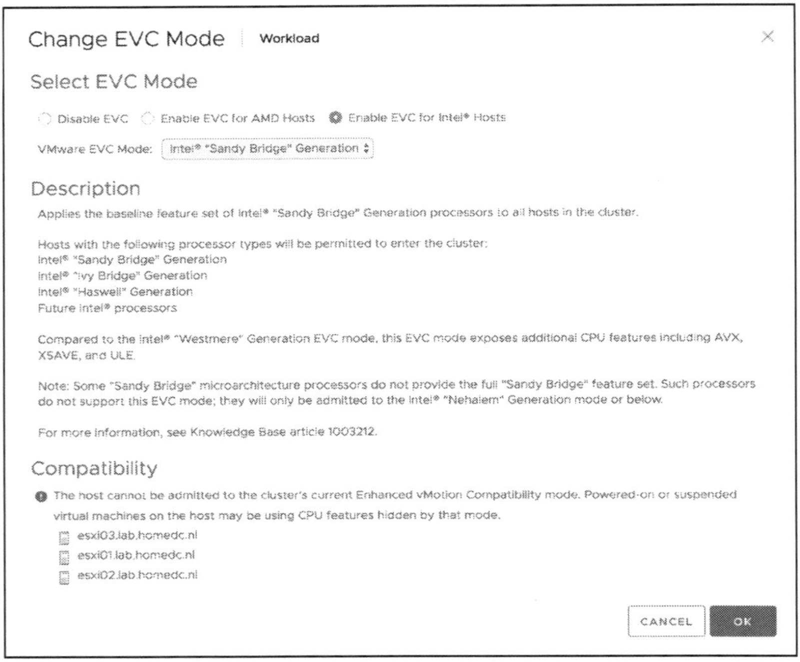

Figure 93: EVC Compatibility Check

Will EVC Impact Application Performance?

Keep in mind that enabling EVC may impact the performance of applications specifically written to benefit from these special instructions masked by EVC. As mentioned before, but never stressed enough, EVC does not affect the number of instructions per second, the number of available cores, hardware acceleration, caching or other CPU features that most software uses.

If your application uses the particular instruction sets such as AVX, it is recommended to test your application with and without EVC baseline attached and determine whether infrastructure scalability and operational simplicity are less or more important than the increase of performance of the instruction set.

If your application is not designed to leverage particular CPU instruction sets, it's highly unlikely to experience performance degradation. But with anything in IT, do not guess! It's important to test, establish a baseline, and make data-driven decisions before enabling a feature.

Enabling and Disabling EVC

EVC can be enabled even when VMs are active. Powered-on virtual machines will not block configuration of EVC for a cluster as long as the VM itself is compatible with the desired EVC mode.

If EVC is disabled, the VMs continue to operate at the same EVC mode and are not forced to restart. If complete removal of the EVC mode is required, the VM must go through a full power-cycle; a reboot is not sufficient.

If EVC is disabled on a cluster containing FT-enabled VMs, their DRS automation settings are changed to Disabled and DRS will be unable to migrate the primary and secondary during load-balancing and maintenance mode operations. If EVC is enabled again, these VMs will once again receive the default cluster DRS automation level.

Power Off VM Instead of Reboot

It is important to remember that EVC baselines are applied only during power-on operations. If the EVC cluster mode is changed, existing VM are required to complete a full power-cycle to receive the new baseline. A VM continues to run if the EVC mode is increased, for example from Intel "Ivy Bridge" generation to Intel "Skylake" generation, but will operate with the knowledge of the instruction set of the original Ivy Bridge generation baseline until it is power-cycled, at which point the new Skylake baseline will be propagated to the VM.

EVC Requirements

To enable EVC on a cluster, the cluster must meet the following requirements:

- All hosts in the cluster must have CPUs from a single vendor, either AMD or Intel.
- All hosts in the cluster must have advanced CPU features, such as hardware virtualization support (AMD-V or Intel VT) and AMD No eXecute (NX) or Intel eXecute Disable (XD) and must be enabled in the BIOS.
- All hosts in the cluster should be configured for vMotion. See the section, host configuration requirements for vMotion.
- All hosts in the cluster must be connected to the same vCenter Server.

Besides, all hosts in the cluster must have CPUs that support the EVC mode you want to enable. To check EVC support for a specific processor or server model, see the VMware Compatibility Guide at: *http://www.vmware.com/resources/compatibility/.*

Conclusion

DRS is a simple to use clustering solution that will allow you to reach higher consolidation ratios while providing optimal utilization of available resources. Understanding the architecture of DRS will enable you to design vCenter and DRS clusters that provides the best performance while operating as efficiently as possible. The following chapters will discuss the fundamental concepts of resource management. We will also review all decision-making moments to ensure you configure DRS in such a way that it meets the requirements of your or your customer's environment.

12

RESOURCE DISTRIBUTION

In this section, we will explain DRS dynamic entitlement and the concepts of resource management. Understanding elements such as dynamic entitlement, resource pools, and resource allocation settings will allow you to troubleshoot DRS behavior more efficiently and gain optimal performance for your virtual machines.

Before diving into DRS and local host resource management, it is essential that we step back and examine the fundamentals of dynamic entitlements.

DRS Dynamic Entitlement

Dynamic entitlement defines a target that represents the ideal amount of resources eligible for use. Both DRS and the host-local schedulers compute this target, and it is up to the virtual machine or resource pool to use the available resources or not. Entitlement consists of static and dynamic elements.

Reservations, shares, and limits define the static part, while estimated VM demand and ESXi host contention levels define the dynamic part. A VM has a separate dynamic entitlement target for CPU and memory.

Dynamic entitlement rests on the configured reservations, shares, and limits settings. These settings not only affect the performance of the VM but could impact the performance of other virtual machines as well. Therefore, it is essential to understand how dynamic entitlement is calculated and how to configure the VM without introducing a denial-of-service for the VM or the rest of the environment.

Both the dynamic and static elements are explained in detail later in this chapter. For now, let's start with the architecture of the scheduler responsible for calculating dynamic entitlements.

Resource Scheduler Architecture

The ESXi host runs multiple host-local resource schedulers within the VMkernel, including the CPU schedulers and the memory scheduler. DRS runs a global scheduler within vCenter. The DRS scheduler provides guidelines to the ESXi resource schedulers.

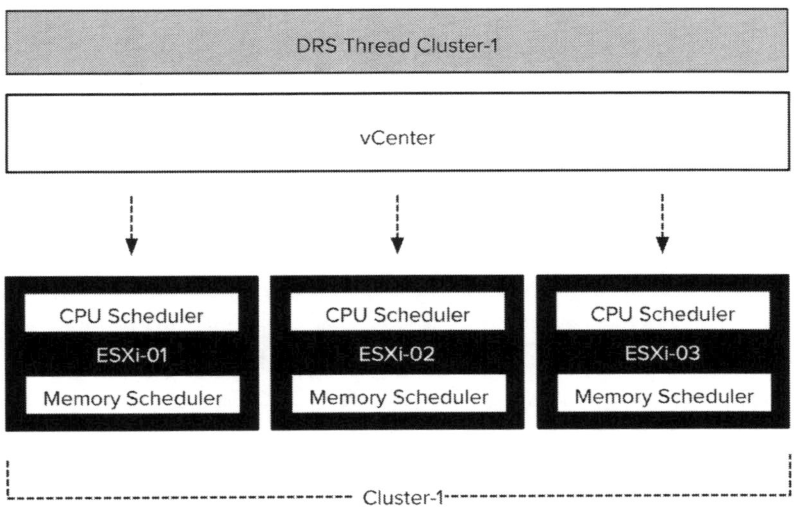

Figure 94: DRS and Host-Local Schedulers

DRS Scheduler

The global scheduler is responsible for dividing the cluster resources. After receiving the active usage and demands of VMs, DRS determines the dynamic entitlement for each VM.

The DRS scheduler computes the ideal CPU and memory entitlements that would have been reached if the cluster were a single large host. DRS relies upon host-level scheduling to implement DRS resource pool and virtual machine-level resource settings.

Host-local resource schedulers are responsible for allocating resources to VMs, requiring translation of cluster resource pool settings to host-level resource pool settings.

DRS solves this by mirroring the cluster resource pool tree to each host and mapping the appropriate resource settings to each resource pool node. The host-local scheduler places the resource pools in the /host/user hierarchy.

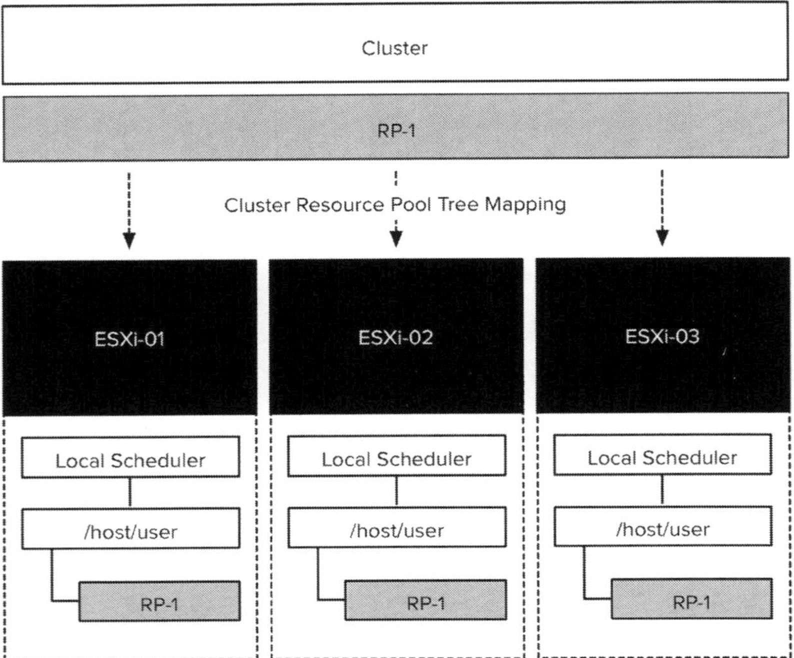

Figure 95: Resource Pool Structure Mapped to ESXi Host-Local RP Tree

DRS sends resource pool settings to each host-local resource pool tree containing the dynamic entitlement of all VMs that are active on that host. DRS trims the resource pool tree and sends the host only the allocations for the VMs running there. In the figure below none of the VMs within resource pool RP1 are active on ESXi-02. Consequently, that specific resource pool tree does not exist on ESXi-02.

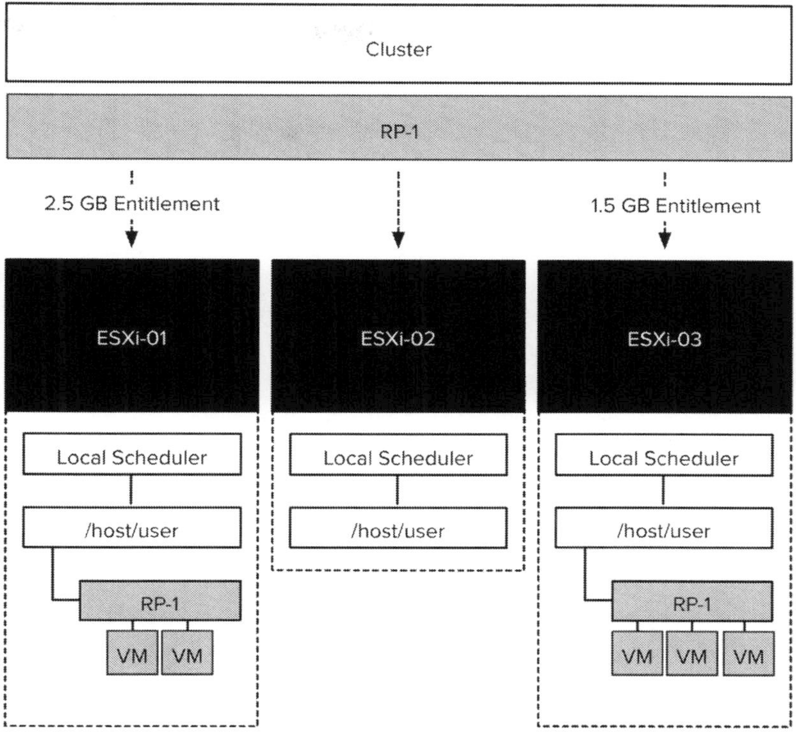

Figure 96: Mapping Resource Pool Structure Across Host-Local RP Trees

Local Scheduler

The local scheduler treats the host-local resource pool tree similar to if the user had set up the tree directly on the host. Following the resource allocation settings of the resource pool tree, the host-local scheduler computes the dynamic entitlement with regards to the tree and flows resources between VMs when that is appropriate. The host-local resource scheduler can allocate additional resources if necessary - if resources are available - and can quickly respond to changes in demand.

Dynamic Entitlement Target

During normal operations in a non-overcommitted cluster, the dynamic entitlement of a VM can fluctuate depending on its activity. In a non-overcommitted cluster, the VM receives all the resources it demands. It does not make sense to limit the VM by the scheduler, as artificially capping resource allocation requires additional calculations from the host-local schedulers. This unnecessary overhead is avoided by the host-local schedulers as much as possible, resulting in a less-restrictive resource allocation policy.

The dynamic entitlement target of a VM increases as the demand of the VM increases. In other words, the VM is effectively capped on resource usage by its maximum configured size (i.e., the number of vCPUs and configured memory size). The dynamic entitlement target consists of demand and usage metrics. By integrating demand metrics in the calculation, both host-local schedulers and DRS understand how many resources the VM wanted to use over how many resources it received.

The metrics used by DRS for dynamic entitlement calculations are CPU active and memory active. CPU active metrics exported by the host-local CPU scheduler include %Run + %Ready. The host-local scheduler includes some parts of the ready time in the active time, depending on the adjustments for specific CPU features such as Hyperthreading and power management.

The host-local memory scheduler exports the active memory metric, and it is the primary memory metric used by DRS to determine the memory entitlement. The active memory represents the working set of the VM, which signifies the number of active pages in RAM. By using the working-set estimation, the memory scheduler determines which of the allocated memory pages are actively used by the VM and which allocated pages are idle. The active memory part also includes the VM's memory overhead. To accommodate a sudden rapid increase of the working set, DRS incorporates 25% of idle consumed memory in the entitlement calculation.

This percentage is key whether you want DRS to load-balance on active memory use or on consumed memory use. If your cluster is designed to back all the virtual memory with physical memory (no memory overcommit), this metric should be set to 100%. The additional option "Memory Metric for Load Balancing" sets the idle consumed memory to 100%.

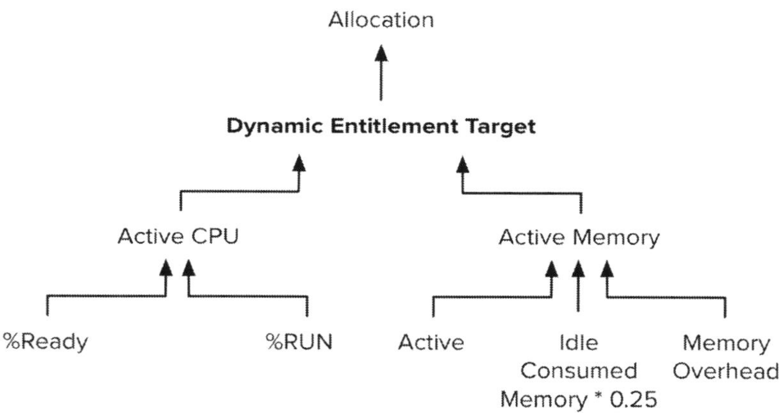

Figure 97: Dynamic Entitlement Target

Let's use a 16 GB VM as an example of how DRS calculates the memory demand. The guest OS running in this VM has touched 75% of its memory size since it was booted, but only 35% of its memory size is active. As a result, the VM has consumed 12288 MB, and 5734 MB of this is the active memory.

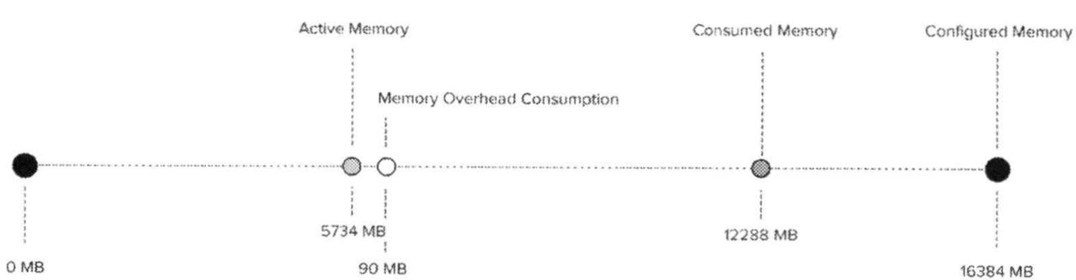

Figure 98: Active - Consumed - Configured Memory

As mentioned, DRS accommodate a percentage of the idle consumed memory to be ready for a sudden increase in memory use. To calculate the idle consumed memory metric, DRS subtracts the 5734 MB active memory from the consumed memory; 12288 MB. Resulting in a total 6554 MB idle consumed memory. By default, DRS includes 25% of the idle consumed memory, i.e. 6554 * 25% = +/- 1639 MB.

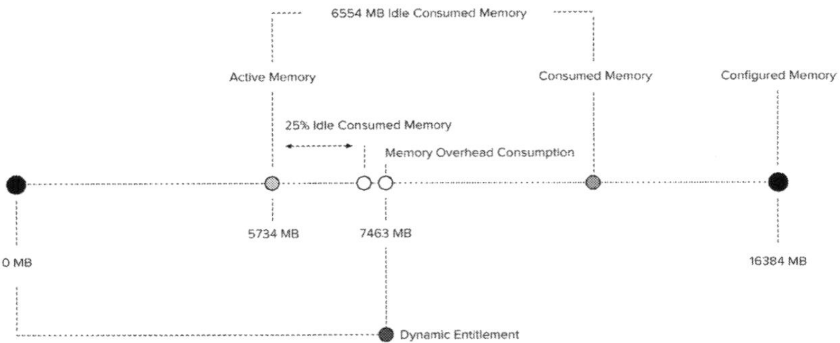

Figure 99: Idle Consumed Memory Calculation

The virtual machine has a memory overhead of 90 MB. The memory demand DRS uses in its load balancing calculation is as follows: 5734 MB + 1639 MB + 90 MB = 7463 MB. As a result, DRS selects a host that has 7463 MB available for this machine if it needs to move this virtual machine to improve the load balance of the cluster.

Memory Metric for Load Balancing Enabled

When enabling the option "Memory Metric for Load Balancing," DRS takes into account the consumed memory + the memory overhead for load balancing operations. In essence, DRS uses the metric Active + 100% IdleConsumedMemory. More info about this feature in chapter 15.

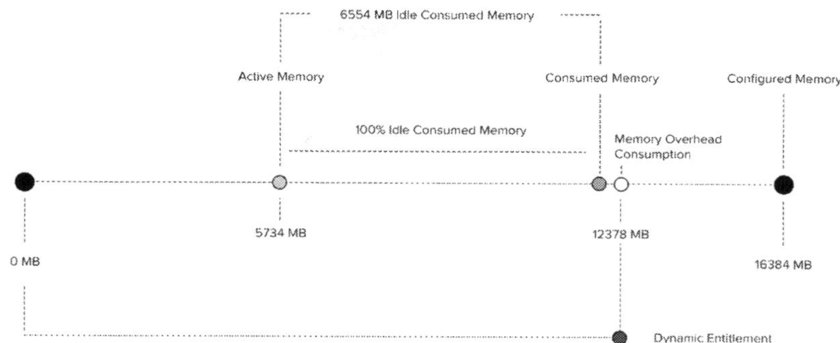

Figure 100: Memory Metric for Load Balancing Enabled

Resource Contention

Resource contention impacts the dynamic entitlement. Resource contention, sometimes called overcommitment, can take all forms and shapes. If the infrastructure is correctly sized, long-term contention does not occur. However, short-term contention can occur when resource usage rapidly increases to the point where demand temporarily exceeds availability.

Host failovers, boot storms, application scheduling, load correlation and load synchronicity can cause contention.

Load correlation is the relationship between loads running in different machines. If an event initiates multiple loads, for example, a search query on front-end web server, this may result in increased load on the supporting stack and backend.

Load synchronicity is often caused by load correlation but can also exist due to user activity such as morning startup routines of users such as login, checking mail and database connectivity.

When contention occurs, both the reservation and share resource allocation settings affect entitlement.

DRS Dynamic Entitlement versus Host-Local Entitlement

Although both DRS and the host-local schedulers compute the dynamic entitlement of a VM, they do not exchange these calculations. They also operate with different scheduling periods. Please note that DRS calculates the average and peak demand for a target for the resource pool tree every 60 seconds. This period is different than the previous versions, in which DRS calculates the entitlement targets every 5 minutes. The shorter period allows DRS to respond better to variations of demand.

Resource Allocation Settings

Resource allocation settings are available for both virtual machines and resource pools. Chapter 13 explains resource pools and resource allocation policies. This section describes the function and impact of virtual machine allocation settings.

SETTING	BEHAVIOR
Reservation	A reservation is the amount of physical resources (MHz or MB) guaranteed to be available for the virtual machine. (Identified in VMkernel as "MIN").
Shares	Shares specify the relative importance of the VM. Shares are always measured against other powered-on sibling VMs and resource pools on the host.
Limit	A limit specifies an upper bound for resources that can be allocated to a VM. (Identified in VMkernel as "MAX").

Table 12: Resource Allocation Settings

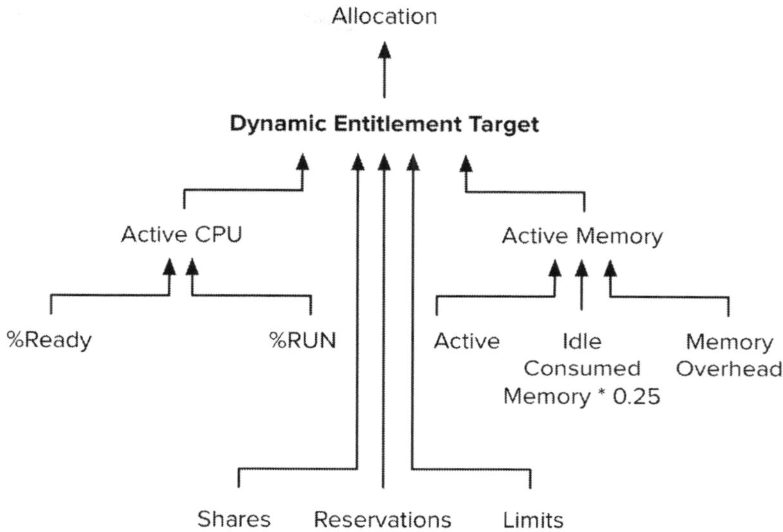

Figure 101: Resource Allocation Settings and Dynamic Entitlement

Reservation

A reservation is the number of physical resources guaranteed available to a virtual machine. When contention occurs, the host-local schedulers need to determine how many resources they can reclaim. The scheduler cannot reclaim resources that are protected by reservation. In other words, a reservation creates a minimum (MIN) dynamic entitlement target that is at least as large as the reservation.

During memory contention, the host-local memory scheduler compares the memory usage of the VM to the dynamic entitlement. If the usage is above the dynamic entitlement, memory is ballooned, compressed or swapped until physical memory usage is at or below the entitlement. Reclamation of resources stops when it reaches the target set by a reservation, as it is the minimum guaranteed dynamic entitlement. the entitlement used to decide memory reclamation is calculated by host-local memory scheduler itself with almost the same algorithm that DRS resource distribution uses.

Continuing with the previous memory example, depicted in figure below. The virtual machine has a dynamic entitlement of 7463 MB. A 6144 MB (6 GB) reservation is set, resulting in a minimum entitlement target of 6144 MB. If contention occurs, the host-local memory scheduler will take the minimum entitlement into account when recalculating a new target and can reclaim memory from the virtual machine up to its minimum entitlement.

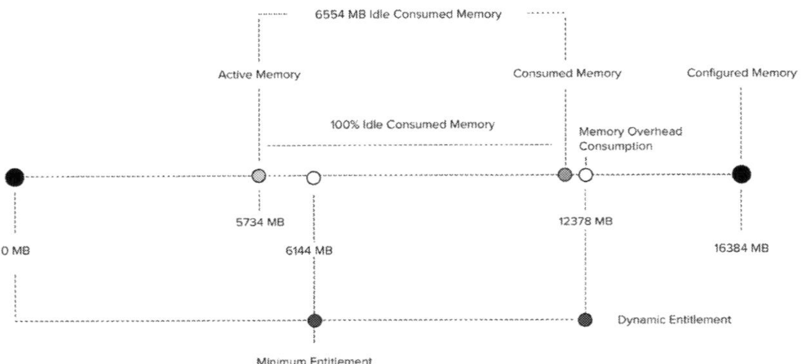

Figure 102: 6 GB Minimum Entitlement

Resource Pool-Level Reservation Behavior

Reservations can exist at both the VM and resource pool levels. Reservations set on a resource pool behave differently than a reservation set on a VM. The resource pool divides its resources amongst the active VMs.

DRS distributes the allocated resources of the resource pool across the host-local RP branches within the cluster. The resources reserved by the host-local resource pool trees are available to each VM and flow between them depending on their dynamic entitlements.

DRS in 6.7 is more aggressive with distributing resources than previous versions. In previous versions, only the resources that cover the dynamic entitlement of the VMs are distributed. For example, if the resource pool is configured with a 30 GB reservation and the VM demand was 20 GB,

DRS distributed 20 GB of the resources across the host-local resource pool trees. In 6.7, DRS distributes the 20 GB to the appropriate RP trees and evenly distributes the remaining 10 GB to ensure the RP has additional resources to satisfy increased demand. A host-local RP tree receives updated resource targets every 60 seconds in vSphere 6.7.

Virtual Machine-Level Reservation Behavior

Virtual machine-level reservations have a less dynamic nature than resource pool-level reservations. Also, a CPU reservation has a different effect than a memory reservation on the availability of resources for other virtual machines.

A reservation set at the VM-level defines the minimum entitlement of that specific VM. During contention, the host-local schedulers can reclaim resources up to the minimum entitlement of the VM. Unlike resource pool-level reservations where resources are provided based on the usage and demand of a VM, the reservations set at the VM level are static. This means that the VM is entitled to have these resources available at all times, whether it uses them or not. This impacts availability of that resource for other VMs.

A difference exists between reserving a resource and using the resource. As reservations are a part of the dynamic entitlement calculation, a VM can use more or less than it has reserved. The static nature of the VM-level entitlement impacts the sharing of resources. By not incorporating usage and demand, reserved resources are static, and the host-local schedulers are not allowed to reclaim any idle resources beyond the dynamic entitlement of a VM.

However, when exactly will a VM hit its full reservation? Popular belief is that the VM hits full reservation immediately when a VM becomes active, but that is not entirely true. A memory reservation on VM-level protects only the consumed physical RAM. Physical RAM only gets allocated to the VM when the virtual RAM is accessed. However, in practice, it depends on the guest OS running inside the VM. During startup, Windows zeroes each page available during boot, hitting the full reservation during boot time. Linux, however, only accesses the memory pages it requires. For example, a 4 GB Linux VM configured with a 2 GB memory reservation and accessing 1 GB would have only 1 GB of physical RAM allocated and protected by the reservation. Its minimum entitlement would be 1GB. A Windows machine with a similar configuration would have the minimum entitlement of 2 GB directly after Windows completed the boot process.

Fortunately, it is not all bad. The agility of the workload determines to share of reserved resources: CPU instructions are transient and can quickly finish. For this reason, the CPU scheduler allows other virtual CPUs to use the physical CPU while the entitled VM is not active. If the entitled VM requests resources, the unentitled VM can be de-scheduled quickly and placed in a queue. Physical RAM holds data, and if memory space was loaned out to other VMs for temporary use, this data needs to be moved if the rightful owner wants to use this memory space. Clearing out this data takes significant time and may delay the entitled VM unfairly. To avoid this, the memory scheduler does not loan out reserved physical memory for temporary use.

Admission Control and Dynamic Entitlement

Dynamic entitlement and admission control are independent mechanisms, but they are both affected by reservations. The admission control mechanism is active before power-on and validates that enough system resources (total system resources - total reservations made by other VMs) are available to meet the CPU and or memory reservation. The power-on operation succeeds only if the admission control is successful whereas dynamic entitlement is active during operation of the VM and doesn't reclaim used resources protected by reservation.

In other words, admission control exists during the first lifecycle phase of the VM (pre-power-on), while dynamic entitlement controls the VM during the operational stage of its lifecycle.

Shares

The scheduler determines the priority of a workload by comparing the share values of the active VMs that share the same parent object that can be a resource pool or the cluster. Shares determine how resources are divided (total system resources - total reservations).

Relative Priorities

Let's use a flat hierarchy as an example; a vSphere cluster contains two VMs. No resource pool exists. The VMs are the child objects of the cluster. The cluster is the parent of both VMs, as they share the same parent, they are considered to be siblings of each other. If contention occurs, the scheduler determines the priority by comparing the shares of both VMs to the outstanding shares within the cluster.

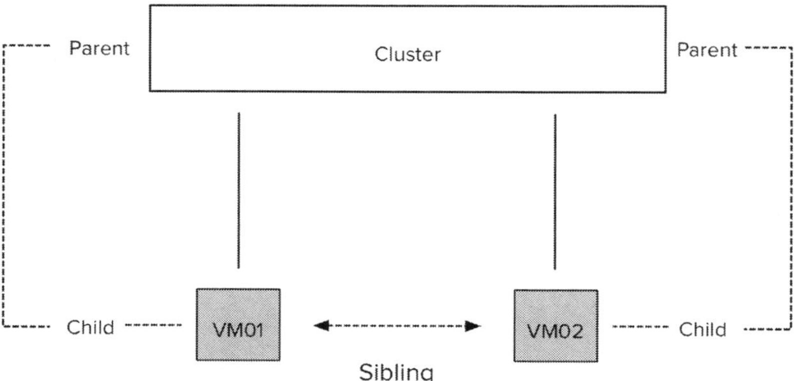

Figure 103: Parent, Child, Sibling Relationship Mapping

Since they signify relative priorities; the absolute values do not matter, comparing 2:1 or 20.000 to 10.000 has the same result.

CPU Shares

After obeying the minimum entitlement of the VMs, shares of CPU are used to divide the available physical CPU resources. If a VM is not using its reserved CPU time, the unused CPU time is available to other VMs. The CPU scheduler calculates an MHzPerShare value for correct distribution of CPU time. This metric is used by the CPU scheduler to identify which VMs are ahead of their entitlement and which VMs are behind and do not fully utilize their entitlement.

When a VM wants to run, the CPU scheduler identifies the progress of the VM and places it in one of its queues. If the VM is behind its entitlement, it is placed it in the main scheduler queue. If it is ahead of its entitlement, the scheduler places the vCPU in the extra queue. Before scheduling, the CPU scheduler compares the MHzPerShare values of the VMs in the main queue and selects the VM with the lowest MHzPerShare value. If no VMs are in the main queue, the scheduler selects a VM from the extra queue.

The scheduler calculates the MHzPerShare as follows:

MHzPerShare = MHzUsed / Shares

MHzUsed is the current utilization of the VM measured in megahertz, while shares indicate the currently configured number of shares of the VM.

For example, VM01 is using 2500 MHz and has 2000 shares, resulting in an MHzPerShare value of 1.25. VM02 is consuming 2500MHz as well but has 1000 shares, resulting in an MHzPerShare value of 2.5. The scheduler places VM01 in front of the queue due to its lower MHzPerShare value.

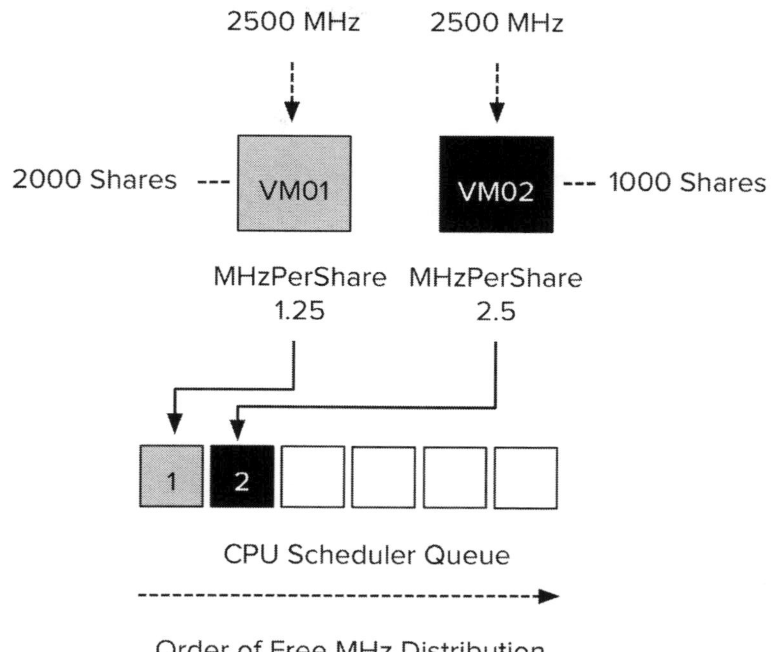

Figure 104: Order of Priority

If the VM with the lowest MHzPerShare value decides not to utilize the cycles, the scheduler allocates the cycles to the VM with the next lower MHzPerShare value. Reservations override shares and guarantee the number of physical resources regardless of the number of active shares present in the pool. As a result, the VM can always use the CPU cycles specified in its reservation, even if the VM has a higher MHzPerShare value. For example, three VMs are present in a resource pool that possesses 8 GHz.

VM	SHARES	RESERVATION
VM01	2000	None
VM02	1000	2500
VM03	2000	None

Table 13: Shares and Reservations Overview

VM01 is running a memory-intensive application and does not require many CPU cycles. Both VM02 and VM03 host a CPU-intensive application. VM01 is running at 500 MHz, with 2000 shares, the MHzPerShare equals 0.25. VM02 owns 1000 shares plus a CPU reservation of 2500MHz. VM03 owns 2000 shares but is powered off. Because VM02 is in need of CPU cycles, the CPU scheduler allocates CPU cycles up to its reservation resulting in an MHzPerShare value of 2.5 (2500/1000). At this point, 5000 MHz remains available in the resource pool.

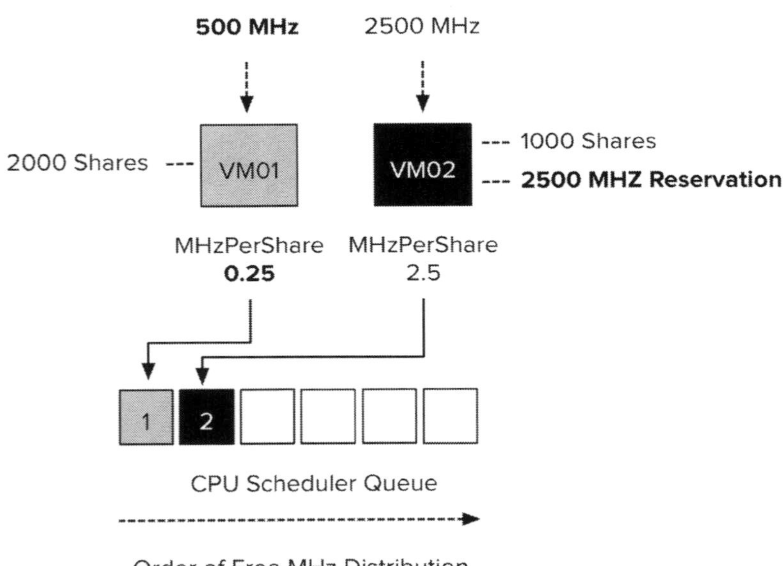

Figure 105: VM02 Claiming Resources Up to its Reservation

In the next scenario VM03 just powered up and is behind its entitlement; the CPU scheduler compares the MHzPerShare values of the VMs and selects the VM with the lowest MHzPerShare value. Step 1 – VM03 has an MHzPerShare of 0 and can claim up to 0.25, the MHzPerShare value of VM01. Step 2 – VM01 does not need additional CPU cycles and forfeits it claim, VM03 can now claim CPU resources until it reaches an MHzPerShare value equal to 2.5 before the CPU scheduler considers providing CPU cycles to VM02. VM03 owns 2000 shares, meaning it can be allocated up to 4500 MHz to reach an MHzPerShare value of 2.5 (4500/2000). The CPU scheduler allocates 4500 MHz to equalize distribution before considering the share value of VM02 to allocate the remaining 500 MHz.

This previous scenario demonstrates that shares of CPU play a significant role in distributing CPU cycles.

Memory Shares

The memory scheduler is invoked every 15 seconds to recompute the dynamic entitlement memory statistics to determine and update the VM memory allocations.

The host-local memory scheduler is responsible for allocating the resources. As mentioned before, every VM is allowed to allocate additional resources if no contention exists.

If contention occurs, the memory scheduler reclaims memory based on the dynamic entitlement of the VM. ESXi determines the level of contention by calculating the free memory state (MinFreePct). Based on the level of contention and the free memory state, the memory scheduler determines which reclamation mechanism to use.

The MinFreePct calculation is extensively covered in the vSphere 6.5 Host Resources Deep Dive, available at Amazon.com or a free ebook at hostdeepdive.com. (Source: vSphere 6.5 Host Deep Dive)

Calculating MinFree

A sliding scale is applied to the available memory that the VMkernel manages. This amount of memory is less than the total amount of memory installed in the system due to overhead of hardware and ESXi itself. The sliding scale is partitioned in four parts: a 256 GB host configuration is used for this example.

PERCENTAGE	MEMORY RANGE	EFFECTIVE RANGE	RESULT
6%	0-4 GB	4096 MB	245.76
4%	4-12 GB	8192 MB	327.68
2%	12-28 GB	16,384 MB	327.68
SUBTOTAL		28,762 MB	901.12
1%	Remaining Memory	233,040 MB	2330.40
Total MinFree			3231.52

Table 14: MinFree Calculation of 256 GB Host

The table is split up in two parts. The first part is the range calculation of the first 28 GB of memory of a host. It is reasonable to assume that servers that run ESXi 6.7 contain more than 32 GB of memory. Therefore, the first three steps are equal for all ESXi 6.5 hosts.

The interesting step in this calculation is the 1% of remaining memory. This is truly the sliding scale part of the equation as it differs for various memory configurations (256 GB, 512 GB, 1024 GB, etc.).
It is dynamically adjusted if the memory configuration of the host is expanded. Using the 256 GB memory configuration as an example.

The 1% is calculated across the range of 233040 MB (261712 MB -/- 28762 MB). This is the result of 261,712 MB of VMkernel managed memory minus the 28,762 MB (4096 MB + 8192 MB + 16384 MB) used for the preceding percentage calculations. MinFree does not do anything by itself. The result of the MinFree calculation is used to derive the memory state of the ESXi host.

Memory State Transition Points

The VMkernel applies one or more memory reclamation techniques when memory pressure occurs. A more aggressive method of memory reclamation is applied with the increase of memory pressure. This may impact VM performance. As a result, memory reclamation is relaxed when memory pressure decreases. To avoid oscillation between two states, different memory state transition points are active with reference to the memory pressure condition. More specifically, the VMkernel uses two transition points for a memory state, one if memory pressure increases and one when memory pressure decreases.

MEMORY STATE	MEMORY PRESSURE INCREASE	MEMORY PRESSURE DECREASE
High	301% of MinFree	401% of MinFree
Clear	300% of MinFree	400% of MinFree
Soft	64% of MinFree	100% of MinFree
Hard	32% of MinFree	48% of MinFree
Low	16% of MinFree	24% of MinFree

Table 15: Memory State Transition Points

As shown, the memory state transition points are derived from the MinFree threshold. It is important to understand that these thresholds are the transition points for that particular level. When memory pressure is increasing, the host enters the listed memory state. Let's use an ESXi host with 256 GB memory as an example.

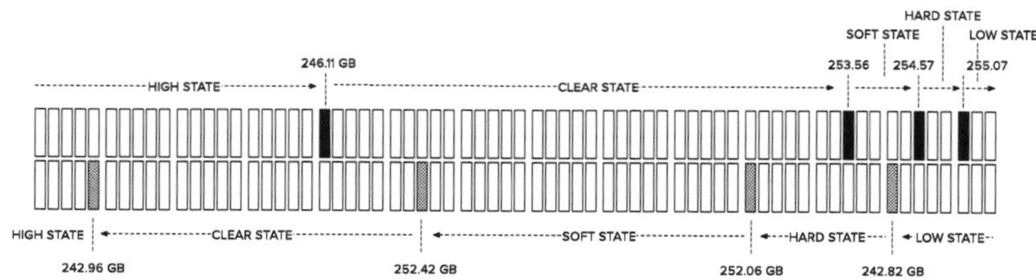

Figure 106: Memory Transition Points Host with 256 GB Memory

Memory Reclamation Techniques per State

Several memory reclamation techniques exist to reclaim memory from VMs. The memory reclamation techniques are transparent page sharing, memory ballooning, memory compression, and memory swapping. Each memory state applies one or more memory reclamation technique.

MEMORY STATE	SHARE	BALLOON	COMPRESS	SWAP	BLOCK
High	X				
Clear	X				
Soft	X	X			
Hard	X		X	X	
Low	X		X	X	X

Table 16: Memory Reclamation Techniques Active per Memory State

The Clear, Soft, and Hard states focus on providing the best performance possible, while each step introduces a more drastic reclamation technique to prevent memory starvation. The Low state is required for correctness. It protects the VMkernel from crashing resulting from memory starvation.

Share-Per-Page

The memory scheduler selects idle memory to reduce the impact of memory reclamation. To determine which physical memory can be redistributed, the memory scheduler computes the Share-Per-Page metric. The memory scheduler reclaims memory from the VM or resource pool that owns the fewest shares per allocated physical memory page.

The memory scheduler determines the Shares-per-Page by dividing the number of shares by the allocation of pages, corrected with the number of active pages and the idle memory tax percentage.

The idle memory tax is applied progressively: the tax rate increases as the ratio of idle memory to active memory for the VM. Adjusting the number of shares with active and idle pages helps to avoid a pure proportional-share state where idle VMs with disproportionate numbers of shares can hoard memory.

Resource Contention

If the free memory state transitions from high to another state such as soft, hard or low, the memory scheduler is invoked and it calculates a new resource allocation target for each VM.

The memory scheduler classifies the working-set memory of a VM as idle or active and uses idle memory tax to adjust the resource allocation target. Although it's possible to reclaim all the unprotected (non-reserved) memory, the memory scheduler keeps a 25% buffer to accommodate rapid increase of the working set.

Assume a 16 GB VM is running Windows. Due to the zero-out technique used by Windows at boot time, the VM allocated memory equal to the configured size. 40% of its configured size is active (6553.6 MB). The VM is configured with a 4 GB memory reservation. After estimating the active memory of the working set size and keeping 25% consumed idle memory as a buffer to be able to respond rapidly to workload increase, the dynamic entitlement is determined at 9101.2 MB for this virtual machine.

The calculation is as follows: 40% of 16384 MB = 6553.6 MB active consumed memory. As all memory is consumed, the calculation of idle consumed memory is: 16384 MB – 6553.6 MB = 9830.4 MB. 25% of idle consumed memory = 9830.4 * 0.25 = 2457.6. The memory overhead reservation is 90 MB, making the total of 6553.6 + 2457.6 + 90 = 9101.2 MB dynamic entitlement.

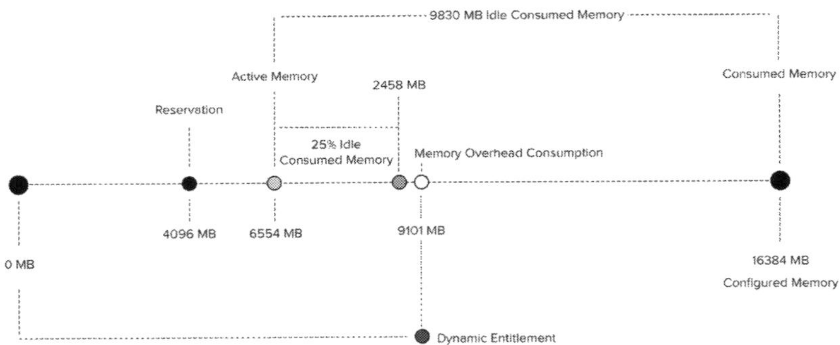

Figure 107: Dynamic Entitlement to Determine Reclamation

The memory scheduler respects the reservation and cannot reallocate memory that is protected by the reservation. Depending on the level of contention, memory is reclaimed from each VM. A low level of contention results in a small number of memory pages reclaimed from each VM on the host. High levels of contention result in increased levels of reclamation. The memory scheduler tries to reclaim pages up to the dynamic entitlement of each VM, but the memory may be reclaimed up to the reservation. This point is typically reached only if memory demand is excessive.

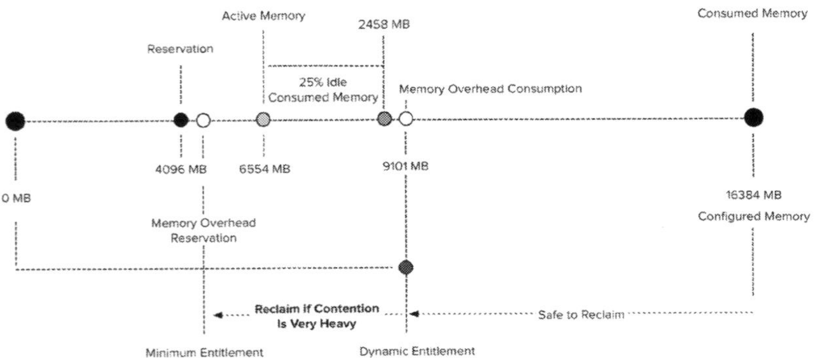

Figure 108: Reclamation and Level of Contention

Worst Case Allocation

When memory is reclaimed up to the minimum entitlement, the VM experiences its worst-case allocation. This value is presented in vCenter as the worst-case scenario column of the resource allocation tab. This value is meant as a theoretical value to help understand how bad resource allocation can become for the virtual machine.

Limits

Limits are a part of the resource allocation settings and define the allowed upper limit of allocation of physical resources. Both the CPU and memory scheduler allocate resources up to the limit. Even if there are enough free resources available, a limit defines the maximum entitlement and is enforced by the host-local resource schedulers. Setting a 10 GB limit on a 16 GB VM running Windows, results in a dynamic target of x, while having a reclaim target of 6 GB. As mentioned before, windows touch the complete memory range during boot. The BIOS reports 16 GB, thus windows will touch 16 GB, the memory scheduler is instructed to allocate physical memory up to 10 GB. How does the VMkernel provide the extra 6 GB? Most of it will be swapped memory, as the other memory reclamation techniques cannot respond fast enough before the boot sequence is finished.

Why Use Limits?

Try not to if you do not have a memory leaking application that cannot be fixed by the vendor or your developers.

Initially, limits were used as a troubleshooting tool by developers to induce a state of overcommitment at the VM level without having to overcommit the entire ESXi host. A limit is a boundary for dynamic entitlement calculations which is not exposed to the guest OS inside the virtual machine. The guest OS resource manager is only aware of the configured size of the virtual machine, i.e. configured memory and number of vCPUs.

CPU Limits: A limit specifies an upper boundary for CPU resources that can be allocated to a virtual machine. If the vCPU exceeds its CPU time, it is descheduled until it is allowed to run again. Possibly wasting CPU cycles while frustrating users due to the underperforming behavior of the application

Memory Limits: The guest OS sizes and tunes its caching algorithms and memory management to the memory it detects. A limit set smaller than the configured memory size hurts performance, as the guest OS or applications within a VM uses memory that is not backed by physical memory. The memory scheduler needs to allocate memory space by ballooning, compressing or swapping, generating overhead on the ESXi host and the storage level if memory is swapped.

Tying it All Together

Reservations, shares, and limits are just components used to calculate the dynamic entitlement. When contention occurs, the VM resource target is at least as large as the reservation. This minimum entitlement identifies the reclamation boundary for host-local schedulers; they cannot reclaim resources beyond this point. Limits define the maximum target for the host-local schedulers and restrict the physical resource allocation. Shares, activity, and contention define the remainder of the entitlement. If a virtual machine's resource usage is either above or below its entitlement, resource reclamation occurs until the VM's usage is at or below the minimum entitlement.

At the deepest level in the world of host-local resource schedulers, reservation, ownership, and shares do not exist. There is only a dynamic target that must be honored. In other words, the host only tries to allocate resources according to the entitlement target.

13

RESOURCE POOLS AND CONTROLS

Clusters aggregate ESXi host CPU and memory resources into resource pools. These resource pools provide an abstraction layer between the resource providers (ESXi hosts) and resource consumers (virtual machines). This form of abstractions provides the ability to isolate resources between pools, but also share resources within pools.

The resource allocation controls: reservations, shares, and limits are instrumental for isolating and sharing of resources. The resource allocation settings are similar to the virtual machine resource allocation settings explained in the previous chapter. This chapter zooms in on how settings work at the resource pool level and what impact they have on virtual machine workloads.

Root Resource Pool

A root resource pool is created at the cluster level when enabling DRS. The host resources are added to the capacity of the root resource pool when an ESXi host joins the cluster. The resources required to run the ESXi virtualization layer are not available to the cluster:

> **The total amount of host resources - virtualization overhead = available resources associated with the cluster.**

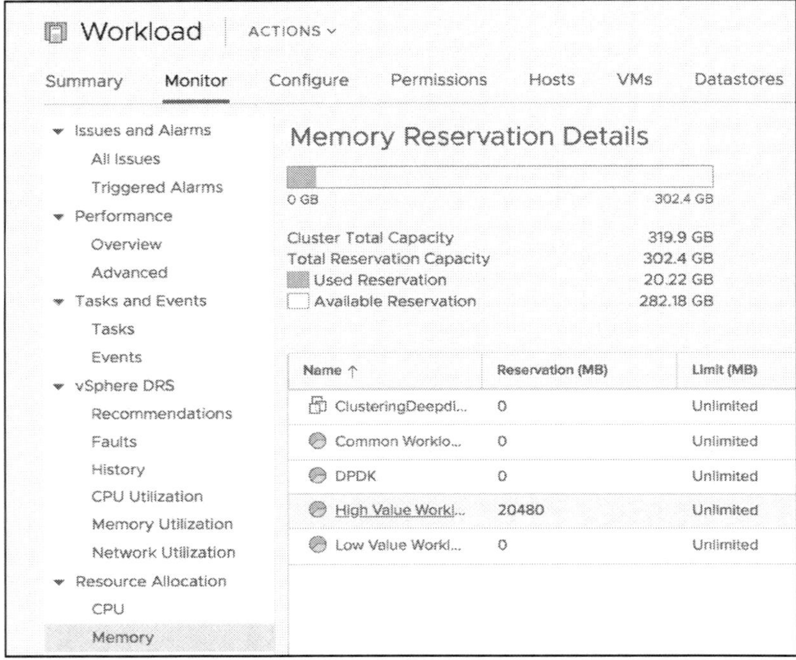

Figure 109: HA Disabled on DRS Cluster

If HA is enabled, resources required satisfying HA failover are drawn from the root resource pool, because HA failover places virtual machines into the root resource pool. The resources required to run the virtualization layer are not visible when reviewing the capacity of the root resource pool, while DRS marks the resources required to satisfy HA failover as reserved resources.

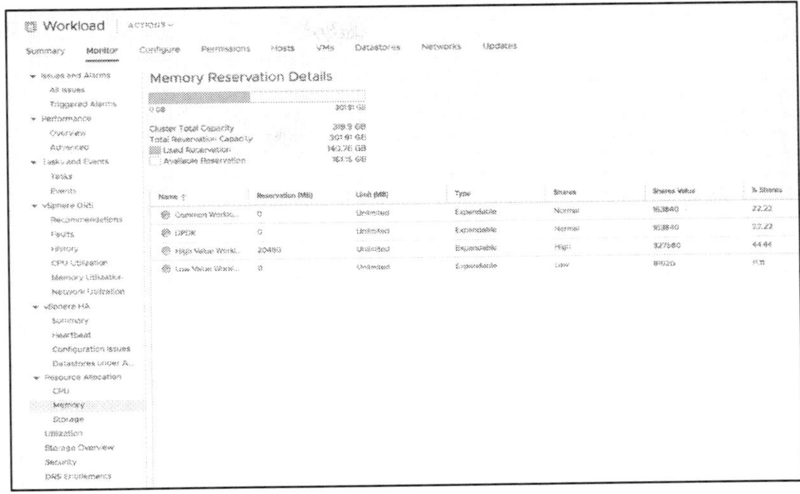

Figure 110: Cluster HA Failover Resources

Resource Pools

As a cluster distributes resources from hosts to VMs, the hosts play the role of resource providers, while VMs are resource consumers. The resource pool plays both roles of a resource provider and consumer as they consume resources from the cluster and in turn, distribute resources to the VMs.

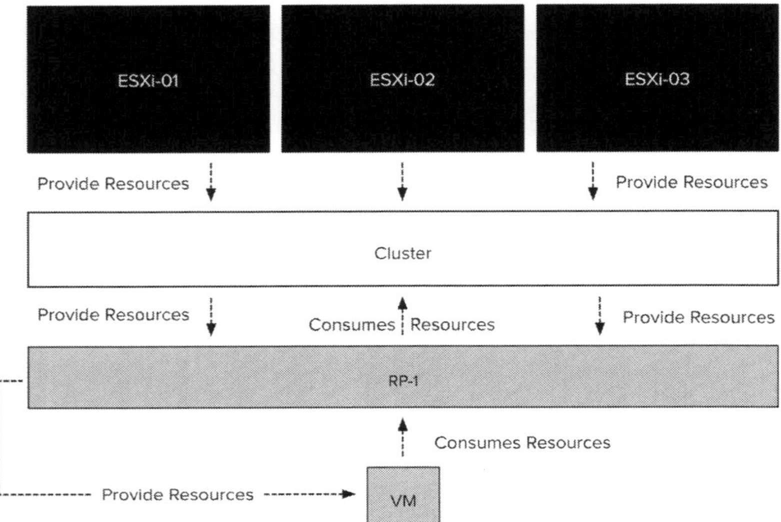

Figure 111: Resource Providers and Consumers

> **It is important to realize that resource pools can be both consumers and providers of resources as this might impact the way you design your resource pools from a shares perspective.**

Inflating or Deflating Resource Pools

Resource pools span the entire cluster. When adding an ESXi host to the cluster, its resources are immediately available to the resource pool. The opposite is true when removing hosts from the cluster: resources provided by the ESXi host are subtracted from the cluster and are not available for use by the resource pool and its child objects.

> **Removing ESXi hosts can place a cluster in an overcommitted state. An overcommitted state occurs when the available cluster resources cannot satisfy the reservations of all resource pools. Resource allocations for the active virtual machines are reduced during an overcommitted state.**

Host-Local Resource Pools

As mentioned in the previous chapter, the cluster hierarchy is mapped to a resource pool structure on each ESXi host within the cluster. If resource allocation settings are applied at the cluster level, these settings are propagated to the host-local resource pool tree. Once these are in place, the host-local CPU and memory scheduler takes care of the actual resource allocation.

Dividing Resources

DRS divides cluster resources with a coarser granularity than the host-local resource schedulers. DRS computes the dynamic entitlement target of all VMs every 60 seconds. ESXi 6.5 introduced a new model for DRS operations. The load-balancing operation and resource distribution operations run separately from each other. Load-balancing operations run every 300 seconds. The resource allocation operation runs every 60 seconds. It's much more frequent than the previous versions, where load-balancing and resource allocation operation ran every 300 seconds. Running it more frequent allows DRS to adjust to resource demand changes better.

During the resource allocation operation, each host conceptually receives a target of resources based upon the dynamic entitlement of its active VMs.

Let's use the host-local memory scheduler as an example. It is responsible for the distribution of available memory within the ESXi. The host-local memory scheduler makes a bottom-up pass over the resource pool tree to compute the demand at each resource pool node.

If the demand of a VM exceeds the amount of memory provided, the dynamic entitlement is adjusted. The memory scheduler makes a top-down pass to compute the new targets for all resource pools and their member virtual machines. The host-local memory scheduler then allows the resource pools to allocate memory to their targets.

Resource Pools Are Not Folders

Resource pools are not folders. They serve as a hierarchy structure for the resource schedulers to determine the resource allocation targets for the VMs inside. Putting VMs into RPs can have a restrictive effect on VM performance.

Often, we come across environments that use resource pools as a folder structure in the "Hosts and Clusters" view of vCenter, because it helps the administrator identify relationships between the VMs. Using resource pools for this purpose generates unnecessary load on both vCenter and the ESXi hosts that can affect application performance.

> **Do not use resource pools as a folder structure in Host and Cluster view, but use the appropriate folder view.**

Resource Pool Tree Structure

For an ESXi host, the maximum resource pool tree depth for user-created pools is 8; 4 levels are taken internally on each ESXi host. These internal resource pools are independent of the DRS resource pools. To avoid complicated proportional share calculations and complex DRS dynamic entitlement calculations, we advise not to exceed a resource pool depth of 2. The flatter the resource pool tree, the easier it is to manage and reduces overhead during dynamic entitlement calculations.

Worst-Case Scenario Should Not Mimic Your Cluster Operational State

In the following sections, we explain the working of shares during a worst-case scenario situation: every virtual machine claims 100% of their configured resources, the system is overcommitted, and contention occurs.

In real life, this situation (hopefully) does not occur very often in your clusters, maybe this state occurs during a severe outage. During normal operations, not every virtual machine is active and not every active virtual machine is 100% utilized. Activity and amount of contention are two elements determining dynamic entitlement of active virtual machines.

To understand true demand and determine whether the resource allocation settings of your resource pools are properly configured, we recommend you to install the VMware Fling "DRS Entitlement Viewer" available at https://labs.vmware.com/flings/.

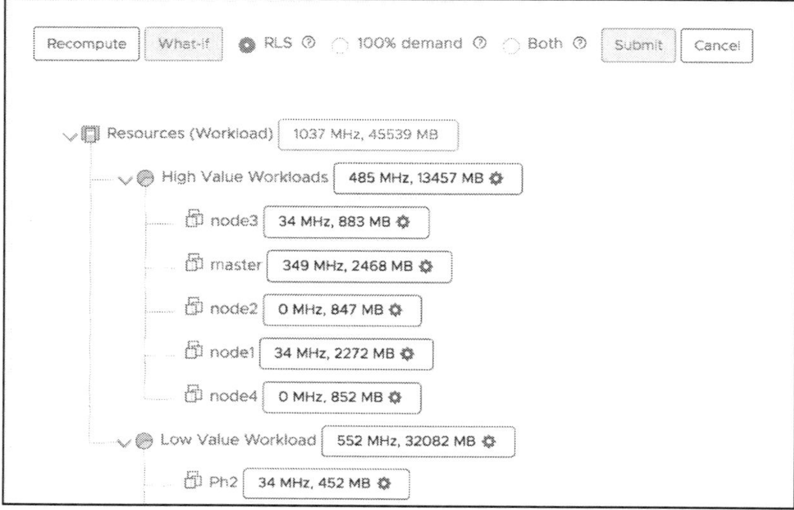

Figure 112: DRS Entitlement Viewer

For ease of presentation, we tried to avoid as many variable elements as possible and used a worst-case scenario situation in each example.

Resource Pool Resource Allocation Settings

Resource pools have similar resource allocation settings to virtual machine-level resource allocation settings. However, their behavior can differ.

SETTING	BEHAVIOR
Reservation	Reservation is the amount of physical resources guaranteed to be available for the VM or resource pool. Reserved resources are not wasted if they are not used. If the utilization is less than the reservation, the resources can be utilized by other running VMs. Units are MB for memory, MHz for CPU. (MIN")
Shares	Shares specify the relative importance of the VM or resource pool. Shares are always measured against other powered-on sibling VMs and resource pools on the host
Limit	A limit specifies an upper bound for resources that can be allocated to a VM or resource pool. The utilization of a resource pool will not exceed this limit, even if there are available resources. ("MAX")
Expandable Reservation	Expandable reservation determines whether or not the reservation on a resource pool can grow beyond the specified value, if the parent resource pool has unreserved resources. A non-expandable reservation is called a fixed reservation. Enabled by default
Low	16% of MinFree

Table 17: Resource Pool Allocation Settings

Shares

Shares determine the priority of a resource pool or VM compared to their siblings. Siblings can be resource pools or virtual machines that exist at the same hierarchical level, i.e., share the same parent.

DRS determines priority by comparing the number of shares to the total number of shares issued by the object's parent. For example, resource pool RP-1 owns 4000 CPU shares. If it is the only object, its parent (the cluster) has issued only 4000 CPU shares. Because the resource pool owns all issued shares, it is entitled to all the CPU resources available in the cluster.

Resource pool RP-2 is added to the cluster and owns 8000 shares. The cluster issues 8000 more shares, increasing the total shares to 12000. RP-1 owns 4000 shares of the outstanding 12000. Thus it owns 33% of the total number of outstanding shares.

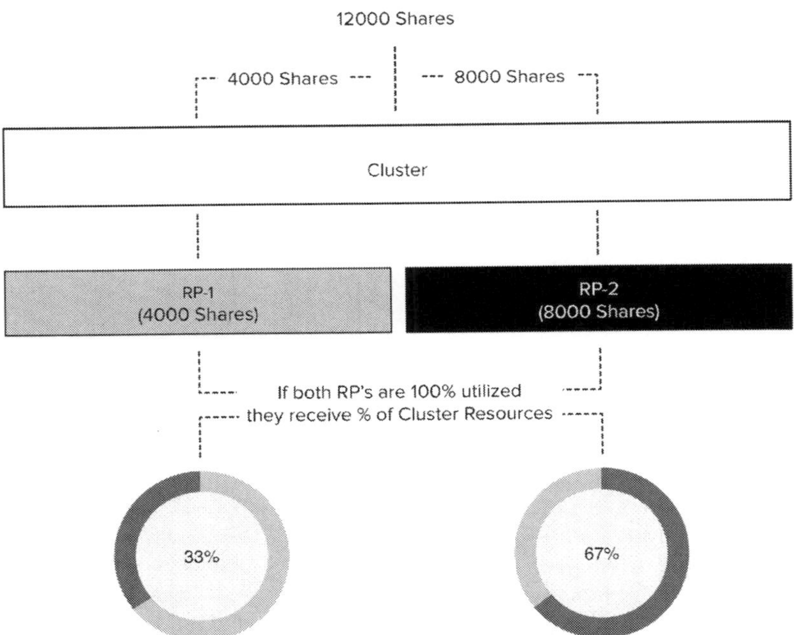

Figure 113: Resource Pool 1 and 2 Share Ratio

If every VM is generating 100% demand, the cluster is in a worst-case scenario state. As a result, DRS distributes the resource to the rightful owners. As Resource pool RP-1 owns 33%, it is entitled to consume 33% of the cluster and distribute it amongst its child-objects.

> **Please note that we are describing a worst-case scenario, typically load varies and resources can flow between resource pools as the targets are updated every minute. The shares do not carve up the resources of a cluster statically. Shares guide the resource distribution in a cluster in the gentlest of ways.**

Shares are a part of the dynamic entitlement calculation. During computation of dynamic entitlement, reservation and limits take precedence over shares, but this does not imply that shares do not play a significant role in resource distribution!

Resource Pool Size

Because resource pool shares are relative to other resource pools or virtual machines with the same parent resource pool, it is important to understand how vCenter sizes resource pools.

The values of CPU and memory shares applied to resource pools are similar to virtual machines. By default, a resource pool is sized like a virtual machine with 4 vCPUs and 16 GB of RAM. Depending on the selected share level, a predefined number of shares are issued. Similar to VMs, four share levels can be selected. There are three predefined settings: High, Normal or Low, which specify share values with a 4:2:1 ratio, and the Custom setting, which can be used to specify a different relative relationship.

SHARE LEVEL	SHARES OF CPU	SHARES OF MEMORY
Low	2000	81920
Normal	4000	163840
High	8000	327680

Table 18: Share Level Overview

Caution must be taken when placing VMs at the same hierarchical level as resource pools, as VMs can end up with a higher priority than intended. For example, in vSphere 6.7, the largest virtual machine can be equipped with 128 vCPUs and 6 TB of memory.

A 128 vCPU and 6 TB VM owns 256000 (128 x 2000) CPU shares and 122 560000 (6128000 x 20) memory shares. In the previous version of the book, we had a nice bar graph that showed the scale between the largest VM and a resource pool with shares level set to high. With these new maximums, it's difficult to create something meaningful while having to deal with the physical dimension of the book. Comparing these two results in a CPU ratio is 32:1 and memory 374:1. The previous is an extreme example, but the reality is that 16 GB and 4 vCPU VM is not uncommon anymore. Placing such a VM next to a resource pool results in sibling rivalry.

Sibling Rivalry

As shares determine the priority of the resource pool or virtual machine relative to its siblings, it is important to determine which objects compete for priority.

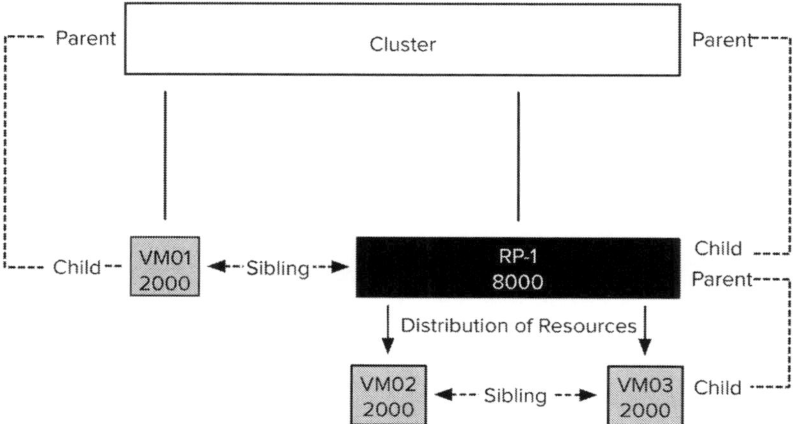

Figure 114: Sibling Rivalry between VM and Resource Pool

In the scenario depicted above, multiple sibling levels are present. VM01 and RP-1 are child objects of the cluster and therefore are on the same sibling level. VM02 and VM03 are child objects of RP-1. VM02 and VM03 are siblings, and both compete for resources provided by RP-1. DRS compares their share values to each other. The share values of VM01 and the other two VMs cannot be compared with each other because they each have different parents and thus do not experience sibling rivalry.

Shares indicate the priority at that particular hierarchical level, but the relative priority of the parent at its level determines the availability of the total amount of resources.

VM01 is a 2 vCPU 8 GB virtual machine. The share value of RP-1 is set to high. As a result, the resource pool owns 8000 shares of CPU. The share value of VM01 is set to Normal and thus it owns 2000 CPU shares. Contention occurs, and the cluster distributes its resources between RP-1 and VM01. If both VM02 and VM03 are 100% utilized, RP-1 receives 80% of the cluster resources based on its share value.

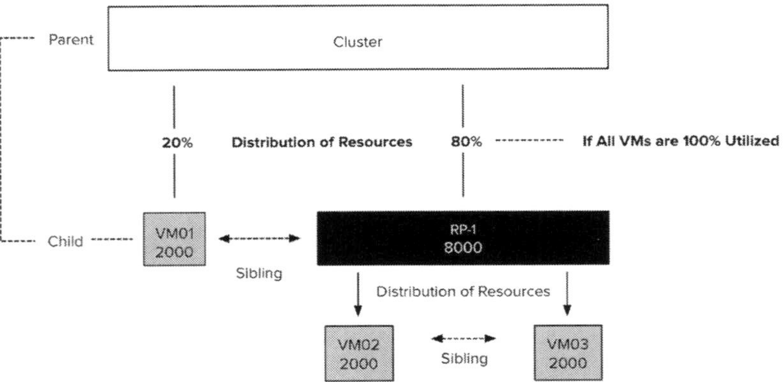

Figure 115: First Level of Resource Distribution

RP-1 divides its resources between VM02 and VM03. Both child-objects own an equal number of shares and therefore receive each 50% of the resources of RP-1.

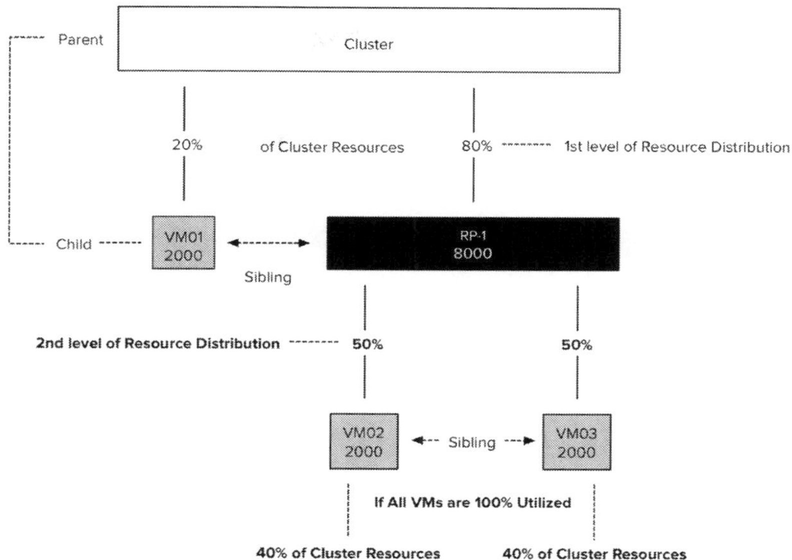

Figure 116: Second Level of Resource Distribution

This 50% of RP-1 resources equals to 40% of the cluster resources. As for now, both VM02 and VM03 are able to receive more resources than VM01. However, three additional VMs are placed inside RP-1. The new VMs own each 2000 CPU shares, increasing the total number of outstanding shares to 10000.

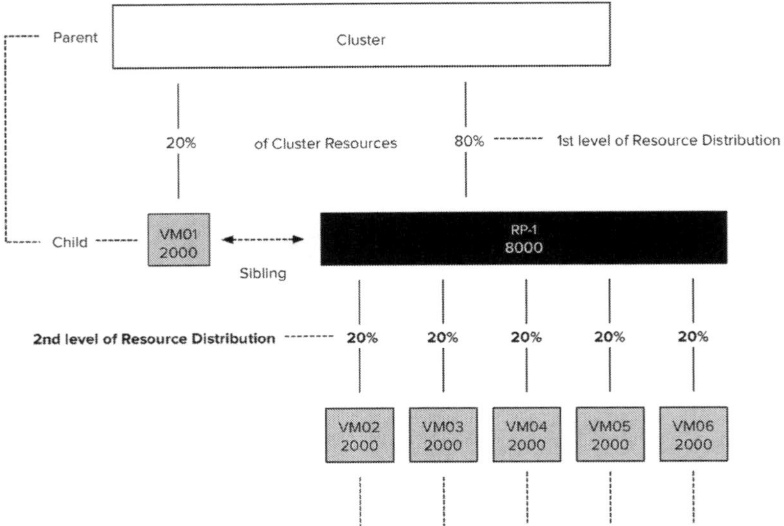

Figure 117: Additional Workload Introduced in Resource Pool RP-1

The distribution at the first level remains the same during contention. The cluster distributes its resources amongst its child-object, VM01 and RP-1; 20% to VM01 and 80% to RP-1. Please note this only occurs when all objects are generating 100% utilized.

If VM01 was generating 50% of its load and the VMs in RP-1 are 100% utilized, the cluster would flow the unused resources to the resource pool to satisfy the demand of its child objects.

The dynamic entitlement is adjusted to the actual demand. The VMs inside RP-1 are equally active, as a result of the reduced activity of VM01; they each receive 2% more resources.

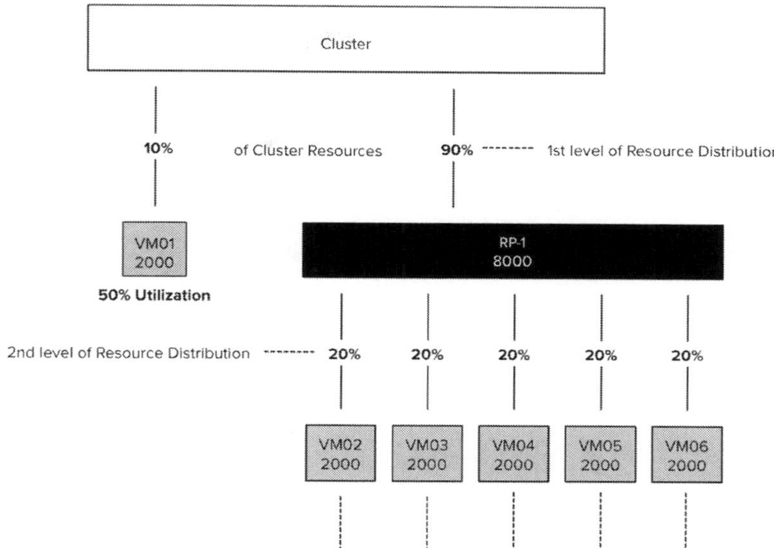

Figure 118: Dynamic Entitlement

VM02, VM03 and VM04 start to idle. The resource pool shifts the entitlement and allocates the cluster resources to the VMs that are active, VM05 and VM06. They each get 50% of 80% of the cluster resources due to their sibling rivalry.

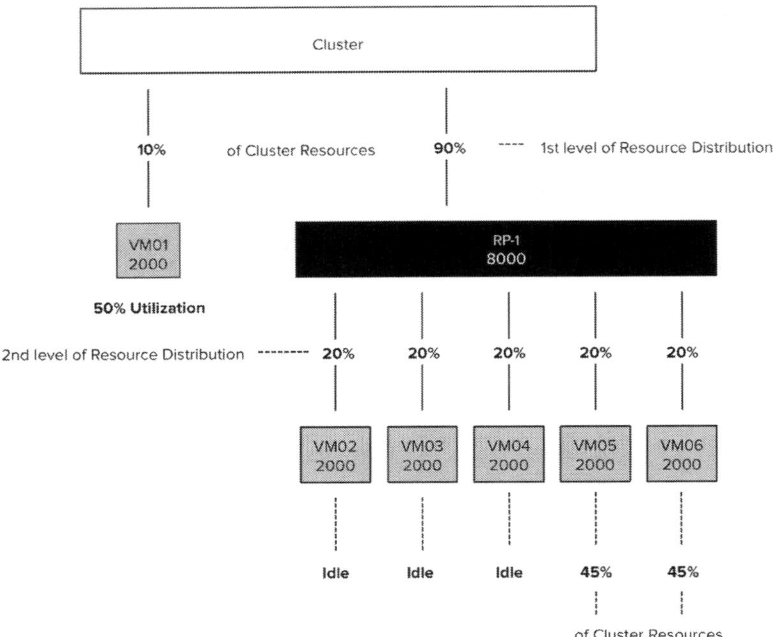

Figure 119: Sibling Rivalry Within RP with Idle and Active VMs

Share Levels are Pre-sets, not Classes

A VM that is placed inside the resource pool, or created in a resource pool, does not inherit the share level of the resource pool. When creating a VM or a resource pool, vCenter assigns the Normal share level by default, independent of the share level of its parent.

Think of share levels as presets of share values. Configure a resource pool or virtual machine with the share-level set to high, and it gets 2000 CPU shares per vCPU. A VM configured with the share level set to low gets 500 CPU shares. If the VM has 4 vCPUs, the VM owns the same number of shares than the 1 vCPU with a share value set to high.

Both compete with each other based on share amounts, not based on share level values.

The Resource Pool Priority-Pie Paradox

As we described in previous sections, at every level, siblings compete for resources and dilute the remaining resources available for every subsequent level.

The amount of resources available to each sibling depends on the number of rivals and their configurations inside the resource pool. This means that a few virtual machines inside a resource pool configured with a Low share level can end up with a higher dynamic entitlement than many virtual machines in a resource pool that is configured with a High share level. Virtual machines depicted in the next figure are all configured identically, and their size is scaled proportionally to their dynamic entitlement within the cluster.

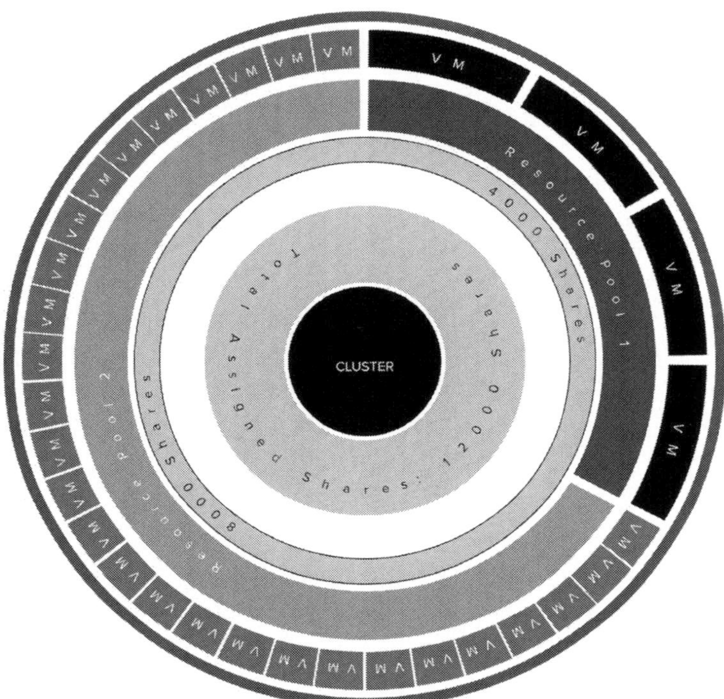

Figure 120: VM Dynamic Entitlement Based on RP Share Value

From Resource Pool Setting to Host-Local Resource Allocation

How do resource pool shares affect VM workloads? As mentioned before, DRS mirrors the resource pool hierarchy to each host and divides the entitled resources of the resource pool across the host-local RP tree based on the number of active VMs, their share amounts, and their current utilization. Once the resource allocation settings are propagated to the host local RP tree, the local host CPU and memory scheduler take care of the actual resource allocation.

For example, a resource pool in a 2-host cluster is configured with a Normal CPU share level. Here, the resource pool RP-1 holds 4000 shares of CPU. Four VMs running inside the resource pool can be configured as follows:

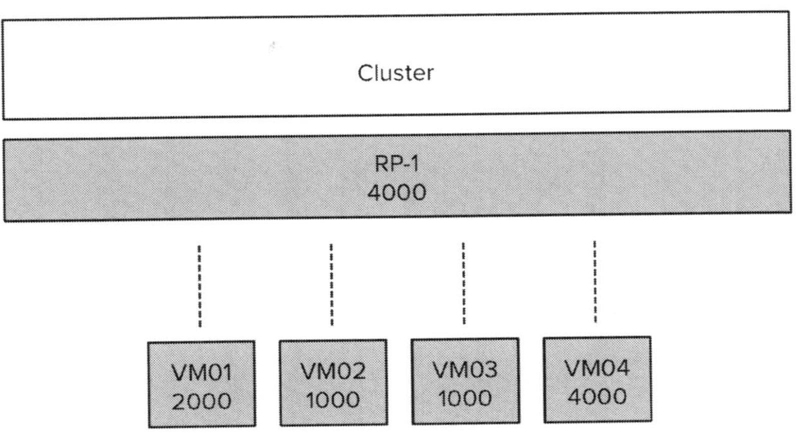

Figure 121: Single Resource Pool Configuration

VM	SHARE LEVEL	NUMBER OF VCPU	SHARES	SHARE RATIO	ESXi HOST
VM01	Normal	2	2000	2/8	ESXi-01
VM02	Low	2	1000	1/8	ESXi-01
VM03	Low	2	1000	1/8	ESXi-01
VM04	High	2	4000	4/8	ESXi-02

Table 19: Share Configuration RP-1 VMs

Assume that all of the VMs equal utilization and stable workloads. DRS balances the virtual machines across both hosts and creates the following resource pool mapping:

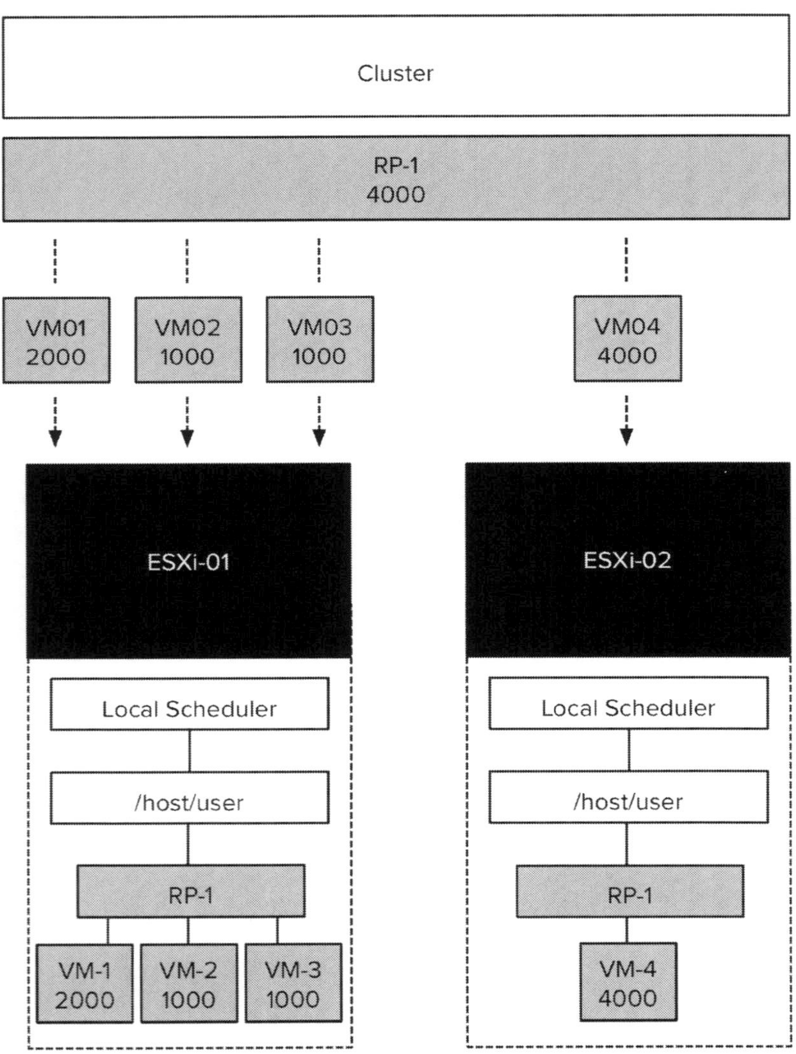

Figure 122: Host-Local Resource Pool Mapping

The number of shares specified on VMs VM01, VM02 and VM03 add up to 4000 and equals to half of the amount of total configured shares inside the resource pool. In this example, DRS places VM01, VM02, and VM03 on ESXi-01 and for that reason assigns 2000 of the total 4000 shares to RP-1 of the host local RP tree. VM04 runs on ESXi host ESXi-02 and receives the other half of the resource pool shares.

At this point resource pool RP-2 is created. RP-2 is configured with a high share level and owns 8000 CPU shares. The VM members of RP-2 are configured identically to the virtual machines in RP-1.

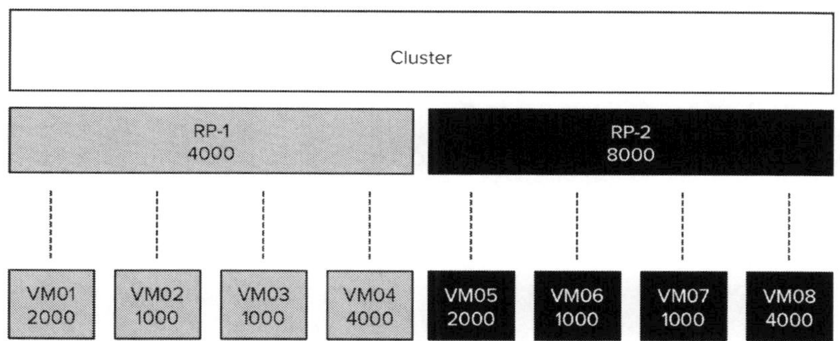

Figure 123: Multiple Resource Pool Configuration

VM	SHARE LEVEL	NUMBER OF VCPUS	SHARES	SHARE RATIO	ESXI HOST
VM05	Normal	2	2000	2/8	ESXi-01
VM06	Low	2	1000	1/8	ESXi-01
VM07	Low	2	1000	1/8	ESXi-01
VM08	High	2	4000	4/8	ESXi-02

Table 20: Share Configuration RP-2 VMs

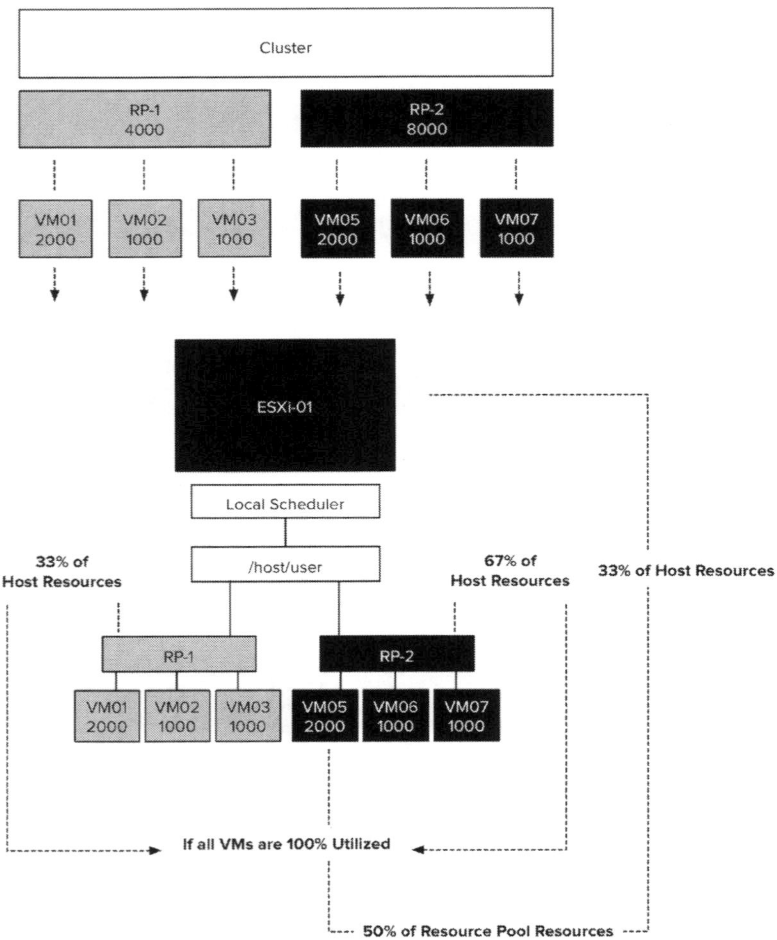

Figure 124: Resource Pool Mapping ESXi-01

The host-local resource pool tree of ESXi-01 is updated with RP-2; RP-2 is configured with twice the number of shares as RP-1. Introducing 4000 more shares increases the total number of shares to 6000. Since RP-2 owns 4000 of the total of 6000, it gets 67 percent of the ESXi host's resources. Due to the 67%- 33% distribution at resource pool level, the local resource scheduler allocates more resources to RP-2 when contention occurs. The resources allocated to RP-2 are distributed across the VMs based on their hierarchical level (sibling rivalry). As a result, virtual machine VM05 is entitled to 50% of RP-2's resources during contention; this translates to 33% of the ESXi host's resources.

The Resource Allocation option in the monitor view of clusters shows the %shares column. This column displays the percentage of resources assigned to the object. This value is related to the total shares issued by the parent and therefore applies only to that particular hierarchical level.

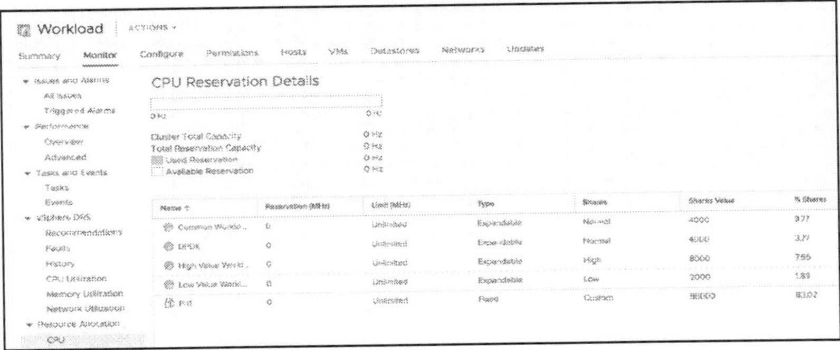

Figure 125: Cluster Resource Allocation Overview

To emphasize, the example used VMs with equal and stable workloads. During normal conditions, some virtual machines have a higher utilization than others. As the active resource utilization is part of the dynamic entitlement calculation, the active workload is taken into consideration when dividing the resource pool shares and resources across hosts and local resource pool trees.

Furthermore, virtual machine utilization often changes and usually affects the resource distribution after each DRS invocation.

Resource Pool-Level Reservation

Setting a reservation guarantees permanent availability of physical resources to the resource pool. Resources protected by a reservation remain available to child objects during contention.

Resource pool-level reservations do not implicitly define a reservation at the child-object layer, but the resource pool distributes protected resources to its child objects. The distribution of protected resources is based on the dynamic entitlement of each child object within the resource pool and therefore can fluctuate for each child object from time to time.

The activity and level of contention play a big part in the distribution of protected resources. By using the virtual machine's dynamic entitlement, resource pool reservations have a dynamic nature and are more in line with the concept of consolidation and fairness.

DRS divides reserved resources among the VMs that require them. The resource pool reserved resource distribution is very conservative in versions before vSphere 6.7. The old model has rigorous control on how many resources to give out to VM. Only resources are provided to satisfy the dynamic entitlement. If there are additional resources in the resource pool, they are not distributed until a VM demands this using its dynamic entitlement. DRS in vSphere 6.7 has two significant improvements over previous versions, first of all, the targets run every 60 seconds, and the resource distribution algorithm is much more aggressive by distributing resources if not used by other child objects. This allows DRS to accommodate sudden VM demand change.

Let's take a closer look at this behavior. A memory reservation is set at 12 GB on RP-1. RP-1 contains four VMs, each configured with 4 GB of memory and no VM reservation. VM02 and VM03 are configured with a Low share level; VM01 has a Normal share level, while VM04 is configured with a High share level. The figure below shows the distribution of protected memory from the resource pool to every single

VM at 08:00 (8 AM). VM01 and VM03 are rather busy, while VM02 and VM04 are each running a very light workload.

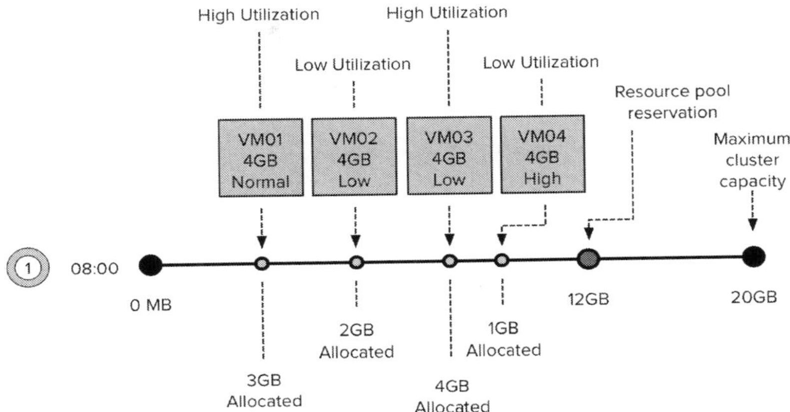

Figure 126: Distribution of Resource Pool Reservation at 08:00 (8 AM)

Although VM03 is configured with a Low share level, the availability of resources and the lack of contention allow VM03 to receive 4 GB of protected memory. In other words, physical memory stores all of VM03's memory pages.

The figure below shows the same environment at 11:00 (11 AM). At that particular time, VM01, VM03, and VM04 are highly utilized. The reserved memory owned by the resource pool is divided based on share level and utilization of each VM. As a result, the resource pool distributes the most memory to VM04 due to its High share level, VM01 gets 3 GB according to its resource demand, and the rest of the reserved memory is divided between VM02 and VM03. As VM03 is highly utilized, its dynamic entitlement is higher than that of VM02, and therefore VM03 can allocate 3 GB of reserved resources.

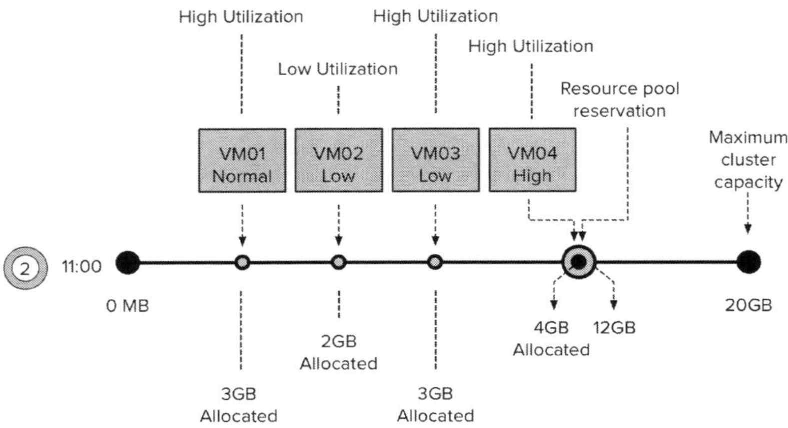

Figure 127: Distribution of Resource Pool Reservation at 11:00 (11 AM)

At 19:00 (7 PM), all systems are idle, except VM02, which is running a backup operation. All memory required is distributed to VM02 while the resource pool has enough reserved memory available to satisfy the dynamic entitlement of the other virtual machines.

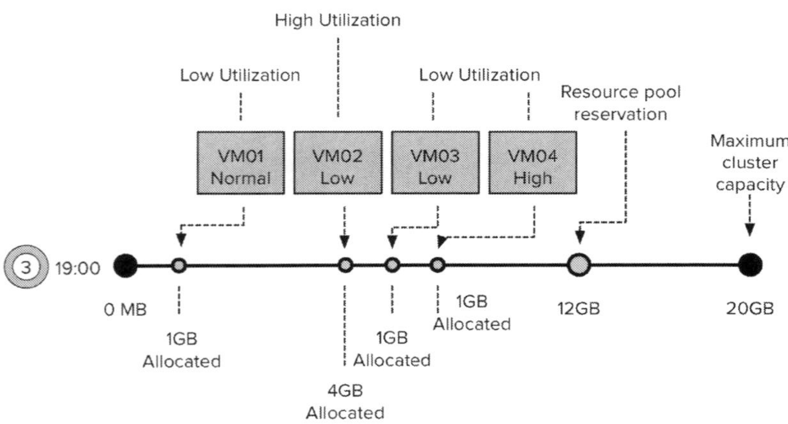

Figure 128: Distribution of Resource Pool Reservation at 19:00 (7 PM)

The dynamic nature of resource pool reservation might not be suitable for specific VMs: virtual machine-level reservations are more suitable if the continuous guaranteed availability of physical resources is required.

Child-Object-Level Reservation Inside a Resource Pool

If a child-object inside a resource pool is configured with a reservation, that reservation is honored by DRS. DRS relies upon host-level scheduling and host-level resource pools to implement DRS-level resource pools and to enforce resource pool and virtual machine-level resource settings. DRS passes virtual machine-level reservations straight through to the host, where the host-level CPU and memory schedulers enforce the reservation.

Any virtual machine-level reservation is withdrawn from the resource pool-level reservation amount and reduces the number of reserved resources available to its siblings. Physical resources allocated by the virtual machine reservation are available only for that virtual machine and is not shared with siblings or VMs and resource pools external to the parent resource pool.

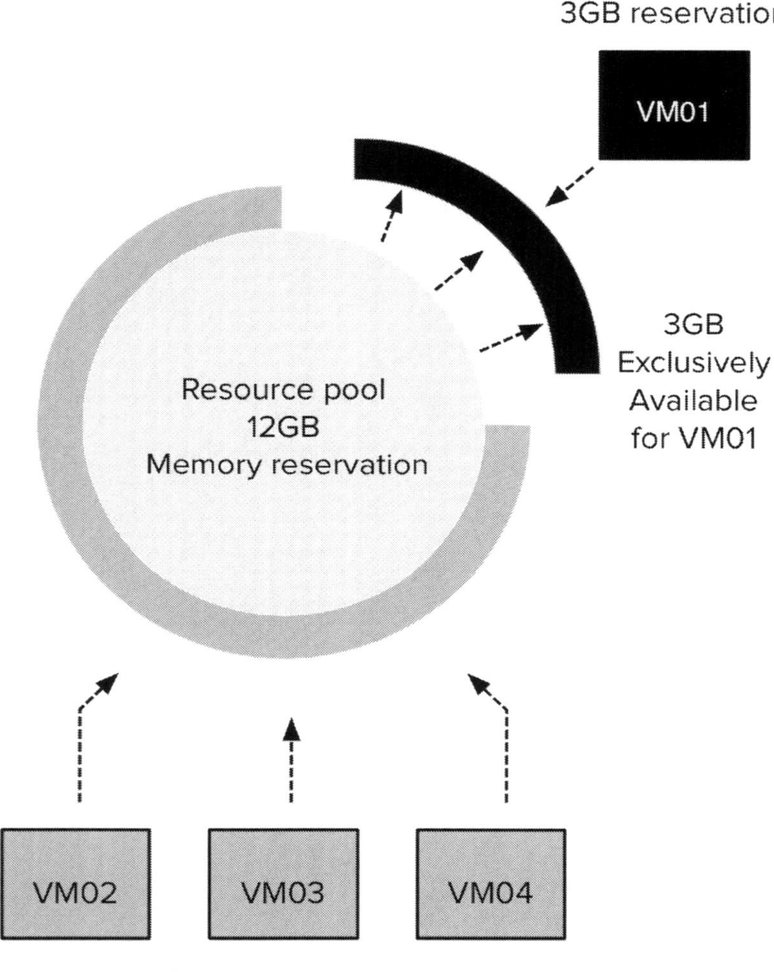

Figure 129: VM Reservation Within a Resource Pool

> **Set per-virtual machine reservations only if a virtual machine absolutely requires guaranteed resources.**

Activation of Reservation

Virtual machine reservations only take effect when a VM is powered on. A resource pool-level reservation applies from the moment it is set. Regardless of child virtual machines' activity. Because of this instant activation, the reservation immediately reduces the number of available unreserved resources at the parent level.

Neither DRS nor the VMkernel power on a VM if it cannot honor its reservation. In addition to virtual machine-level reservations, the VMkernel requires unreserved memory to satisfy the memory overhead of each VM. Configuring resource pool-level reservations can impact the consolidation ratio of VMs in the cluster.

> **We recommend to right-size resource pool-level reservations to avoid unnecessary reduction of the pool of unreserved resources. Adjust resource pool-level reservations according to the requirements of the current virtual machines. A great tool for this is the DRS entitlement viewer fling available at *http://labs.vmware.com/flings*.**

Memory Overhead Reservation

For each running VM, ESXi reserves physical memory for its virtualization overhead. ESXi requires this extra space for the internal VMkernel data structures like VM frame buffer and a mapping table for memory translation. Two kinds of VM overheads exist:

Static Overhead
Static overhead is the minimum overhead that is required for the VM to startup. DRS and the host-local memory scheduler use this metric for admission control and vMotion calculations. The destination ESXi host must be able to accommodate the sum of the VM reservation and the static overhead otherwise the vMotion fails.

Dynamic Overhead

Once a VM starts up, the virtual machine monitor (VMM) can request additional memory space. The VMM requests the space, but the VMkernel is not required to supply it. If the VMM does not obtain the extra memory space, the VM continues to function, but this could lead to performance degradation. The VMkernel treats overhead reservation the same as VM-level memory reservation, and it won't reclaim this memory once it's used.

To power-up VMs in the resource pool, a pool of reserved resources needs to be available. If no resource pool-level reservation is set, the resource pool is required to allocate unreserved resources from its parent. To allow resource pools to retrieve unreserved resources, enable the Expandable Reservation setting on the resource pool.

> **Memory overhead reservations need to be taken into account while designing the cluster and resource pool structure.**

The vSphere Resource Management guide lists the overhead memory of virtual machines. The table listed below is an excerpt from the Resource Management guide (page 34) and lists the most common ones.

MEMORY	1 vCPU	2 vCPU	4 vCPU	8 vCPU
256	20.29	24.28	32.23	48.16
1024	25.90	29.91	37.86	53.82
4096	48.64	52.72	60.67	76.78
16384	139.62	143.98	151.93	168.60

Table 21: VM Memory Overhead

Engineering spends much time reducing the memory overhead, for example, an 8 vCPU virtual machine with 4096 MB vRAM would consume on average a memory overhead of 561.52 MB on older versions, in the 6.x versions, the overhead is down to 76.78 MB.

Please be aware of the fact that memory overheads may vary with each new release of ESXi, so keep this in mind when upgrading to a new version. Verify the documentation of the VM memory overhead and check the specified memory reservation on the resource pool.

Memory Overhead Reservation Appears as Resource Pool Reservation

When a virtual machine powers on, the memory overhead reservation is added to the total amount of resource pool reservation. If a resource pool is configured without a reservation, the total amount of memory overhead reservation is displayed in the resource pool summary.
In the example below, you see the resource pool named Common Workload. In the left part of the image, no VMs are powered on. The resource pool has no memory reservation configured. The VM DCX0is powered on, it has no reservation as well, yet the Used Reservation is now listing 230 MB. This is the memory overhead reservation to run the VM, and it is accounted towards the resource pool.

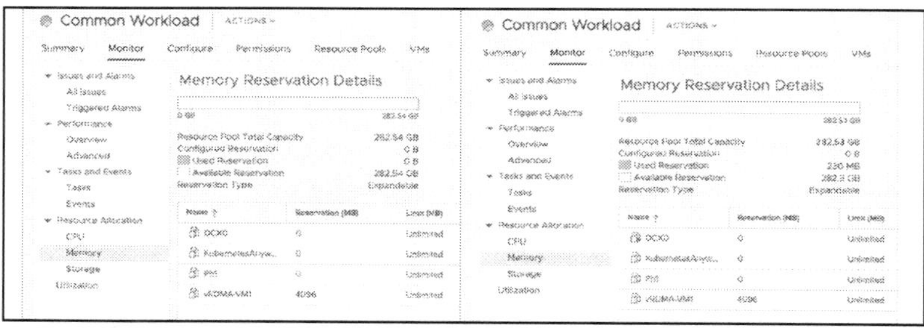

Figure 130: Memory Overhead Reservation

Right Size Virtual Machines

Although the VMkernel requires a small amount of memory to satisfy the memory overhead reservation of a VM, a significant amount of memory can be required when running many virtual machines. Right-sizing VMs can save a lot of reserved and non-shareable memory.

Expandable Reservation

The Expandable Reservation option allows a resource pool to acquire unreserved resources from its parents to satisfy VM-level and memory overhead reservations.

If the Expandable Reservation setting is enabled, Admission Control considers the capacity in the parent resource pool tree available for satisfying VM-level reservations. If the Expandable Reservation setting is not enabled, Admission Control considers only the available resources of the resource pool to satisfy the reservation.
In the following scenario, the expandable reservation option is disabled for the memory configuration of the resource pool. The UI list the reservation type as fixed instead of expandable.

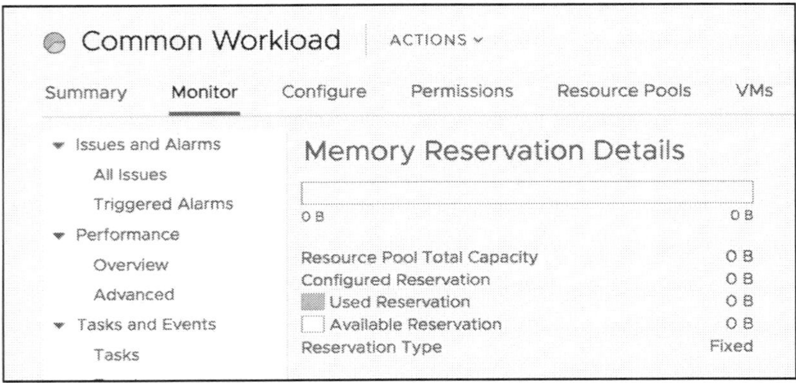

Figure 131: Reservation Type Fixed

The resource pool has no reserved memory configured. When powering on a VM, the following error shows:

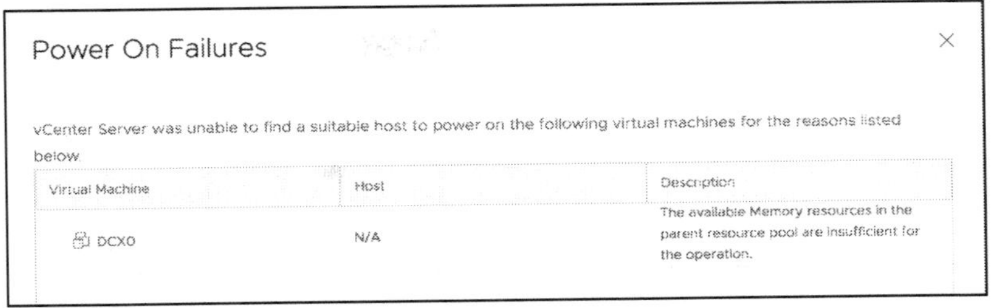

Figure 132: Power On Failure

To verify whether the resource pool can satisfy the reservations, add the virtual machine-level reservations and static overhead reservations of every active virtual machine in the resource pool. The result of the calculation cannot exceed the resource-pool level reservation, unless Expandable is checked. DRS uses the following decision matrix:

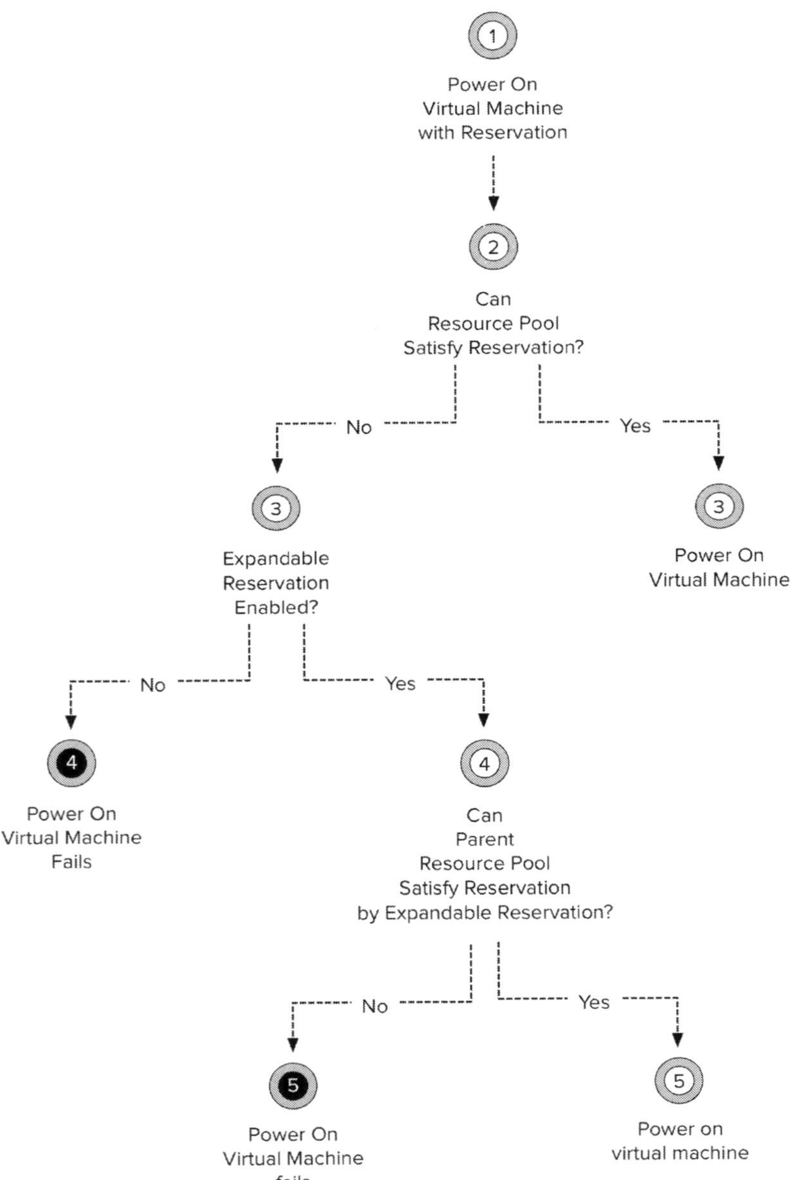

Figure 133: Power On Decision Workflow

Traversing the Parent Tree

Admission Control only considers unreserved resources from parents, not siblings. The search for unreserved capacity halts at a resource pool configured with a limit or if Expandable Reservation is not enabled. If the requested capacity would allocate more resources than the limit of the parent resource pool specifies, vCenter rejects the request, and the VM does not start.

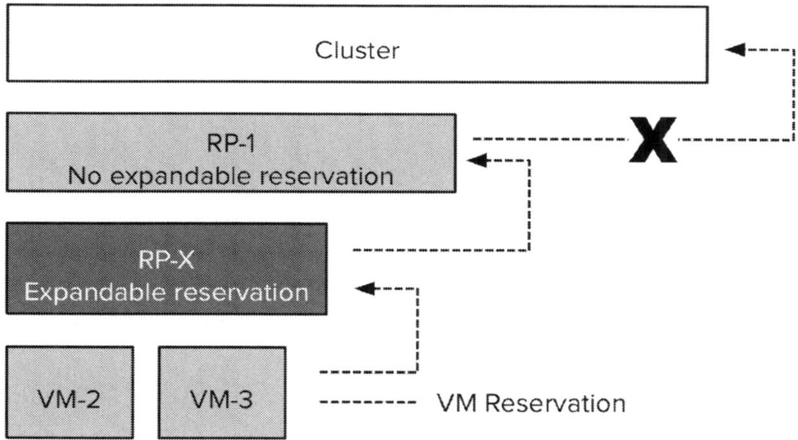

Figure 134: Traversing the Parent Resource Pool Tree

> **To satisfy memory overhead reservations, enable Expandable Reservation if no reservations are set at the resource pool-level.**

Reservations are Not Limits

A reservation at the resource pool-level defines the amount of protected physical resources; it does not define the maximum amount of available physical resources. Child-objects can allocate resources beyond the specified reservation. However, allocating additional resources is based on share value, and this does not guarantee that the required resources are available for use.

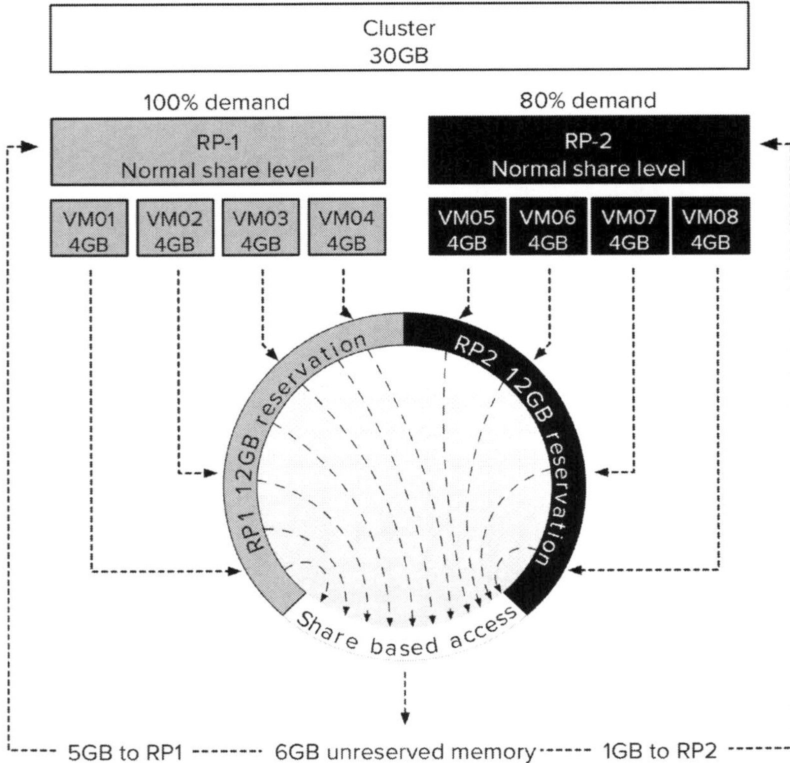

Figure 135: Reservation and Shares

In the figure above, RP-1 has a 12 GB memory reservation configured, but the total configured memory of its VMs is higher than the reservation (Configured memory + memory overhead reservation = +/- 17 GB). RP-1 relies on the shares to obtain the remaining 5 GB to satisfy resource demand of the VMs inside the pool.

Both resource pools have an equal number of shares, providing them with equal chances of obtaining resources. Due to the difference in activity of VMs, RP-1 receives 5 GB, while RP-2 receives 1 GB. Although it appears equal distribution based on shares is not the case in this scenario, both resource pools get the resources they require, as 80% demand of 16 GB equals to 12.8 GB.

Resource Pool Limit

A limit defines the maximum amount of available physical resources that can be allocated. Limits are an excellent way of specifying a boundary with regards to physical resource utilization of objects. The limit prohibits a resource pool from allocating more physical resources than the configured amount, even when they are available. Setting limits on resource pools or VMs can not only affect the performance of the virtual machines, but can negatively affect the rest of the environment.

Limits associated with resource pools apply to all the child-objects within the resource pool collectively. Resource pool-level limits do not implicitly define a limit at the child-object layer, but instead adjust the maximum amount of resources any child object can utilize. Because a resource pool limit does not become a static setting on the child-object, the availability of resources capped by the limit can fluctuate for each child object from time to time. As a result, the dynamic entitlement of a virtual machine can fluctuate depending on the level of contention inside the resource pool.

The resource pool limit is divided amongst its children based on the dynamic entitlement of each child-object. Because allocation is based on dynamic entitlement, actual activity and level of contention play a big part in the availability of resources.

Limits, Reservations and Memory Overhead Reservation

A limit must be equal to or exceed the configured reservation. If VMs are configured with a reservation, that reservation is directly subtracted from the resource pool unreserved memory pool. To power-on, a VM vCenter must be able to reserve the defined amount of reserved memory plus the memory overhead of the VM.

> **When calculating the limit on a resource pool, take both reservations and memory overhead reservations into account.**

Expandable Reservation and Limits

As explained in the previous section, Expandable Reservation is used to allocate unreserved memory for VM reservations and VM memory overhead reservations on behalf of the VMs inside the resource pool. If the resource pool is unable to provide enough unreserved resources, it traverses the ancestor tree to allocate sufficient unreserved resources.

However, when a limit is set at the resource pool level, the resource pool cannot allocate more physical resources than defined by its limit setting. Although the expandable reservation setting allows the resource pool to allocate additional unreserved resources, the limit parameter prohibits the resource pool from allocating more physical resources than the configured limit.

14

CALCULATING DRS RECOMMENDATIONS

DRS takes several metrics into account when calculating migration recommendations to load balance the cluster: the current resource demand of the VMs, host resource availability and high-level resource policies. The following section explores how DRS uses these metrics to create a new and better placement of VMs than the current location of the VMs, while still satisfying all the requirements and constraints.

When is DRS Invoked?

DRS calculates resource allocation targets every 60 seconds, while the load-balancing operation runs every 300 seconds by default. During the load-balancing operation DRS computes and generates recommendations to migrate VMs.

DRS retires each recommendation that is not applied at the next load balancing operation. Please note that DRS might generate the same recommendation again if the imbalance is not solved.

Recommendation Calculation

DRS performs multiple calculations and passes to generate migration recommendations. DRS determines the cluster imbalance and makes a selection of suitable VMs to migrate to solve the imbalance.

Constraints Correction

Before determining the current load imbalance, DRS checks for constraint violations. The constraint correction pass determines whether DRS needs to:

- Evacuate hosts that the user requested to enter Maintenance or Standby mode
- Correct Mandatory VM-Host affinity/anti-affinity rule violations
- Correct VM/VM anti-affinity rules violations
- Correct VM/VM affinity rules violations
- Correct host resource overcommitment (Rare, since DRS is controlling resources)

These constraints are respected during load balancing. Understand that constraints may cause an imbalance, which may not be fixable while respecting these constraints. The imbalance information on the cluster summary page informs the administrator if an unfixable imbalance was identified.

Imbalance Calculation

To establish cluster imbalance, DRS compares the *Current Hosts Load Standard Deviation* (CHLSD) metric to the *Target Host Load Standard Deviation* (THLSD). If the CHLSD exceeds the THLSD, the cluster is considered imbalanced.

Current Host Load Standard Deviation

DRS determines the *Current Host Load Standard Deviation* (CHLSD) by computing the average and standard deviation of the normalized entitlement across all active hosts in the cluster.

Normalized entitlement is the measure of the utilization of available capacity. DRS receives the usage and demand of each VM to compute its dynamic entitlement then sums the entitlements of all VMs on the host and divides this by the capacity of the host. The available capacity of the host is the number of resources remaining after subtracting the resources required for running the virtualization layer.

$$Normalized\ entitlement = \frac{VM\ entitlements}{Capacity\ of\ host}$$

Because the virtual machine entitlement contains demand metrics, such as %ready time for CPU and %idle for memory, the standard deviation of the normalized entitlement is very similar to the state of a cluster that does not experience contention.

Target Host Load Standard Deviation

DRS derives the Target Host Load Standard Deviation (THLSD) from the DRS migration threshold, which defines the cluster imbalance tolerance level.

DRS Migration Threshold

The migration threshold determines the maximum value under which the load imbalance is to be kept under. The DRS migration threshold offers five levels, ranging from Conservative to Aggressive.

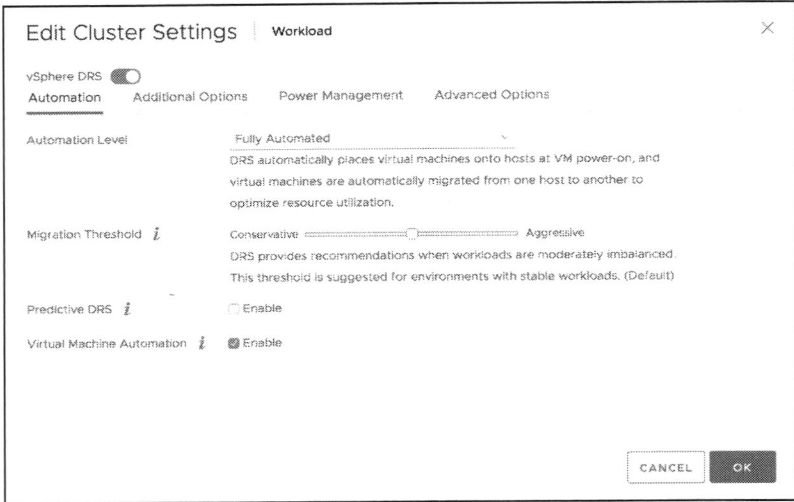

Figure 136: Migration Threshold

Each threshold level sets an imbalance tolerance margin. The Aggressive threshold sets a tight margin allowing for little imbalance, while the more conservative thresholds tolerate bigger imbalances. The most conservative threshold does not compute a THLSD and only recommends mandatory moves to correct constraint violations. More information about thresholds can be found later in the chapter.

A higher frequency of migrations can be expected when selecting a more aggressive migration threshold as DRS is required to keep the CHLSD lower than the THLSD.

The metric Current Host Load Standard deviation is presented in vCenter, while CHLSD is often referred as the Load Imbalance Metric inside DRS. In the next section, Load Imbalance Metric is interchangeable with CHLSD.

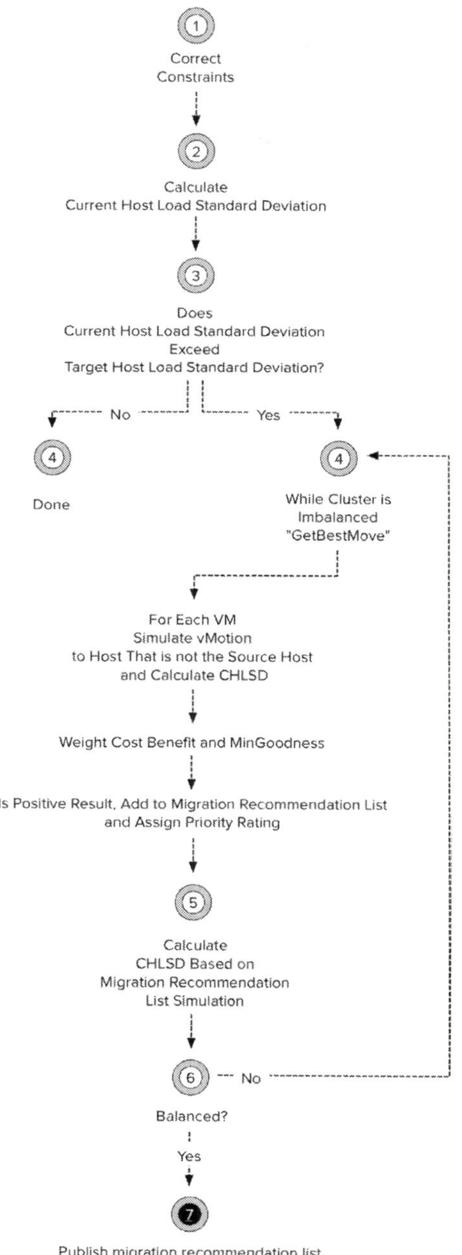

Figure 137: DRS Migration Recommendation Workflow

If the Current Hosts Load Standard Deviation exceeds the Target Hosts Load Standard Deviation, DRS will initiate the *GetBestMove*.

```
while (load imbalance metric > threshold) {
move = getbestmove();
if no good migration is found:
stop;
else:
add move to the list of recommendations;
update representation of cluster to the state after the move is
added; }
```

The algorithm adds all the recommendations to the list before allowing vCenter or the user to execute the recommendations list.

GetBestMove

The GetBestMove procedure aims to find the VM that gives the best improvement in the cluster-wide imbalance. The GetBestMove procedure consists of the following instructions:

```
GetBestMove() {
for each virtual machine v:
  for each host h that is not source host:
    if h is lightly loaded compared to source host:
      if cost-benefit and risk analysis accepted
        simulate move v to h
        measure new cluster-wide load imbalance metric as g
        return move v that gives least cluster-wide imbalance g.
}
```

This procedure determines which migration offers the most improvement. DRS cycles through each DRS-enabled VM and each host that is not the source host. The source host is the ESXi host currently running the VM under consideration. DRS compares the normalized entitlement of the source host to each destination host. Hosts with a lower normalized entitlement are selected for further simulations. After the GetBestMove is completed and the result is positive, DRS selects an ESXi host from the previous normalized entitlement selection and simulate a migration. DRS computes the possible CHLSD of both hosts after the simulated migration and, if they still exceed the DRS Migration threshold, DRS repeats the procedure but selects a different target host. DRS repeats this procedure for every VM-to-host combination. The migration recommendation lists the migrations that result in the most significant reduction in load imbalance.

Cost-Benefit and Risk Analysis Criteria

The purpose of the cost-benefit and risk analysis is to filter out expensive and unstable migrations. The term "unstable migration" indicates the effect of the migration on the cluster load balance and examines the stability of the workload pattern of the virtual machine. Please note it does not imply the vMotion process itself is unstable.

DRS invokes a cost-benefit risk analysis to throttle migrations and avoid a constant stream of vMotions. Both the source and destination hosts incur costs when performing a vMotion and continuously initiating vMotions can nullify the benefit of migrating a virtual machine.

The cost-benefit and risk analysis also prevent spiky workloads from affecting the recommendations. If a virtual machine's workload changes directly after the recommendation, the recommendation becomes useless and creates a situation where the virtual machine is selected over and over again, resulting in "Ping-Pong" migrations.

Cost

The vMotion process reserve 30% of a CPU core if a 1GbE connection is used. If 10GbE is available to the vMotion Portgroup, it reserves 100% of a CPU core. This reservation is set to a host-local resource pool and is created on both source and destination hosts. If multiple vMotions are running, this reservation is shared between the vMotion tasks. A shadow VM is created on the destination host during the vMotion process; the memory consumption of this shadow VM is also factored into the cost of the recommendation.

Benefit

By moving a VM, resources on the source host are released and made available for other VMs. The migrated VM benefits due to the lower normalized entitlement on its new host. The migration of workloads identified by DRS results in a much more balanced cluster.
If any host is overcommitted on a particular resource, DRS gives a higher benefit weight to that resource for all migrations. For example, if contention occurs primarily on CPU, DRS applies a higher benefit weight on CPU to resolve contention. DRS re-examines overcommitment on a particular resource during each invocation.

Risk

Risk accounts for the possibility of irregular loads. Irregular load indicates inconsistent and spiky demand workloads.

Combining the Cost-Benefit Risk

DRS recommends migrations for rebalancing if their estimated cost is lower than their potential benefit for current and recent VM demand and to the relative imbalance between hosts. DRS combines the cost benefits and risk to compute a new placement of virtual machines that satisfies all constraints and improves load balance.
The cost-benefit and risk analysis determines the resource gain of migration, whether positive or negative.

To determine if migration has a positive result, the workload characteristics of the VM over the last 5 minutes are analyzed. This is called the "stable time" and indicates how long the VM has used resources similar to the active workload metric. A conservative estimation is used for the remaining time within the invocation period (invocation period duration – stable time). DRS assumes the VM runs at its worst possible load and uses the peak value from the last 60 minutes. DRS includes the cost of migration and considers the resource gain of both the source and destination hosts. DRS only recommends a migration if the cost-benefit and risk analysis produces a positive result.

MinGoodness

Besides the Cost-Benefit analysis, DRS calculates a Goodness value for each move. This value indicates the positive or negative effect of a move on the load balance of the cluster. For both the Cost-Benefit and Goodness metrics, DRS uses the same rating system:

RATING	DESCRIPTION
-2	Strongly reject
-1	Accept only if the other metric is rated strongly accept
0	Neutral, leave the decision to the other metric
+1	Accept, if the other metric is neutral or above
+2	Strongly accept, reject only if other metric rating is definitely reject

Table 22: DRS Rating System

Each move gets a goodness rating that is related to current load balance and the minimum migration threshold. If a move severely hurts the load balance, the move receives a rating of -2. A move that slightly reduces the load balance gets a -1 rating. One that improves the load balance but does not improve it enough to reach the minimum threshold receives a neutral rating. A move that improves the load balance slightly (0.1) receives a +1 rating. Moves with a goodness rating of +2 improve the load balance by a significant amount.

As mentioned before, DRS uses the same values to weight the cost-benefit of a move. These ratings are applied as follows: A move that reduces resource availability by at least 10% receives a -2 rating. A move that could have a slight decrease in resource availability receives a value of -1. If a move has a neutral effect on resource availability, i.e., it doesn't hurt or help, receives a 0 value. If a move improves resource availability, a +1 rating is awarded, while a move that improves resource availability by at least 10% receives a +2 rating.
Before presenting the recommendations, the goodness ratings are compared to the cost-benefit ratings. As the cost-benefit algorithm is more conservative than the goodness algorithm, it is highly unlikely to see DRS recommend moves with a neutral or less goodness rating.

Therefore, recommendations made by DRS are usually moves with positive cost-benefit and goodness ratings.

Filtering moves by goodness (MinGoodnessFiltering) and cost-benefit (CostBenefitFiltering) could prevent DRS from recommending moves when a cluster is severely imbalanced. A cluster is regarded as severely imbalanced when any host's load differs more than 0.2 from the target host load deviation.

If you notice that DRS is not recommending any load balancing moves in your environment, it could be that each move has a too little impact on the cluster imbalance. It is possible that no possible move significantly improves the cluster-wide balance (controlled by the MinGoodnessFiltering), or that the moves which improve the cluster-wide imbalance have costs that are too high (controlled by the CostBenefitFiltering).

To solve this situation, DRS is equipped with three additional steps in the load-balancing algorithm. These steps are RelaxMinGoodness, RelaxCostBenfitFiltering and DropCostBenefitFiltering. How does this work?

		COST-BENEFIT RATINGS				
		-2	-1	0	1	2
Goodness Ratings	-2	Reject	Reject	Reject	Reject	Reject
	-1	Reject	Reject	Reject	Reject	Reject
	0	DCB	RCB	RMG	Accept	Accept
	1	DCB	RCB	Accept	Accept	Accept
	2	DCB	Accept	Accept	Accept	Accept

Table 23: DRS Invocation Steps

During normal operations, moves with neutral or negative Goodness ratings are **rejected (Reject)**; however, they can be reconsidered and **accepted (Accept)** if the cluster remains severely imbalanced.

If the cluster remains severely imbalanced after the DRS load balancing step, and if the load balancing operation isnot limited by the migration limit (MaxMovesPerHost), load balancing is re-run with the **RelaxMinGoodness (RMG)** flag activated. This means that a DRS considers recommending moves with a neutral goodness and cost-benefit rating previously dropped by MinGoodNessFiltering.

If the analysis shows that the cluster remains severely imbalanced, even after considering moves that improve the cluster-wide balance in a small - but still positive way, DRS sets the **RelaxCostBenefitFiltering (RCB)** flag.

In this situation, moves are considered that would improve load balance on a small to medium scale, even if they have a slightly negative Cost Benefit value. If these additional moves do not solve the severe imbalance, DRS sets the **DropCostBenefit (DCB)** flag and considers moves that would have been strongly rejected during regular load balancing runs.

Please note that these additional moves only appear if the cluster is in a state of severe imbalance. In essence, this feature is an automated way of implementing the manual workaround of setting minGoodness=0 and costBenefit=0. However, DRS applies this mechanism only during states when it's necessary; enabling these settings manually could hurt VM performance.

Calculating the Migration Recommendation Priority Level

The migration threshold specifies the tolerance of imbalance of the Current Host Load Standard Deviation (CHLSD) relating to the Target Host Load Standard Deviation (THLSD). The migration threshold factor is configured via the DRS setting on the cluster level. Priority levels are used to make the migration threshold setting simpler to understand.

During its calculations, DRS assigns a priority level to each recommendation and this priority level is compared to the migration threshold. If the priority level is less than or equal to the migration threshold, the recommendation is displayed or applied, depending on the automation level of the cluster. If the priority level is above the migration threshold, the recommendations are either not displayed or discarded. You can think of the migration threshold as a filter for recommendations generated by DRS.

Level 1 (conservative)
When selecting the conservative migration threshold level, only mandatory moves, priority-one recommendations, are executed. This means that the DRS cluster does not invoke any load-balancing migrations. Mandatory moves are issued when:

- The ESXi host enters maintenance mode
- The ESXi host enters standby mode
- An (anti-) affinity rule is violated
- The sum of the reservations of the virtual machines exceeds the capacity of the host

It is possible that a mandatory move causes a violation on another host. If this happens, DRS moves VMs to fix the new violation at the next DRS invocation. This scenario is possible when multiple rules exist on the cluster. It is not uncommon to see several migrations required to satisfy the configured DRS rules.

Level 2 (moderately conservative)
The level 2-migration threshold only applies priority-one, and priority-two recommendations, priority two recommendations promise a very good improvement in the cluster's load balance.

Level 3 (moderate)
The level 3-migration threshold is the default migration threshold when creating DRS clusters. The moderate migration threshold applies priority-one, -two and priority-three recommendations, promising a good improvement in the cluster's load balance.

Level 4 (moderately aggressive)
The level 4-migration threshold applies all recommendations up to priority level four. Priority-four recommendations promise a moderate improvement in the cluster's load balance.

Level 5 (aggressive)
The level 5-migration threshold is the right-most setting on the migration threshold slider and applies all five priority level recommendations; every recommendation which promises even a slight improvement in the cluster's load balance is applied.

> **The default moderate migration threshold provides a higher tolerance for migrations, while offering sufficient balance. The algorithm generates only recommendations that are worthwhile according to the tolerance. The default setting is typically aggressive enough to maintain workload balance across hosts without creating unnecessary overhead caused by too-frequent migrations.**

Pair-Wise Balancing Thresholds

vSphere 6.5 introduced an additional load balancing threshold that helps to minimize the load difference between hosts in the cluster. This threshold is tied to the migration threshold and determines the maximum load difference between the least utilized host and the most utilized host within the cluster. This setting is called pair-wise balancing.

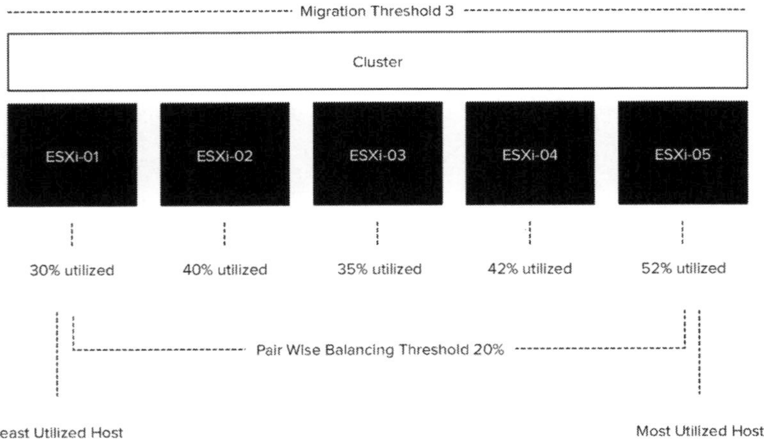

Figure 138: Pair-Wise Balancing Threshold

In this scenario, DRS compares the host load of each host and determines that the least utilized host is ESXi-01 with 30% utilization. The most utilized host is ESXi-05, which is 52% utilized. The difference in load exceeds the threshold of 20% that related to from the migration threshold. The table below lists the Tolerable Resource Utilization Difference Between Host Pair and its relationship with the migration threshold level.

MIGRATION THRESHOLD LEVEL	TOLERABLE RESOURCE UTILIZATION DIFFERENCE BETWEEN HOST PAIR
1 Conservative	Not available
2	30%
3 (Default)	20%
4	10%
5	5%

Table 24: DRS Migration Threshold Level

DRS migrates VMs to reduce the load difference. DRS is not bound to migrate the workload from ESXi-05 to ESXi-01. It can move VMs from ESXi-05 to any other host in the cluster. Standard load-balancing logic is applied, and therefore DRS takes all the constraints into account when finding the most suitable candidate for migration.

Network Aware DRS

vSphere 6.5 introduced Network-Aware DRS. The DRS initial placement and load-balancing algorithms take host network utilization and the VM network usage in account when determining the best ESXi host for VM placement.

> **It is crucial to understand that DRS in vSphere 6.7 does not migrate VMs when there is a network load imbalance. DRS balances on CPU and memory imbalance and uses network utilization metrics to fine-tune the VM placement. It makes sure that the VM is placed on a host that provides the compute resources and the host does not have a saturated network connection. In essence, network-aware is a filter for host selection; network utilization is not a first-class citizen in the DRS algorithms like CPU and memory.**

Initial Placement Enhancement

During Initial Placement, DRS creates a list of ESXi host based on compatibility, compute utilization, constraints, and resource requirements of the VM. DRS sorts the list and selects the ESXi host that satisfies the resource utilization of the VM (100% utilization of compute resource configuration) and have the least network utilization.

Load-Balancing Enhancement

During Load Balancing, DRS generates the list of migration recommendations. Network-aware DRS prunes the list of migration recommendations that contains hosts that are network saturated.

After pruning, DRS selects the migration recommendation that improves the cluster balance from a compute perspective. If the cluster contains hosts that are network saturated, DRS selects the migration recommendation that improves cluster balance and that improves the network resource availability of the source host. Due to this new selection of hosts, DRS only shows a single host recommendation if the VM is set to manual DRS automation level.

Network Saturation Threshold

The network saturation threshold is set to 80% by default. It's important to understand that Network-aware DRS uses the total network capacity and usage of the host, it accounts for all the physical uplinks that are connected to a switch and in an 'up' state. It doesn't distinguish between portgroups or vSwitches.

For example, your ESXi host has four physical 1 GbE NICs. Two NICs are connected to vSwitch0 that handles infrastructure network traffic, such as management network traffic, vMotion traffic and IP-storage traffic. The two remaining physical NICs are attached to vSwitch1, solely created to isolate VM traffic. You can argue that Network-aware DRS should only consider the utilization of vSwitch1. Unfortunately, vSwitch configuration and higher-level objects are not visible to network-aware DRS. Thus, it just aggregates the bandwidth of all the active physical NICs.

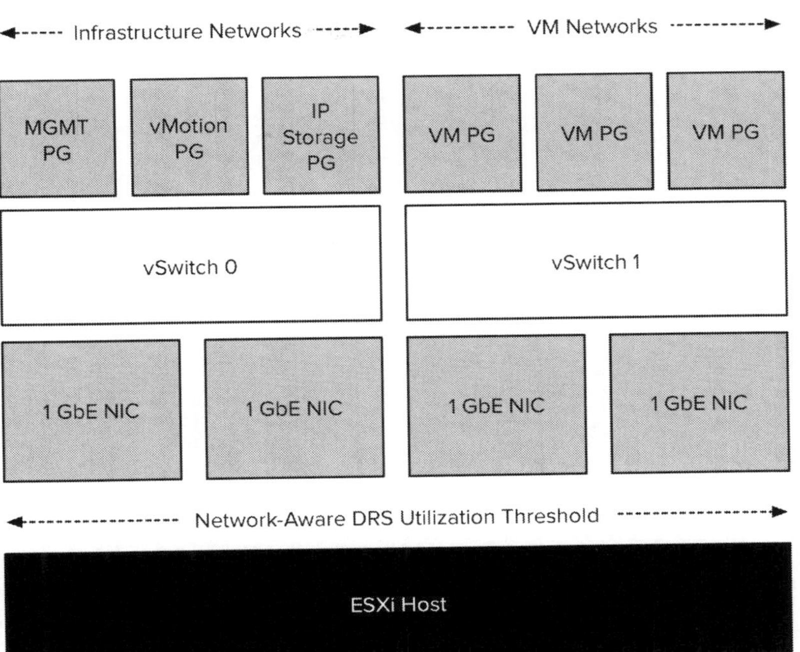

Figure 139: Network-Aware DRS Thresholds on Logically Separated NICs

Today most new servers are equipped with converged network adapters or 2 x 10GbE NICS, logically partitioned by VLANs. In these situations, Network-Aware DRS functions more accurately as VM networks are able to use all the network bandwidth available to the ESXi host.

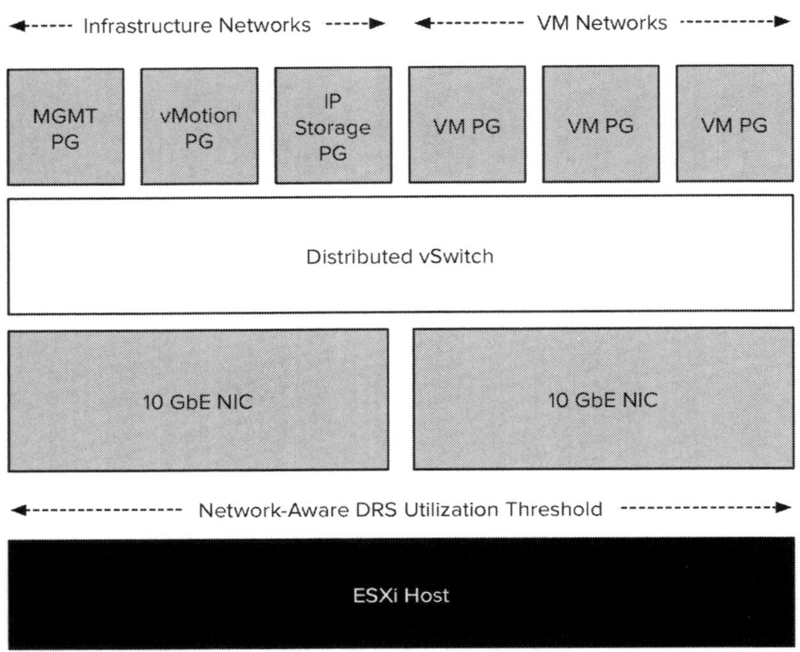

Figure 140: Network-Aware DRS Thresholds 10 GbE NICs Configuration

Advanced Setting

You can change the threshold with the following advanced setting: `NetworkAwareDrsSaturationThresholdPercent`. By default, it is set to 80%. Lowering the threshold might be helpful if the ESXi hosts have an abundance of bandwidth. But as always, please test it first in a test environment before using advanced settings in production.

15

IMPACTING DRS RECOMMENDATIONS

Some DRS settings and features can influence the DRS migration recommendations. This chapter takes a closer look at the various settings and the impacts they can have on the DRS calculations and load balancing process.

DRS Additional Options

To simplify DRS tuning, DRS exposed three new policies grouped under the name Additional Options. These options provide customizations to the DRS load-balancing algorithm and translate into advanced settings. Each of these options is listed in the advanced settings tab of the cluster UI. These options are available at Cluster | Configure | vSphere DRS | Edit.

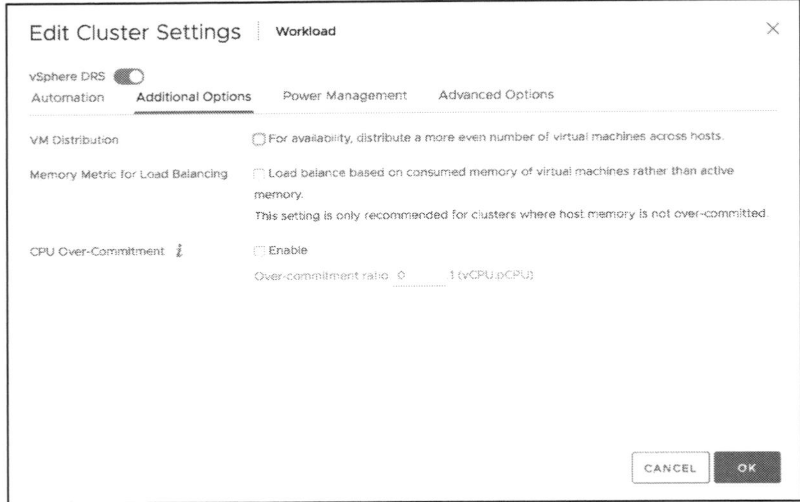

Figure 141: DRS Cluster Additional Options

VM Distribution

The VM Distribution (TryBalanceVmsPerHost) setting instructs DRS to distribute the VMs equally across the cluster. This policy replaces the advanced settings `LimitVMPerESXHost` and `LimitVMsPerESXHostPercent` introduced in vSphere 5.5.

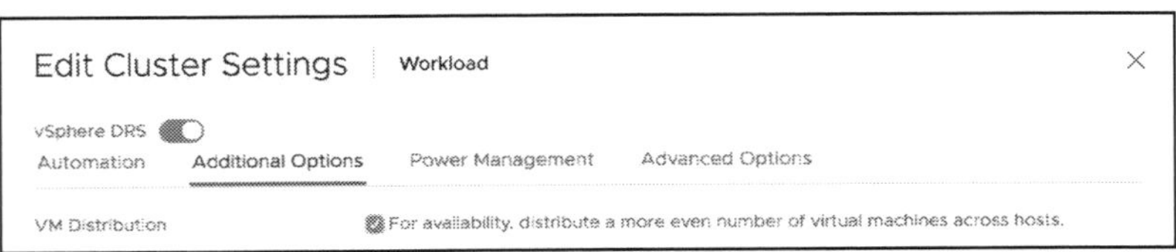

Figure 142: VM Distribution

Fundamentally, the VM Distribution setting keeps the number of VMs on any host below the (number of VMs)/(number of hosts).
The setting is a soft setting, meaning that DRS attempts to distribute the VMs evenly with the best effort. It still honors and applies the full load-balancing algorithm. The cluster should not get in a state that it is severely imbalanced.

The setting only applies to load-balancing operations. Imbalance can occur if a group of VMs is powered on simultaneously. During the next load-balancing operation, the imbalance is solved. During this load-balance operation, DRS determines which VM has the lowest entitlement (small VM) and moves this to less loaded host. The move still needs to improve the overall load balance. Thus you won't see DRS migrate VMs randomly.

This option is primarily meant for availability purposes, averaging out the number of VMs per host in the cluster. The side effect of selecting this option is the increasing number of vMotions, to keep the number of VMs per host balanced.

Memory Balancing in Non-Overcommitted Clusters

DRS is aligned with the premise of virtualization, resource sharing and overcommitment of resources. DRS goal is to provide compute resources to the active workload to improve workload consolidation on a minimal compute footprint. However, virtualization surpassed the original principle of workload consolidation to provide unprecedented workload mobility and availability.

With this change of focus, many customers do not overcommit on memory. Many customers design their clusters to contain (just) enough memory capacity to ensure all running virtual machines have their memory backed by physical memory. In this scenario, DRS behavior should be adjusted as it traditionally focusses on active memory use.

vSphere 6.5 and 6.7 provides this option in the DRS cluster settings. By ticking the box “Memory Metric for Load Balancing” DRS uses the VM consumed memory for load-balancing operations.

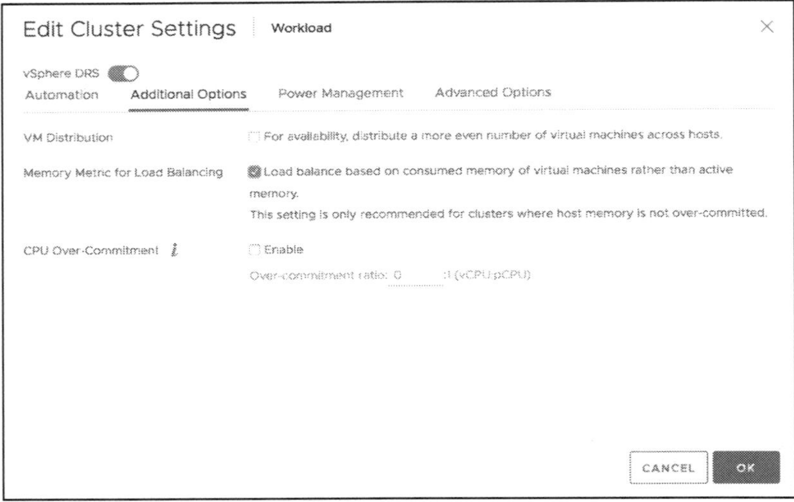

Figure 143: DRS Memory Metric for Load Balancing

> **Please note that DRS is focused on consumed memory, not configured memory! DRS always keeps a close eye on what is happening rather than accepting static configuration. Let's take a closer look at DRS input metrics of active and consumed memory.**

Out-of-the-box DRS Behavior

As described in the chapter "Resource Distribution" DRS calculates the active memory demand of the VMs in the cluster during load balancing operation. The active memory represents the working set of the VM, which signifies the number of active pages in RAM. By using the working-set estimation, the memory scheduler determines which of the allocated memory pages are actively used by the virtual machine and which allocated pages are idle. To accommodate a sudden rapid increase of the working set, 25% of idle consumed memory is allowed. Memory demand also includes the virtual machine's memory overhead.

Let's use a 16 GB VM as an example of how DRS calculates the memory demand. The guest OS running in this virtual machine has touched 75%

of its memory size since it was booted, but only 35% of its memory size is active. This means that the virtual machine has consumed 12288 MB and 5734 MB of this is used as active memory.

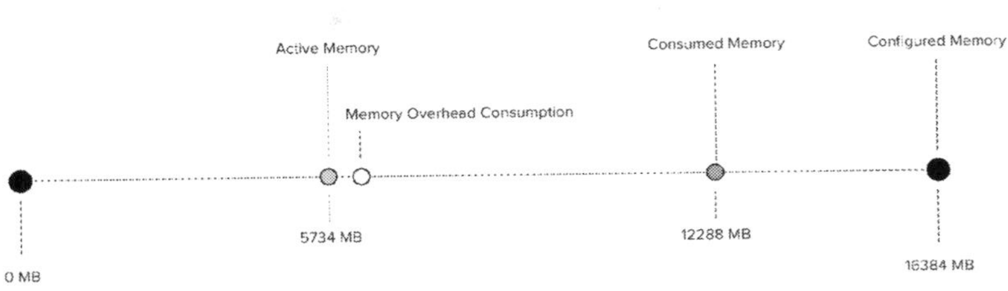

Figure 144: Active, Consumed and Configured Memory

As mentioned, DRS accommodate a percentage of the idle consumed memory to be ready for a sudden increase in memory use. To calculate the idle consumed memory, the active memory 5734 MB is subtracted from the consumed memory, 12288 MB, resulting in a total 6554 MB idle consumed memory. By default, DRS includes 25% of the idle consumed memory, i.e. 6554 * 25% = +/- 1639 MB.

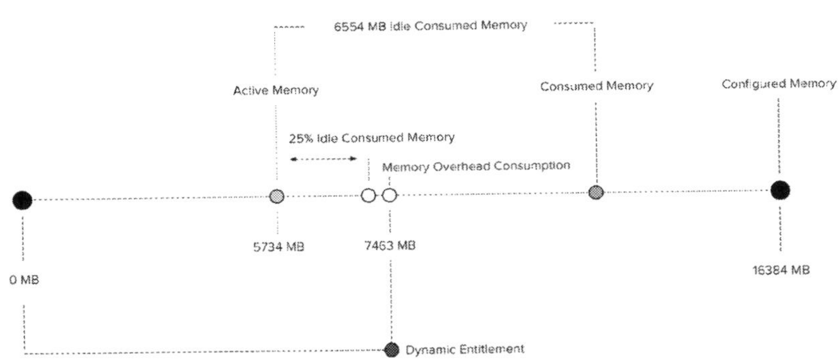

Figure 145: Default Dynamic Entitlement Calculation

The VM has a memory overhead of 90 MB. The memory demand DRS uses in its load balancing calculation is as follows: 5734 MB + 1639 MB + 90 MB = 7463 MB. As a result, DRS selects a host that has 7463 MB available for this machine if it needs to move this VM to improve the load balance of the cluster.

Memory Metric for Load Balancing Enabled

When enabling the option "Memory Metric for Load Balancing", DRS takes into account the consumed memory + the memory overhead for load balancing operations. In essence, DRS uses the metric Active + 100% IdleConsumedMemory.

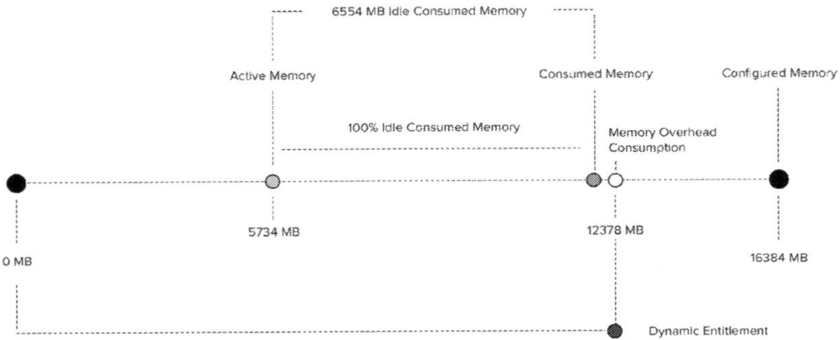

Figure 146: 100% Idle Consumed Memory

The UI client from vSphere 6.5 update 1d and up allows you to get better visibility in the memory usage of the virtual machines in the cluster. The memory utilization view can be toggled between active memory and consumed memory.

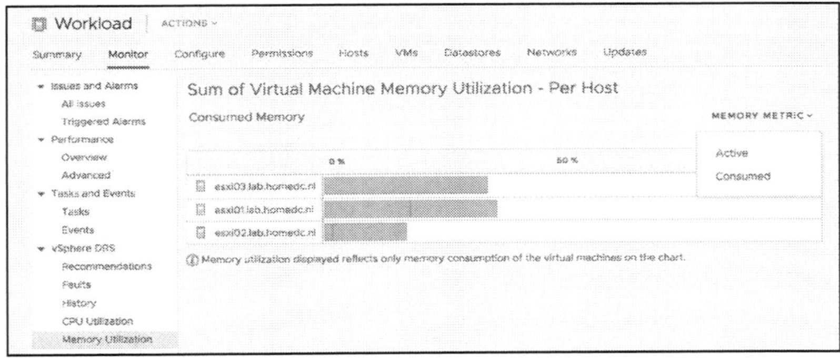

Figure 147: Cluster Memory Utilization Consumed View

When reviewing the cluster, it shows that the cluster is pretty much balanced.

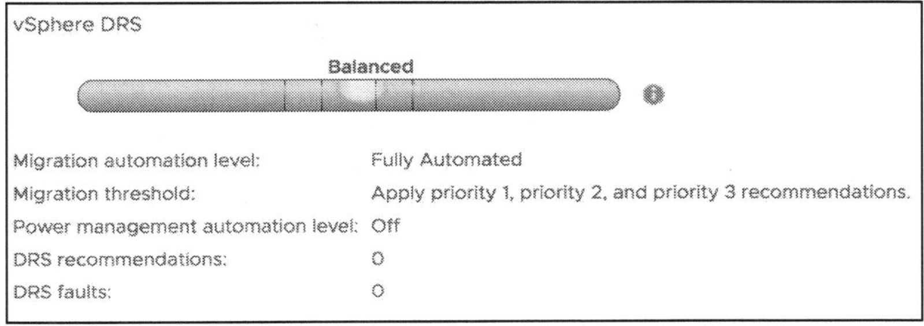

Figure 148: Cluster Balanced State

When looking at the default view of the sum of VM memory utilization (active memory), it shows that ESXi host ESXi-02 is busier than the others.

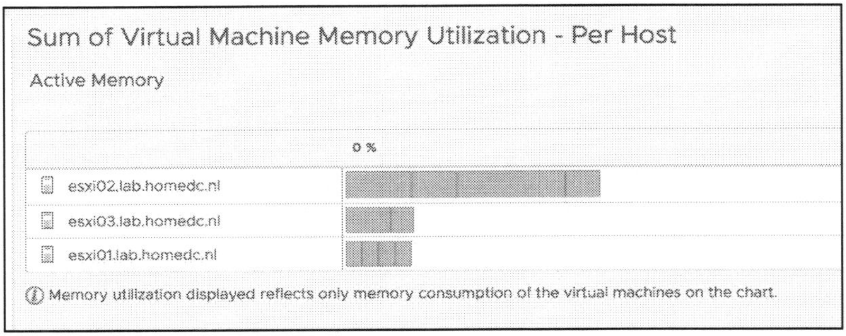

Sum of Virtual Machine Memory Utilization - Per Host

Active Memory

0 %

esxi02.lab.homedc.nl

esxi03.lab.homedc.nl

esxi01.lab.homedc.nl

Memory utilization displayed reflects only memory consumption of the virtual machines on the chart.

Figure 149: Sum of VM Memory Utilization Based on Active Memory

Since the active memory of each host is less than 20% and each virtual machine is receiving the memory they are entitled to, DRS does not move VMs around. Remember, DRS is designed to create as little overhead as possible. Moving one VM to another host to make the active usage more balanced, is just a waste of compute cycles and network bandwidth. The VMs receive what they want to receive now, so why take the risk of moving VMs?

However, a different view of the current situation is when you toggle the graph to use consumed memory.

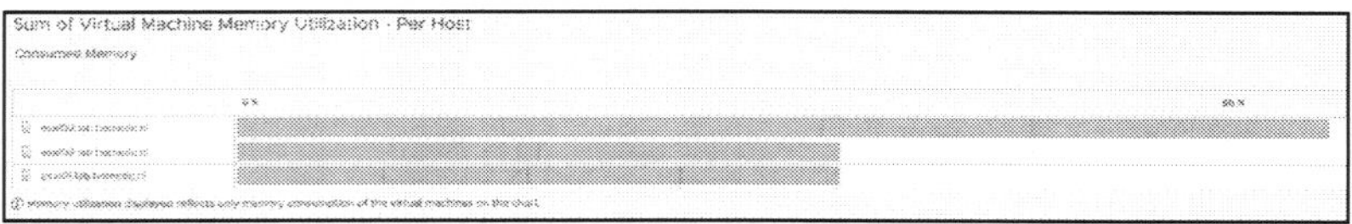

Figure 150: Sum of VM Memory Utilization Based on Consumed Memory

Now we see a more significant difference in consumed memory utilization. Much more than 20% between ESXi-02 and the other two hosts. By default, due to pair-wise balancing DRS tries to clear a utilization difference of 20% between hosts. However, since DRS focuses on Active memory usage, Pair-Wise Balancing won't be activated with regards to the 20% difference in consumed memory utilization. After enabling the option "Memory Metric for Load Balancing" DRS rebalances the cluster with the optimal number of migrations (as few as possible) to reduce overhead and risk.

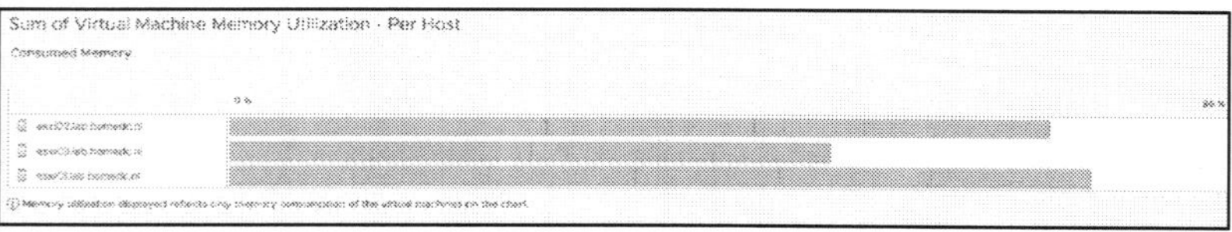

Figure 151: Memory Metric for Load Balancing Enabled

> **If you design your cluster with no memory overcommitment as guiding principle, we recommend testing out the DRS option "Memory Metric for Load Balancing". You might want to switch DRS to manual mode, to verify the recommendations first.**

Please note that these additional options override any equivalent cluster advanced options. For example, if you set cluster advanced option `PercentIdleMBInMemDemand` to some value, and then enable the memory metric option for load balancing, the advanced option is cleared to give precedence to the new memory metric option.

CPU Over-Commitment (DRS Additional Option)

DRS provides the CPU over-commitment option for applications that benefit from lower CPU latency (CPU scheduling time). By reducing the number of virtual CPUs per physical CPU, you skew the cluster more towards performance than providing the best economics.

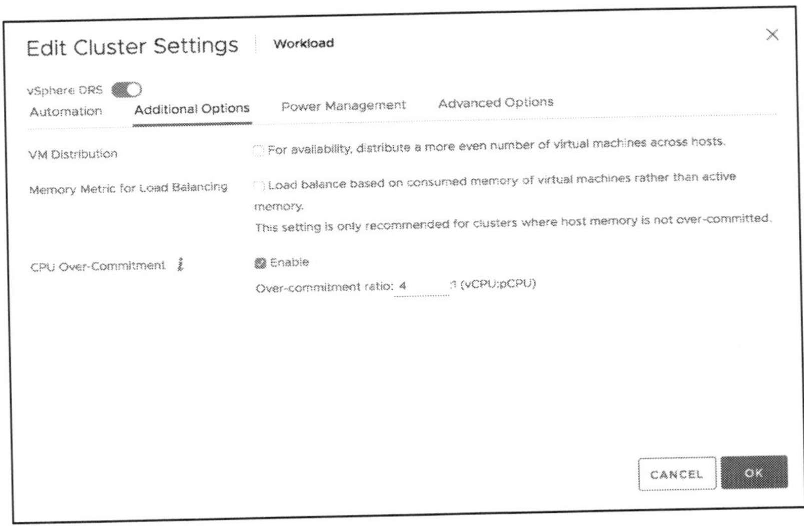

Figure 152: Setting the CPU Over-Commit Ratio 4:1

When setting the CPU Over-Commitment option of the DRS cluster, you configure an advanced option. Depending on the client use, the advanced option is different.

CLIENT TYPE	HTML 5 CLIENT	WEB CLIENT
Focus	Host-Based vCPU to pCPU ratio	Cluster-wide CPU over-commitment ratio
Advanced Setting	MaxVcpusPerCore	MaxVCPUsPerClusterPct
Minimum Value	4	0
Maximum Value	32	500

Table 25: vSphere Client Variation

Maximum vCPUs per CPU Core

This DRS additional option control is available via the H5 client and is active at the ESXi host level. No ESXi host in the cluster is allowed to violate this setting. The UI allows settings between 0 and 500. However, the minimum value is 4, the maximum value is 32. The maximum setting is in line with ESXi host maximum vCPU to pCPU limit of 32.

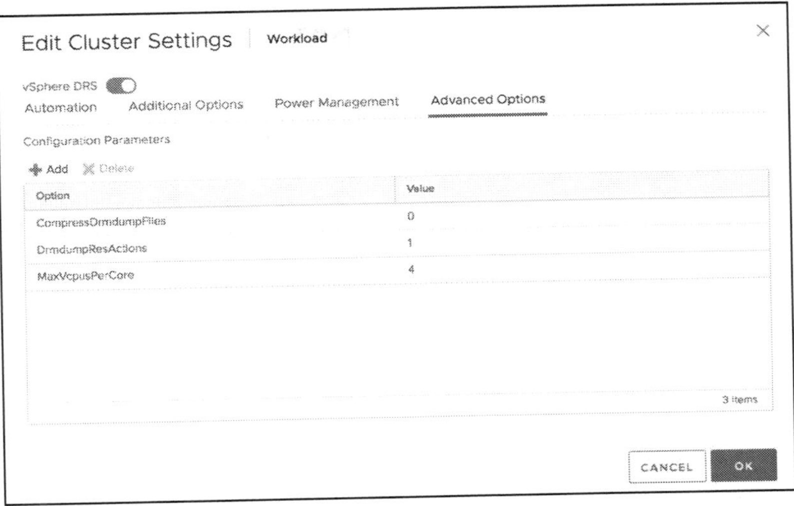

Figure 153: MaxVcpusPerCore Advanced Option

Maximum vCPU Per Cluster Percentage

This DRS additional options control is applied when using the (not-recommended) web client. This setting applies a cluster-wide vCPU to pCPU overcommitment ratio. The setting is a percentage based on the calculation of total number of vCPUs in the cluster / total number of pCPUs in the cluster divided by 100.

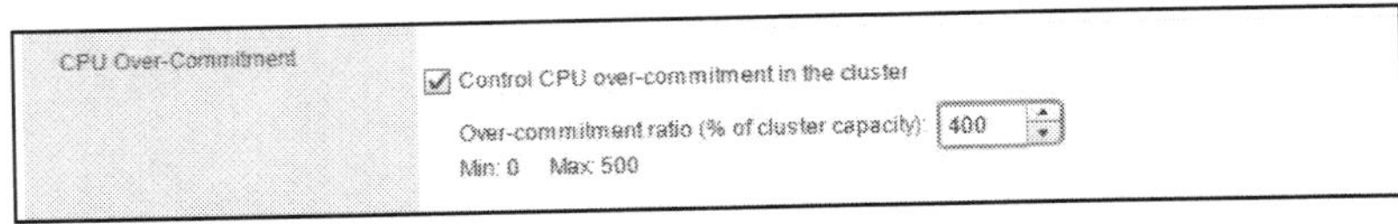

Figure 154: Web Client Option

You are allowed to use the minimum value of 0. However, this restricts the cluster from running any vCPU on the cluster. You are manually creating a cluster-wide denial of service. A use-case might be a temporary ban on workloads to make room for cluster-wide upgrade operations. Other than that, we cannot come up with a use-case.

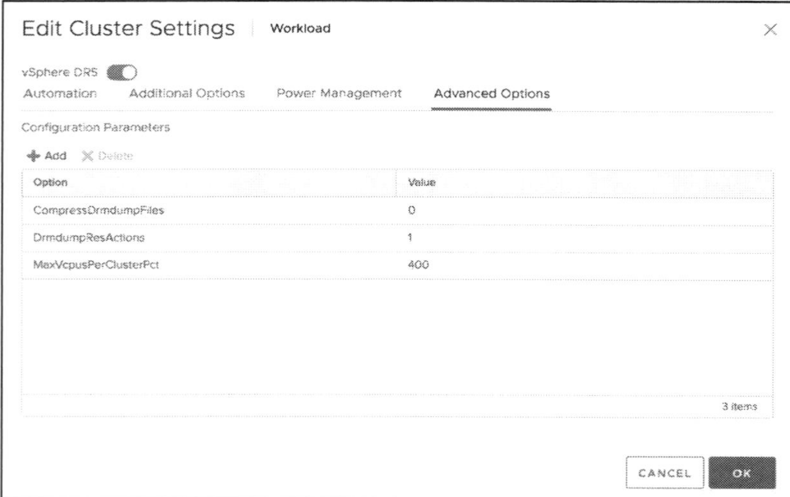

Figure 155: MaxVcpusPerClusterPct

In general, it is recommended to use the H5 client as much as possible. However, the difference in behavior could force you to load the web client. If you want to reduce the over-commitment ratio of 4:1 or less use the web client. If you want to be more lenient, but still restrict it to less than 32, use the H5 client. It is expected that future updates of the vSphere versions provide a more uniform experience.

AggressiveCPUActive

> **Stated multiple times in the book, but noting it again, please only use advanced settings unless there is an absolute need for it. Especially the AggressiveCPUActive setting, test properly, before applying it in production environments.**

The AggressiveCPUActive setting changes the CPU balancing behavior of DRS. It's designed to handle spiky CPU workloads by changing the statical input for DRS to base its recommendations on. By default, DRS uses the CPU active percentage statistic, averaged over five minutes to determine the CPU entitlement. When an application is generating stable load, this average provides an adequate representation of the workload. Using such a sample size allows vCenter to handle high volumes of stats, which ramp up quickly when you realize DRS uses 20 quikstat counters per VM with a 60 minutes length of history.

However, if the workload generates short-lived spikes of workload, the average stat can smooth out spikes and are missed by DRS to generate a migration recommendation to find a more suitable host.

When enabling AggressiveCPUActive (AggressiveCPUActive=1), DRS uses five one-minute samples of average CPU active. DRS sorts these statistics in ascending order and selects the second highest value in the interval. It means that DRS uses the 80th percentile value of the last 5 minutes of active CPU usage of the VM.

For example, a VM is running a workload that is using 60%, 5%, 80%, 5% and 40%. With the default 5 minutes quickstat, DRS determine the demand of the VM is 38%. When enabling AggressiveCPUActive, DRS sorts the quickstats in ascending order, 5%,5%,40%,60% and 80% and selects the 4th value (80th percentile). DRS uses 60% as CPU active demand for this VM.

Using this setting can help to avoid ready time for particular VMs, but please be aware that this more aggressive DRS behavior increases overhead at the vCenter level and it skews the behavior of DRS recommendation. It can be compelling, but it can also introduce unwanted behavior. Please test accordingly.

VM Size and Initial Placement

When a VM powers on, DRS selects a target host to place the VM. DRS prefers the registered host as long as the placement of the VM on this host does not cause a cluster imbalance.

During initial placement, DRS applies a worst-case scenario because it does not have historical data of the resource utilization of the virtual machine. DRS assumes that both the memory demand and CPU demand is equal to its configured size. I.e., powering on a 4 vCPU 16 GB VM introduces 400% CPU load and consumes 16 GB of memory.

VMs that are oversized can introduce a temporary cluster imbalance. If none of the cluster members can provide the full 100% of the resources requested DRS defragments the cluster's resources, migrating VMs to make room.

If the actual utilization of a VM is comparable to its configured size, the new migrations are expected behavior as they help the cluster reach a balanced state as quickly as possible. However, if a VM is oversized (its active utilization does not compare to DRS's initial expectation), a number of migrations throughout several DRS rounds may occur to rebalance the cluster.

We are aware that many organizations still size their VMs based on assumed peak loads happing in the (late) life cycle of that service or application. This is similar to the policy historically used for sizing physical machines. One of the benefits of using VMs is the flexibility it offers with regards to resizing a machine during its lifecycle. We recommend leveraging these mechanisms and incorporating this into your service catalog and daily operations. To most effectively utilize your resources, size a VM according to its current or near-future workload.

MaxMovesPerHost

DRS evaluates the cluster and recommends migrations based on demand and cluster balance state. This process repeats each invocation period. To minimize CPU and memory overhead, DRS limits the number of migration recommendations per DRS invocation period. Ultimately, there is no advantage in recommending more migrations that can complete within a single invocation period. On top of that, the demand could change after an invocation period which would render the previous recommendations obsolete.

vCenter calculates the limit per host based on the average time per migration, the number of simultaneous vMotions and the length of the DRS invocation period (PollPeriodSec).

PollPeriodSec: By default, PollPeriodSec – the length of a DRS invocation period – is 300 seconds, but can be set to any value between 60 and 3600 seconds.

> **Decreasing:** The interval increases the overhead on vCenter due to additional cluster balance computations. It also reduces the number of allowed vMotions due to a smaller time window, resulting in more extended periods of cluster imbalance.
>
> **Increasing:** The interval decreases the frequency of cluster balance computations on vCenter and allows more vMotion operations per cycle. Unfortunately, this may also leave the cluster in a more prolonged state of cluster imbalance due to the prolonged evaluation cycle.

Simultaneous vMotions: vSphere allows you to perform 8 concurrent vMotions on a single host with 10GbE capabilities. For 1GbE, the limit is 4 concurrent vMotions.

Multi-NIC vMotion: Assigns multiple active NICs to the vMotion portgroup that allows vMotion to leverage the available bandwidth for vMotion operations. Even a single vMotion can utilize all available NICs to decrease the amount of time required for a vMotion.

Estimated total migration time: DRS considers the average migration time observed from previous migrations. The average migration time depends on many variables, such as source and destination host load, active memory in the VM, link speed, available bandwidth and latency of the physical network used by the vMotion process.

> **When designing a DRS cluster, take the requirements of vMotion into account. By providing enough bandwidth, the cluster can reach a balanced state more quickly, resulting in better resource allocation (performance) for the VMs.**

Placement Rules

To control VM placement, vSphere 6.7 offers both Virtual Machine-to-Virtual Machine (VM-VM) rules and Virtual Machine to Host (VM-Host) rules.

- VM-VM affinity rules specify whether VMs should stay together and run on the same hosts (affinity rules) or that they are not allowed to run on the same host (anti-affinity).
- A VM-Host affinity rule specifies whether the members of a VM DRS group can or should run on the members of a Host DRS group.

VM-VM Affinity Rules

A VM-VM affinity rule specifies which VMs should run on the same ESXi host.

Affinity rules are used to keep multiple VMs on the same ESXi host, typically to eradicate network latency. For example, by keeping both the front-end and back-end servers of an application on the same host, internal application network traffic remains inside the virtual switch, reducing latency and decreasing load on physical network links and components.

VM-VM Anti-Affinity Rules
A VM-VM anti-affinity rule achieves the opposite of an affinity rule: it specifies which VMs are not allowed to run on the same host.
Anti-affinity rules can be used to offer host failure resiliency to services provided by multiple VMs; examples of such services are Active Directory

domain controllers, DNS servers, and web server farms. By running these VMs on separate hosts, it is possible to maintain service availability during an ESXi host failure.

VM-VM Affinity Rules – impact on HA

Note that VMware HA is unaware of VM-VM affinity and anti-affinity rules. Following a host failure, VMware HA may restart the VMs on the same host, but DRS corrects this violation during the next invocation.

VM-VM Affinity Rules – impact on DRS

VM-VM affinity rules limit migration choices and place more constraints on VM mobility. DRS obeys affinity rules and correct constraint violations first before determining optimal VM placement to achieve cluster balance. In small clusters or large clusters with a large number of rules, this behavior can lead to sub-optimal cluster balance and resource allocation. Although DRS may temporarily violate VM-VM affinity rules if necessary for placement, it corrects the violation during the next invocation period if possible, probably affecting resource allocation again.

VM-Host Affinity Rules

A VM-Host affinity rule specifies whether the VMs, belonging to a VM Group, must (not) or should (not) run on the ESXi hosts in a Host Group. VM-Host affinity rules establish an association between a group of VMs and a group of ESXi hosts. Please note that VMs listed in the VM Group can independently run on the ESXi host listed in the Host Group, they are not required to run all on the same hosts within the Host Group – unless the Host Group contains only one host, of course.

VM-Host affinity rules can be used to isolate VMs inside cluster-subsets of hosts to comply with ISV license regulations. A VM-Host Anti-affinity rule may be used to separate VMs across different failure domains for increased availability. An example of a failure domain could be a server blade chassis or hosts or sets of racks connected to the same power supplies. A VM-Host affinity rule consists of three components:

- VM Group
- Host Group
- Type (i.e., Must/Should run on)

VM-Host affinity and anti-affinity can be configured as either mandatory rules, presented in the UI as "Must (not) run on" or preferential rules, presented as "Should (not) run on".

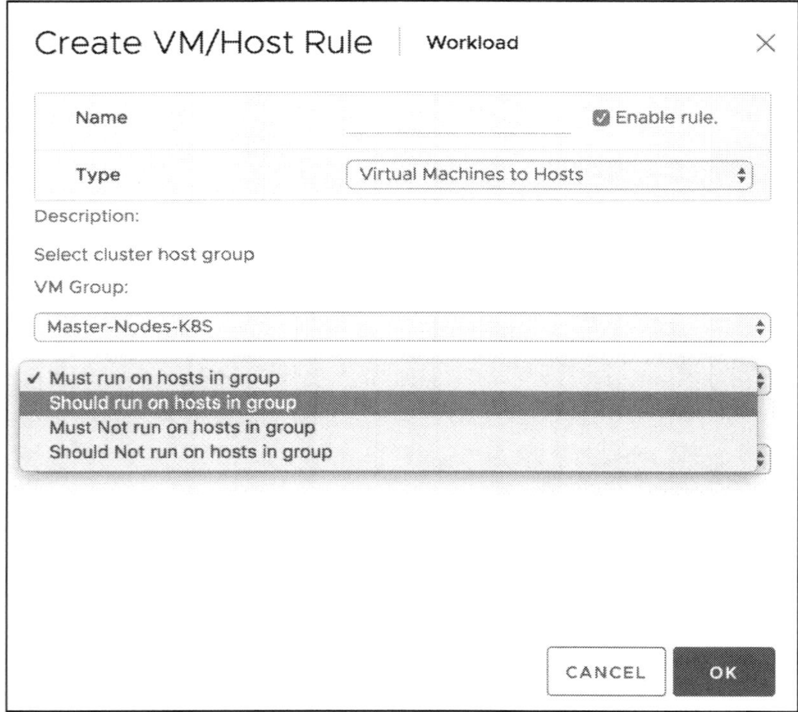

Figure 156: VM to Host Affinity Rule

> **VM-Host affinity rules apply to a specific cluster. Therefore, they can only contain virtual machines and ESXi hosts belonging to that specific cluster.**

VM Group: The VM group contains the VMs to which the rule applies. Please note that if a VM is removed from the cluster, it is automatically removed from the VM Group. The VM is not automatically re-added to the group if it is returned to the cluster.

Host Group: The Host Group contains the ESXi hosts to which the rule applies. Similar to VM behavior, if an ESXi host is removed from the cluster, it is automatically removed from the Host Group. The host is not automatically returned to the group if the host re-added to the cluster.

Type: Two different types of VM-Host rules are available, a VM-Host affinity rule can either be a "must" rule or a "should" rule.

Should (not) run on: The "should" rule is a preferential rule for DRS and DPM. DRS and DPM use best effort trying to satisfy these rules, but DRS and DPM can violate should rules if necessary.

Must (not) run on: The "must"-rule is a mandatory rule for HA, DRS, and DPM. It forces the specified VMs to run on or not run on the ESXi hosts specified in the ESXi Host Group.

Should Run - Preferential Rules

Preferential rules are designed to influence DRS migration recommendations. DRS executes preferential rules if it does not over-utilize the CPU or memory demand of the host. During load-balancing calculations, DRS runs the preferential rules. If they violate any other requirement, DRS drops the rule list and reinitializes a load-balance calculation without the preferential rules.

DRS does not provide any information regarding preferential rules to HA. Since HA is unaware of these "should" rules, it may unknowingly violate these rules during placement after a host failure. During the next DRS invocation cycle, DRS identifies the constraint and issues a (4 stars - priority 2) migration recommendation to correct this violation, if possible. Depending on the automation level of DRS, it will either display the recommendation or correct the situation itself.

Must Run - Mandatory Rules

A mandatory rule applies to DRS, DPM, HA, and user-initiated operations. DRS takes the mandatory rules into account when generating or executing operations. DRS never produces any recommendations that violate the mandatory rule set. For example, DRS rejects the request for Maintenance Mode if it would violate a mandatory rule.

If a reservation is set on a VM, DRS takes both the reservation and the mandatory rules into account. Both requirements must be satisfied during placement or power on operation. If DRS is unable to honor either one of the requirements, the VM is not powered on or migrated to the proposed destination host.

When a mandatory rule is created, and the current VM placement is in violation of a rule, DRS corrects this violation or reports an error if the violation cannot be corrected.

It is important to realize that HA does not violate mandatory rules during a VM restart following a host failure; HA will failover VMs, if possible. If vCenter is available, HA sends an action list (which VM needs to failover) to vCenter. Periodically HA checks if vCenter has freed up enough resources so that HA can handle the failover operations. If HA cannot restart the VMs after a configurable number of retries, it generates an error.

A user operation, such as a vMotion of a VM to a host external to the Host Group, violates the mandatory rule and fails with an error indicating host incompatibility.

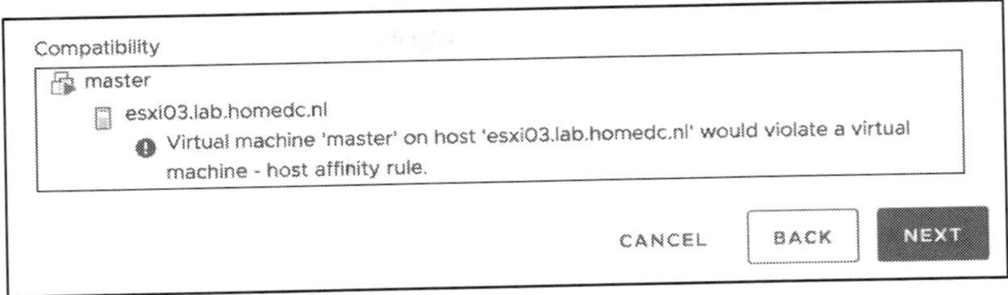

Figure 157: vMotion Compatibility Check

Compliance with mandatory rules is deemed crucial by vSphere, and mandatory rules are not removed when DRS is disabled. That bears repeating: even after disabling DRS, mandatory rules are still in effect for HA and user operations. The cluster continues to track, report and alert if these mandatory rules are violated. For example, if a vMotion operation would violate a mandatory rule, the cluster rejects the migration operation, citing host incompatibility as the reason. Mandatory rules can only be disabled if the administrator explicitly does so. If the administrator intends to disable DRS, he should remove mandatory rules before disabling DRS.

Please note that once DRS is disabled, vCenter no longer displays the DRS options, prohibiting the user from viewing or managing the rules. When DRS is enabled once again, the rules are displayed; disabling DRS does not permanently orphan the rules.

DPM does not place an ESXi host into standby mode if the result would violate a mandatory rule. Moreover, DPM powers-on ESXi hosts if these are needed to meet the requirements of the mandatory rules.

Mandatory rules place more constraints on VM mobility, restricting the number of hosts a VM can run on. HA and DPM operations are constrained as well. For example, mandatory rules will:

- Limit DRS in selecting hosts to load-balance the cluster
- Limit HA in selecting hosts to power up the VMs
- Limit DPM in selecting hosts to power down

Mandatory VM-Host affinity rules reduce the placement options for DRS when defragmenting the cluster. When using HA "Percentage based" admission control, resource fragmentation can occur. During a failover, HA can request defragmentation of cluster resources. To satisfy this request, DRS migrates VMs to free up enough resources to power-on all of the failed VMs. During defragmentation, DRS is allowed to use multi-hop migrations, which creates a chain of dependent migrations. For example, VM-A migrates to host 2 and VM-B migrates from host 2 to host 3. Mandatory rules reduce the options by allowing VMs to only move around within their associated DRS host groups.

A VM that is a member of multiple mandatory rule sets is constrained to run only on the host(s) listed in both DRS host groups. For example, rule 1 allows the VM02 to run on 4 hosts ESXi-01, -02, -03 and ESXi-04. Rule 2 allows the virtual machine to run on host ESXi-03, -04, -05 and ESXi-06. The net result is that the VM is only allowed to run on the compatibility subset that contains ESXi-03 and ESXi-04.

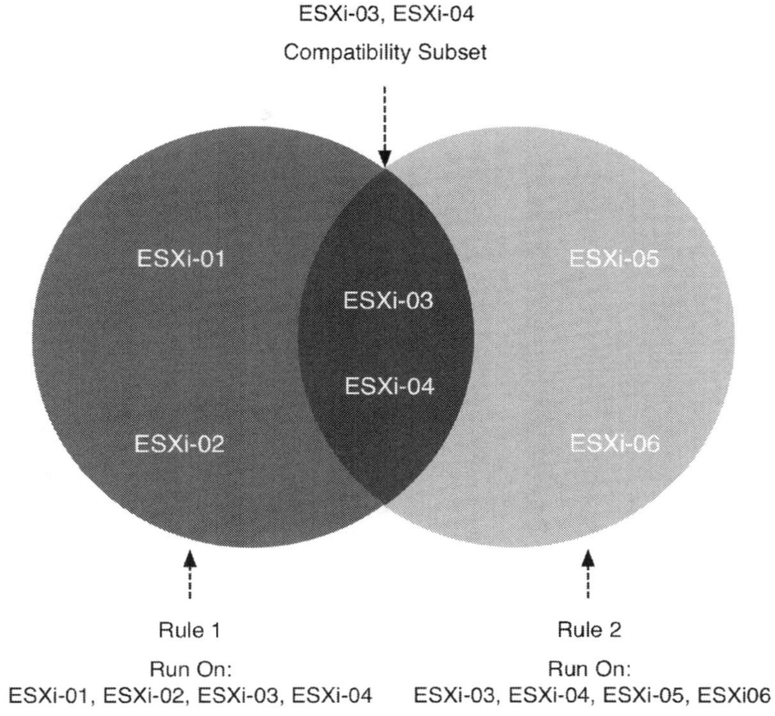

Figure 158: Compatibility Subset

Rule Behavior

Mandatory rules are obeyed, and preferential rules are executed if they do not overcommit the host or cause constraint violations. Rules impact DRS in its goal of achieving a load-balanced cluster. As you can imagine, mandatory affinity rules can complicate troubleshooting in specific scenarios. For example, trying to determine why a VM is not migrated from a highly utilized host to an alternative lightly utilized host in the cluster.

If you create a rule that conflicts with an existing rule, the old rule overrides the newer rule, and DRS disables the new rule. When creating a new rule, a message displays the conflicting rule, and the new rule is visibly disabled.

Due to their limiting behavior, mandatory rules should be used sparingly and only for specific cases, such as licensing requirements. Preferential rules can be used to méet availability requirements such as separating VM between blade enclosures, racks, or other failure domains.

> **Use VM-Host and VM-VM affinity rules sparingly, as rules can have an impact load balancing operations. The configured rules introduce constraints for load balancing.**

Backup Your Affinity Rules

Many users create rules but forget to create a backup or to document them. Anti-affinity rules can play an important role in satisfying SLA or BC/DR requirements. Using PowerCLI, the rules can easily be extracted from the vCenter database. Ben Liebowitz (@ben_liebowitz) created a nice script that exports the rules from multiple vCenters. You can find his script here: *http://www.thelowercasew.com/script-to-backup-your-vcenter-drs-rules*

VM Overrides

VM Overrides allows you to change the behavior of HA and DRS for a specific VM. VM Overrides options is available at Cluster | Configure | Configuration | VM Overrides.

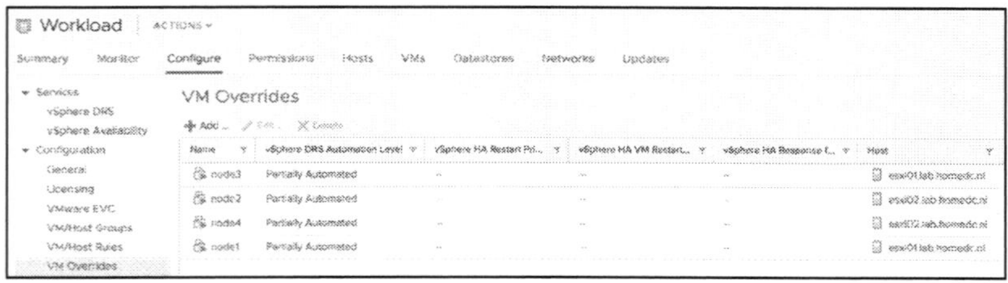

Figure 159: VM Overrides

It allows you to customize automation levels for individual VMs to override the DRS cluster automation level.

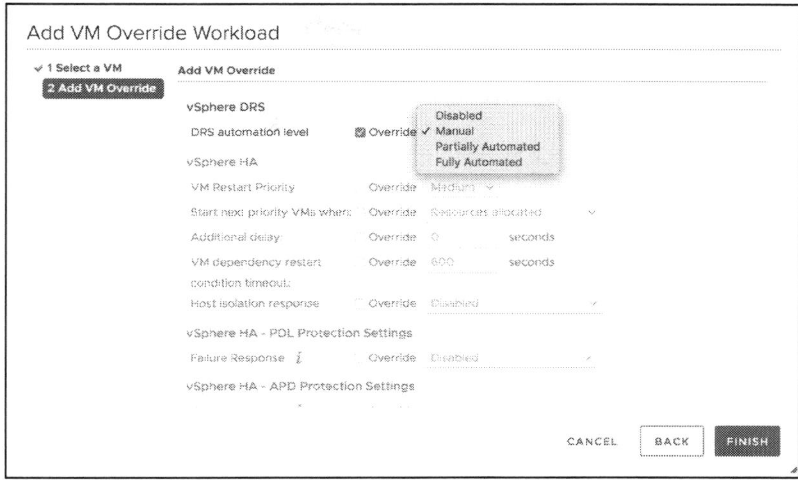

Figure 160: DRS Automation Level

There are four automation level modes:

- Disabled
- Manual
- Partially Automated
- Fully Automated

Disabled Automation Level

If you select the disabled automation level, then DRS operations are disabled for that specific VM. DRS does not generate a migration recommendation or generate an initial placement recommendation. The VM powers-on on its registered host. A powered-on VM with its automation level set to disabled impacts the DRS load balancing calculation as it consumes cluster resources.

During the recommendation calculation, DRS ignores the VMs set to disabled automation level and selects other VMs on that host.

Manual Automation Level

If you select the manual automation level, DRS generate both initial placement and load balancing migration recommendations. However, the user needs to manual approve these recommendations.

> **If you have very active VMs that you want to pin down on a single host, we recommend you to use VM-Host affinity rules instead. DRS does not consider that VM for moving as that would violate the affinity rule and thus looks for other VMs to improve the balance.**

Partially Automation Level

DRS automatically places a VM with a Partially Automated level. However, it generates a migration recommendation, which requires manual approval.

The Impact of DRS Automation Levels on Cluster Load Balance

When selecting any other automation level than disabled, you create a contract with DRS stating that you are the one executing the recommendations. As a result, DRS continues to include the VMs in the analysis of cluster balance and resource utilization. During the analysis DRS simulates VM moves inside the cluster, DRS includes every VM that is not disabled in the migration recommendations selection process.

If a particular move of a VM offers the highest benefit and the least amount of cost and lowest risk, DRS generates a migration recommendation for this move. Because DRS is limited to a specific number of migrations, it might drop a recommendation of a VM that provides almost similar goodness.

The problem with this scenario is that the recommended migration might be a VM configured with a manual automation level, while the VM with near-level goodness is configured with the default automation level. This should not matter if the user monitors each and every DRS invocation and reviews the migration recommendations when issued. It is unrealistic to expect this, as DRS runs 288 times per day.

We have seen a scenario where a group of the VMs were configured with manual mode. It resulted in a host becoming a "trap" for the VMs during an overcommitted state. The user did not monitor the DRS tab in vCenter and was missing the migration recommendations. This resulted in resource starvation for the VMs itself, but even worse, it impacted multiple VMs inside the cluster. Because DRS generated migration recommendations, it dropped other suitable moves and could not achieve an optimal balance.

Disabled versus Partially and Manual Automatic Levels

Disabling DRS on VMs has some negative impact on other operation processes or resource availability, such as placing a host into maintenance mode or powering up a VM after maintenance itself. As it selects the registered host, it might be possible that the VM is powered on a host with ample available resources while more suitable hosts are available. However disabled automation level avoids the scenario described in the previous paragraph.

Partially automatic level automatically places the VM on the most suitable host, while manual mode recommends placing the VM on the most suitable host available. Partially automated offers the least operational overhead during placement, but can together with manual automation level introduce lots of overhead during normal operations.

Risk versus Reward

Selecting an automation level is almost a risk versus reward game. Setting the automation level to disabled might impact some operation procedures, but allows DRS to neglect the VMs when generating migration recommendations and come up with alternative solutions that provide cluster balance as well. Setting the automation level to partially or manual offers you better initial placement recommendations and a more simplified maintenance mode process, but creates the risk of unbalance or resource starvation when the DRS.

16

DISTRIBUTED POWER MANAGEMENT

Distributed Power Management (DPM) Provides power savings by dynamically sizing the cluster capacity to match the VM resource demand. DPM dynamically consolidates VMs onto fewer ESXi hosts and powers down excess ESXi hosts during periods of low resource utilization. If the resource demand increases, ESXi hosts are powered back on and the VMs are redistributed among all available ESXi hosts in the cluster.

DPM is disabled by default and can be enabled by selecting the power management modes Manual or Automatic. DRS must be enabled first because of DPM's dependency on DRS for moving VMs around the cluster.

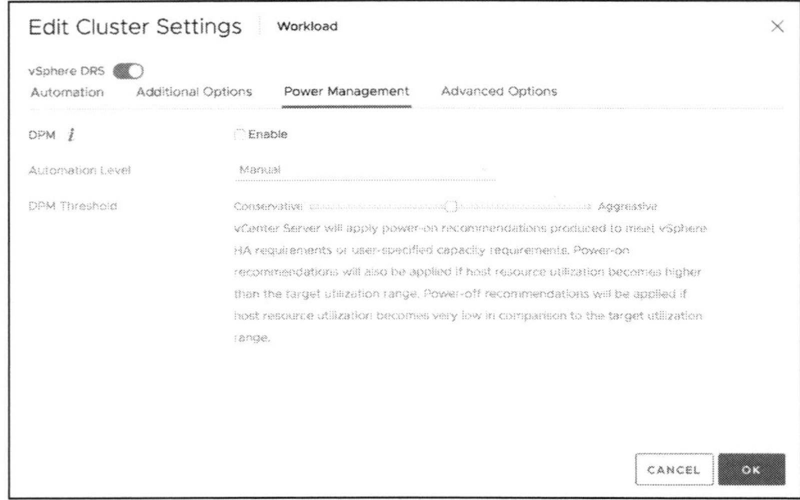

Figure 161: Enable DPM

DPM can be set to Manual or Automatic mode. All hosts inside the cluster will inherit the default cluster setting, but DPM settings can be configured on at the host-level as well. Host-level settings override the cluster default setting.

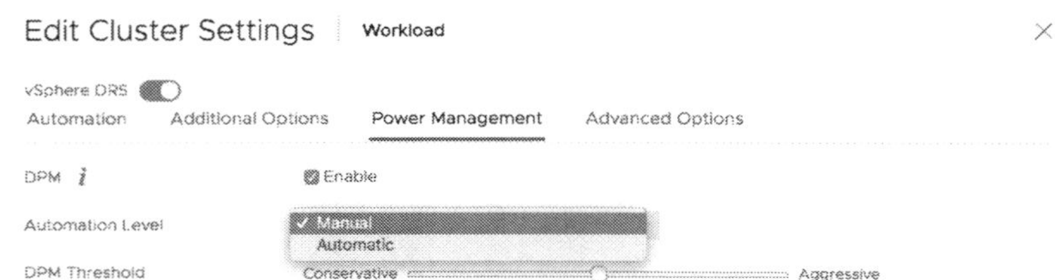

Figure 162: DPM Automation Level

DPM Host Power Management options is available at Cluster | Configure | Configuration | Host Options.

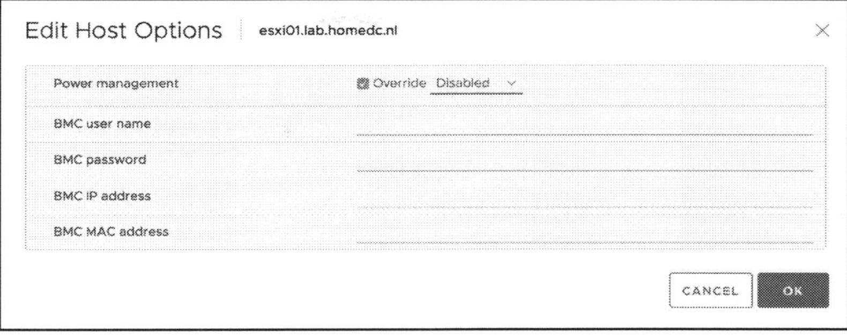

Figure 163: DPM Host Power Management Option

A reason for overriding DPM cluster default is virtual machine template placement. While DPM leverages DRS to migrate all active VMs on a host before powering it down, the registered templates are not moved. This means that templates registered on the ESXi host placed in standby mode are not accessible as long as the host is in standby mode.

Each power management mode operates differently:

AUTOMATION LEVEL	DESCRIPTION
Disabled	No power recommendation is issued
Manual	A power recommendation is generated; the user must manually confirm the recommendation
Automatic	A power recommendation is generated and is executed automatically; no user intervention required

Table 26: DPM Automation Levels

DRS and DPM management modes are distinct and can differ from each other: DRS can be set to automatic while DPM is set to manual or vice versa. Both DRS and DPM generate recommendations, and each combination of management modes results in different behavior regarding initial placement and migration recommendations or operations. Keep in mind that certain combinations, while valid, do not make much sense to implement.

DRS LEVEL	DPM LEVEL	EFFECT
Manual	Manual	Recommendations generated for placement of VMs and power-on/off hosts; manual action required to apply all recommendations
Automatic	Manual	Recommendations generated for power-on/off hosts; automatic placement of VMs
Manual	Automatic	Recommendations generated for power-on/off hosts, but user must confirm VM migrations before DPM will place ESXi host into standby mode. DPM will automatically power-up host if resources are needed
Automatic	Automatic	Fully automatic placement of virtual machines and automatic power-on/off of ESXi hosts.

Table 27: DRS and DPM Automation Levels

The goal of DPM is to keep the cluster utilization within a specific target range, but at the same time take various cluster settings, VM settings and requirements into account when generating DPM recommendations. After DPM has determined the maximum number of hosts needed to handle the resource demand and HA requirements of the VMs, it leverages DRS to distribute the VMs across that number of hosts before placing the target ESXi hosts into standby mode.

Calculating DPM Recommendations

DPM attempts to keep the resource utilization of each ESXi host in the cluster within a specified Target Resource Utilization Range, offering an optimum mix of resource availability and power savings. If the resource utilization of an ESXi host in the cluster is below the target resource utilization range, DPM evaluates and provide power-off recommendations if necessary. Conversely, if resource utilization is above the resource utilization target range, DPM provides power-on recommendation after evaluation.

Evaluating Resource Utilization

DPM evaluates each ESXi host and calculates whether the CPU and memory resource utilization of the ESXi host is within the specified target utilization range. DPM computes the target utilization range as follows:

Target Resource Utilization Range = DemandCapacityRatioTarget ± DemandCapacityRatioToleranceHost

Resource utilization: DPM calculates the resource utilization of an ESXi host based on the VM demand and the available ESXi host capacity. The available capacity of a host is the number of resources remaining after subtracting the resources required for running the virtualization layer. DPM calculates the resource demand as the sum of each active virtual machine over a historical period of interest plus two standard deviations. DPM uses different historical periods for recommending power-on recommendations than for calculating power-off recommendations.

Similar to DRS, the calculation of demand is a combination of active usage plus unsatisfied demand during periods of contention. By using historical data over a more extended period instead of using only the current demand of active virtual machines, DPM ensures that an evaluated virtual machine demand is representative of the virtual machines' normal workload behavior. Using shorter periods of time may lead to unnecessary power state change recommendations. Not only does this impact the power-saving efficiency, but it also impacts DRS as it attempts to load-balance the active VMs across a continually changing landscape of available hosts.

DemandCapacityRatioTarget is the utilization target of the ESXi host. By default, this is set at 63%.

DemandCapacityRatioToleranceHost specifies the tolerance around the utilization target for each host, by default, this is set at 18%.

DPM attempts to keep the ESXi host resource utilization centered at the 63% sweet spot, plus or minus 18%, creating a range between 45 and 81%. The sweet spot of 63% is based on in-house testing and feedback from customers. If the ESXi hosts' resource utilization of each resource is below 45%, DPM evaluates power-off operations. If the resource utilization exceeds the 81% of either CPU or memory resources, DPM evaluates power-on operations of standby ESXi hosts.

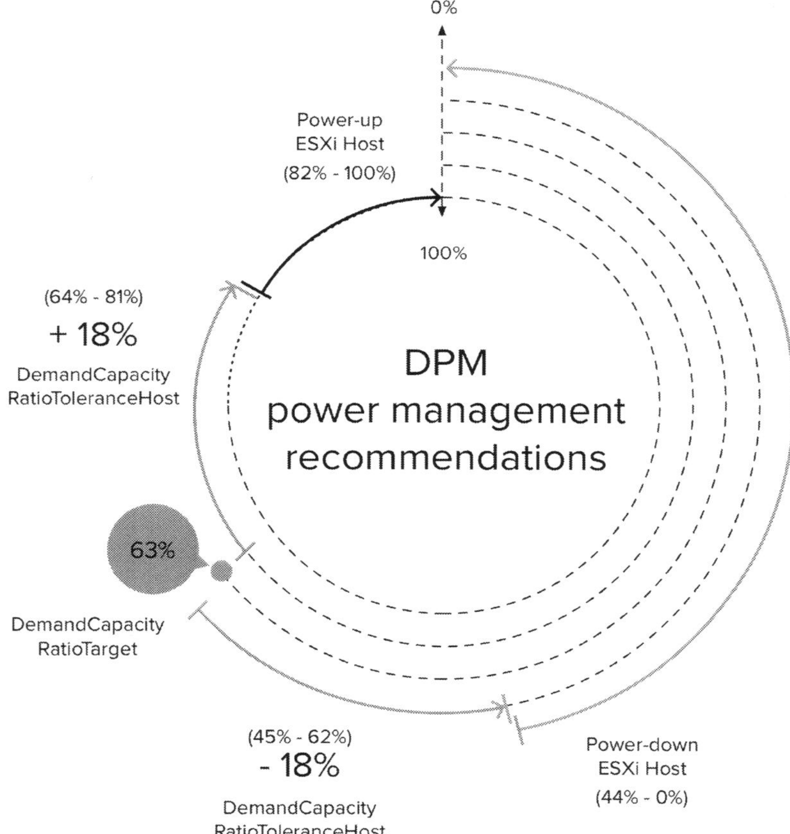

Figure 164: Power Operations Regarding to Host Utilization Levels

Advanced options

At DRS advanced options, the user can specify a different `DemandCapacityRatioTarget` and `DemandCapacityRatioToleranceHost` value.

`DemandCapacityRatioTarget` and can be set from 40% to 90%, while `DemandCapacityRatioToleranceHost` and can be set from 10% and 40%.

> **It is recommended to use the default values and to only modify the values when you fully understand the impact.**

The advanced options can be found at the DRS cluster settings. DPM Host Power Management options is available at Cluster | Configure | vSphere DRS | Edit | Advanced Options.

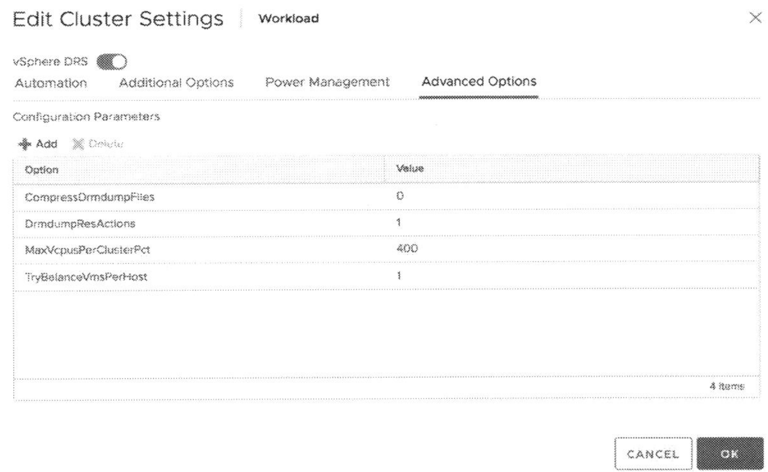

Figure 165: DRS Cluster Advanced Options

Finding a proper balance between supply and demand can be quite tricky as underestimating resource demand can result in lower performance while overestimating resource demand can lead to less optimal power savings.

Historical Period of Interest

As mentioned before, DPM determines the VM average demand by calculating the demand over a historical period of interest. DPM uses two periods of interest when calculating the average demand:

DPM uses a shorter period for evaluating power-on recommendations, allowing itself to respond to demand increases relatively quickly.

Power-on recommendations: The period of interest in evaluating VM demand for power-on operations is 300 seconds (5 minutes).

The longer period used to evaluate power-off operations ensures that DPM responds more slowly to a decrease in workload demand.

Power-off recommendations: DPM uses a longer period of evaluating resource demand for power-off operations; DPM evaluates the VM workload of the past 2400 seconds (40 minutes).

DPM must be sure that it will not negatively impact VM performance. Providing adequate resources for workload demand is considered more important by DPM than a rapid response to decreasing workloads, so performance receives a higher priority by DPM than saving power. This becomes visible when reviewing the rules of power-on and power off operation recommendations; a power-off recommendation is only applied when the ESXi host is below the specified target utilization range, AND there are no power-on recommendations active.

Evaluating Power-On and Power-Off Recommendations

If the resource utilization evaluation indicates low or high resource utilization, DPM generates power-state recommendations that reduce the distance between the current resource utilization and the target resource utilization range. In other words, optimizing and aligning the power demand to the workload demand.
Both DRS and DPM evaluate every ESXi host in the cluster for power-state recommendations. Hosts are placed in a particular order for evaluation to optimize the evaluation and selection process. Candidate host can be rejected if they violate any DRS constraint, such as affinity rules or any resource reservation.

Power-Off Recommendations

Before selecting ESXi hosts for power off operations, DPM reviews the active hosts inside the cluster and sorts them in a specific order for its power off evaluation process. If the cluster contains hosts in both DPM automatic mode and manual mode, they are placed into separate groups. Hosts inside the automatic mode group are considered before the hosts inside the manual mode group.

If the cluster contains homogeneous-sized hosts, DPM considers hosts in order of lower VM evacuation costs: hosts inside the automatic mode group with a lower number of VMs or smaller VMs are considered before heavily-loaded hosts in the same group.

If the cluster contains heterogeneous-sized hosts, DPM considers hosts in order of critical resource capacity. For power-off recommendations, smaller capacity hosts are favored over larger capacity hosts.

To generate Host Power-Off Recommendations, DPM evaluates the candidate hosts and uses DRS to run simulations in which the candidate hosts are powered off in the cluster.

These simulations are used by DPM to determine the impact of the power-off operations. DPM examines the positive gain of reducing the number of lightly loaded hosts and reducing the distance of the current utilization to the target resource utilization while minimizing the increase of utilization on the remaining hosts

To measure the amount of resource utilization under the target resource utilization range, DPM calculates a value for CPU and memory resources called cpuLowScore and memLowScore. To measure the amount of resource utilization above the target resource utilization range, DPM computes the resource HighScores called cpuHighScore and memHighScore.

The formula used for each resource is similar and calculates the weighted distance below or above the target utilization. DRS calculates the memLowScore as follows:

MemLowScore = Sum across all hosts below target utilization (target utilization – host utilization)

DPM compares the LowScore value of the cluster with all the candidate hosts' active workloads to the LowScore value of the simulations. DPM includes the critical resource state in this evaluation. If the hosts are overcommitted on memory, DPM determines that memory is the critical resource and will prioritize memory over CPU recommendations. If a simulation offers improvement of the LowScore and if the HighScore value does not increase, DPM generates a power-off recommendation. This power-off recommendation also contains VM migration recommendations for the virtual machines running on this particular host.

Rejection of Host Power-Off Recommendations

DPM does not power down a host if it violates the minimum powered-on capacity specified by the settings MinPoweredOnCpuCapacity and MinPoweredOnMemCapacity.

OPTION	DESCRIPTION
MinPoweredOnCpuCapacity	The minimum amount of powered-on CPU capacity maintained by VMware DPM
MinPoweredOnMemCapacity	The minimum amount of powered-on memory capacity maintained by VMware DPM

Table 28: DPM Advanced Options

By default, both settings have a value of 1 MHz and 1 MB respectively, which ensures that at least one host is kept powered-on. If these settings are altered, it might happen that DPM and DRS do not require all of the powered-on physical resources to run the VMs at a proper level. An ESXi host may be idle, leading to less efficient power utilization.

The CPU capacity kept powered on might not match the required CPU characteristics. If this setting is used in a cluster with different CPU configurations, enable EVC to guarantee that the available CPU resources are compatible with all VMs.

> **Enable EVC when adjusting MinPoweredOnCapacity settings with heterogeneous CPU/Memory configurations inside a cluster.**

Another reason for DPM to not select a specific candidate host is based on DRS constraints or objectives. For example, a host might be rejected for power off if the VMs that need to be migrated can only be moved to hosts that become too heavily utilized. This situation can occur when multiple DRS (anti) affinity rules are active in the cluster.

A third factor is that DPM does not select a candidate host to power down based on the negative or non-existing benefit indicated by the power-off cost/benefit analysis run by DPM. DPM continues to run simulations as long as the cluster contains ESXi hosts below the target utilization range.

DPM Power-Off Cost/Benefit Analysis

Before DPM generates a power-off recommendation, it calculates the costs associated with powering down a host. The following costs are taken into account:

- Migrating VMs off the candidate host
- Power consumed during the power-down period
- Unavailable resources of candidate host during power-down
- Loss of performance if candidate host resources are required to meet workload demand while candidate host is powered off
- Unavailability of candidate host resources during the power-up period
- The power consumed during the power-up period
- Cost of migrating VMs to the candidate host

DPM runs the power-off cost/benefit analysis that compares the costs and risks associated with a power-off operation to the benefit of powering off the host. DPM only accepts a host power-off recommendation if the benefits meet or exceed the performance impact multiplied by the PowerPerformanceRatio setting.

The default value of PowerPerformanceRatio is 40 but can be modified to a value in the range between 0 and 500. A user-specified PowerPerformanceRatio is set at the DRS advanced options interface. As always, do not change these settings unless you understand the true impact of modifying them. Both cost and benefit calculations include CPU and memory resources.

Power-Off Cost and Benefit Analysis Calculation

The power-off benefit analysis calculates the StableOffTime value, which indicates the amount of time the candidate host is expected to be powered-off until the cluster needs its resources because of an anticipated increase in VM workload.

StableOffTime = ClusterStableTime – (HostEvacuationTime + HostPowerOffTime)

The time that the VM workload is stable and no power-up operations are required is called the ClusterStableTime. DPM will use the VM stable time, calculated by the DRS cost-benefit-risk analysis, as input for the ClusterStableTime calculation.

The time it takes from applying the power-off recommendation to the power-off state is taken into account as well. The analysis breaks this time down into two sections and calculates this as the sum of the time it takes to migrate all active VMs off the host (HostEvacuationTime), and the time it takes to power off the host (HostPowerOffTime).

The power-off cost is calculated as the summation of the following estimated resource costs:

- Migration of the active VMs running on the candidate host to other ESXi hosts
- Unsatisfied VM resource demand during power-on candidate host at the end of the ClusterStableTime
- Migration of VMs back onto the candidate host

DPM can only estimate the last two bullet points; DPM calculates the number of hosts required to be available at the end of the ClusterStableTime. This calculation is, to some extent, a worst-case scenario as DPM expects all the VMs to generate heavy workloads at the end of the ClusterStableTime, as a result of this generating a conservative value.

As previously mentioned, DPM only recommends a power-off operation if there is a significant gain in resource utilization efficiency. It might be possible that the ClusterStableTime is low, and this can result in a StableOffTime equal to or even less than zero. During this scenario, DPM stops evaluating the candidate host for a power-off operation recommendation because it does not offer any benefit.

Power-On Recommendations

Host Selection for Power-On Recommendations

Similar to power-off recommendations, ESXi hosts in automatic mode are evaluated before ESXi hosts in manual mode for power-on recommendations. In a cluster containing heterogeneous-sized hosts, the ESXi hosts with a larger capacity with regards to the critical resources are favored.

If the sort process discovers equal hosts concerning the capacity or evacuation cost, DPM randomizes the order of hosts, done for a wear-leveling effect. Be aware that sorting of the hosts for power-on or power-off recommendations does not determine the actual order for the selection process to power-on or power-off hosts.

Host Power-On Recommendations

If the resource utilization evaluation indicates a host with high utilization inside the cluster, DPM considers generating host power-on recommendations.

Before selecting an ESXi host for power on, DPM reviews the standby hosts inside the cluster and sorts them in a specific order for DPM power on evaluation process.

DPM continues by evaluating each standby host and invokes DRS to run simulations. The simulations distribute current VMs across all hosts regardless if they are active or standby. By using the HighScore calculation, DPM determines the impact of a power-up operation on the current utilization ratio. It needs to determine how much improvement each power-up operation has on the distance of the resource utilization from the target utilization or the possible reduction of the number of highly utilized hosts. DPM compares the HighScore value of the cluster in its current state (standby host still down) to the HighScore value of the simulations. If a simulation offers an improved HighScore value when a standby host is powered-on, DPM generates a power-on recommendation for that specific host.

DPM does not strictly adhere to its host sort order if doing so would lead to choosing a host with capacity far more significant than needed if a smaller capacity host that can adequately handle the demand is also available. Sometimes a host is not selected if DPM expects that the candidate cannot offer the simulated load-reduction.

For example, if it is not possible to migrate specific virtual machines to the candidate due to vMotion incompatibility, the simulated reduction may not be achievable.

DPM continues to run simulations as long as there are hosts in the cluster exceeding the target utilization range. DPM is very efficient in homogeneous-sized clusters as DPM skips every host that is identical regarding physical resources or vMotion compatibility to any host who is already rejected for power-on operation during the simulation.

> **Use homogeneous clusters, as DPM operates more efficiently.**

Impact of Advanced Settings on Host Power-On Recommendations

Advanced options can be set to specify a particular minimum amount of CPU or memory capacity is kept powered on regardless of DPM recommendations.

If the user sets a custom value in the advanced settings, `MinPoweredOnCpuCapacity` and `MinPoweredOnMemCapacity`, DPM needs to adjust its power-on operation recommendations to fulfill the requirements defined in these settings.

Contrary to a power-off recommendation, redistribution of VMs among the powered-on hosts is not included in a power-on recommendation. To satisfy that need, DPM relies on future invocation rounds of DRS.

Recommendation Classifications

The DPM threshold slider works similarly to the DRS slider. Like DRS, threshold options range from conservative to aggressive. DPM recommendation priority levels can be compared to the DRS priority levels.

The aggressive level of DPM corresponds with the aggressive level of DRS in that it generates DPM recommendations up to priority 5. Similarly, the conservative level of DPM corresponds with the conservative level of DRS: selecting the conservative level threshold causes DPM to generate priority level 1 recommendations only. The following warning is displayed below the threshold slider when the conservative DPM level is selected:

> **Apply only priority 1 recommendations. vCenter applies power-on recommendations produced to meet HA requirements or user-specified capacity requirements. DPM will only automatically apply the power-on recommendations.**

In this scenario, DPM does not generate power-off recommendations; this effectively means that the automatic DPM power saving mode is disabled. The user can place the server in the standby mode manually, but DPM will only power-on ESXi hosts when the cluster fails to meet specific HA or custom capacity requirements or constraints.

Priority Levels

The power-off and power-on recommendations are assigned priorities ranging from priority one-recommendations to priority-five recommendations.

Priority level ratings are based on the resource utilization of the cluster and the improvement that is expected from the suggested host power state recommendation. It may be interesting to note that different ranges are applied to power-on recommendations than power-off recommendations: power-off recommendations can range from priority 2 to priority 5 while power-on recommendations range from priority 1 to priority 3.

PRIORITY LEVEL	POWER-OFF RECOMMENDATION	POWER-ON RECOMMENDATION
1		X
2	X	X
3	X	X
4	X	
5	X	

Table 29: Priority Levels Range of Power State Recommendations

Power-Off Recommendations

Recommendations with higher priority levels results in more power-savings if the recommendations are applied. The highest power-off priority level 2 results in the most significant reduction of excess capacity headroom, while applying a priority level 5 power-off recommendation results in a modest reduction in excess capacity headroom. Priority level 1 recommendations are not generated for power-off recommendations as providing adequate resources for workload demand is considered more important by DPM than rapid response to decreasing workloads.

Power-On Recommendations

A priority level 1 is generated when conforming to vSphere High Availability requirements or powered-on capacity requirements set by the user. Power-on priority level 2 indicates a more urgent recommendation to solve higher host utilization saturation levels than priority level 3.

Be aware that the generated migration recommendations are not mandatory. If DRS is set to the conservative migration threshold, these migration recommendations are ignored and effectively disables DPM.

> **Do not set DRS to the conservative migration threshold if DPM is required.**

Guiding DPM Recommendations

DPM Standby Mode

The term "Standby mode" used by DPM specifies a powered down ESXi host. The term is used to indicate that the ESXi host is available to be powered on should the cluster require its resources. DPM requires the Host to be able to awake from an ACPI S5 state via Wake-On-LAN (WOL) packets or one of the two supported out-of-band methods: Intelligent Platform Management Interface (IPMI) version 1.5 or HP Integrated Lights-Out (iLO) technology. Both IPMI and iLO require the availability of a Baseboard Management Controller (BMC) providing access to hardware control functions and allowing the server hardware to be accessed from the vCenter server using a LAN connection. To use WOL, the ESXi host must contain a Network Interface Card that supports the WOL protocol. If the host does not offer the hardware support and configurations of any of these protocols, it cannot be placed into standby mode by DPM.

DPM WOL Magic Packet

If the ESXi host is not an HP server supporting iLO, does not support IPMI version 1.5, or if the appropriate credentials for using iLO or IPMI have not been configured and set up in vCenter, DPM uses Wake-On-LAN Packets to bring the ESXi host out of standby mode. The "magic packet," the network packet used to bring the server back to life, is sent over the vMotion network by another currently powered on ESXi server in the cluster. For this reason, DPM keeps at least one host powered on in the cluster at all times, managed by the DPM advanced controls, MinPoweredOnCpuCapacity and MinPoweredOnMemCapacity, both configured with the respective default values of 1 MHz and 1 MB. Because the magic packet is sent across the vMotion network to a powered-off server, DPM impacts the configuration of the vMotion network as well. Because most NICs support WOL only if they can switch to 100 Mb/s, the switch port used by the vMotion NIC must be set to auto-negotiate link speed instead of setting the port to a fixed speed/duplex such as 1000 Mb/s Full. Industry best practices advise setting both NIC and switch ports to identical settings, so ensure that vmknic speed is set to auto-negotiate as well.

Baseboard Management Controller

If both a BMC wake method (IPMI or iLO) and WOL are present and both are operational, DPM attempts to use a BMC wake method as default. To ensure IPMI is operational, configure the BMC over LAN channel to always be available, some BMC LAN channels require the availability to send operator-privileged commands. Some BMC boards require IPMI accounts set in the BIOS.

DPM uses MD5- or plaintext-based authentication with IPMI. If the BMC reports that it supports MD5 and has the operator role enabled, only then vCenter uses MD5 authentication. vCenter switches to plaintext authentication if none or only one requirement is met. If neither MD5 nor plaintext is enabled or supported, vCenter does not use IPMI and attempts to use Wake-On-LAN.

Protocol Selection Order

1. If the server is configured for IPMI or iLO, DPM uses the protocols in the order IPMI, iLO and then WOL.
2. If vCenter is unable to successfully power on the ESXi host with the IPMI, it uses the second protocol, iLO.
3. If this attempt fails, DPM tries to power on using the Wake-On-LAN and instructs a powered-on ESXi host to send the magic packet.

It is essential to understand that placing the ESXi host into standby mode does not use any power management protocols; vCenter initiates a graceful shutdown of the ESXi host.

P3

VSPHERE STORAGE DRS

17

INTRODUCTION TO VSPHERE STORAGE DRS

Storage DRS resolves some of the operational challenges associated with VM provisioning, migration and cloning. Historically, monitoring datastore capacity and I/O load have proven to be very difficult. As a result, it is often neglected, leading to hot spots and over- or underutilized datastores. *Storage I/O Control* (SIOC) solves part of this problem, by providing a datastore-wide disk-scheduler that allows for proportional allocation of I/O resources to VMs based on their respective shares during times of contention.

Storage DRS brings this to a whole new level by providing smart virtual machine placement and load balancing mechanisms based on both space and I/O capacity. In other words, where SIOC reactively throttles hosts and VMs to ensure fairness. SDRS proactively generates recommendations preventing imbalances from both space utilization and latency perspectives. There are five key features that Storage DRS offers:

- Resource aggregation
- Initial Placement
- Load Balancing
- Datastore Maintenance Mode
- Affinity Rules

Resource Aggregation

Resource aggregation is the critical component that all other Storage DRS features depend on. Resource aggregation enables grouping of multiple datastores into a single, flexible pool of storage called a datastore cluster.

A datastore cluster is a construct that provides access to Storage DRS functionality. The datastore cluster separates the physical from the logical. It dramatically simplifies storage management by allowing adding and removing datastores dynamically from the cluster. In turn, this allows you to deal with maintenance, performance or out of space conditions more quickly and efficiently. The Storage DRS load balancer provides automatic initial placement of VM disk files and economical use of datastores.

Initial Placement

The goal of initial placement is to place *virtual machine disk files* (VMDK) based on the existing load on the datastores, ensuring that neither space nor the I/O capacity is exhausted prematurely.

Initial placement provides a more straightforward provisioning process by automating the selection of an individual datastore and leaving the user with the much smaller-scale decision of selecting a datastore cluster. Storage DRS selects a particular datastore within a datastore cluster based on actual space utilization and I/O capacity.

In an environment with multiple seemingly identical datastores, initial placement can be a time-consuming and challenging task for the administrator. In many environments, the standard practice is to find a datastore with the most free space and use that one. This is not always the best choice. Not only does a datastore with adequate available disk space need to be identified, but it is also crucial to ensure that the introduction of this new VM does not result in I/O bottlenecks.

Storage DRS takes care of all of this and substantially reduces the amount of operational effort required to provision VMs; that is the actual value of Storage DRS.

Load Balancing

Storage DRS can operate in two distinct load-balancing modes: No Automation (manual mode) or Fully Automated. Where initial placement reduces complexity in the provisioning process, load balancing addresses imbalances within a datastore cluster. Before Storage DRS, placement of VMs was often based on current space consumption or the number of VMs on each datastore. I/O capacity monitoring and space utilization trending are often regarded as too time-consuming. Over the years, we have seen this lead to performance problems in many environments, and in some cases, even result in downtime because a datastore ran out of space.

Storage DRS load balancing helps prevent these unfortunately common scenarios by generating placement recommendations based on both space utilization and I/O capacity. The load balance process is initiated periodically, by default every 8 hours. Placement recommendations are generated if the space utilization or I/O latency of a datastore exceeds the thresholds configured at the datastore cluster level. Depending on the selected automation level, these recommendations will be automatically applied by Storage DRS or will be presented to the administrator who then can decide to apply them manually.

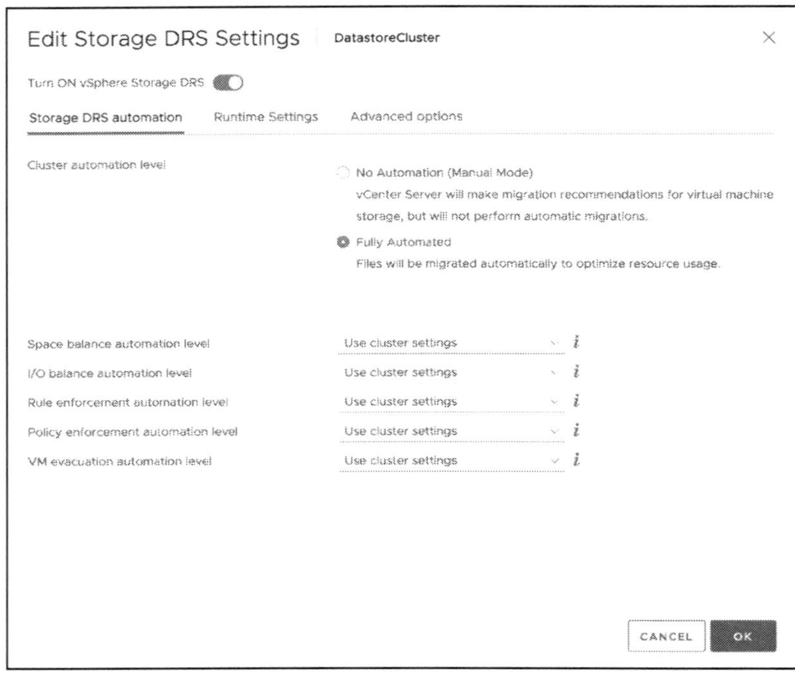

Figure 166: Storage DRS Automation Level

Although we see load balancing as a single feature of Storage DRS, it consists of two separately configurable options. When either of the configured thresholds for utilized space or I/O latency is exceeded, Storage DRS makes recommendations to resolve the imbalance within the datastore cluster. In the case of I/O capacity load balancing, monitoring can be explicitly disabled.

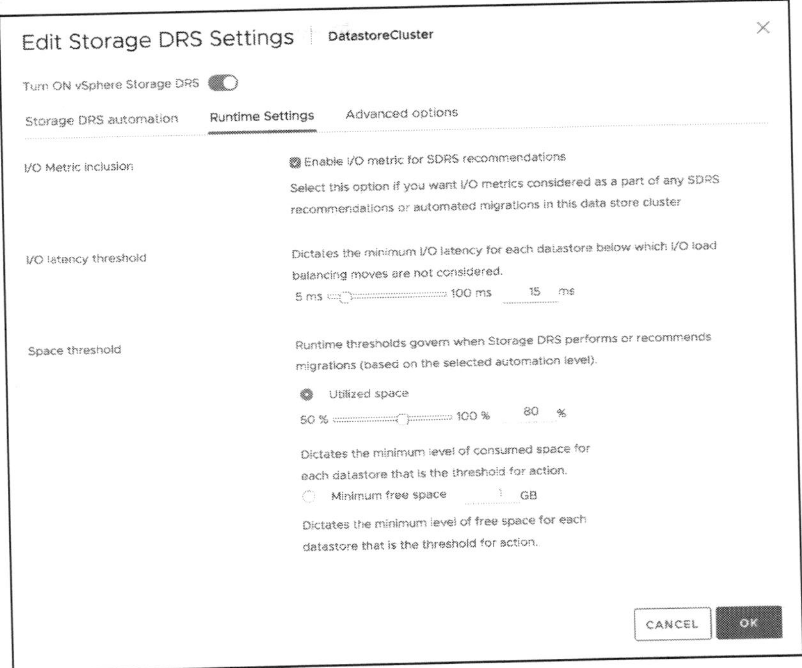

Figure 167: I/O Metric for Storage DRS Recommendations

Storage DRS functionality can be enabled on fully populated datastores and environments without downtime. It is also possible to add fully populated datastores to existing datastore clusters. It is a great way to solve actual or potential bottlenecks in any environment with minimal required effort or risk.

Affinity Rules

Affinity Rules enable control over which VMDKs should or should not be placed on the same datastore within a datastore cluster following your best practices and availability requirements. By default, all of a virtual machine's VMDKs are kept together on the same datastore.

Datastore Maintenance Mode

Datastore maintenance mode can be compared to host maintenance mode: when a datastore is placed in maintenance mode, all registered VMDKs on that datastore are migrated to the other datastores in the datastore cluster. Typical use cases are data migration to a new storage array or maintenance on a LUN, such as migration to another RAID group.

Requirements

For Storage DRS to function correctly, the environment must meet the following requirements:

- VMware vCenter Server 5.0 or later
- VMware vSphere ESXi 5.0 or later
- VMware vCenter Cluster (recommended)
- VMware vSphere Enterprise Plus license
- Shared VMFS or NFS datastore volumes
- Shared datastore volumes accessible by at least one ESXi host inside the cluster*
- Datastores must be visible in only one data center

* Full cluster connectivity is recommended, however, this is not enforced.

18

STORAGE DRS INITIAL PLACEMENT

Storage DRS can automate the initial placement of a VM to avoid disk space imbalances and I/O hotspots on the datastores. By providing automatic datastore selection, Storage DRS initial placement minimizes the risk of over-provisioning a datastore, creating I/O bottlenecks or negatively impacting performance of the VMs.

User Interaction

Initial placement speeds up the process for the user by automating the datastore selection. Datastores used in a datastore cluster are by default not visible when selecting a datastore during the VM creation process; only datastore clusters or "unclustered" datastores are available for selection.

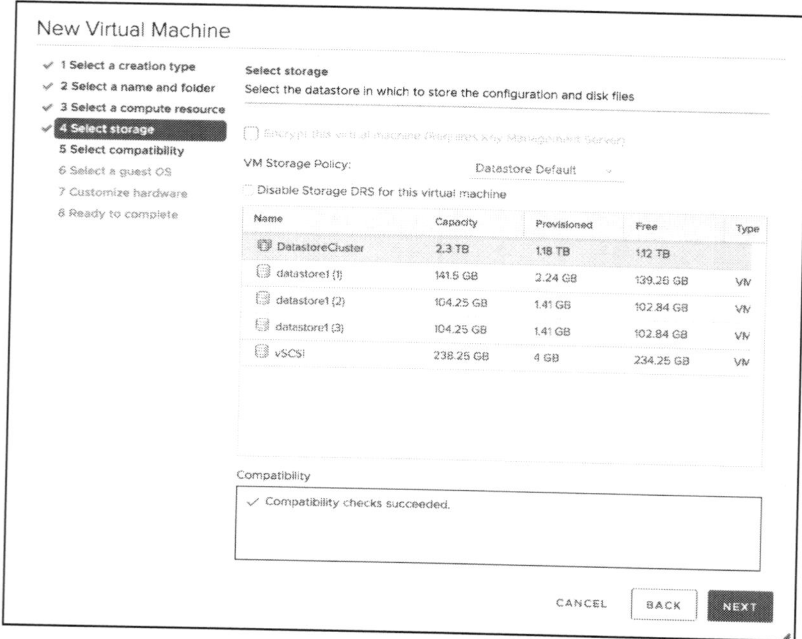

Figure 168: Selecting Storage During VM Creation Process

Affinity Rules

By default, Storage DRS place a VM and its VMDKs on datastore(s) within a datastore cluster according to the datastore cluster affinity rules. VMDK affinity rule is the default setting for the datastore cluster.

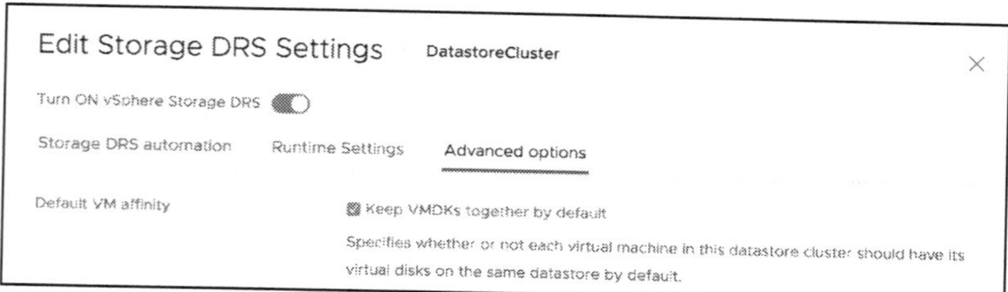

Figure 169: Default VM Affinity Rule

The default can be changed, from affinity to anti-affinity by deselecting the option box. Please note that the new standard rule only applies to newly created VMs.

Cluster Automation Level

Datastore clusters can be configured either with manual load balancing or automatic load balancing. There is no partially automated mode available in Storage DRS. Automated initial placement is excluded in both modes: Storage DRS generates an Initial placement recommendation that always requires a manual confirmation.

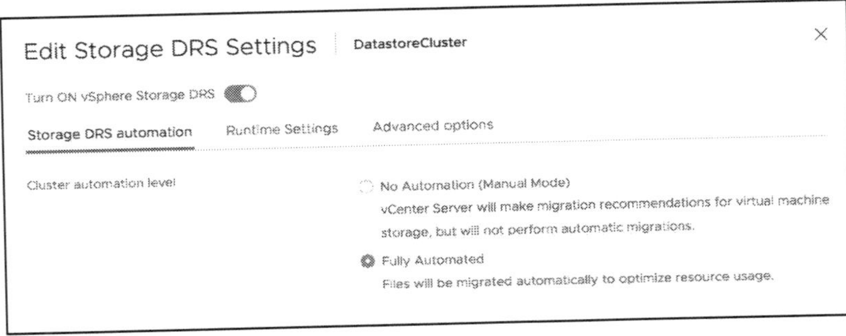

Figure 170: Cluster Automation Level

DRS Mobility and Datastore Connection

When connecting a datastore cluster to a DRS cluster, Storage DRS is in charge of VM placement. It is responsible for VM placement on compute and storage level. Storage DRS checks the datastore connectivity of all hosts within the DRS cluster to ensure that the VMs have the highest mobility on both host and datastore levels.

Storage DRS prefers datastores that are connected to all hosts of a DRS cluster (fully connected), before considering datastores that are connected to a subset of hosts within the DRS cluster (partially connected).

If a VM is placed on a partially connected datastore, it impacts the compute mobility perspective (DRS) of the VM. DRS can only move the VM to hosts that are connected to that particular datastore.

Space and I/O Load Consideration

When selecting a datastore, initial placement takes both DRS and Storage DRS threshold metrics into account. It selects the host with the least utilization and the highest connectivity to place the VM.

For datastores, Storage DRS takes the utilization of the datastores of the datastore cluster into account and combines space and IO metrics using a dynamic weighting.

If space is running low, it attempts to balance the space more than I/O (and vice versa). If neither resources are constrained the weight of both metrics is the same. For example, if the available datastores are close to the space utilization threshold, the weight of the space metric becomes higher, and it is more likely that initial placement is based on space balancing.

Space Utilization Threshold

During initial placement, Storage DRS checks the total amount of free space at datastore cluster level and datastore level. When placing VMs, Storage DRS avoids violating the space utilization threshold. It is essential to understand that the space utilization threshold set on a datastore cluster applies to each datastore separately, not to the collective whole of the datastore cluster. This means that each datastore has a buffer space which initial placement tries to avoid using.

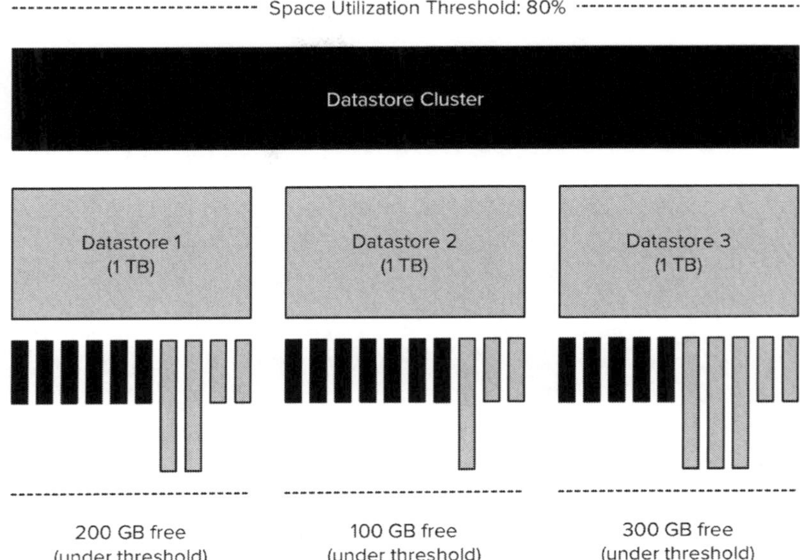

Figure 171: Datastore Space Utilization Threshold

Setting the space utilization threshold to 80% on a datastore cluster containing a single 1 TB datastore allows Storage DRS to place VMs that consume space up to 800 GB. In this scenario, 600 GB of the Datastore 1 is used. As a result, Storage DRS considers this datastore to have 200 GB free. The placement of a VM bigger than 200 GB violates the threshold. If all the datastores are at or above the threshold, initial placement proceeds if there is a datastore that can fit the incoming VM. For example, if there is an incoming VM of 150 GB, and all the other datastores have also exceeded the space threshold, then this VM can be placed at Datastore 1.

Datastore Cluster Defragmentation

Storage DRS considers both free space at datastore and datastore cluster levels. If enough free space is available in the datastore cluster but not enough space is available per datastore, the datastore cluster is considered fragmented. During this state, Storage DRS migrates existing VMs from one or more datastores to free up space if it cannot place the new VM on any datastore.

Depth of Recursion

Storage DRS uses a recursive algorithm for searching alternative placement combinations. To keep Storage DRS from trying an extremely high number of combinations of VM migrations, the "depth of recursion" is limited to 2 steps. What defines a step and what counts towards a step? A step can be best defined as a set of migrations out of a datastore in preparation for (or to make room for) another migration or placement into that same datastore. A step can contain migration of one VMDK, but can also contain migrations of multiple VMs with multiple VMDKs attached. In some cases, free space must be created on that target datastore by moving a VM out to another datastore, which results in an extra step. The following diagram visualizes the process.

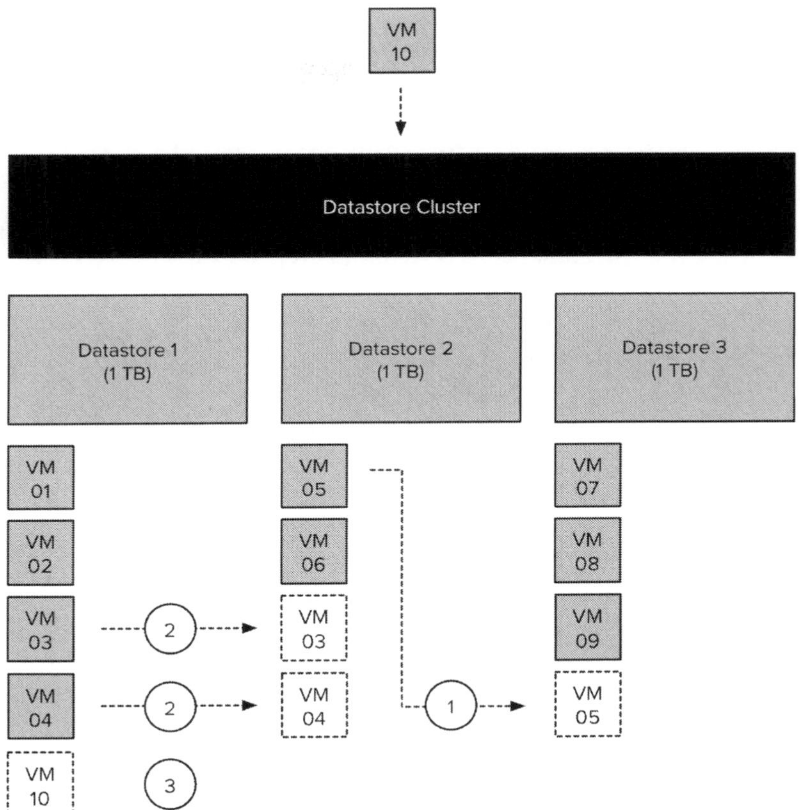

Figure 172: Depth of Recursion

Storage DRS has calculated that a new VM, VM10, can be placed on Datastore 1 if VM3 and VM4 are migrated to Datastore 2, however, placing these two VMs on Datastore 2 violates the space utilization. Therefore room must be created. As a result, VM5 is moved out of Datastore 2 as part of a step of creating space. This results in Step 1, moving VM5 out to Datastore 3, followed by Step 2, moving VM3 and VM4 to Datastore 2, and finally placing the new VM on Datastore 1.

Storage DRS stops its search if there are no 2-step moves to satisfy the storage requirement of initial placement. An advanced setting can be set to change the number of steps used by the search. As always, changing the defaults is strongly discouraged since many hours of testing has been invested in researching the setting that offers excellent performance while minimizing the impact of the operation. If you have a strong case for changing the number of steps, set the Storage DRS advanced configuration option `MaxRecursionDepth`. The default value is 1 the maximum value is 5. Because the algorithm starts counting at 0, the default value of 1 allows 2 steps. Please note that this is a per-Datastore Cluster option.

Goodness Value

Storage DRS reviews all datastores in the datastore cluster and initiates a search for space on each datastore. A search generates a set of prerequisite migrations if it can provide space that allows the VM placement within the depth of recursion. Storage DRS evaluates the generated sets and awards each set a goodness value. The set with the least amount of cost (i.e., migrations) is the preferred migration recommendation and shows at the top of the list.

Scenario

The datastore cluster contains 3 datastores; each datastore has a size of 1000 GB and contains multiple VMs with various sizes. The space consumed on the datastores range from 550 GB to 650 GB, while the space utilization threshold is set to 80%. Datastore 1 has 150 GB of free space before hitting the threshold (*T*). Datastore 2 has 250 GB and Datastore 3 has 225 GB of free space below the threshold.

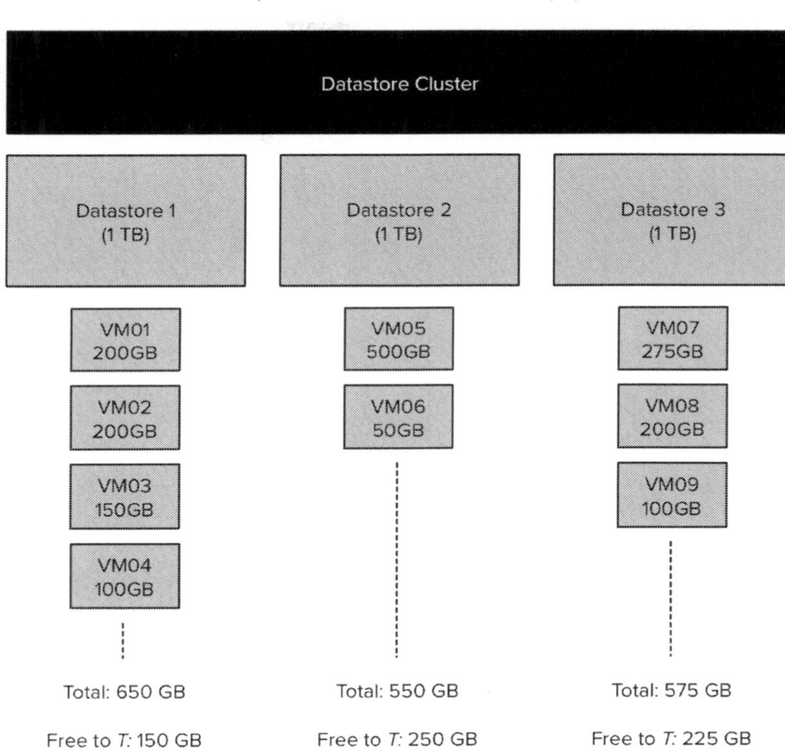

Figure 173: Space Utilization Datastore Cluster Prior to Initial Placement

At this point, the administrator creates VM10 that requests 350 GB of space. Although the datastore cluster itself contains 1225 GB of free space, Storage DRS avoids placing the VM "as is" on any of the three datastores because placing the VM without taking precautionary actions would violate the space utilization threshold of the datastores.

As each ESXi host provides information about the overall datastore utilization and the VMDK statistics, Storage DRS has a clear view of the most up to date situation and uses these statistics as input for its search.

In the first step, it simulates all the necessary migrations to fit VM10 in Datastore 1. The prerequisite migration process with least number of migrations to fit the virtual machine on to Datastore 1 looks as follows:

- Step 1: VM03 from Datastore 1 to Datastore 2
- Step 1: VM04 from Datastore 1 to Datastore 3
- Place VM10 on Datastore 1

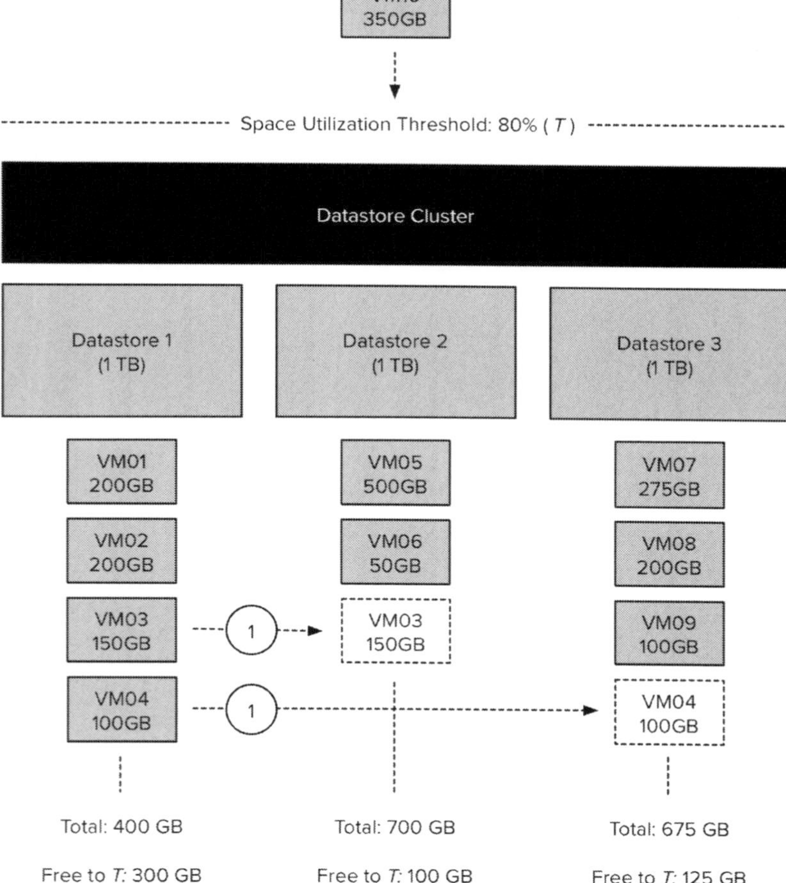

Figure 174: Datastore 1 Simulation Prerequisites Migrations

Although VM03 and VM04 are each moved out to a different datastore, both migrations are counted as a one-step prerequisite migration because both VMs migrate out of a SINGLE datastore (Datastore 1).

In a new simulation, Storage DRS evaluates Datastore 2. Due to the size of VM05, Storage DRS is unable to migrate VM05 out of Datastore 2 because it immediately violates the utilization threshold of any selected destination datastore.

One of the coolest parts of the algorithm is that it considers inbound migrations as valid moves. In this scenario, migrating VMs into Datastore 2 would free up space on another datastore to provide enough free space to place VM05, which in turn frees up enough space on Datastore 2 to allow Storage DRS to place VM10 onto Datastore 2.

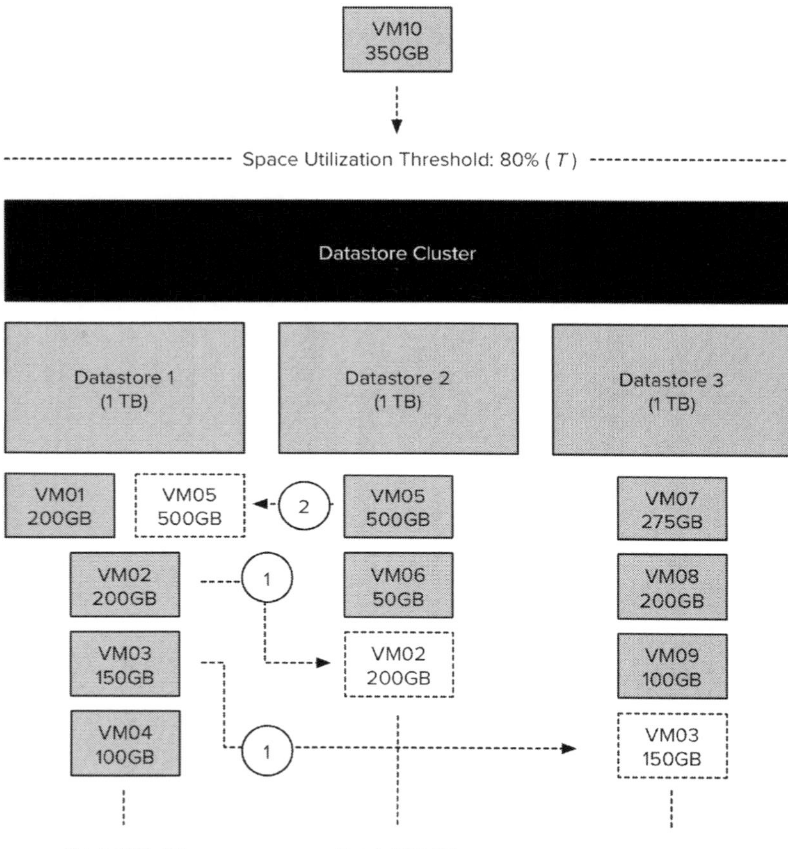

Figure 175: Datastore 2 Simulation Prerequisite Migrations

The prerequisite migration process with least number of migrations to fit the VM on Datastore2 looks as follows:

- Step 1: VM02 from Datastore 1 to Datastore 2
- Step 1: VM03 from Datastore 1 to Datastore 3
- Step 2: VM05 from Datastore 2 to Datastore 1
- Place VM10 on Datastore 2

The analysis of Datastore 3 generates a single prerequisite migration. Migrating VM08 from Datastore 3 to Datastore 2 will free up enough space to allow placement of VM10. Selecting VM09 would not free up enough space and migrating VM07 generates more cost than migrating VM08. By default, Storage DRS attempts to migrate the VMDK(s) with a size that is closest to the required space.

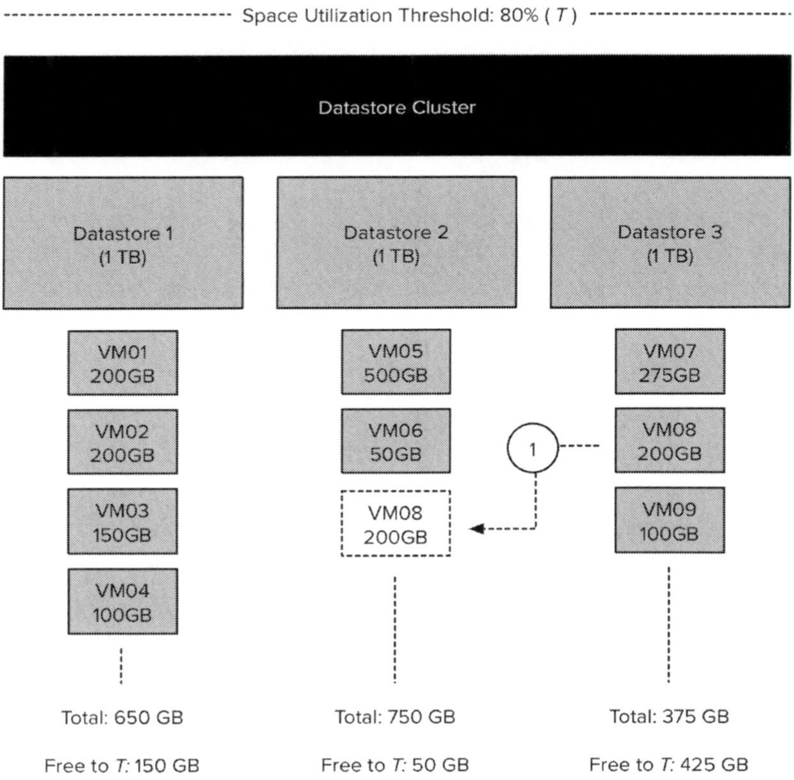

Figure 176: Datastore 3 Simulation Prerequisite Migrations

The prerequisite migration process with least number of migrations to fit the VM on to Datastore 3 looks as follows:

- Step 1: VM08 from Datastore 3 to Datastore 2
- Place VM10 on Datastore 3

After analyzing the cost and benefit of the three search results, Storage DRS assigns the highest goodness factor to the migration set of Datastore 3. Although each search result can provide enough free space after moves, the recommendation set of Datastore 3 results in the least number of moves and migrates the smallest amount of data. All three results are shown; the most highly recommended set is placed at the top.

A placement recommendation screen is displayed. Note that you can apply only the complete recommendation set and that applying the recommendation triggers the prerequisite migrations before the initial placement of the VM occurs.

Adding a New Disk to an Existing VM in a Datastore Cluster

When adding a new disk, Storage DRS triggers the initial placement process for that disk. Storage DRS reviews the configured affinity rule of the VM. Storage DRS never can violate the affinity or anti-affinity rule of the VM. For example, if the datastore cluster default affinity rule is set to "keep VMDKs together" then all the files are placed on the same datastore. Therefore, if you add a new disk to the VM, that disk must be stored on the same datastore in order not to violate the affinity rule.

Storage DRS will defragment the datastore cluster if individual datastores do not have enough free space below the threshold. Therefore in a datastore cluster, you will never see Storage DRS splitting up a VM if it's configured with an affinity rule, but you will see pre-requisite moves, migrating VMs out of the datastore to make room for the new VMDK.

Manually Migrating VMs within the Datastore Cluster

If a VM is placed inside the datastore cluster, you cannot easily migrate the VM to another datastore. When selecting a storage migration, the datastore destination in the select storage window shows the datastore cluster as the destination.

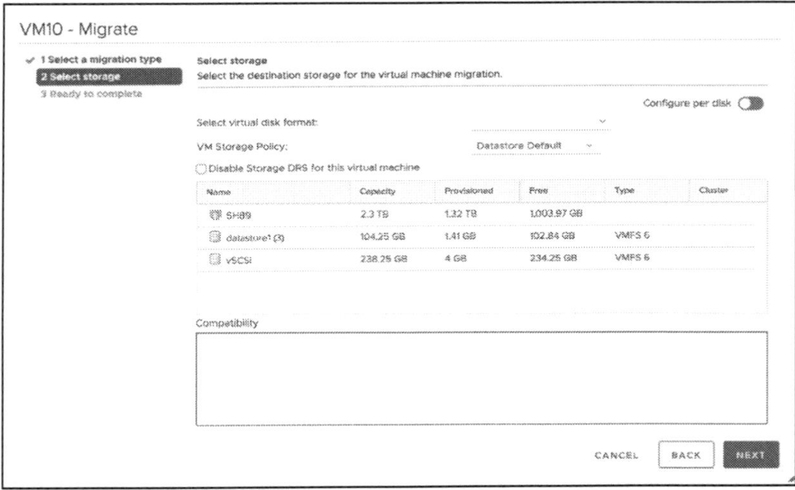

Figure 177: Datastore Cluster as Destination

Until you activate the "Disable Storage DRS for this virtual machine", the window will show you the individual datastores within the datastore cluster. It nicely orders the datastores based on their compatibility with the storage profile that is attached to the VM (chapter 21 covers storage profiles).

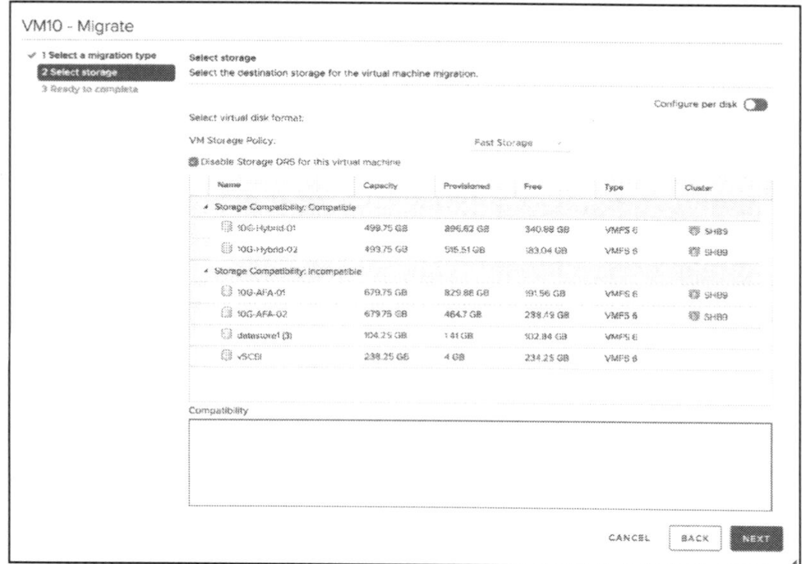

Figure 178: Disable Storage DRS Reveals Individual Datastores

Why must you disable automation for this VM when migrating between datastores inside a datastore cluster or when selecting a datastore during placement of a new VM?

It is all about intent. When migrating a VM into a datastore cluster, you are migrating the VM into a load-balancing domain (the datastore cluster). You trust Storage DRS to provide you an environment that provides an optimum load balanced state where the VMs receive the overall best I/O performance and the optimal placement regarding space utilization.

If the user wants to migrate the VM to a different datastore inside the datastore cluster, Storage DRS is capturing this intent, as "user knows best". The way this is designed is that if a datastore is selected, then user is telling us that the selected datastore is the best, i.e., user knows something Storage DRS doesn't. And to prohibit any future migration recommendation to other datastores, Storage DRS is disabled to ensure permanent placement.

This behavior also applies when migrating a virtual machine into a datastore cluster. During initial placement it is expected that the user selects the datastore cluster, if the user wants to select a specific datastore it has to select "Disable Storage DRS for this virtual machine" in order to be able to select a member datastore.

During the initial placement operation, Storage DRS runs a simulation to understand the impact of the VM placement. During this simulation, Storage DRS retrieves the current datastore free space values.

Storage DRS uses this "snapshot" of free space during this simulation. The snapshot works perfectly for a single VM as the begin state of the operation is the actual state of the datastore cluster. But what if you want to deploy multiple VMs in one transaction? The datastore utilization changes after placing the first VM, but all following VM placement is now done with an incorrect view of the datastore cluster utilization state. Let's use an example that explains this behavior.

In this scenario the datastore cluster contains three datastores, the size of each datastore is 1 TB, no VMs are deployed yet, and therefore they each report a 100% free space. When deploying a 500 GB VM, storage DRS selects the datastore with the highest reported number of free space, and as all three datastores are equal, it will pick the first datastore, Datastore 1. Until the deployment process is complete, the datastore remains to report 1000 GB of free space.

When deploying a single VM, this behavior is not a problem. However, when deploying multiple VMs, this might result in an unbalanced distribution of virtual machine across the datastores.

To solve this problem Storage DRS (since 5.1) applies a storage lease when deploying VMs on a datastore. This lease "reserves" the space and making deployments aware of each other, thus avoiding suboptimal/invalid placement recommendations.

The same datastore cluster configuration is used, each datastore if empty, reporting 1000 GB free space. Three virtual machines, VM01,

VM02, and VM03, are deployed. Respectively they are 100 GB, 200 GB and 400 GB in size. During the provisioning process, Storage DRS selects a datastore for each VM. As the main goal of Storage DRS is to balance the utilization of the datastore cluster, it determines which datastore has the highest free space value after each placement during the simulation.

During the simulation, VM01 is placed on Datastore 1, as all three datastores report an equal value of free space. Storage DRS then applies the lease of 100 GB and reduces the available free space to 900 GB.

When Storage DRS simulates the placement of VM02, it checks the free space and determines that Datastore 2 and Datastore 3 each have 1000 GB of free space. Datastore 1 reports 900 GB. Although VM02 can be placed on Datastore 1 as it does not violate the space utilization threshold, Storage DRS prefers to select the datastore with the highest free space value. Storage DRS will choose Datastore 2 in this scenario as it picks the first datastore if multiple datastores report the same free space value.

The simulation determines that the optimal destination for VM03 is Datastore 3, as this reports a free space value of 1000 GB, while Datastore 2 reports 800 free space and Datastore 1 reports 900 GB of space.

This lease is applied during the simulation of placement for the generation of the initial placement recommendation and remains applied until the placement process of the VMs is completed or when the operation times out.

19

STORAGE DRS LOAD BALANCING

Storage DRS takes both space and I/O load into consideration when recommending load-balancing recommendations: Storage DRS generates a unified load-balance recommendation.

Storage DRS generates migration recommendations when space utilization or I/O response time thresholds have exceeded, and a significant space or I/O imbalance exists. However, if Storage DRS cannot correct the threshold violation, it balances the load within the datastore cluster as much as possible.

The datastore cluster settings displays both space and I/O load balancing configuration options.

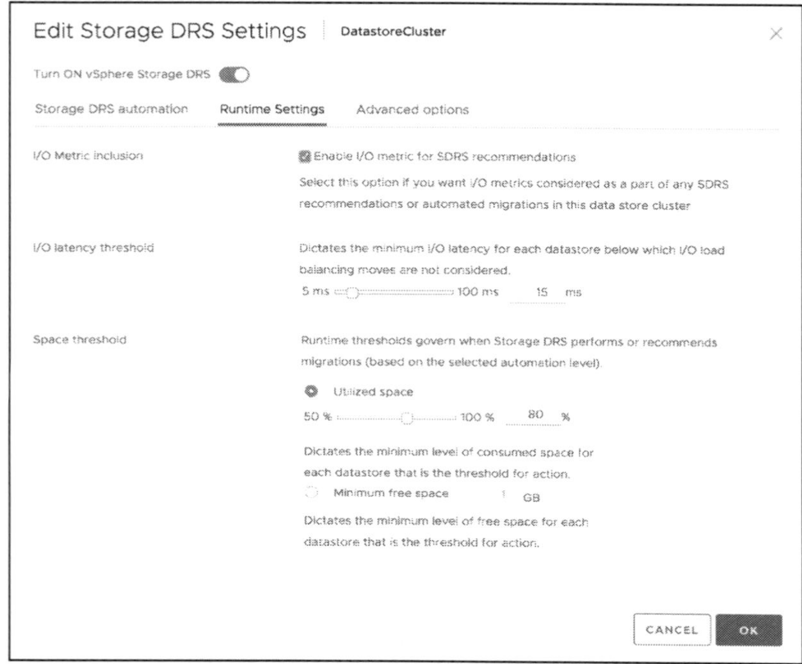

Figure 179: Storage DRS Thresholds

Storage DRS uses these settings to determine if migrations are required to balance workload across datastores. Each of the load balancers generates recommendations independently. Storage DRS considers both recommendations before providing a unified recommendation. The following section examines each load balancer separately before expanding upon unified recommendations.

Space Load Balancing

Storage DRS distributes space utilization of the VMs across the datastores of the datastore cluster. The workflow is repeated for each space-overloaded datastore, and more than one migration may be recommended to reduce the load on a datastore. The space balance workflow looks as follows:

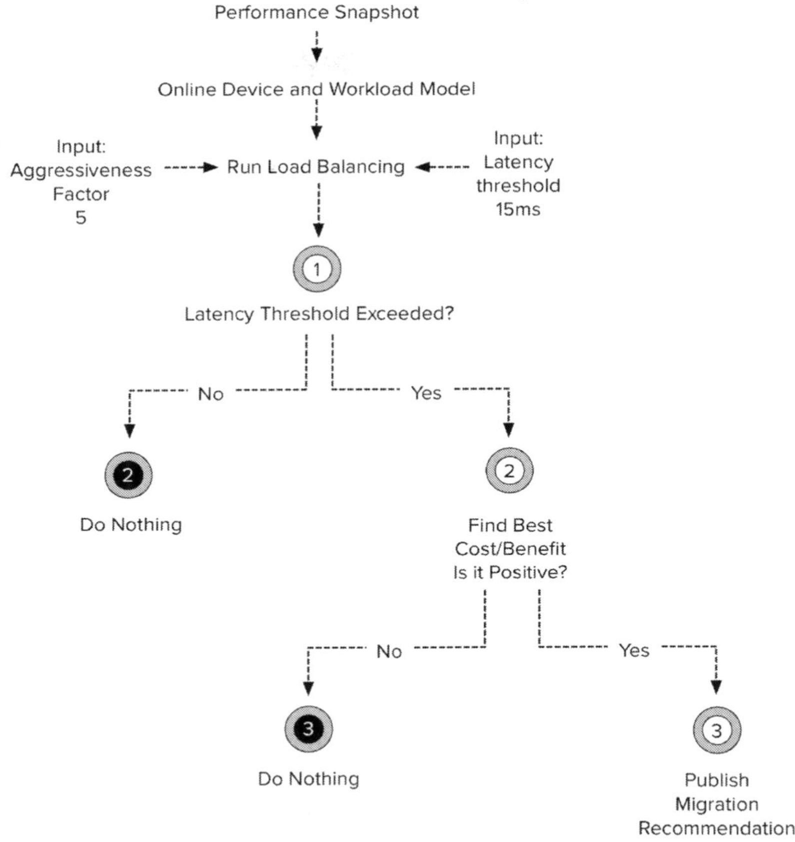

Figure 180: Space Load Balance Workflow

Collecting Statistics

Storage DRS retrieves **VM statistics** from the vCenter database every two hours. The host on which the VM is registered provides vCenter detailed information regarding the files associated with the VM. Storage DRS collects this information from the vCenter database to understand the disk usage and file structure of each VM.

Each ESXi host reports the **datastore utilization** at a frequent interval, and this information is stored in the vCenter database. Storage DRS checks whether the datastore utilization is above the user-set threshold. The user-set threshold – space utilization ratio threshold – defines the maximum acceptable space load of the VMFS datastore. The space load is the sum of the total consumed space on the datastore, divided by the capacity of the datastore.

> **Space load = (total consumed space on the datastore)/(datastore capacity)**

By default, the space utilization ratio is set to 80%, which indicates that the total consumed space on the datastore must not exceed 80% of the capacity of the datastore. To avoid unnecessary migrations from one overloaded datastore to a datastore that is near the threshold, Storage DRS uses the space utilization ratio difference threshold to determine which datastores should be considered as destinations for VM migrations.

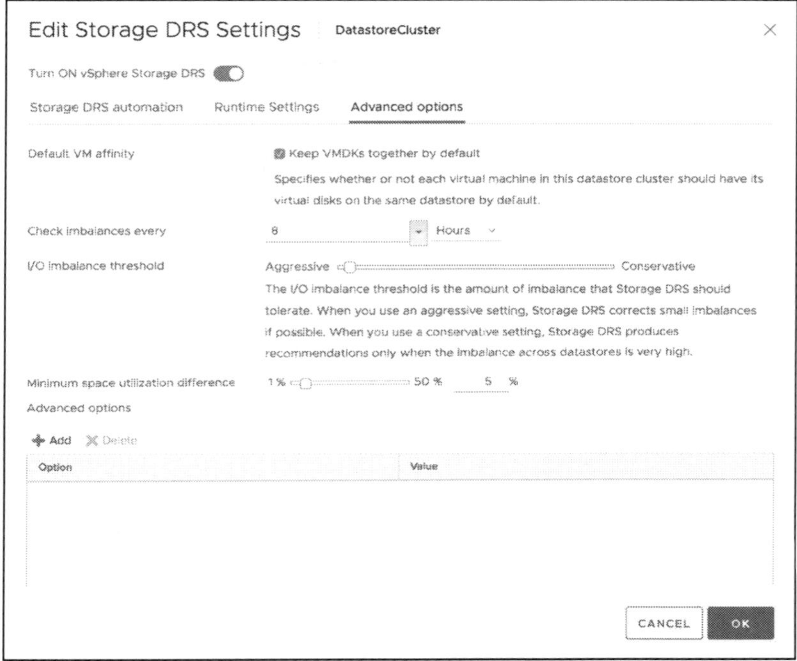

Figure 181: Minimum Space Utilization Difference

The space utilization ratio difference threshold indicates the required difference of utilization ratio between the destination and source datastores. The difference threshold value is set by default to 5%. Utilization is usage * 100/capacity. If the space used on Datastore 1 is 82% and Datastore 2 is 79%, the difference is 3%. Storage DRS will not make migration recommendations from Datastore 1 to Datastore 2 until it exceeds the threshold.

Cost Benefit-Risk Analysis

Similar to DRS, Storage DRS uses a cost-benefit metric to identify suitable migration candidates and to determine if the datastore cluster benefits from the move.

Benefit: The increase of free space after a VM moves out of the datastore.

Cost: The size of the VMDK and activity of I/O workload impacts the cost calculation. The number of mirrored writes to the datastores and the expected duration of the migration are considered as the overhead of a migration.

Risk: Risk is involved when generating migration recommendations for VMs configured with thin-provisioned disks. Storage DRS considers the allocated disk space instead of the provisioned amount (configured size) when determining if load balancing is required. The data-growth rate is considered a risk when migrating thin disks. Storage DRS attempts to avoid migrating VMs with data-growth rates that will likely cause the destination datastore to exceed the space utilization threshold in the near future.

The growth rate is estimated by means of historical usage samples; with recent samples weighing more than older samples. The "Near future" is a defined time window and defaults to 30 hours. If the benefit outweighs the cost, Storage DRS considers the move for a recommendation.

Migration candidate selection

When a datastore exceeds the space utilization threshold, Storage DRS attempts to move the number of megabytes out of the datastore to correct the space utilization violation. In other words, Storage DRS attempts to select a VM that is closest in size required to bring the space utilization of the datastore to the space utilization ratio threshold.

To minimize overhead, Storage DRS prefers moving powered-off VMs to powered-on VMs. The advantage of moving powered-off VMs is that Storage DRS does not have to track any block changes inside the VMDK during relocation and does not have to calculate the performance degradation on the VM workload.

To reduce the overhead even more, if the VM swap files are stored in a location explicitly specified by the user, Storage DRS does not move these files. After evaluation of statistics, space utilization and utilization ratio thresholds, the Storage DRS space load-balancing algorithm selects a candidate VM. This VM offers the highest benefit with the lowest overhead. However, Storage DRS does not apply or display the load balancing recommendation straight away; it considers the I/O load balancing recommendations before generating the actual recommendations.

On-Demand Space Load Balancing

Although Storage DRS load-balancing runs every 8 hours, a load balancing process is triggered by Storage DRS when the consumed space in a datastore exceeds the utilization ratio threshold. Storage DRS monitors utilization of the datastores and decides when the algorithm invocation needs to be scheduled. Depending on the fill-rate of the volume and the associated risk, Storage DRS decides if a load-balancing process needs to take place. It is possible that the threshold is violated, but due to a slow fill-rate, space load balancing is not immediately necessary. This behavior avoids generating unnecessary overhead.

I/O Load Balancing

The I/O load balancer's goal is to resolve the imbalance of performance delivered from datastores in a datastore cluster. To generate an I/O load balancer migration, Storage DRS runs the workflow outlined in the next figure. Similar to the space-balancing algorithm, this algorithm runs for all overloaded datastores, and the algorithm may recommend one or more migrations for each overloaded datastore.

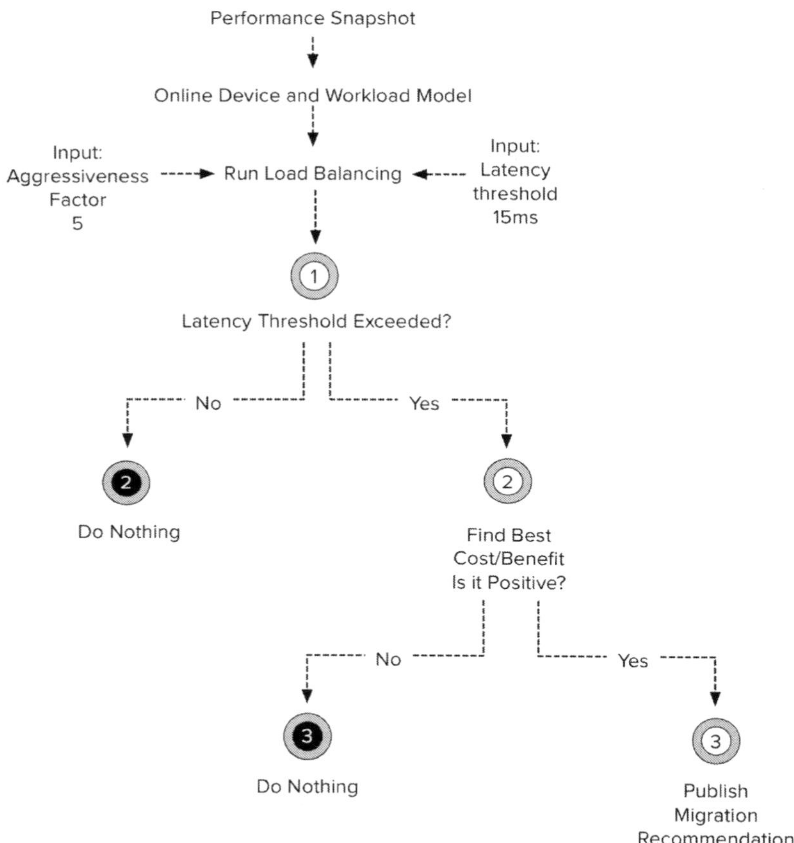

Figure 182: I/O Load Balancing Workflow

Stats Collection – Performance Snapshot

The main metric used by Storage DRS to represent performance is the average latency on each datastore. To solve the uneven distribution of average latency within the datastore cluster, Storage DRS requires input to recommend migrations. The required input is acquired by collecting a set of various statistics from vCenter. This set of statistics is commonly referred to as the "performance snapshot". Storage DRS uses the performance snapshot for its online device and workload modeling.

Online Device and Workload Modelling

To achieve better and more efficient utilization of storage resources in a datastore cluster, Storage DRS creates an online device and workload model. This model helps Storage DRS determine overall device performance capability and analyzes the impact of a specific set of workload data points on the latency of the datastore.

Device Modelling

Storage DRS captures device performance to create its performance models. Most storage devices hide RAID level and device characteristics from ESXi hosts and only present latency and the total capacity of a disk. It is essential to understand that not every disk is the same and that device performance can vary due to a wide variety of configuration differences. For example, a 2 TB disk spanning a disk group containing thirty-two 15K RPM Fibre-Channel disks usually offers better performance than a 2 TB disk spanning eight 7.2K RPM SATA disks. To understand and learn the performance of each device, Storage DRS uses a workload-injector and a reference workload to measure outstanding I/O's and latency. Paired together, they indicate the relative performance capability of a datastore.

> **Please remember that Storage DRS does not require any support from the storage array to determine device characteristics. No additional third-party software is required to run Storage DRS.**

Workload Modelling

The workload modeling process creates a workload metric of each virtual disk. Per virtual disk, 4 data points are collected:

- Number of Outstanding I/Os
- I/O size
- Read / Write ratio
- % Randomness

Storage DRS analyzes the impact of each data point on latency and returns an overall workload model metric.

Normalized Load

The device metric and workload metric are used to define the normalized load of a datastore. The normalized load allows Storage DRS to base its load balancing recommendation on both the intensity of the workload and the capabilities of the connected devices. The standard deviation of the normalized load of each datastore allows Storage DRS to determine the datastore cluster load imbalance.

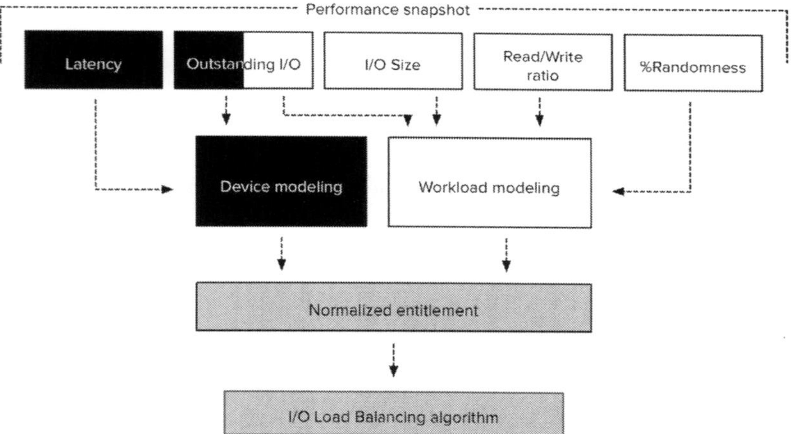

Figure 183: I/O Load-Balancing Input

This performance snapshot contains read and write latency samples captured by the SIOC injector on the previous day. Although Storage DRS is invoked every 8 hours, the I/O load Storage DRS evaluates the same performance data from the previous day during each invocation. Effectively, I/O load balancing recommends moves based on whole-day stats. This could lead to I/O load-balancer-related migrations once a day.

Data Points

To avoid having its data polluted by peak load moments, Storage DRS does not use real-time statistics. Instead, it aggregates all the data points collected over a period of time. Storage DRS reviews the data points, and if the 90th percentile I/O latency measured over a day for the datastore is higher than the threshold, Storage DRS considers the datastore as overloaded. By using the 90th percentile, Storage DRS uses the busiest 10% of the measurement period as a basis for its I/O load balancing decision.

As workloads shift during the day, enough information needs to be collected to make an accurate assessment of the workloads. Therefore, Storage DRS must have at least 16 hours of data before recommendations are made. By using at least 16 hours of data, Storage DRS has enough data of the same timeslot so it can compare utilization of datastores.

For example Datastore 1 to Datastore 2 on Monday morning at 11:00. As 16 hours is 2/3 of the day, Storage DRS receives enough information to characterize the performance of datastores on that day. However, how does this tie in with the 8-hour invocation period?

8-hour invocation period and 16 hours worth of data Storage DRS uses 16 hours of data. However, this data must be captured in the current day otherwise the performance snapshot of the previous day is used. How is this combined with the 8-hour invocation periods?

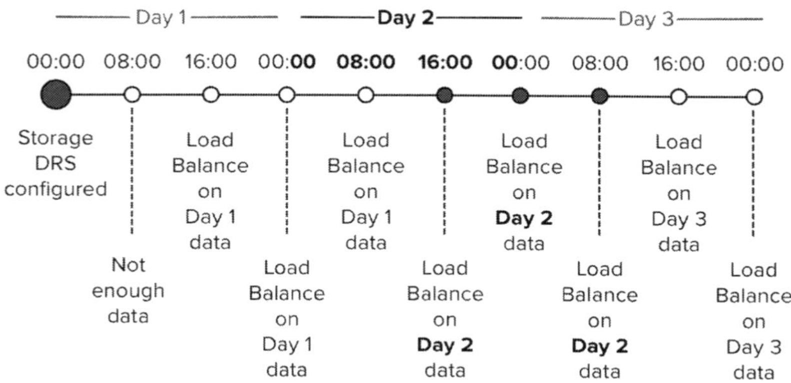

Figure 184: Invocation Period Overview

I/O load balancing is technically performed every 16 hours. Usually after midnight, after the day date, the stats are fixed and rolled up, this is called the rollover event. The first invocation period (08:00) after the rollover event uses the 24 hours statistics of the previous day. After 16 hours of the current day have passed, Storage DRS uses the new performance snapshot and may evaluate moves based on the new stats.

> **Storage DRS always uses past-day statistics regardless of the selected invocation period. For example, if the invocation period is set to 72 hours, Storage DRS still reviews the data collected from the previous 16 hours.**

Load Imbalance Recommendations

The I/O latency threshold defines the trigger point for considering load balancing to reduce latency. To do this, Storage DRS identifies the normalized load of each datastore. If a normalized load exceeds the user-set I/O latency threshold, Storage DRS reviews the load differences between the datastores in the datastore cluster and compares that to the value of tolerated imbalance set by the I/O imbalance threshold. If the load difference between the datastores matches or exceeds the tolerated imbalance, Storage DRS initiates the process to recommend migrations.

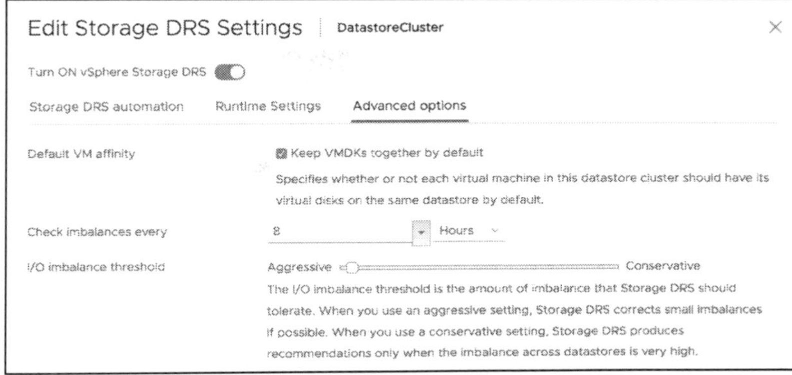

Figure 185: I/O Imbalance Threshold

The I/O imbalance threshold can be set from Conservative to Aggressive by moving the slider to the appropriate side. A more conservative setting causes Storage DRS to generate recommendations only when the imbalance across the datastores is very high while selecting a more aggressive setting would make Storage DRS generate recommendations to solve even small imbalances.

Cost-Benefit Analysis

The cost-benefit analysis is similar to the cost-benefit analysis of the space load balancer.

Cost: The cost is related to the duration of the Storage vMotion, which by itself is dependent on the size of the VM disk files.

Benefit: The benefit is the estimated improvement of I/O latency that is achieved on the source disk after the VM is migrated to the destination disk. If, after subtracting the cost from the benefit, the benefit remains greater than zero, Storage DRS generates an I/O load balance recommendation. If the imbalance is very low between the source and destination datastores and the VMDK files are large, the value can be zero because the estimated Storage vMotion time is so high that it does not make sense to recommend the move.

Ignoring Peak Moments

Storage DRS starts to generate I/O load-related recommendations once an imbalance persists for some period of time, usually at least 10% of a day (or approximately 2.4 hours). This timeframe prevents Storage DRS from being impacted by peak load moments. The duration of the imbalance period depends on the workload and the I/O imbalance threshold.

SIOC Latency and Storage DRS Latency

Although SIOC is leveraged by Storage DRS, its latency threshold setting is decoupled from Storage DRS. The configured latency threshold for Storage DRS is used by Storage DRS to classify a datastore as being overloaded and make recommendations to prevent bottlenecks and hotspots. The configured latency threshold for SIOC is used by SIOC to detect contention and throttle hosts based on this information to ensure each VM receives the number of resources it is entitled to.

To compute the latency metric, Storage DRS uses the vmObservedLatency metric while SIOC only uses the device latency metric. vmObservedLatency is the time between the hypervisor receiving an I/O request from the VM and getting I/O response back from the datastore. By using vmObservedLatency, Storage DRS is also aware of any queuing delays (wait time) occurring inside the host.

To leverage vmObservedLatency, all hosts connected to the datastore cluster should be vSphere 5.1 or higher. This metric is included in the SIOC Performance Charts in the vSphere UI.

To avoid misaligned latency threshold settings, SIOC automatically determines the latency threshold for each device. The default latency threshold for datastores in a datastore cluster is based on the device model. This threshold corresponds to 90% of peak IOPS of the disks backing the datastore. SIOC does not set the threshold lower than the specified I/O latency threshold when the I/O metric is enabled.

> **If you set the SIOC latency manually, set the SIOC latency higher than Storage DRS latency threshold, because Storage DRS latency is about correcting to reduce and avoid contention, whereas SIOC latency is about throttling workloads in a fair way when there is contention.**

Datastore Correlation Detector

IO load balancing operations avoid recommending migration of VMs between two performance-correlated datastores. Performance-correlated datastores are datastores that share the same backend resource such as disk- or RAID-groups. When multiple datastores share the same disk- or RAID-group, their performance characteristics could be interrelated, i.e., if one datastore experiences high latency, the other datastores sharing the same disks might experience similarly high latency since the same disks service I/O's from both datastores.

Storage DRS uses the SIOC injector for datastore correlation detection. How does it work? The datastore correlation detector measures performance during isolation and when concurrent IOs are pushed to multiple datastores. For example, Datastore 1 and Datastore 2 belong to the same datastore cluster. The SIOC injector uses a synthetic workload to measure to average I/O latency of Datastore 1 in isolation. Next, it measures the average I/O latency of Datastore 2 in isolation. The third step uses the same workload on both datastores simultaneously.

The first two steps are used to establish the baseline for each datastore. If the average latency of each datastore in step 3 has increased significantly, the datastores are marked as performance-correlated. If there is no performance correlation, concurrent I/O to one datastores should have no effect on the other datastore. If two datastores are performance-correlated, the concurrent I/O streams should amplify the average I/O latency on both datastores.

When two datastores are marked as performance-correlated, Storage DRS does not generate IO load balancing recommendations between those two datastores. However, Storage DRS can still generate recommendations to move VMs between two correlated datastores to address out of space situations or to correct rule violations.

Load Balancing Recommendations

Storage DRS generates both space and I/O load balancing recommendations separately. However, it weighs and combines both recommendations to provide a unified recommendation.

Unified Recommendations

A migration recommendation should not violate any user-set threshold. For example, migrating a VM to resolve an I/O load imbalance should not create a situation that results in a space load balance violation on the destination datastore and requires Storage DRS to generate another migration recommendation to resolve the space imbalance.

To avoid this scenario, Storage DRS calculates the space and I/O load imbalances for each candidate migration and selects the migration that improves the I/O load imbalance while not decreasing the space balance. To address any conflicting goals, each move is awarded a goodness metric that represents the weighted sum of the improvements to the I/O load and space load imbalances.

If the space load metric of each datastore is substantially below the space utilization threshold, the I/O load metric becomes the dominant factor in migration recommendations. However, if the space utilization of a datastore is above the threshold, the space metric receives more weight than the I/O load metric. Likewise, if I/O is overcommitted, the I/O load metric receives more weight than the space metric. Otherwise, both metrics receive equal weight.

If both thresholds are exceeded, Storage DRS can still decide not to generate migration recommendations if, for example, no valid moves exist. This can occur due to VM anti-affinity rules or because the cost of each move outweighs the benefit of that move. For example, the benefit value of a move can be zero if migrating VMs with large disks is the only way to solve a very low I/O imbalance. In this scenario, the cost of the Storage vMotion time would exceed the improvement on the I/O load balance in the datastore cluster.

Dependent Migration Recommendations

Dependent migration recommendations consist of multiple recommendations that must be executed in order, as a whole, to achieve a positive gain (load balanced). It is entirely possible that partial executions of this set may lead to a negative gain (worse imbalance). Storage DRS does not generate dependent migration recommendations during load balancing operations; however, Storage DRS may generate multiple independent moves which can lead to a positive gain of load balance. These independent moves can be executed in any order and still result in an improvement of load balance. Applying a subset of recommendations may also lead to an improvement, but with a smaller positive gain than applying the full set of recommendations.

Note that initial placement and migrations of virtual disks is based on the space availability and that the Storage DRS algorithm can issue multiple Storage vMotion actions as part of its recommendation to accommodate a virtual disk within a datastore. See the cluster defragmentation section for more information.

Cultivation Time

Storage DRS migration recommendations are delayed after Storage DRS is enabled for the first time. As mentioned in the data points section, Storage DRS requires at least 16 hours worth of data before it can use the performance snapshot for migration recommendations. On top of this, Storage DRS uses a “warm-up” period in which it determines the capabilities of connected storage array(s) and the characteristics of the active workloads. This results in delays before the first set of migration recommendations is generated.

In general, Storage DRS is being conservative about issuing load-balancing recommendations before it has collected enough information about the environment.

Invocation Triggers

The I/O load balancing algorithm is automatically invoked every 8 hours. When the invocation interval expires, Storage DRS computes and generate recommendations to migrate VMs. Each recommendation that is not applied is retired at the next invocation of Storage DRS; Storage DRS might generate the same recommendation again if the imbalance is not resolved.

The invocation period can be changed via the user interface and can range between 60 minutes and 43200 minutes (30 days). If the invocation period is set to 0, periodic load balancing is turned off. Changing the default value is strongly discouraged. A less frequent interval might reduce the number of Storage vMotion operations and result in less overhead, but may lead to longer datastore cluster imbalance. Shortening the interval will likely generate extra overhead while providing little additional benefit.
Besides periodic scheduling according to the configured invocation frequency, the Storage DRS imbalance calculation is also performed when it detects changes, such as:

- The datastore cluster configuration is updated
- A datastore is entering maintenance mode
- During initial placement [No load balancing]
- A datastore is moved into a datastore cluster
- A datastore exceeds its configured space threshold
- When “Run Storage DRS” is invoked

Cluster Configuration Change

If the thresholds or invocation period is changed, Storage DRS triggers a new imbalance calculation.

Datastore Maintenance Mode

When triggering maintenance mode, Storage DRS leverages vCenter APIs to retrieve a list of registered VMs on a given datastore. Storage DRS generates the migration recommendations and, depending on the automation level. It presents the list directly to vCenter for execution or presentation to the user.

> **If there are any faults generated after putting the datastore into maintenance mode, manual override kicks in. In this case, the user must cancel the request to enter maintenance mode or approve the recommendations and agree to manually address the faults.**

Because Storage DRS retrieves information via vCenter APIs, and uses the vCenter APIs to move VM files, it only generates migration recommendations for VMs that are registered in vCenter. Orphaned VMs or other non-related files are not migrated. When executing migration recommendations, vCenter only considers the remaining datastores of the datastore cluster as destinations. Datastores outside the cluster are not considered as suitable and compatible destinations.

Initial Placement

Initial placement of a VM or virtual disk triggers the Storage DRS imbalance calculation when:

- A VM is created
- A VM is cloned
- A virtual disk is added to a VM
- A VM or virtual disk is migrated into the datastore cluster

Exceeding Threshold

An invocation of Storage DRS is scheduled to run when a host reports datastore usage above the user-set threshold or when a thin-provisioning out-of-space alarm is triggered.

Invocation Frozen Zone

Each ESXi host reports datastore space utilization statistics to vCenter on a regular basis. vCenter compares the utilization statistics to the imbalance threshold and schedules a Storage DRS invocation if the utilization exceeds the threshold.

Because ESXi hosts do not report on a synchronous basis, vCenter might keep on receiving utilization statistics while a VM is being migrated to solve the space utilization violation. To counter possible Storage DRS schedule requests from vCenter due to space threshold issues, an invocation "frozen zone" is introduced. After each Storage DRS invocation, Storage DRS invocation cannot be scheduled for at least 10 minutes.

Future Storage DRS invocations take these recommendations into account; the best practice would be to apply such recommendations as soon as possible.

Recommendation Calculation

Storage DRS performs multiple calculations and passes to generate migration recommendations. Storage DRS determines the datastore cluster imbalance and selects suitable VMs to migrate to solve the imbalance. It monitors both space load and I/O performance to generate the migration recommendation. Before generating recommendations, Storage DRS checks for constraint violations.

The constraint correction pass determines whether Storage DRS needs to recommend mandatory Storage vMotions:

- To correct VMDK-VMDK anti-affinity rule violations
- To correct VMDK-VMDK affinity rule violations
- To correct VM-VM anti-affinity rule violations

If no acceptable move can be found to fix a violation, Storage DRS displays the reason why it cannot fix the violation in a fault message located in the Storage DRS view.

How to Create a "New Storage DRS recommendation generated" Alarm

One of the drawbacks of manual mode is the need to monitor the datastore cluster on a regular basis to discover if new recommendations are generated. As Storage DRS is generated every 8 hours and doesn't provide insights when the next invocation run is scheduled, it's become a bit of a guessing game when the next load balancing operation has occurred.

To solve this problem, it is recommended to create a custom alarm and configure the alarm to send a notification email when new Storage DRS recommendations are generated. Here's how you do it: Go to Storage | Storage DRS Cluster| Configure | More | Alarm Definitions | Add.

Name and Description
Provide the name of the alarm as this name will be used by vCenter as the subject of the email. Provide an adequate description so that other administrators understand the purpose of this alarm.

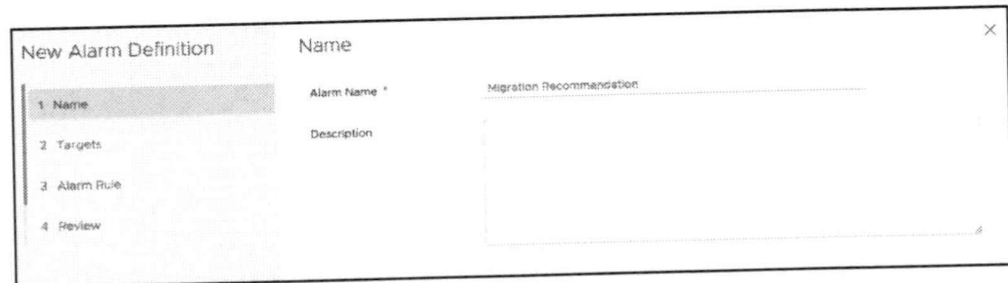

Figure 186: Alarm Name and Description

Targets
Since you already selected the Datastore Cluster, the target type and target are prefilled.

Figure 187: Alarm Targets

Alarm Rule

Select the drop down box at the IF statement and select “New Storage DRS recommendation generated”. Select the severity of the alarm level, we guess you don’t want a migration recommendation listed as critical, thus we selected the warning type in this example. Fill out the email address if you want to be notified via an email message. Or if you want it plugged into your monitoring systems you can configure SNMP traps or use a script.

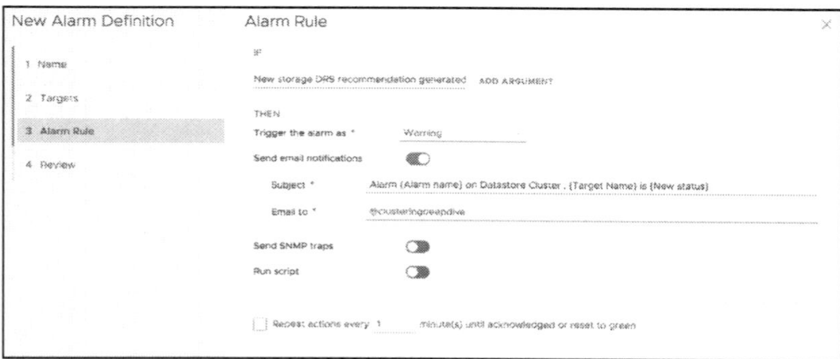

Figure 188: Alarm Rule

Review

Click on next to review the alarm and create to finish this process. Make sure the option at the left bottom “Enable this alarm” is indicated as green.

20

DATASTORE CLUSTER CONFIGURATION

Datastore clusters form the basis of Storage DRS and can best be described as a collection of datastores aggregated into a single object. Once configured, you manage a datastore cluster instead of the individual datastores. Please be aware that datastore clusters are referred to as “storage pods” in the vSphere API.

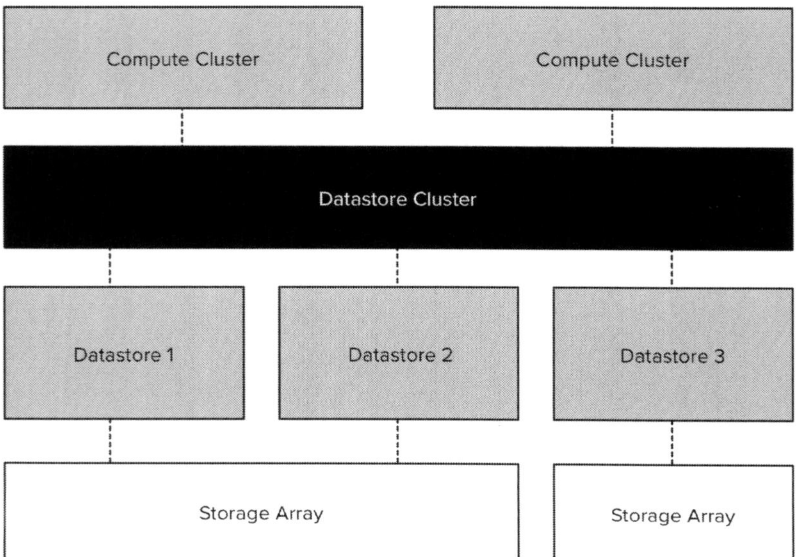

Figure 189: Datastore Cluster Ecosystem Architecture

A datastore cluster is used as the storage destination during the provisioning process. The provisioning process not only refers to the creation of a VM, but also to adding a disk to an existing VM, cloning a VM or moving a VM by Storage vMotion operation into the datastore cluster.

The datastore cluster becomes a load-balancing domain once Storage DRS is enabled. The load balancing algorithm issues migration recommendations when thresholds are exceeded.

The workflow for creating a datastore cluster is straightforward.

Creating a Datastore Cluster

Before we show the eight steps that need to be taken when creating a datastore cluster, we want to list some constraints and our recommendations for creating datastore clusters.

Constraints:

- VMFS and NFS cannot be part of the same datastore cluster
- Use Similar disk types inside a datastore cluster
- Maximum of 64 datastores per datastore cluster
- Maximum of 256 datastore clusters per vCenter Server
- Maximum of 9000 VMDKs per datastore cluster

Recommendations:

- Group disks with similar characteristics (RAID-1 with RAID-1, Replicated with Replicated, 15k RPM with 15k RPM, etc.)
- Pair I/O latency threshold with disk type: SSD disk 10-15ms, FC/SAS 20-40ms, SATA disk: 30-50ms
- Full connectivity of datastores, all ESXi hosts of DRS cluster are connected to all datastores within datastore cluster
- Leverage information provided by vSphere Storage APIs - Storage Awareness

Configuration Workflow

1. Go to the Home screen.
2. Go to Storage.
3. Right click on Datacenter object or select Datacenter object and select Actions.
4. Select Storage.
5. Click on “New Datastore Cluster”.
6. Provide the datastore cluster with a name and leave “Turn On Storage DRS” enabled.
7. Select Automation level.
8. Enable or Disable I/O load balancing.
9. Configure the I/O latency threshold if I/O load balancing is enabled and select the appropriate threshold based on the disk architecture that back the datastores.
10. Set space threshold, please note that the setup screen only offers the percentage based setting. The setting screen of the datastore cluster allows you to configure an absolute number (i.e. 50 GB instead of 20%).

11. Select the hosts and clusters you wish to connect to.
12. Select the appropriate datastores.
13. Validate the selected configuration and click finish.

The datastore cluster is created literally in seconds. If "Storage DRS" is not enabled, a datastore cluster is created which lists the datastores underneath, but Storage DRS won't recommend any placement action for provisioning or migration operations on the datastore cluster.

Name and Location

The first steps are to enable Storage DRS, specify the datastore cluster name and check if the "Turn on Storage DRS" option is enabled.

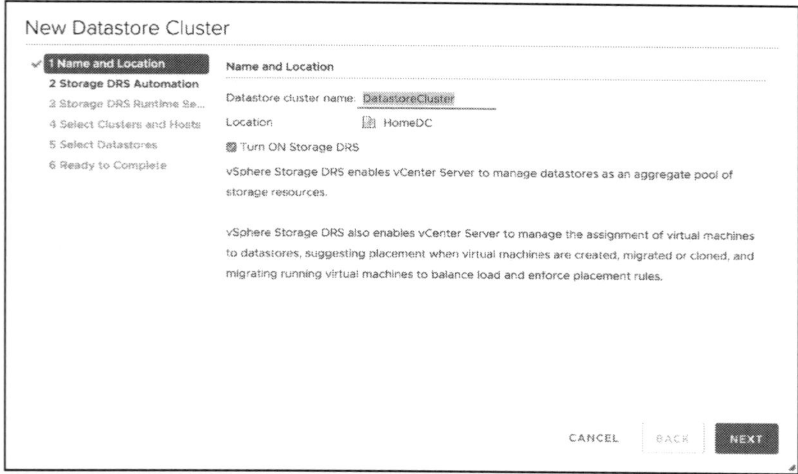

Figure 190: Datastore Cluster Name and Location

When "Turn on Storage DRS" is activated, the following functions are enabled:

- Initial placement for virtual disks based on space and I/O workload
- Space load balancing among datastores within a datastore cluster
- IO load balancing among datastores within a datastore cluster

The "Turn on Storage DRS" checkbox enables or disables all of these components at once. If necessary, I/O balancing functions can be disabled independently. When disabling Storage DRS by disabling the "Turn On Storage DRS" checkbox, all the Storage DRS settings, e.g., automation level, aggressiveness controls, thresholds, rules and Storage DRS schedules are saved so they may be restored to the same state it was in when Storage DRS was disabled.

Storage DRS Automation

Storage DRS offers two automation levels:

No Automation (Manual Mode)
Manual mode is the default mode of operation. When the datastore cluster is operating in manual mode, placement and migration recommendations are presented to the user but are not executed until they are manually approved.

Fully Automated
Fully automated allows Storage DRS to apply space and I/O load-balance migration recommendations automatically. No user intervention is required. However, initial placement recommendations still require user approval.

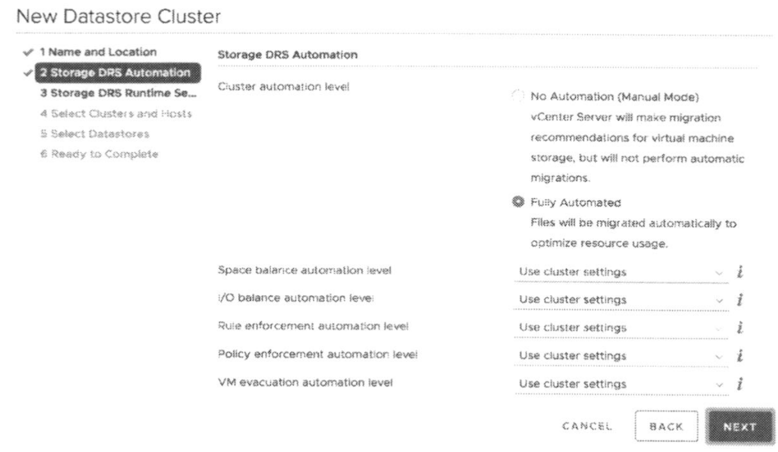

Figure 191: Storage DRS Automation

Select a cluster automation level for cluster level and, if necessary, fine-tune the behavior of the individual algorithms and features. This screen allows you to configure Storage DRS that automatically applies storage load balance operations while providing the user I/O load balancing recommendations. The user has to approve the I/O load balance recommendations manually in this configuration.

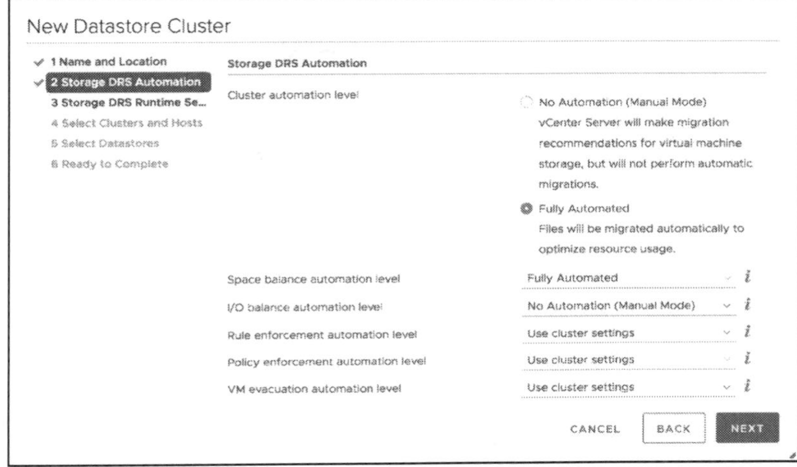

Figure 192: Customized Storage DRS Automation Settings

Rule enforcement automation level: Specifies the Storage DRS behavior when it generates recommendations for correcting affinity rules violations in a datastore cluster. Since an affinity rule is a constraint, a rule of behavior for Storage DRS to obey to, these recommendations are marked as the highest priority and should be executed as fast as possible. It's recommended to set this to fully automated.

Policy enforcement automation level: Specifies the Storage DRS behavior when it generates recommendations for correcting storage and VM policy violations after a datastore is coming out of maintenance mode. If you use Storage Policy, it's recommended to set this to fully automated.

VM evacuation automation level: Specifies the Storage DRS behavior when it generates recommendations for VM evacuations from datastores in a datastore cluster. This applies to the behavior of Storage DRS when putting a datastore in maintenance mode. Do you want automatic migrations of VMs when putting a datastore in maintenance mode, if yes, select fully automated.

> **Partially Automated is Missing Storage DRS does not offer partially automated automation that provides automatic initial placement of the VMs. Initial placement recommendations must always be approved manually, regardless of the selected automation level. The automation level only specifies the approval-automation of space and I/O load balancing recommendations.**

Storage Run Runtime Settings

Configure the I/O latency threshold if I/O load balancing is enabled and select the appropriate threshold based on the disk architecture that back the datastores.

Set space threshold; please note that the setup screen only offers the percentage-based setting. The setting screen of the datastore cluster allows you to configure an absolute number (i.e. 50 GB instead of 20%)

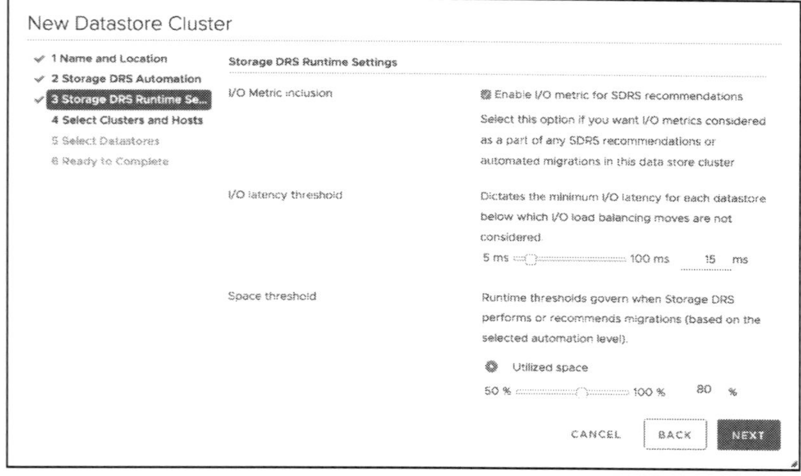

Figure 193: Storage DRS Runtime Settings

Select Clusters and Hosts

The "Select Hosts and Clusters" view allows the user to connect the datastore cluster to one or more DRS clusters. Only clusters within the same vSphere datacenter can be selected, as the vCenter datacenter is storage DRS boundary.

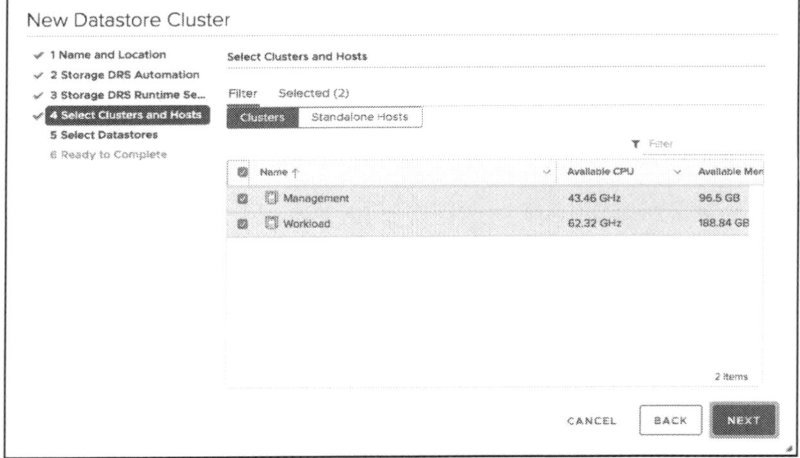

Figure 194: Cluster and Host Selection Screen

Please note that datastores shared across multiple data centers cannot be included in a datastore cluster. A datastore cluster is managed by a single vCenter, as Storage DRS runs in a single vCenter. If two vCenters can both see the datastore cluster, then the Storage DRS operations would conflict between the vCenters.

Select Datastores

By default, only datastores connected to all hosts in the selected DRS cluster(s) are shown. The Show datastore dropdown menu provides the options to show partially connected datastores.

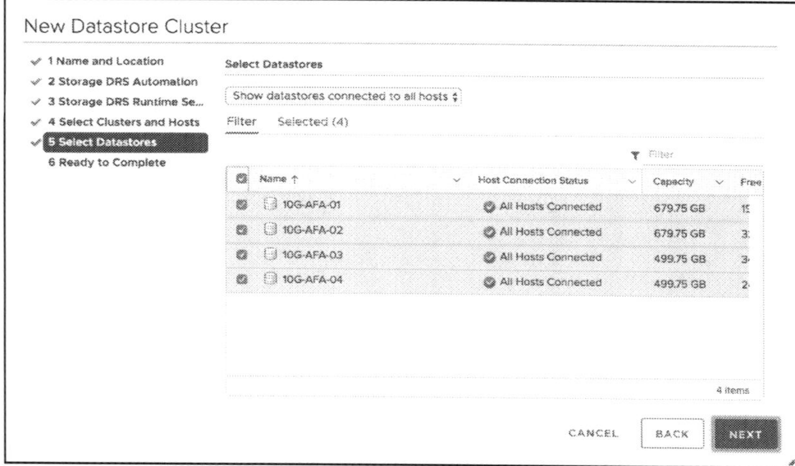

Figure 195: Select Datastores

> **If the overview shows a datastore that is not connected to all host, now is the time to fix this! Partially connected datastores limit DRS and Storage DRS load balancing effectiveness.**

Ready to Complete

The “Ready to Complete” screen provides an overview of all the settings configured by the user.

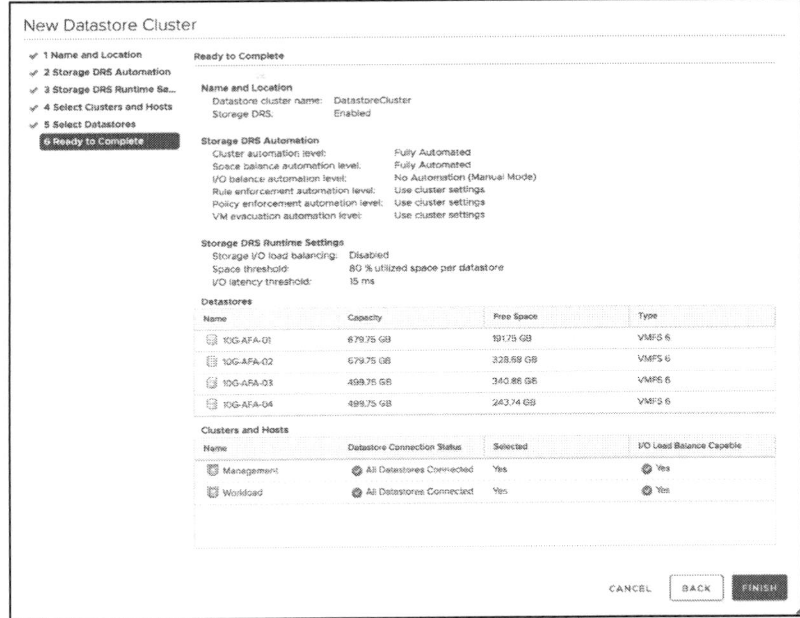

Figure 196: Ready to Complete

Click on Finish to create the Datastore Cluster.

21

ARCHITECTURE AND DESIGN OF DATASTORE CLUSTERS

Connectivity

When introducing a datastore cluster into the infrastructure, care must be taken regarding the connectivity of the datastore cluster. There are multiple aspects of connectivity that must be considered: connectivity of a datastore cluster to hosts within a compute cluster, connectivity to multiple compute clusters and connectivity to multiple arrays. For example, spanning a datastore cluster across multiple storage arrays is possible and supported, but what are the benefits and pitfalls of such a configuration?

Host Connectivity

Connectivity between ESXi hosts and datastores affects initial placement and load balancing decisions made by both DRS and Storage DRS. Although connecting a datastore to all ESXi hosts inside a cluster is a recommended practice. We still come across partially connected datastores in virtual environments. Let's start with the basic terminology.

Fully connected datastore clusters: A fully connected datastore cluster is one that contains only datastores that are available to all ESXi hosts in a DRS cluster. This design is a recommendation, but it is not enforced.

Partially connected datastore clusters: If any datastore within a datastore cluster is connected to a subset of ESXi hosts inside a DRS cluster, the datastore cluster is considered a partially connected datastore cluster.

What happens if the DRS cluster is connected to partially connected datastore clusters? It is essential to understand that the goal of both DRS and Storage DRS is resource availability. The key to offering resource availability is to provide as much mobility as possible.

> **Storage DRS does not generate any migration recommendations that reduces the compatibility (mobility) of a VM regarding datastore connections. VM-to-host compatibility is calculated and captured in compatibility lists.**

Compatibility List

A VM-host compatibility list is generated for each VM. The compatibility list determines which ESXi hosts in the cluster have network and storage configurations that allow the VM to come online successfully. The membership of a mandatory VM-to-Host affinity rule is listed in the compatibility list as well. If the VM's configured network port group or datastore is not available on the host, or the host is not listed in the host group of a mandatory affinity rule, the ESXi server is deemed incompatible to host that VM.

Both DRS and Storage DRS focus on resource availability and resource outage avoidance. Therefore, Storage DRS prefers datastores that are connected to all hosts. Partial connectivity impacts both DRS and Storage DRS load balancing capabilities.

If DRS selects a host (ESXi-01) that is partially connected, it limits the mobility of the VMDK within the datastore (Datastore 2 and Datastore 3) If Storage DRS selects Datastore 1, it limits the mobility of the VM within the DRS cluster (ESXi-02 and ESXi-03).

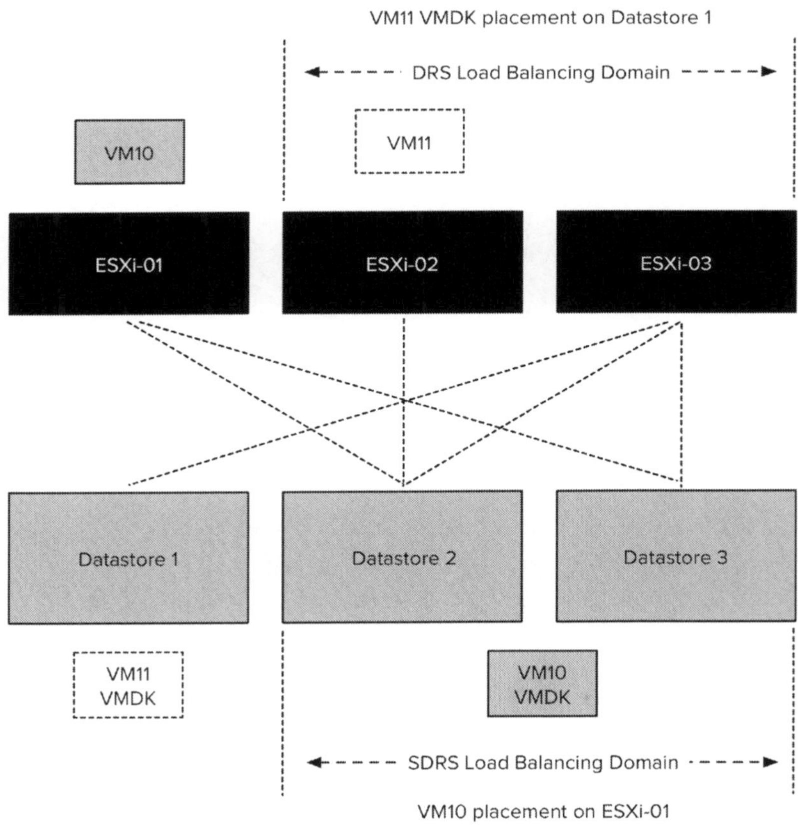

Figure 197: VM and VMDK Mobility in a Partially Connected Architecture

During the process of generating migration recommendations, DRS selects a host that can provide enough resources to satisfy the VM's dynamic entitlement, while lowering the imbalance of the cluster. DRS might come across a host with much lower utilization, than other hosts inside the cluster. If that lightly utilized host is not connected to the datastore containing the VM's files, (the poor connection situation might even be the reason for the low utilization rate) DRS does not consider the host due to the incompatibility. While this host might be a desirable option to solve resource imbalance from a DRS resource load balancing perspective, its lack of connectivity prevents it from being more effectively utilized. Also, keep in mind the impact of this behavior on VM-Host affinity rules, DRS does not migrate a VM to a partially connected host inside the host group (DRS cluster). Similar imbalances can happen with Storage DRS load balancing using partially connected datastores.

Partially connected datastores are not recommended when fully connected datastores are available that do not violate the space Storage DRS threshold.

I/O load balancing in Partially Connected Datastore Clusters

You might wonder why the space Storage DRS threshold is explicitly mentioned and not the latency threshold: that's because I/O load balancing is disabled when a partially connected datastore is detected in the datastore cluster. Not only on that single, partially connected datastore, but the entire datastore cluster. This limitation effectively disables a complete feature set of your virtual infrastructure.

Partially Connected Datastores and the Invocation Period

The connectivity status is extremely important when the Storage DRS interval expires. During the migration recommendation calculation, the connectivity state of each datastore is checked. If a partially connected datastore is detected during the check, Storage DRS disables I/O load balancing and space load balancing might not consider that datastore as a valid destination.

A temporary all-paths-down status or a rezoning procedure might not have an effect on Storage DRS load-balancing behavior, but what if good old Murphy decides to give you a visit during the invocation period? Keep this in mind when scheduling maintenance on the storage platform; it might be wise to temporarily disable Storage DRS.

> **Connect all datastores within a datastore cluster to all ESXi host within a compute cluster.**

Cluster Connectivity

A long-time best practice is to connect datastores to a single DRS cluster. When introducing a new cluster, new datastores were created to contain the VMs provisioned onto that new cluster. This best practice was recommended primarily to reduce the number of SCSI-locks. As VAAI functionality replaces old SCSI locks, connecting datastores to multiple clusters becomes a possibility without impacting performance. With that in mind, sharing datastore clusters across multiple compute clusters is a supported configuration. Minimizing the number of datastore clusters makes initial placement of VMs increasingly simple. During VM placement, the administrator must select the destination DRS cluster and Storage DRS selects the host that can provide the most resources to the VM.

A migration recommendation generated by Storage DRS does not move the VM at the host level. Consequently, a VM cannot move from one compute cluster to another DRS cluster by any operation initiated by Storage DRS.

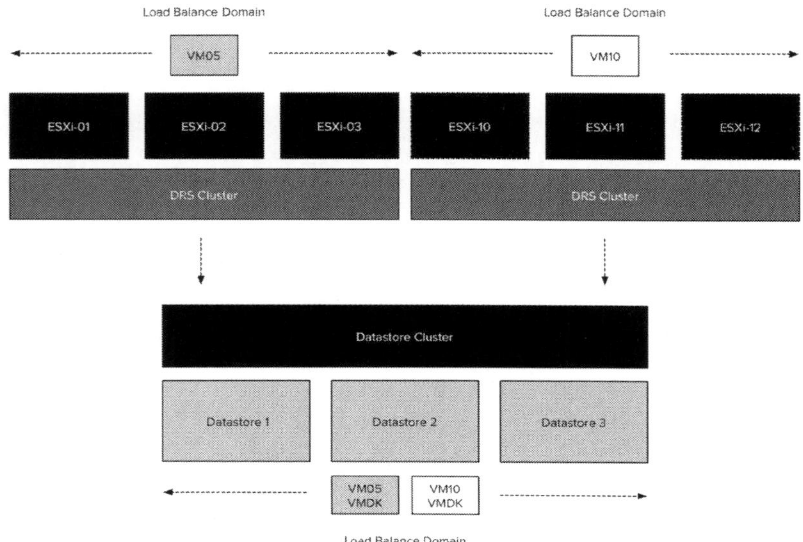

Figure 198: DRS and Storage DRS Load Balancing Domains

Multiple Compute Clusters and SIOC

VMs of various clusters can safely share datastores of a datastore cluster, as SIOC and its shares are datastore focused. SIOC is unaware of and unaffected by the cluster membership of a host. SIOC uses virtual disk shares to distribute storage resources fairly, and these are applied on a datastore-wide level, regardless of host clustering. In short, cluster membership of the host has no impact on SIOC's abilities to detect violations of the latency threshold or manage the I/O stream to the datastore.

Maximum Number of Hosts per Volume

The maximum supported number of hosts connected to a VMFS datastore is 64. Keep this in mind when sizing compute clusters or connecting multiple compute clusters to datastore clusters using VMFS datastores. The maximum number of hosts connected to an NFS datastore depends on the maximums of the NFS filer.

Array Connectivity

What if multiple arrays are available to the virtual infrastructure? Are there any drawbacks to spanning the datastore cluster across multiple arrays, or would there be more benefits associated with creating a datastore cluster per array?

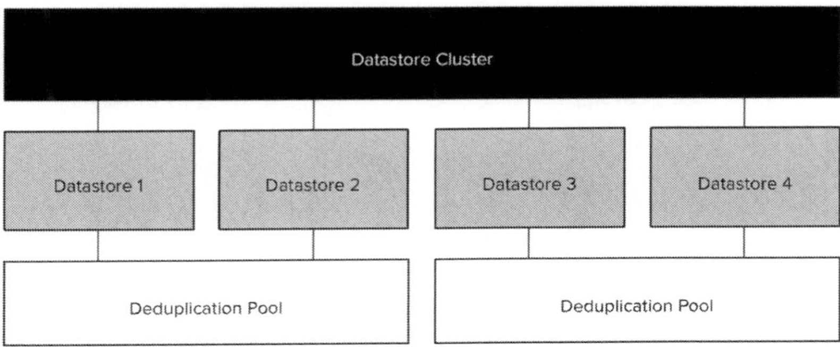

Figure 199: Array Connectivity

Combining datastores located on different storage arrays into a single datastore cluster is a supported configuration. Such a configuration could be used during a storage array data migration project where VMs must move from one array to another, but also when using multiple arrays on a permanent basis. The key areas to focus on are the homogeneity of configurations of the arrays and datastores.

When combining datastores from multiple arrays, it is highly recommended to use datastores that use similar types of arrays, disks, and RAID levels. Using similar types of arrays provide comparable performance and redundancy features. Although RAID levels are standardized by SNIA, implementation of RAID levels by different vendors may vary from the actual RAID specifications. An implementation used by a particular vendor may affect the read and/or write performance and the degree of data redundancy compared to the same RAID level implementation of another vendor.

APIs for Storage Awareness

Would *vSphere APIs for Storage Awareness* (VASA) and Storage profiles be any help in this configuration? VASA enables vCenter to display the capabilities of the LUN/datastore. This information could be leveraged to create a datastore cluster by selecting the datastores that report similar storage capabilities. Keep in mind that the actual capabilities surfaced by VASA are being left to the individual array storage vendors. This means that the storage capability detail and description could be similar, yet the performance or redundancy features of the datastores may differ.

Would this be harmful, or will Storage DRS stop working when aggregating datastores with different performance levels? Storage DRS will work and will load balance VMs across the datastores in the datastore cluster. However, Storage DRS load balancing focuses on distributing the VMs in such a way that the configured thresholds are not violated and getting the best overall performance out of the datastore cluster. By mixing datastores providing different performance levels, VM performance may not be consistent when migrated between datastores belonging to different arrays.

Hardware Offloading

Another caveat to consider is the impact of migrating VMs between datastores on different arrays: *vSphere API for Array Integration* (VAAI) hardware offloading is not possible. Storage vMotion will be managed by one of the datamovers in the vSphere stack. As storage DRS does not identify "locality" of datastores, it does not incorporate the additional overhead incurred when migrating VMs between arrays.

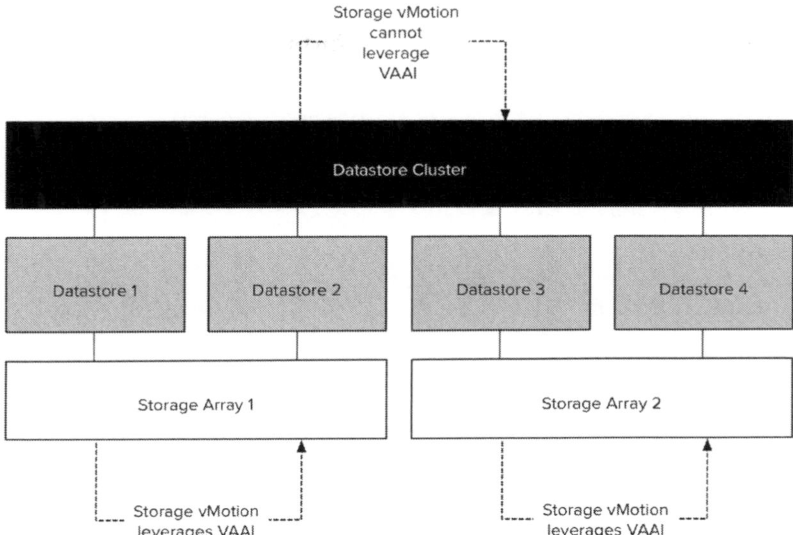

Figure 200: VAAI Hardware Offloading within Arrays

If designing an environment that provides a stable and continuous level of performance, redundancy and low overhead, could datastores from multiple arrays be aggregated into a single datastore cluster? Datastores and array should have the following configuration:

- Identical vendor
- Identical firmware/code
- Identical number of spindles backing diskgroup/aggregate
- Identical RAID Level
- Same replication configuration
- All datastores connected to all hosts in compute cluster
- Equal-sized datastores
- Equal external workload (best none at all)

We recommend creating multiple datastore clusters. Group datastores belonging to each storage array into their own datastore cluster. It reduces the complexity of both the design and ongoing operations.

When spanning multiple arrays, the configuration of the storage arrays need to be kept as identical, impacting the management of the storage arrays. Keep firmware versions identical across arrays in addition to maintaining array functional parity and synchronizing downtime during maintenance windows. Besides reducing operational overhead, keep the datastore clusters confined within a storage array leverages VAAI. This helps to reduce the load on the storage subsystem.

Datastores

The maximum number of datastores and the disk footprint of VMs are usually the primary drivers of the datastore design. If a configuration standard exists within your company, be aware of the possible impact the maximum number of datastores could have on the consolidation ratio of VMs on a datastore cluster.

Space Utilization Threshold and the Space Safety Buffer

One of the primary considerations in the consolidation ratio of the VMs to datastores is the space safety buffer. A common practice is to assign a big chunk of space as safety buffer to avoid an out of space situation on a datastore, which might lead to downtime of the active VMs. We have seen organizations using requirements of 30% free space on datastores. As Storage DRS monitors space utilization, the free space used as a safety buffer can be greatly reduced. Each ESXi host reports the VM space utilization and the datastore utilization; Storage DRS triggers an invocation if the configured space utilization threshold is violated.
By reducing slack space, a higher consolidation ratio can be achieved (if I/O performance allows this). Reclaiming slack space can provide additional space for extra datastores within the datastore cluster.
The availability of more datastores benefits Storage DRS by offering more load balancing options: more datastores increases the number of storage queues available, which benefits I/O management at the ESXi level as well as SIOC at the cluster level.

Scale Up or Scale Out Datastores

The maximum number of datastores supported in a datastore cluster is 64. If there is no predefined (company IT-standard) datastore size standard, a suitable datastore size needs to be determined. Datastore size depends on multiple variables: consolidation ratio of VMs per datastore cluster, VM disk footprint and storage array performance to name a few. As mentioned in the previous paragraph, more datastores means more scheduling options for storage DRS. Selecting a smaller datastore size could result in more migrations if the space utilization threshold of datastores is violated.

Storage DRS supports datastores up to 64 TB. Extents are supported as well, although there are some drawbacks introduced when using extents in datastore clusters. Extending a datastore does not offer extra load balancing options to Storage DRS, just a single datastore grows in size. Storage DRS disables SIOC on an extended datastores, which in turns result in disabled I/O load balancing for that particular datastore.

> **Storage DRS does not support combining NFS and VMFS datastores into a single datastore cluster. You need to commit to one type of file system per datastore cluster.**

VM Configuration

The VM configuration impacts the load balancing ability of storage DRS as well as the consolidation ratio of VMs to datastore clusters.

Datastore Cluster Default Affinity Rule

Storage DRS allows you changing the default affinity rule for the datastore cluster. By default, Storage DRS recommends an Intra-VM affinity rule. If you deselect this rule, Storage DRS spreads the VM files and VMDKs across different datastores.

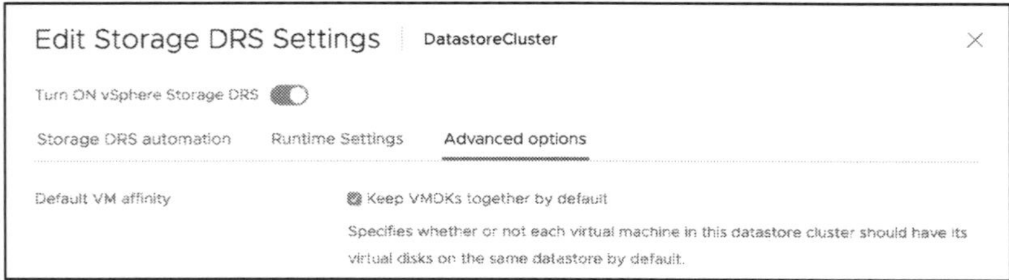

Figure 201: Default VM Affinity

Affinity rules are covered more in detail in the next chapter. The Intra-VM affinity rule keeps the VM files, such as VMX file, log files, vSwap and VMDK files together on one datastore.

VM10
350GB

Initial Placement Selects Appropriate Datastore

Datastore Cluster

Datastore 1
(1 TB)

Datastore 2
(1 TB)

Datastore 3
(1 TB)

VM10
VMDK1

VM10
VMDK2

VM Files

Affinity Rule

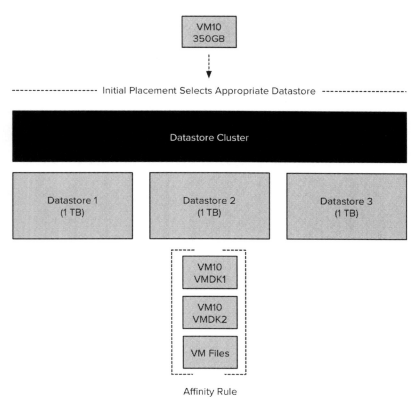

Figure 202: Initial Placement with Default Affinity Rule

Keeping all files together on one datastore helps ease troubleshooting. However, Storage DRS load balance algorithms may benefit from the ability to distribute the VM across multiple datastores. Let's zoom in how Storage DRS handles VMs with multiple disks when the Intra-VM affinity rule is removed from the VM.

DrmDisk

Storage DRS uses the construct "DrmDisk" as the smallest entity it can migrate. A DrmDisk represents a consumer of datastore resources. This means that Storage DRS creates a DrmDisk for each VMDK belonging to the VM. The interesting part is how it handles the collection of system files and swap file belonging to VMs: Storage DRS creates a single DrmDisk representing all of the system files. If, however, an alternate swapfile location is specified, the vSwap file is a separate DrmDisk. Load balancing is disabled on this swap DrmDisk. For example, for a VM with two VMDK's and no alternate swapfile location configured, Storage DRS creates three DrmDisks:

- A separate DrmDisk for each VM Disk File
- A DrmDisk for system files (VMX, Swap, logs, etc)

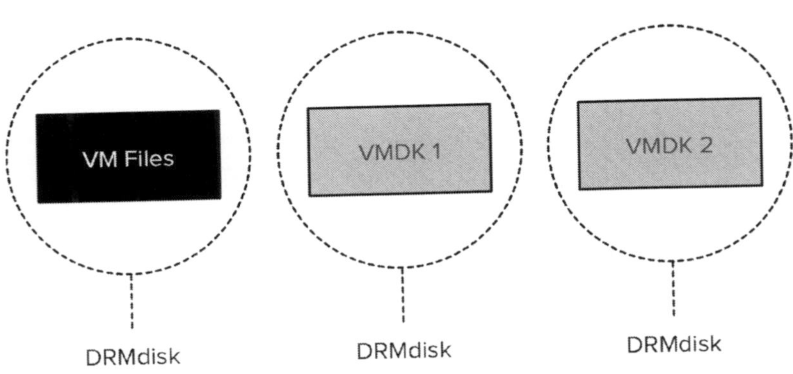

Figure 203: DrmDisk of a VM

When deploying a new virtual machine into the datastore cluster, Storage DRS generates the following datastore recommendation:

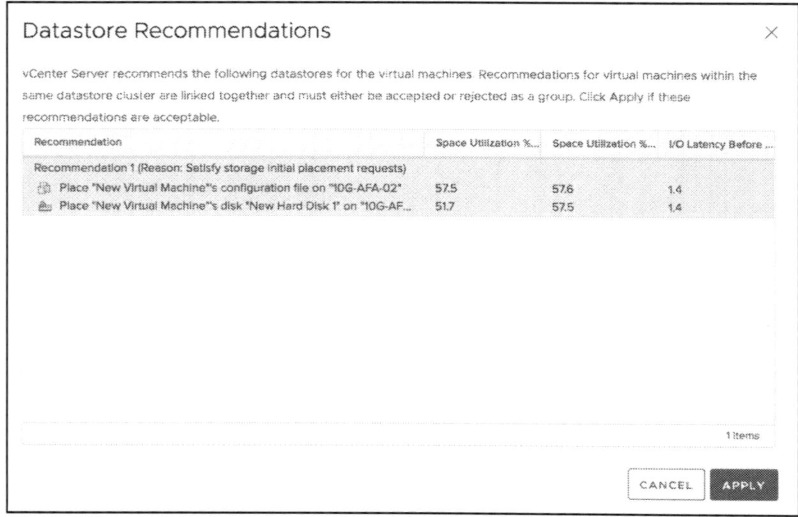

Figure 204: Datastore Recommendation with Affinity Rules Disabled

Notice the separate recommendation for "New Virtual Machine configuration file"? This is the DrmDisk containing the system files.

Increasing Granularity

Initial placement and Space load balancing benefit tremendously from separating virtual disks across datastores. Instead of searching for a suitable datastore that can hold the VM as a whole, Storage DRS is able to search for appropriate datastores for each DrmDisk file separately. You can imagine that this increased granularity means that datastore cluster fragmentation is less likely to happen and, if prerequisite migrations are required, the number of migrations is expected to be a lot lower.

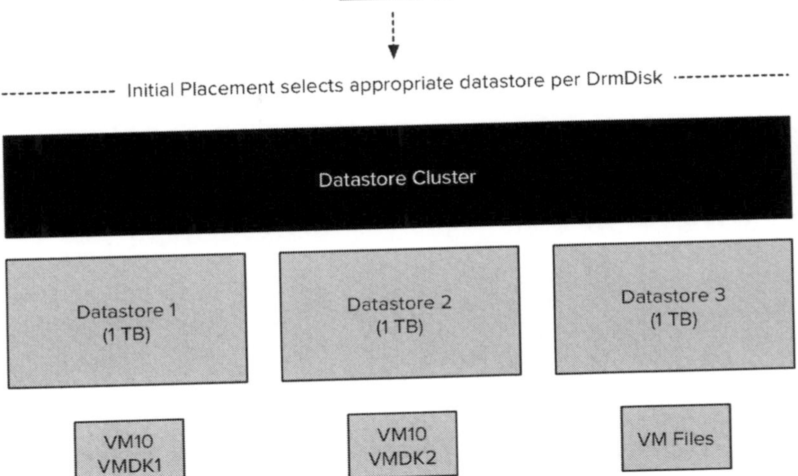

Figure 205: Initial Placement with VMDK Anti-Affinity Rule Enabled

I/O Load Balancing with Anti-Affinity Rules

Similar to initial placement and load balancing, I/O load balancing benefits from the greater granularity. Using smaller units, it can find a better fit for each workload generated by the VMDK files. The system file DrmDisk will not be migrated very often as it is small in size and does not generate a lot of I/O. Storage DRS analyzes the workload of each DrmDisk, then decides on which datastore it should place the DrmDisk to keep the load balance within the datastore cluster while also providing enough performance to each DrmDisk.

If Intra-VM affinity rules are used, Space balancing is required to find a datastore that can store the VM without exceeding the space utilization threshold. If I/O load balancing is enabled, this datastore also needs to provide enough performance to keep the latency below the I/O latency threshold after placing the three DrmDisks. You can imagine it is a lot less complicated when space and I/O load balancing are allowed to place each DrmDisk on a datastore that suits their specific needs.

Disk Types

Storage DRS supports the following disk types:

- Thick
- Thin
- Independent disk
- vCloud Linked Clones
- Snapshot

Thick Disk

By default vSphere configures a VM with the thick format. During initial placement and load balancing operations, the provisioned space is used to calculate the necessary space available on the datastore. Because allocated and provisioned space are the same, the calculation is simple.

Thin Provisioned Disk

Storage DRS supports thin provisioned disks. As mentioned in the load-balancing algorithm chapter, it uses the committed space of a thin provisioned disk instead of the provisioned space. One caveat is that during the initial placement process, Storage DRS uses the provisioned space in its calculations. This safeguards Storage DRS from violating the space utilization threshold directly after placement.

Independent Disk

By default, Storage DRS does not move VMs with independent disks. Independent disks can be shared or not. Determining whether the disks are shared is a costly operation within the algorithm, as Storage DRS needs to investigate every VM and its disks in the datastore cluster. To reduce the overhead generated by Storage DRS on the virtual infrastructure, Storage DRS does not recommend such moves.
When using VMs that have disks set to independent and are placed in a

datastore cluster, attempting to enter Storage DRS maintenance mode for a datastore result in the error "Storage DRS is unable to move independent disks." An advanced parameter allows the use of non-shared independent disks in a datastore cluster.

The option `sdrs.disableSDRSonIndependentDisk` needs to be added to the vpxd.cfg file to use non-shared independent disks in a datastore cluster. By default, this option is not listed in the vpxd.cfg and is treated as true. When specified and set to false, Storage DRS moves independent disks and the error "Storage DRS is unable to move independent disks" does not appear.

Remember that adding this option to the VPXD.cfg file it automatically applies to all datastore clusters managed by that vCenter server! Please note that this option should only be used with non-shared independent disks! Moving shared independent disks is not supported.

Avoiding VMDK Level Over-Commitment While Using Thin Disks and Storage DRS

The behavior of thin provisioned disk VMDKs in a datastore cluster is quite impressive. Storage DRS supports the use of thin provisioned disks and is aware of both the configured size and the actual data usage of the virtual disk. When determining the placement of a VM, Storage DRS verifies the disk usage of the files stored on the datastore. To avoid getting caught out by instant data growth of the existing thin disk VMDKs, Storage DRS adds a buffer space to each thin disk.

This buffer zone is determined by the advanced setting `PercentIdleMBinSpaceDemand`. This setting controls how conservative Storage DRS is with determining the available space on the datastore for load balancing and initial placement operations of VMs.

IdleMB
The advanced option "PercentIdleMBinSpaceDemand" specifies the amount of IdleMB a thin-provisioned VMDK disk file contains.

- When a thin disk is configured, the user determines the maximum size of the disk (capacity). This configured size is the "**Provisioned Space**".
- When a thin disk is in use, it contains data. The size of the actual data inside the thin disk is the "**Allocated Space**".
- The space between the allocated space and the provisioned space is called identified as the **IdleMB**.

Let's use this in an example. VM10 has a single VMDK on Datastore 1. The total configured size of the VMDK is 6 GB. VM10 written 2 GB to the VMDK, this means the amount of IdleMB is 4 GB.

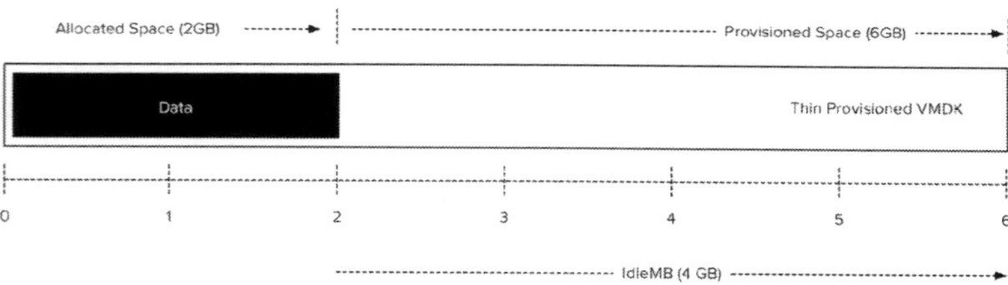

Figure 206: Thin Provisioned Disk

PercentIdleMBinSpaceDemand

The PercentIdleMBinSpaceDemand setting defines the percentage of IdleMB that is added to the allocated space of a VMDK during free space calculation of the datastore. The default value is 25%. When using the previous example, the PercentIdleMBinSpaceDemand is applied to the 4 GB unallocated space, 25% of 4 GB = 1 GB.

Entitled Space Use

Storage DRS adds the result of the PercentIdleMBinSpaceDemand calculation to the consumed space to determine the "Entitled Space Use". In this example the entitled space use is: 2 GB + 1 GB = 3 GB.

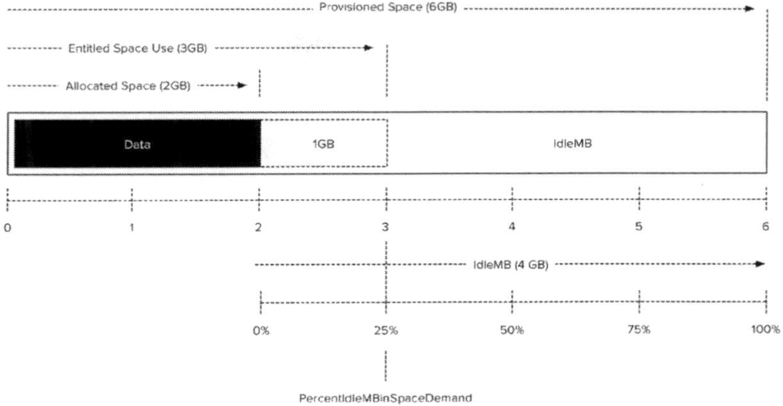

Figure 207: Entitled Space Use

Calculation During Placement

The size of Datastore1 is 10 GB. VM10 entitled space use is 3 GB, this means that Storage DRS determines that Datastore 1 has 7 GB of available free space. The Space Utilization Threshold set on the Datastore Cluster applies to each datastore. Thus, the load-balancing algorithm kicks in when the datastore thin provisioned disks entitled space use exceeds 8 GB.

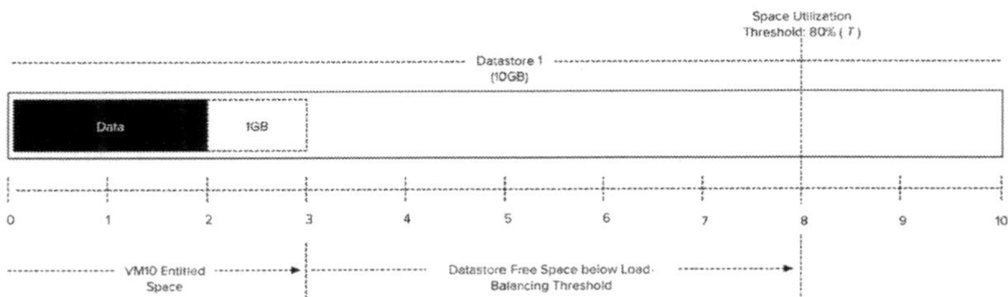

Figure 208: Datastore Free Space

Changing the PercentIdleMBinSpaceDemand Default Setting

Any value from 0% to 100% is valid. This setting applies to the datastore cluster level. There can be multiple reasons to change the default percentage. By using 0%, Storage DRS will only use the allocated space, allowing high consolidation. This is might be useful in environments with static or extremely slow data increase.

There are multiple use cases for setting the percentage to 100%, effectively disabling over-commitment on VMDK level. Setting the value to 100% forces Storage DRS to use the full size of the VMDK in its space usage calculations. Many customers are comfortable managing over-commitment of capacity only at storage array layer. This change allows the customer to use thin disks on thin provisioned datastores.

Use case 1: NFS Datastores
A use case is for example using NFS datastores. Default behavior of vSphere is to create thin disks when the VM is placed on a NFS datastore. This forces the customer to accept a risk of over-commitment on VMDK level. By setting it to 100%, Storage DRS uses the provisioned space during free space calculations instead of the allocated space.

Use case 2: Safeguard to Protect Against Unintentional Use of Thin Disks
This setting can also be used as safeguard for unintentional use of thin disks. Many customers have multiple teams for managing the virtual infrastructure, one team for managing the architecture, while another team is responsible for provisioning the virtual machines. The architecture team does not want over-commitment on VMDK level, but is dependent on the provisioning team to follow guidelines and only use thick disks. By setting "PercentIdleMBinSpaceDemand" to 100%, the architecture team ensures that Storage DRS calculates datastore free space based on provisioned space, simulating "only-thick disks" behavior.

Use-case 3: Reducing Storage vMotion Overhead While Avoiding Over-commitment
By setting the percentage to 100%, no over-commitment will be allowed on the datastore. However, the efficiency advantage of using thin disks remains. Storage DRS uses the allocated space to calculate the risk and the cost of a migration recommendation when a datastore avoids its I/O or space utilization threshold. This allows Storage DRS to select the VMDK that generates the lowest amount of overhead. vSphere only needs to move the used data blocks instead of all the zeroed out blocks, reducing CPU cycles. Overhead on the storage network is reduced, as only used blocks need to traverse the storage network.

VM Automation Level

Automation levels for individual VMs can be customized to override the Storage DRS cluster automation level. There are four automation levels for VMs:

- Fully Automated
- Manual
- Default (cluster automation level)
- Disabled

If the automation level of a VM is set to Disabled, Storage DRS does not migrate that VM or provide migration recommendations for it. By setting the automation mode of the VM to Manual, Storage recommendations are generated, but all recommendations need to be approved by the user before any action is taken.

Impact of VM Automation Level on Load Balancing Calculation
A VM set to Disabled automation level still has an impact on space and I/O load balancing as both space, and I/O metrics are still captured both at the datastore level and per VM. With the VM automation level set to Disabled, Storage DRS refrains from generating migration recommendations for that VM.

Interoperability

Array Features

vSphere 6.0 introduced Deep integration with *vSphere APIs for Storage Awareness* (VASA) 2.0 and this removed many of the interoperability concerns Storage DRS had with Array-based features. When the VASA plugin for your storage system is configured then Storage DRS will understand what capabilities are enabled on your storage system and more specific your datastores. From 6.0 and up Storage DRS is capable of understanding:

- Array-based auto-tiering
- Array-based deduplication
- Array-based replication
- Array-based thin-provisioning

Array-Based Auto-Tiering

By default, Storage DRS runs every 8 hours and uses performance data captured over more than a 16-hour period to generate I/O load balancing decisions. Many array-based auto-tiering features use a different timeframe to collect, analyze and move workload.

Storage DRS expects that the behavior of a LUN remains the same for at least 16 hours and it will perform its calculations using this assumption. Auto-tiering solutions might change the underlying structure of the datastore based on its algorithms and timescales, conflicting with these calculations.

VASA identifies datastores with auto-tiering and Storage DRS treats these datastores differently for performance modeling purposes. Storage DRS backs of at that moment. It becomes very conservative with generating recommendations. Storage DRS lets the array deal with the SLA guarantees because it's dealing at the block level and this is much more efficient than at the VMDK level.

Storage DRS increases the latency in such a way that it allows the storage Array to remediate and rectify the problems. Even after doing everything it can to solve the imbalance, and the latency is still growing, that's the moment Storage DRS helps to solve the I/O latency imbalance. The SIOC threshold is set even higher. The SIOC threshold is a part of this solution as well, as it can help to throttle the I/O load at the Host level.

Array-Based Deduplication

Deduplication offers space savings due to the elimination of duplicate data based on the actual content. This is achieved by indexing of the actual stored data on a datastore and storing only the index for the shared data.

As a result, all identical blocks will be replaced by a single block and the rest will be replaced by pointers to that block. Pre-vSphere 6.0 Storage DRS was not aware of the deduplication behavior of the underlying datastores.

Moving data out of a deduplicated datastore might inflate the actual storage use on the storage array, but moving data between datastores backed by the same deduplicated pool may potentially cause inefficiencies as well. For example, if a VMDK is moved from datastore 1 to datastore 2 where both datastores are sharing a common deduplication pool:

The entire content of the VMDK will be accessed to make the copy. This operation is less efficient on a deduplicated datastore. The deduplication engine will re-index the incoming VMDK on datastore 2. This is completely unnecessary due to sharing of the deduplication pool by 1 and 2. These moves have no net benefit and may potentially cause a great deal of overhead.

VASA identifies the datastores that share a common deduplication pool, and Storage DRS avoids any space balancing move operation between two datastores sharing the same deduplication pool. However, Storage DRS is capable of moving VMs out of the deduplicated pool as a last resort. Typically this depends on the VASA provider functionality of the storage array vendor, the VASA provider can identify how efficient the deduplication process is and Storage DRS can decide to move less-efficient VMs to other datastores. This functionality is not a VASA requirement, thus verify with your storage vendor if they have implemented this extra functionality.

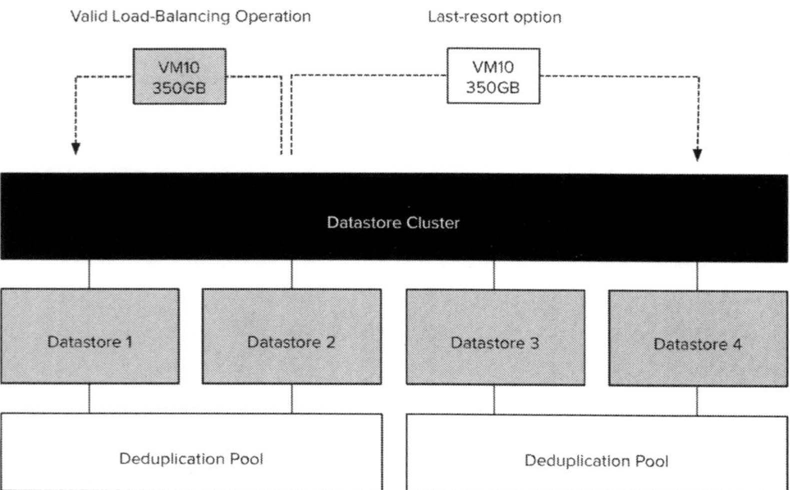

Figure 209: VMDK Migration within Deduplication Pools

Array-Based Replication

When replication is enabled and your datastore is part of a Storage Array consistency group then Storage DRS will ensure that the VM is only migrated to a datastore that belongs to the same consistency group.

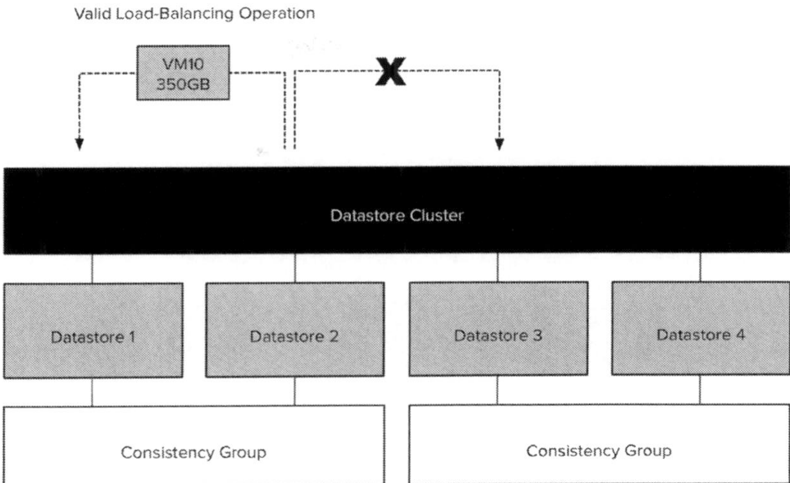

Figure 210: VMDK Migration within Same Consistency Group

Array-Based Thin-Provisioning

Pre vSphere 6.0 version used VASA to provide a thin-provisioning threshold. If the datastore exceeded the threshold (75%), then VASA triggered the thin-provisioning alarm. Storage DRS marked the datastore and did not move any VMs into this datastore via initial placement or load-balancing operations.

Since 6.0 VASA informs Storage DRS which datastores share the same thin-provision pool at the storage array level. VASA allows the storage array to report the available capacity within the thin-provisioning pool. This allows Storage DRS to generate recommendations based on the actual space rather than the reported capacity of the datastore. Storage DRS migrates the VMDK to a datastore backed by a different thin-provisioning pool if there is a physical space problem at the array level.

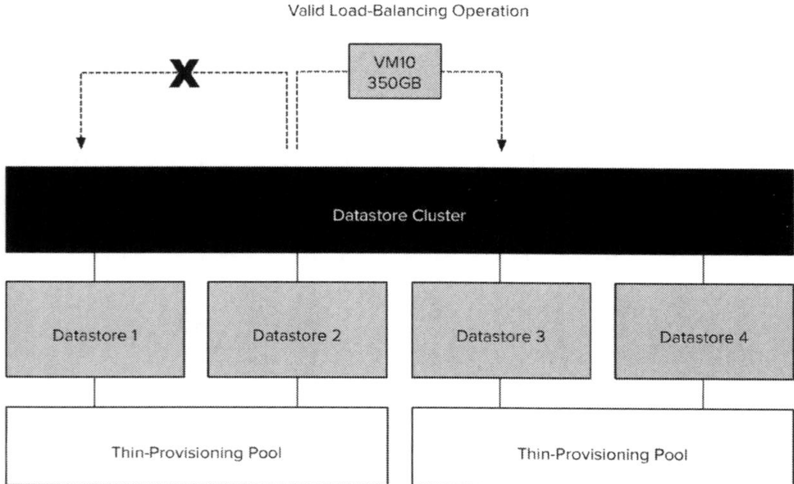

Figure 211: VMDK Migration between Thin-Provisioning Pools

Storage DRS Integration with Storage Profiles

Storage Policy Based Management (SPBM) allows you to specify the policy for a VM that is enforced by Storage DRS. Datastore clusters can be tagged or use VASA to expose the capabilities of the storage array's LUNs backing these datastores. If the VMs have storage profiles associated with them, Storage DRS can enforce placement based on underlying datastore capabilities.

This makes it much easier to select appropriate datastores for virtual machine placement or the creation of datastore clusters. It can also facilitate the troubleshooting process or conversations between you (vSphere administrator) and the storage administrators by automatically providing vCenter with details such as RAID level, thin/thick provisioned, replication state and much more.

Profile-Driven Storage

Prior to the availability of Profile-Driven Storage, managing datastores and matching the SLA requirements of VMs with the appropriate datastores was challenging, to say the least. Profile-Driven Storage allows for rapid and intelligent placement of VMs based on pre-defined storage profiles. These profiles usually represent a storage tier and are created through a vCenter feature called "VM Storage Profiles." Typically, characteristics like RAID level, replication, performance, deduplication and thin/thick provisioned are used to define different tiers. An example of these tiers would be:

- Latency Sensitive - All Flash Array
- Fast - Hybrid Array
- Economic - Hybrid Array - Deduplication enabled

Using VM Storage Profiles, different storage characteristics, provided through the Storage APIs (system defined) or manually entered (user defined), can be specified in a VM Storage Profile. These VM Storage Profiles are used during provisioning, cloning and Storage vMotion to ensure that only those datastores or datastore clusters compliant with the VM Storage Profile are made available.

This is shown in the figure below where the VM Storage Profile "Latency Sensitive" is selected and the datastore cluster "SHB9" is presented as compliant with this VM Storage Profile.

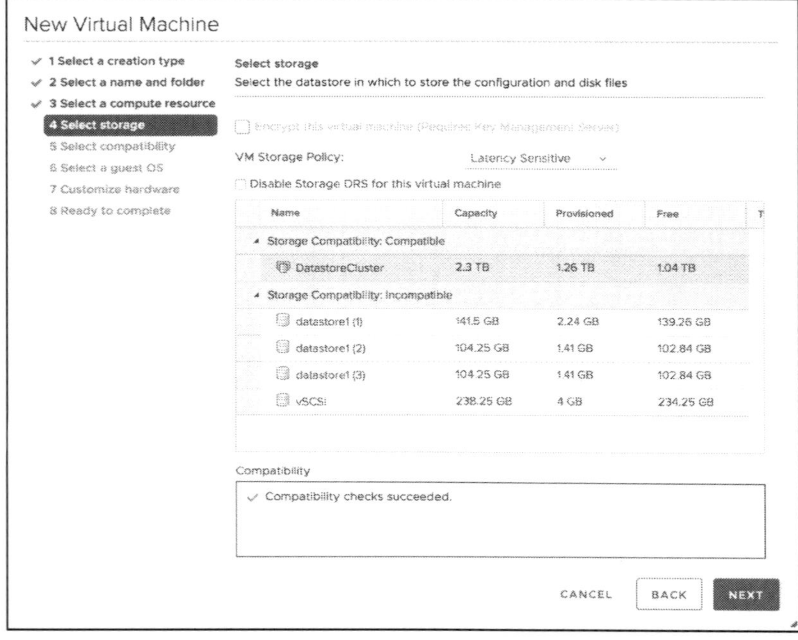

Figure 212: Compatible Datastore Cluster

The reason we are discussing this feature is that Profile-Driven Storage helps select the correct datastore cluster. Only datastore clusters that are compliant with the VM Storage Profile is presented. A requirement for this to work, however, is that similar type datastores are selected during the creation of the datastore cluster.

> **Please note that Datastore Clusters should be seen as a pod of service. It's a load-balancing domain! Meaning datastores within that datastore cluster should provide the same level of service or performance. You can tag a datastore cluster or the individual datastores. You can even tag a subset of datastores with different tags within that cluster. In that scenario, neither the datastores or the datastore cluster will show up as a compatible storage destination during the initial placement of the VM.**

If you desire to build a datastore cluster with datastores that offer different storage services, you can still tag the individual datastores separately. The only challenge is that the datastore cluster or datastore is not directly displayed as compatible datastore.

In this example the datastore cluster groups four datastores into a single load-balancing domain, two datastores are backed by a diskgroup containing only flash devices. These datastores, 10G-AFA-01 and 10G-AFA-02 are tagged with the tag AFA, and this Tag is linked to the storage policy "Latency Sensitive". The datastore cluster contains two datastores that are backed by a diskgroup that contains AFA and spindles (Hybrid solution). Not as fast as the AFA, but lightyears faster than an old all-spindle array. The tag Hybrid is applied to these datastores and the storage policy "Fast Storage" uses this tag.

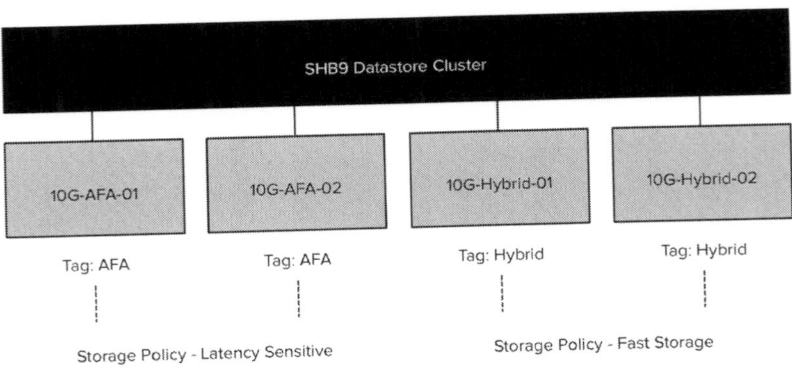

Figure 213: Multiple Storage Policies in Single Datastore Cluster

VM10 is not running a latency sensitive application, but prefers fast responding storage. The hybrid datastores are sufficient for the workload requirements of VM10. During the deployment process, the Fast Storage storage policy is applied to VM10. The UI list no compatible datastore.

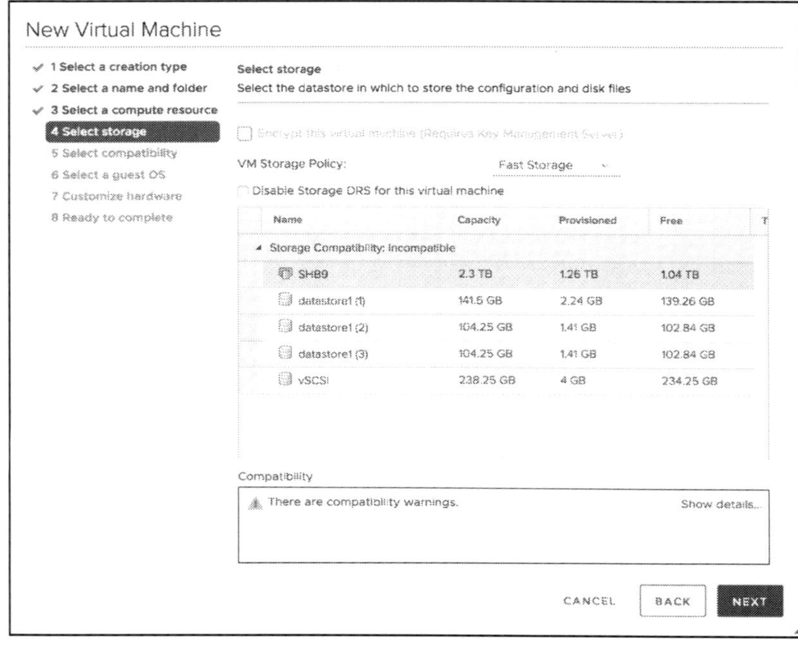

Figure 214: Incompatible Datastores

We know that there are datastores within the datastore cluster and select SHB9 and continue the deployment process. (You can argue that this screen should bubble up the two datastores, but again, a datastore cluster is intended to be a consistent load-balancing domain. The ready to complete screen shows that there are datastore recommendations.

New Virtual Machine

- ✓ 1 Select a creation type
- ✓ 2 Select a name and folder
- ✓ 3 Select a compute resource
- ✓ 4 Select storage
- ✓ 5 Select compatibility
- ✓ 6 Select a guest OS
- ✓ 7 Customize hardware
- 8 Ready to complete

Ready to complete

Click Finish to start creation.

Provisioning type	Create a new virtual machine
Virtual machine name	VM10
Folder	HomeDC
Cluster	Workload
Datastore	SHB9 [10G-Hybrid-02] (Recommended) more recommendations

Figure 215: Datastore Selection Recommendations

By clicking on the link of more recommendation, the deployment process displays the compatible datastores for the VM to be placed on.

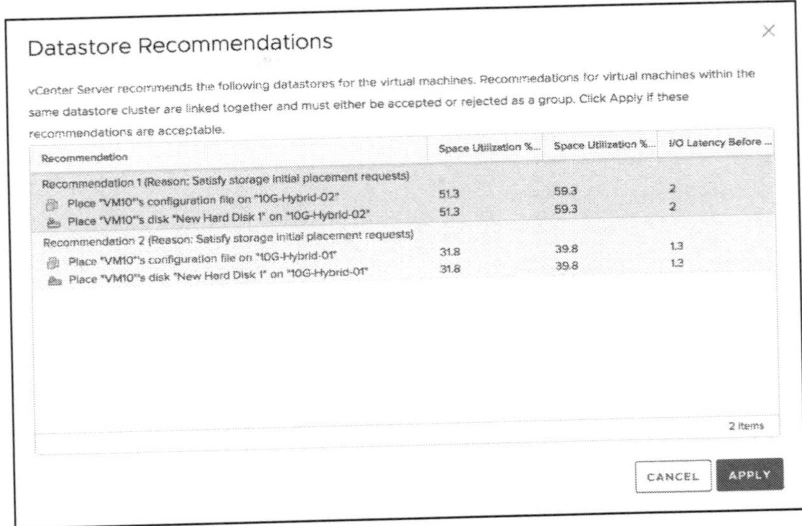

Figure 216: Compatible Datastore List

As proven, it can work, but we are not sure this is the way to use storage policies. Interesting fact, I/O load balancing is disabled, yet Storage DRS still displays the I/O latency to allow you to make a well-informed decision.

Storage Policy Compliancy

The status screen of the VM shows which VM storage policy is applied to the VM and if the VM configuration is compliant with the storage policy.

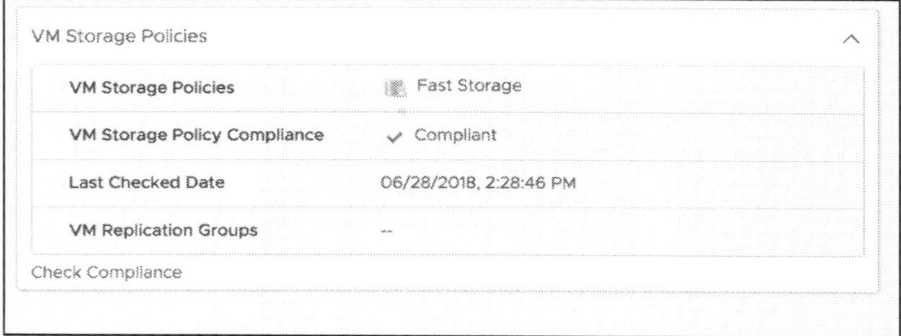

Figure 217: VM Storage Policy Compliance Status

As part of Storage DRS integration with storage profiles, the Storage DRS cluster level advanced option `EnforceStorageProfiles` is introduced.

Advanced option `EnforceStorageProfiles` takes one of these integer values: 0,1 or 2. The default value is 0. When the option is set to 0, it indicates that there is no storage profile or policy enforcement on the Storage DRS cluster. **For example, Load balancing can move the VMs to a datastore that is not compliant with the storage policy.**

When the option is set to 1, it indicates that there is a storage profile or policy soft enforcement on the Storage DRS cluster. This is analogous with DRS soft rules. Storage DRS will comply with storage profile or policy in the optimum level. Storage DRS will violate the storage profile compliant if it is required to do so. Storage DRS affinity rules will have higher precedence over storage profiles only when storage profile enforcement is set to 1. **For example, if the anti-affinity rule is active, it may happen that a single disk will violate the storage policy.**

When the option is set to 2, it indicates that there is a storage profile or policy hard enforcement on the Storage DRS cluster. This is analogous with DRS hard rules. Storage DRS will not violate the storage profile or policy compliant. Storage profiles will have higher precedence over affinity rules. Storage DRS will generate fault: could not fix anti-affinity rule violation. **For example, VMs will not be moved out a datastore if no other compliant datastores are available.**

Prerequisites
By default, Storage DRS will not enforce storage policies associated with a VM. Please configure EnforceStorageProfiles option according to your requirements. The options are Default (0), Soft (1) or Hard (2).

> **Please note that Storage DRS does not remediate any current violations of storage policies immediately. Thus if a VM violates the policy, Storage DRS does not move the VM after setting EnforceStorageProfiles. During the load-balancing invocation, Storage DRS will generate the recommendation for moving the VM to a compliant datastore.**

22

AFFINITY RULES

By default, Storage DRS applies an Intra-VM affinity rule (VMDK affinity) that specifies storing all files belonging to a VM on one datastore. After configuring a datastore cluster, the advanced options allow you to change this default VM affinity rule.

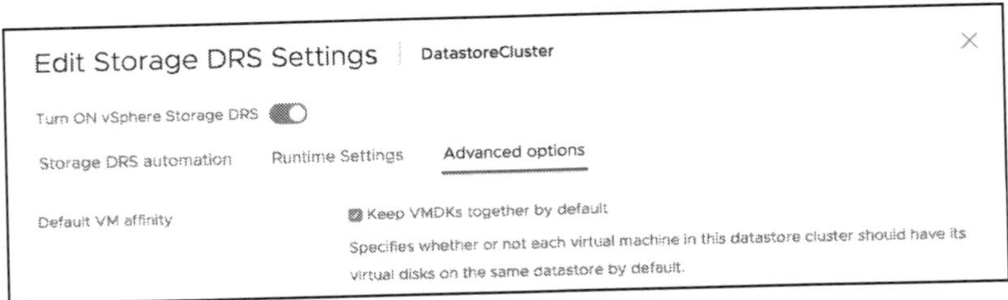

Figure 218: Default VM Affinity

By deselecting the Default VM affinity section's "Keep VMDKs together by default" option, all new VMs are configured with an anti-affinity rule, meaning that Storage DRS initial placement and load balancing keeps the VM files and VDMK files stored on separate datastores. This chapter takes a closer look at the affinity rules provided by Storage DRS, how they can impact initial placement and load balancing operations and how to configure them.

Storage DRS Rules

Storage DRS provides the option to control the placement of virtual disks. The affinity rule keeps virtual disks of a VM together on the same datastore, and this rule is considered to be a VMDK affinity rule. Anti-Affinity rules in datastore clusters are available for VMDK level and VM-VM level. Storage DRS rules are available at Storage | Storage DRS Cluster| Configure | Configuration | Rules.

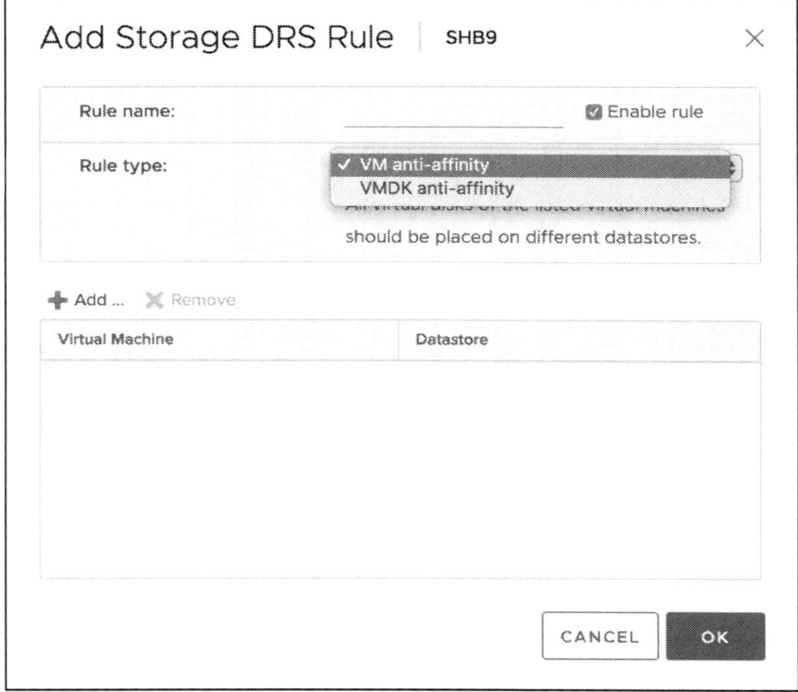

Figure 219: Storage DRS Rules

> **All rules are enforced during initial placement and Storage DRS-recommended Storage vMotions, but they are not enforced on user-initiated Storage vMotions.**

VMDK Affinity Rule

Storage DRS applies a VMDK affinity rule to each VM by default. The VMDK affinity rule keeps the VMDKs belonging to a VM stored together on the same datastore.

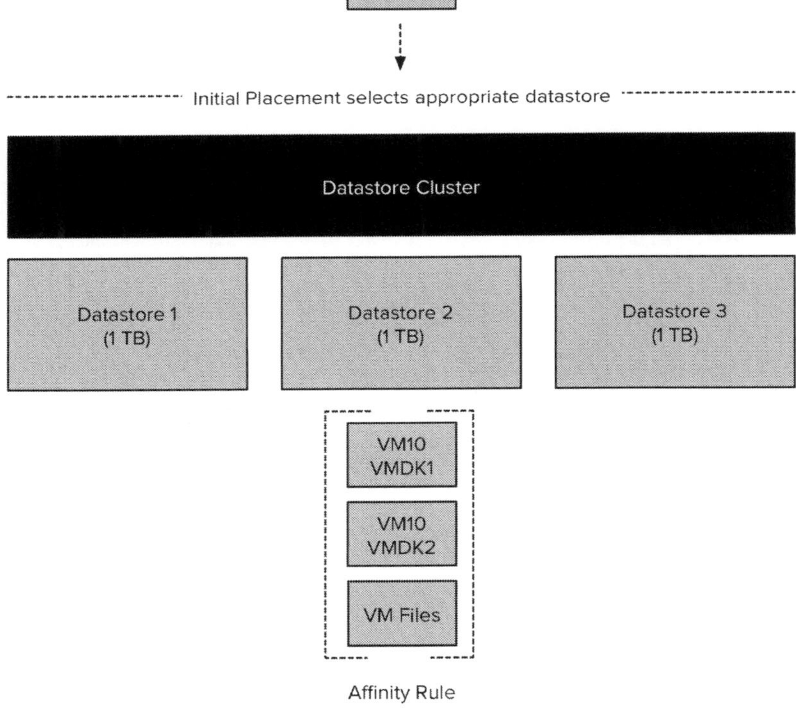

Figure 220: Initial Placement with Default Affinity Rule

VMDK Anti-Affinity Rule

The Intra-VM VMDK anti-affinity rule keeps the specified VMDKs belonging to a VM on separate datastores.

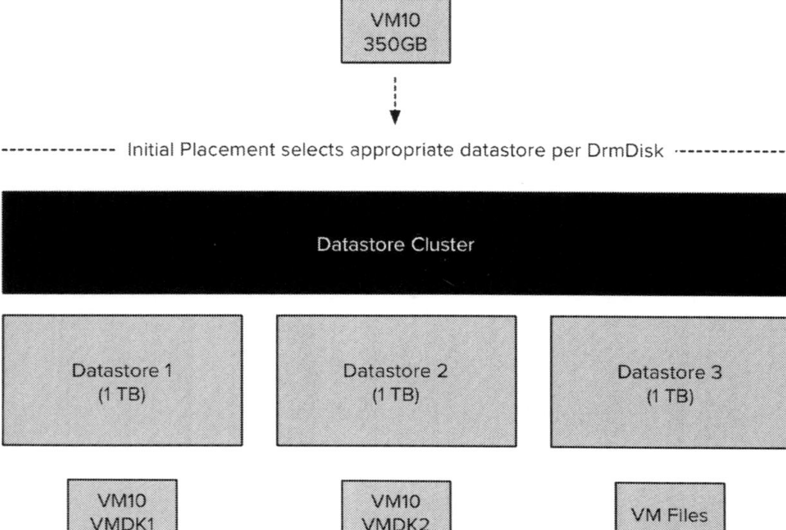

Figure 221: Initial Placement with VMDK Anti-Affinity Rule Enabled

When the default VM affinity rule option at datastore cluster level is deselected, Storage DRS places each VM disk file on a separate datastore. During the creation of a new VM, Storage DRS recommends placing the VMDK files on different datastores.

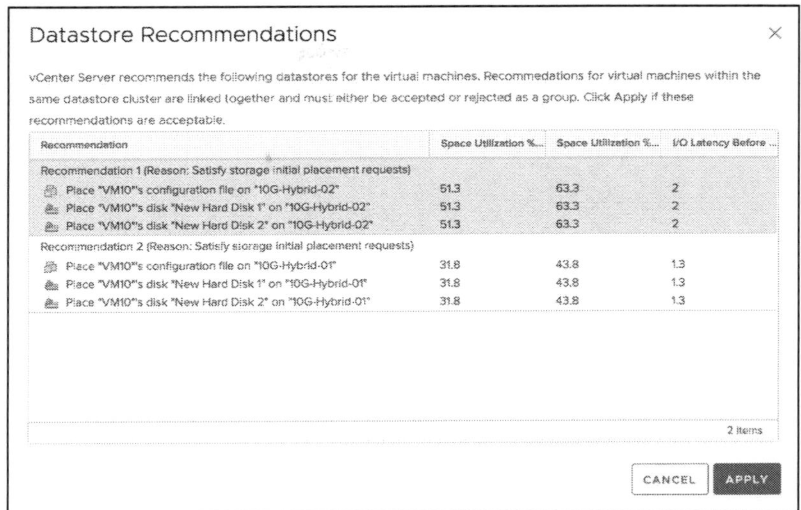

Figure 222: Datastore Recommendation with Default Anti-Affinity

VM Anti-Affinity Rule

The Storage DRS VM anti-affinity rule keeps the specified VMs on different datastores. This rule can help maximize the availability of a collection of related VMs. The availability of the set of VMs is increased by not allowing Storage DRS to place the VMs on the same datastore. For example, web servers in a load-balanced cluster or domain controllers.

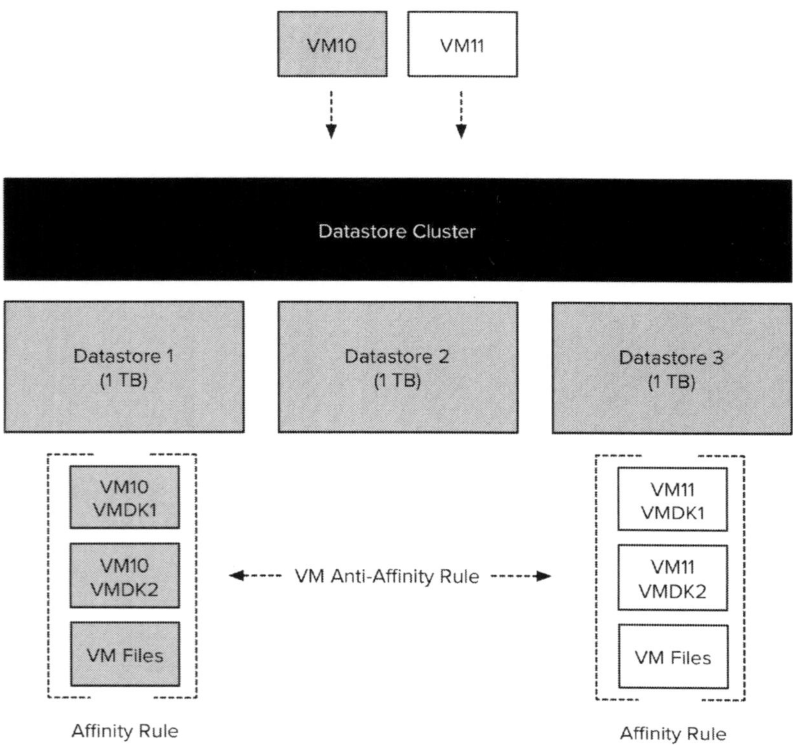

Figure 223: VM to VM Anti-Affinity Rule

Storage DRS VM anti-affinity rules can contain two or more VMs. We recommend applying VM anti-affinity rules sparingly. Anti-Affinity rules place limitations on Storage DRS initial placement, maintenance mode, and load-balancing operations by reducing the possibilities it has to reach a steady and balanced state.

VMs that are associated with an Inter-VM VM anti-affinity rule must be configured with an Intra-VM affinity rule. If a VM is configured with an Intra-VM anti-affinity rule, this could be due to the cluster-wide default anti-affinity rule, vCenter displays the following warning and the user is required to fix the violation manually.

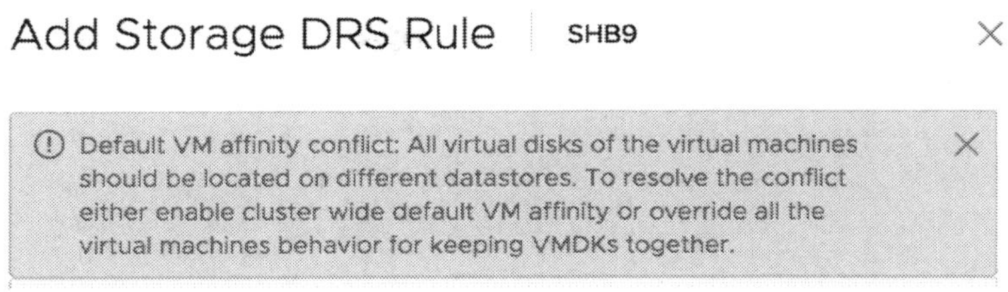

Add Storage DRS Rule | SHB9

Default VM affinity conflict: All virtual disks of the virtual machines should be located on different datastores. To resolve the conflict either enable cluster wide default VM affinity or override all the virtual machines behavior for keeping VMDKs together.

Figure 224: Default VM Affinity Conflict

Violate Anti-Affinity Rules

Initial placement, I/O, and space load balancing do not violate anti-affinity rules; however, when generating migration recommendations for datastore maintenance mode, Storage DRS may provide recommendations that potentially violate the affinity and anti-affinity rules.

Storage DRS generates migration recommendations with the rules intact and provides these recommendations to the user if no faults are generated. If the fully automatic mode is selected, maintenance mode does not require manual approval unless there is a fault.

Configuring an intricate and elaborate set of rules in a datastore cluster with a small number of datastores may lead Storage DRS to generate faults. If there are faults, Storage DRS reruns the algorithm but drops the affinity and anti-affinity rules, which may lead to recommendations that violate the affinity rule set.

Anti-Affinity Rules with Datastore Correlation

Datastore correlation typically indicates resource sharing. It is best to avoid using two correlated datastores to enforce an anti-affinity rule (VM-VM or VMDK-VMDK).

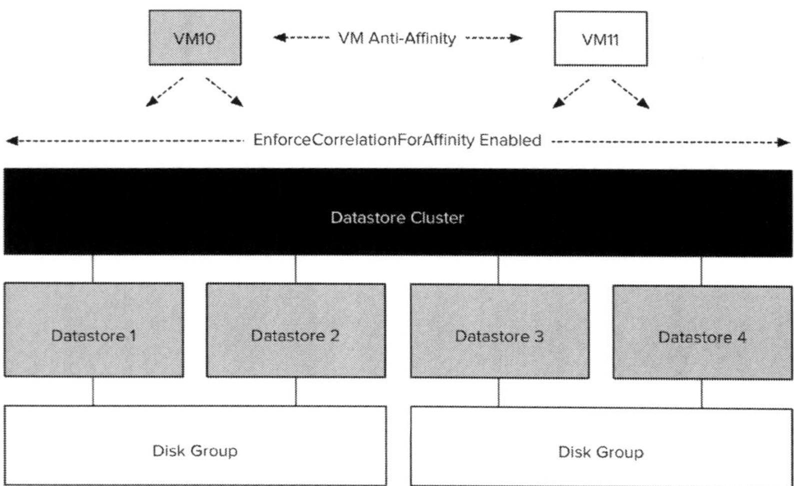

Figure 225: EnforceCorrelationForAffinity Enabled

Storage DRS allows controlling affinity rules when performance correlation is detected. Set the `EnforceCorrelationForAffinity` in the advanced options of the datastore cluster:

VALUE	ENFORCEMENT	DESCRIPTION
0	None	No consideration for correlations
1	Soft	Do not use any correlated datastores unless it is necessary when fixing an anti-affinity rule violation
2	Hard	Do not use correlated datastores. If the rule can't be fixed without using correlated datastores, generate faults

Table 30: EnforceCorrelationForAffinity Settings

Overriding Datastore Cluster Default

Storage DRS provides the ability to override the default datastore cluster affinity rule at the VM level. This can be done during the creation of a VM or when the VM is placed inside the datastore cluster. When the VM is created, the affinity rule can be changed via the VM override option of the datastore cluster settings page or by editing the settings of the VM directly.

VM Overrides

The VM Overrides function allows you to configure a different VMDK affinity rule. The VM Overrides option is available Storage | Storage DRS Cluster| Configure | Configuration | VM Overrides. Click add to select the VM you want to configure and select the appropriate options.

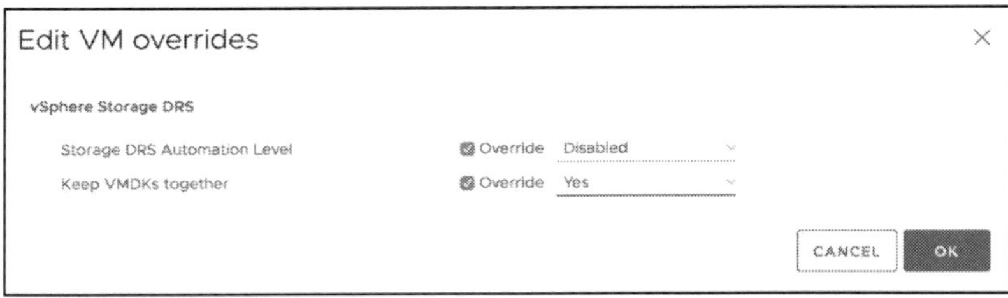

Figure 226: VM Overrides

Storage DRS Rules

Affinity rules can be changed in the Storage DRS Rules window. The advantage of changing rules at the datastore cluster level is that multiple VMs can be selected and changed at once.

Moving a VM into a Datastore Cluster

If an existing VM is moved into a datastore cluster, the application of an Intra-VM affinity rule depends on the disk layout configuration of the VM and the method of introduction. A VM can be moved into a datastore cluster by either Storage vMotion or by adding the datastore(s) containing its disks to a datastore cluster.

VMDK CONFIGURATION	MIGRATION METHOD	RULE ACTIVATE	DISK LAYOUT
All VMDKs on single DS	SvMotion	Yes	All VMDKs on single DS
VMDKs on multiple DS	SvMotion	Yes	All VMDKs on single DS
All VMDKs on single DS	Add Datastore	Yes	All VMDKs on single DS
VMDKs on multiple DS	Add Datastore	No	**VMDKs on multiple DS**

Table 31: Overview Storage vMotion of Various VM Storage Layouts

Be aware of the result of these actions when migrating to a datastore cluster. When a VM is moved into a datastore cluster by Storage vMotion, placement of the VMDKs associated with the VM is made in accordance of the cluster wide default affinity rule. If a VMDK affinity rule is configured as cluster wide default rule, Storage DRS will consolidate all of the VMDKs onto a single datastore, regardless of the original layout.

When adding datastores to the cluster, Storage DRS configures the existing VMs with VMDKs stored on a single datastore. If the VMDK files associated with a VM span multiple datastores, Storage DRS disables the default affinity rule (if there is one) for the VM configuration. This is done to avoid an SvMotion storm when moving a datastore into a datastore cluster if the datastore contains existing VMDKs that are not kept together.

23

DATASTORE MAINTENANCE MODE

Datastore maintenance mode is similar to Host Maintenance Mode. When a datastore is placed in Maintenance Mode, all registered VMs on that datastore are migrated to other datastores in the datastore cluster.

By using the vCenter datastore API, Storage DRS learns which registered VMs are using the datastore. Storage DRS uses this list as input for generating migration recommendations. Because Storage DRS depends on vCenter's inventory, VMs that are not registered in vCenter will not be migrated off the datastore. The same is true for any other files on the datastore that are not related to registered VMs, such as ISO files.

Automation Mode

Depending on the Storage DRS automation mode, or the VM Evacuation automation level vCenter automatically executes Storage vMotions for the VMs if Storage DRS is configured in Fully Automated mode. Otherwise, vCenter generates a recommendation list and presents this to the user for validation.

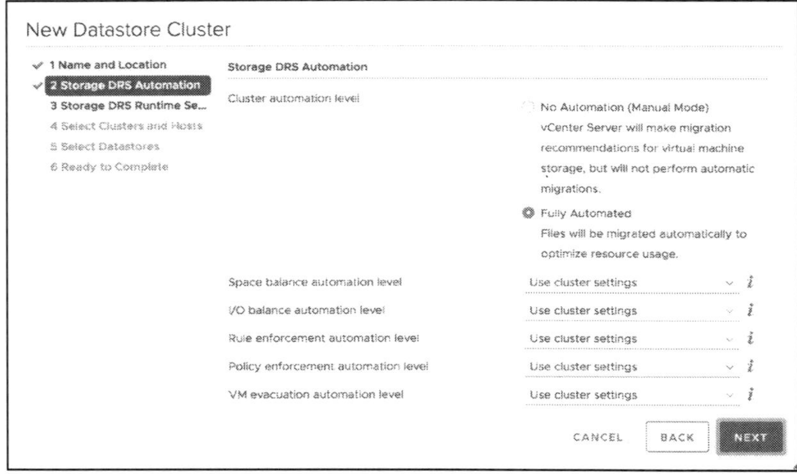

Figure 227: VM Evacuation Automation Level

VM evacuation automation level: Specifies the Storage DRS behavior when it generates recommendations for VM evacuations from datastores in a datastore cluster. This applies to the behavior of Storage DRS when putting a datastore in maintenance mode. Do you want automatic migrations of VMs when putting a datastore in maintenance mode, if yes, select fully automated.

Using Datastore Maintenance Mode for Migration Purposes
Datastore maintenance mode can be used to safely migrate VMs out of the datastore for storage array related maintenance operations such as migrating a LUN to another RAID group or migrating multiple VMs to datastores hosted by a new Storage Array.

Manually moving a large group of VMs manually out of datastore is a time-consuming operation. Selecting the datastore cluster as the migration target, initial placement helps you select the appropriate datastore. However, you still need to manually start a Storage vMotion process for each VM and manage the migrations until the last VM is migrated.

Datastore Maintenance Mode on a Datastore

When the datastore inside a datastore cluster is placed into maintenance mode, migration recommendations are generated to empty the datastore. Storage DRS reviews the VMs on the datastores and distributes them across the other datastores in the datastore cluster. Storage DRS finds an optimal placement based on the space and I/O utilization of the VMs and moves them to selected datastores while keeping the datastore cluster as balanced as possible concerning space and I/O load.

Depending on the Storage DRS automation mode, it generates a list of recommendations (Manual mode) and automatically execute migrations of the VMs (Fully Automated).

After all the VMs have been migrated, Storage DRS will indicate that the datastore is in maintenance mode. At this point you can remove the datastore from the datastore cluster.

Throttle the Number of Storage vMotion Operations

When enabling datastore maintenance mode, Storage DRS move VMs out of the datastore as fast as it can. The number of VMs that can be migrated into or out of a datastore is 8 and is controlled by the operation costs and limits defined at various levels. This is related to the concurrent migration limits of hosts, network, and datastores. To manage and limit the number of concurrent migrations, either by vMotion or Storage vMotion, a cost and limit factor is applied. Although the term "limit" is used, a better description would be "maximum cost." For a migration operation to be able to start, the cost of the operation cannot exceed the maximum cost (limit) configured on the resources. In this case, vMotion and Storage vMotion are considered operations and the ESXi host, network and datastore are considered resources. A resource has both a maximum and an in-use cost. When an operation is requested, the in-use cost plus the new operation cost cannot exceed the maximum cost.

The operation cost of a storage vMotion on a host is 4, the max cost of a host is 8. If one Storage vMotion operation is running, the in-use cost of the host resource is 4, allowing one more Storage vMotion process to start without exceeding the host limit.

As a storage vMotion operation also hits the storage resource cost, the max cost and in-use cost of the datastore needs to be factored in as well. The operation cost of a Storage vMotion for datastores is set to 16, the max cost of a datastore is 128. This means that 8 concurrent Storage vMotion operations can be executed on a datastore. These operations can be started on multiple hosts, not more than 2 storage vMotion from the same host due to the max cost of a Storage vMotion operation on the host level.

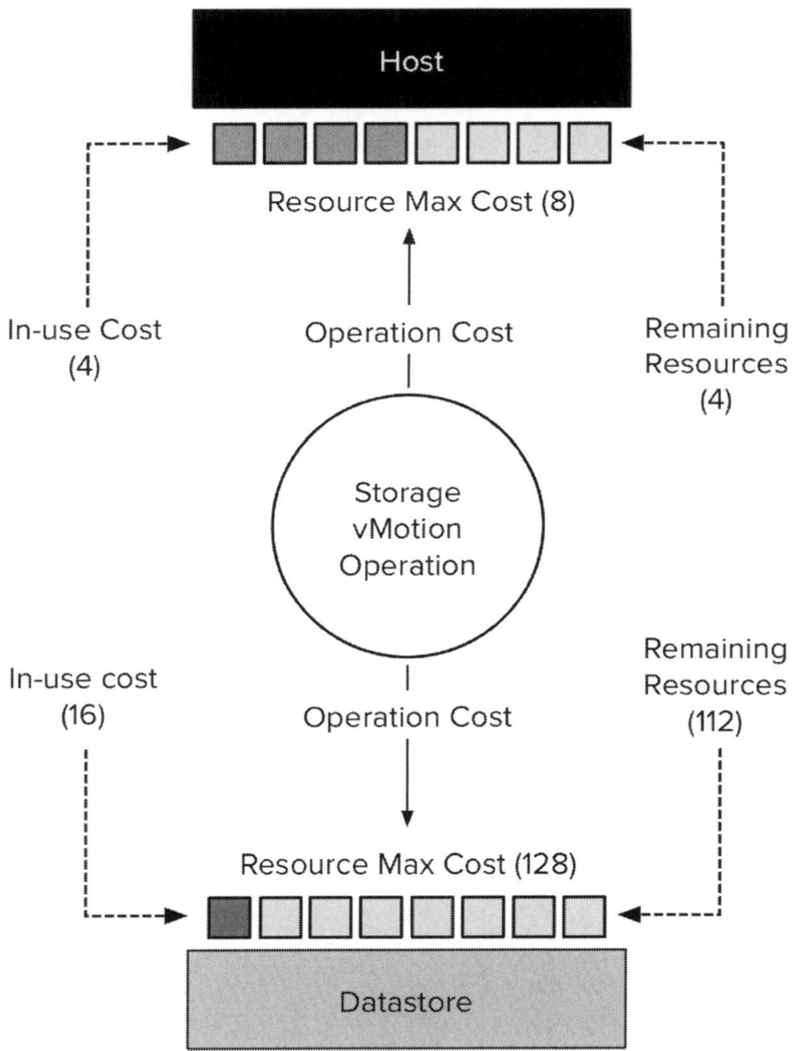

Figure 228: Storage vMotion in Progress

How Do You Throttle The Number of Storage vMotion Operations?

You may want to throttle the number of storage vMotion operations to reduce the I/O hit on a datastore during maintenance mode. The preferred method for doing so is to reduce the max cost for provisioning operations to the datastore. Adjusting host costs is strongly discouraged. Host costs are defined according to host resource limitation issues and adjusting host costs can impact other host functionality that is unrelated to vMotion or Storage vMotion processes. Adjusting the max cost per datastore can be done by editing the vpxd.cfg or via the advanced settings of the vCenter Server Settings in the administration view.

If done via the vpxd.cfg, the value vpxd.ResourceManager.MaxCostPerEsx6xDS should be added as follows:

```
< config >
< vpxd >
< ResourceManager >
< MaxCostPerEsx6x1DS > new value < /MaxCostPerEsx6xDS >
< /ResourceManager >
< /vpxd >
< /config >
```

Please note that the setting changed names starting vSphere 6.0, this setting used to be called MaxCostPerEsx41DS.
Please remember to leave some room for vMotion when resizing the max cost of a datastore since the vMotion process has a datastore cost as well. During the stun/unstun of a VM, the vMotion process hits the datastore, and the cost involved with this process is 1.

As an example, changing the MaxCostPerEsx6xDS to 112, allows 7 concurrent Storage vMotions against a given datastore in the vCenter inventory. If 7 concurrent Storage vMotions are started on this datastore, a vMotion process of a VM using this datastore will be queued as the vMotion process would violate the max cost of the datastore. 7 x 16 =

112 + 1 vMotion = 113. The moment a Storage vMotion is completed, the vMotion process will resume as resources become available.

Please note that cost and max values are applied to each migration process, impact normal day-to-day DRS and Storage DRS load balancing operations as well as the manual vMotion and Storage vMotion operations occurring in the virtual infrastructure managed by the vCenter server.

As mentioned before, adjusting the cost at the host side can be tricky as the costs of operations and limits are relative to each other and can even harm other host processes unrelated to migration processes. Think about the impact on DRS if you adjust the cost at the host side! When increasing the cost of a Storage vMotion operation on the host, the available "slots" for vMotion operations are reduced. This might impact DRS load balancing efficiency when a storage vMotion process is active and should be avoided at all times.

P4

QUALITY CONTROL

24

STORAGE I/O CONTROL

Virtualization infrastructures commonly operate shared storage platforms to serve datastores to VMware ESXi hosts. We are moving towards distributed storage systems that allow for easier performance and capacity scaling, like with VMware vSAN. However, a significant portion of the market is still using storage arrays that present LUNs or NFS shares as datastores towards the ESXi hosts.

> **A general consensus in our industry is that most virtualization performance issues originate in latency issues caused by the storage backend.**

Storage arrays are evolving, flash becoming the de facto standard in today's data center. Flash storage continues to grow more dense, meaning that more and more capacity is available in the same amount of rack units. On the other hand, the application landscape is also changing. Demand for capacity and performance is increasing. That leaves us with the same challenges we had since we began to utilize shared storage systems in our vSphere environments.

When using shared storage, the fundamental storage architecture remains the same. Multiple ESXi hosts are connected to storage controllers within storage arrays that utilize spindles and flash media to store data.

Storage administrators today are still faced with the challenge of making sure all workloads can consume their much-needed storage resources. Looking at infrastructures with VMs running on the same shared datastore, served by a storage array, we need to make sure to enforce a level of storage fairness between the various VMs.

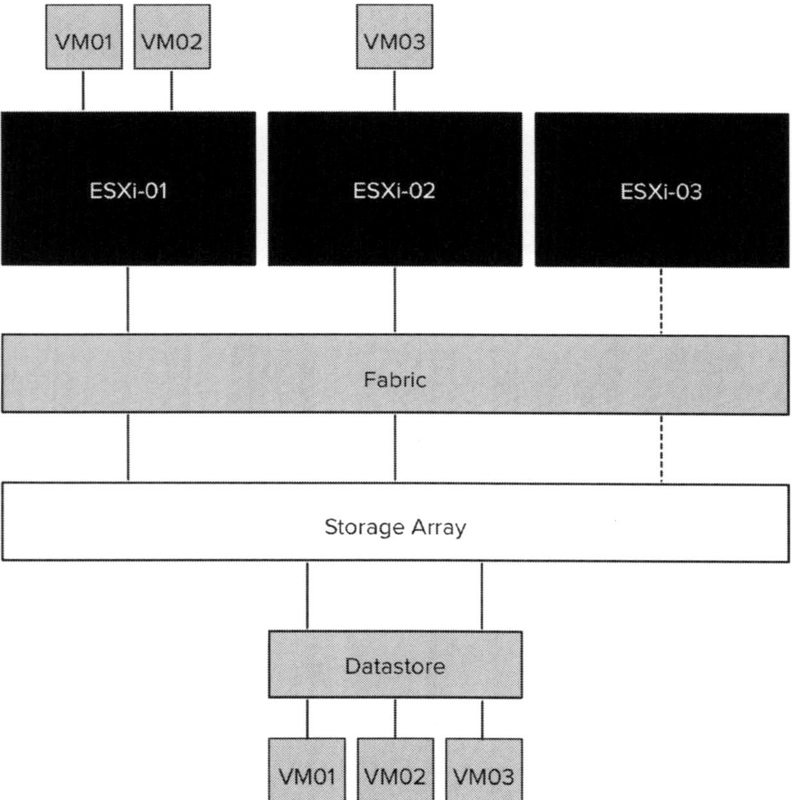

Figure 229: Basic Shared Storage Architecture

Without storage fairness, it is entirely possible that VM3 running on one ESXi host gets more storage performance entitlement relative the other two VMs running on the ESXi-01 host.

> **A general recommendation is not to have datastores shared across multiple vSphere clusters or other physical workloads. This way, we will be able to benefit from vSphere storage quality control mechanisms to the fullest.**

The following diagram shows an example of unbalanced storage I/O consumption on the datastore. The ESXi-01 server hosts two VMs, while the ESXi-02 server only hosts one VM. When all three VMs are consuming similar I/O on the same shared datastore, VM03 will have 50% of the storage I/O entitled to it while VM01 and VM02 both get 25%, sharing the 50% designated from the ESXi-01 host to the datastore.

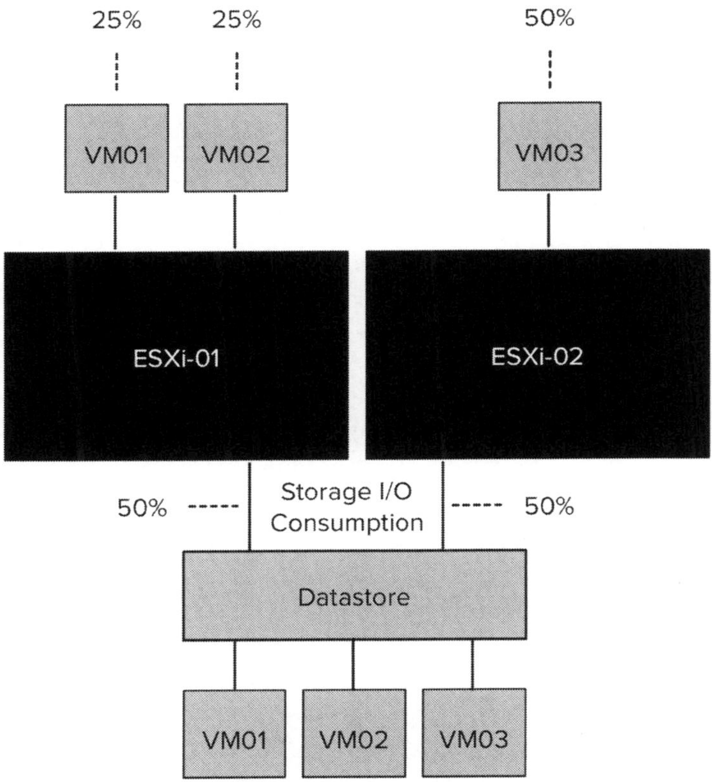

Figure 230: Unbalanced Storage I/O Consumption

The more desirable storage I/O distribution would be to throttle down the storage I/O entitlement of VM03, making sure it can consume the same I/O in relation to what VM01 or VM02 are entitled to.

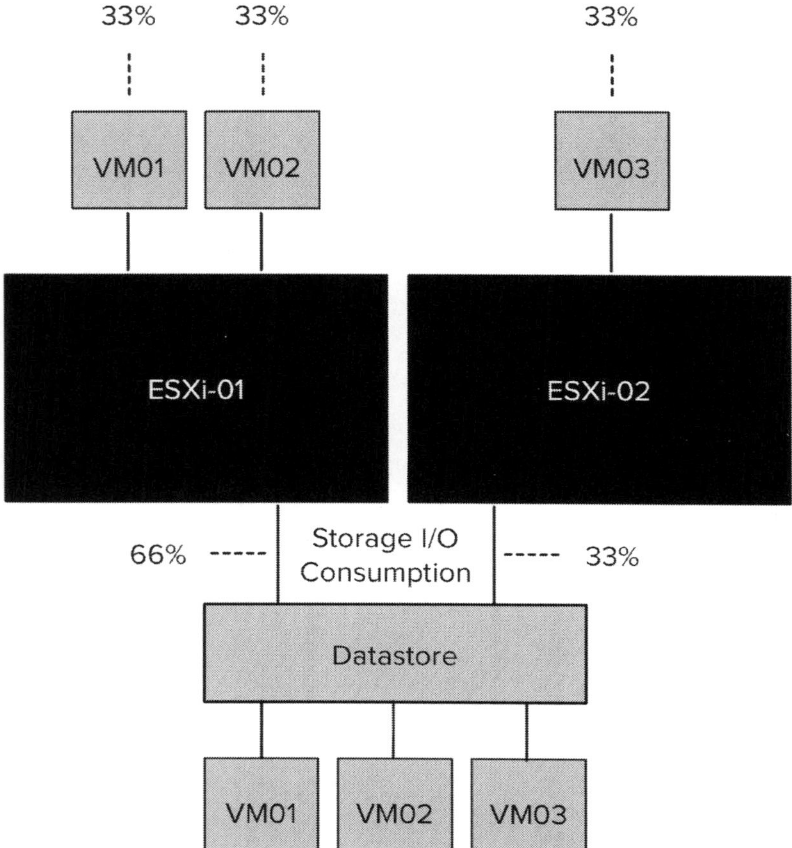

Figure 231: Balanced Storage I/O Consumption

The exemplary situation we just described uses a mechanism to control storage fairness, making sure all VMs are equally treated when it comes to storage I/O consumption. It will prevent one VM from monopolizing the datastore by leveling out all other I/O requests the datastore receives.

In the extent of storage fairness, we would like to be able to prioritize specific workloads. How do we make sure our business-critical workloads are preferred over lower class workloads when it comes to shared storage performance? All the more reason why we need vSphere Storage I/O Control.

SIOC Explained

Storage I/O Control (SIOC) was first introduced in vSphere 4.1, supporting *Virtual Machine File System* (VMFS) datastores only. As of vSphere 5.0, SIOC also included support for *Network File System* (NFS) datastores.

The release of vSphere 6.5 saw an improved SIOC implementation, most noticeable is the use of the *vSphere APIs for I/O Filtering* (VAIO) framework. More about this topic in an upcoming chapter.

> **SIOC is disabled by default and is enabled per datastore. It is available with vSphere Enterprise+ licensing.**

Storage Fairness

SIOC introduced a datastore-wide scheduler, allowing distribution of queue priority against the VMs located on multiple ESXi hosts that are connected to a datastore. Before SIOC, disk I/O scheduling was done only at ESXi host level.

SIOC is designed to help you in situations where storage contention occurs. If necessary, SIOC will divide the available queue slots across the ESXi hosts to satisfy the storage I/O requirements based on VM priorities. SIOC measures the latency from the datastore inside the VMkernel to the storage media inside the storage array. It is not designed to migrate VMs to other hosts in the cluster to reduce latency or bandwidth limitations incurred by the data path.

> **The goal of Storage DRS I/O load balancing is to fix long-term prolonged I/O imbalances, VMware vSphere Storage I/O Control addresses short-term burst and loads.**
> Source: https://kb.vmware.com/s/article/2149938

Even though there are similarities between Storage DRS and SIOC, they are not alike. SIOC is all about managing storage queues whilst Storage DRS is about intelligent storage placement and avoiding bottlenecks.

SIOC Defaults

When enabling SIOC you will be presented with several options. By default, SIOC is using the congestion threshold option set to 90% of the peak throughput.

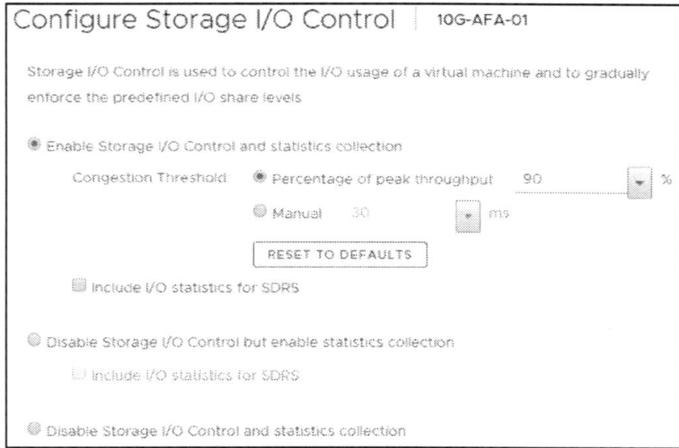

Figure 232: Default SIOC Configuration Values

As the percentage based congestion threshold is the only dynamic option, it is typically a good idea to leave SIOC by its default setting. If you have specific requirements or need to manually enforce the latency threshold, configured as *milliseconds* (ms), you can do so. The following table consists of some guidelines on what value to use when using the manually set threshold, depending on the type of storage media used.

STORE MEDIA TYPE	RECOMMENDED LATENCY THRESHOLD
Flash	5-15 ms
Fibre-channel	15-25 ms
SAS	20-30 ms
SATA	30-50 ms

Table 32: Latency Recommendations

More information about the "Include the I/O statistics for SDRS" option is discussed in the Storage DRS chapter in this book.

A general recommendation is to enable SIOC on all datastores used in a cluster. Let us emphasize; SIOC only kicks in when contention occurs. But when that happens, SIOC is there to help you to throttle down that noisy neighbor VM. It does so by adjusting the queue depth to storage on a per-VM basis. It is important to understand that once latency comes back down below the threshold value, all ESXi hosts and VMs can have their full queue depth as SIOC will stop throttling.

Latency Threshold Computations

When SIOC is enabled on a datastore, all ESXi hosts monitor the device latency when communicating with that datastore. Only when the device latency exceeds the default or custom latency thresholds, it is considered to be congested. As a result of SIOC taking the average device latency of all ESXi hosts connected to the datastore into account, it understands the overall picture when determining the correct queue depth for the VMs. Keep in mind; SIOC throttling will only occur during contention.

Automatic or Manual Threshold

When you want SIOC to automatically assess the latency threshold, as it would be when you enable SIOC, the I/O-injector is used. However, datastore latency is determined by statistics of its esxtop equivalent (DQLEN) when the congestion threshold is set to a manual value.

Because the automatic latency threshold computation feature leverages the I/O-injector, it learns the peak value of a datastore and adjusts the SIOC threshold accordingly. The SIOC threshold will be set to 90% of its peak value. Due to a regular re-run of the I/O-injector, SIOC will keep the actual workloads and the storage backend in mind. If something changes on either end, it will adapt its threshold values.

I/O Injector

The I/O-injector was first introduced in vSphere 5.0 as part of SIOC. As mentioned, when SIOC operates in automatic threshold computation mode, the I/O-injector mechanism is used. It allows SIOC to characterize datastore performance.

> **The I/O-injector mechanism, previously used to automatically determine the latency threshold of a given datastore, has been enhanced to also determine the IOPS (4K, random read) of a given datastore.**
> Source: *cormachogan.com/2013/06/20/storage-io-control-workload-injector-behaviour/*

Datastore latency is determined by the used storage backend model and configuration. When storage tiers within a storage array are defined, configuration details like the number of disks or flash media backing each datastore makes a difference in performance behaviour. Even a small difference in the number of storage disks or flash media (for example seven vs nine spindles) may cause a substantial difference in performance. On top of that, some arrays use large disk pools and stripe LUNs across these pools.

The I/O-injector process takes about 30 seconds and is triggered once every 24 hours per datastore. Let us stress that the I/O-injector tries to characterize a datastore when it is idle. Even though an injector process has started, it will stop and retry later to try to minimize the overhead on the storage backend. The I/O-injector will trigger random read I/O's using a variety of *Outstanding I/O* (OIO) numbers to determine datastore latency. In other words, random read I/O is injected using a different number of outstanding I/O every time. Since this is a recurring process,

SIOC is adaptive and will update the datastore latency value when storage backend configurations change. The outcome of the I/O-injector process is plotted in the following diagram.

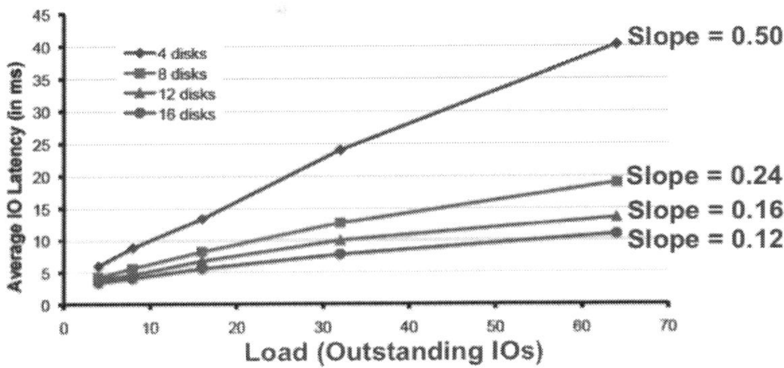

Figure 233: Device Modeling using Different Number of Disks

As this example demonstrates, when the number of Outstanding I/O increases, the latency also increases for each device. The rates at which the increases occur are different.

> **In mathematics, the slope or gradient of a line describes its steepness, incline, or grade. A higher slope value indicates a steeper incline.**

We would like to refer those who want to read more on this topic to the BASIL academic paper written by the Storage DRS engineering team: *https://www.usenix.org/conference/fast-10/basil-automated-io-load-balancing-across-storage-devices*

Auto-Tiering Algorithms

The SIOC I/O-injector feature is a powerful tool. However, auto-tiering solutions migrate LUN segments (blocks) to different disk types based on the usage pattern. Hot segments (frequently accessed) typically move to a faster storage tier while cold segments move to slower tiers. Depending on the array type and vendor, there are different kind of policies and thresholds for these migrations.

Each vendor uses different time-cycles to collect and analyze workloads before moving LUN segments: some auto-tiering solutions move blocks based on real-time workload while other arrays move chunks after collecting performance data for 24 hours. This means that auto-tiering solutions alter the landscape in which the SIOC injector performs its test.

For example, SIOC is primarily opening datastore blocks located in the Tier-1 disk group. As the datastore isn't using these segments that often (cold blocks) the auto-tiering solution decides to migrate these segments to a lower tier. In this case, the segments are migrated from SDD devices to 15K disks.

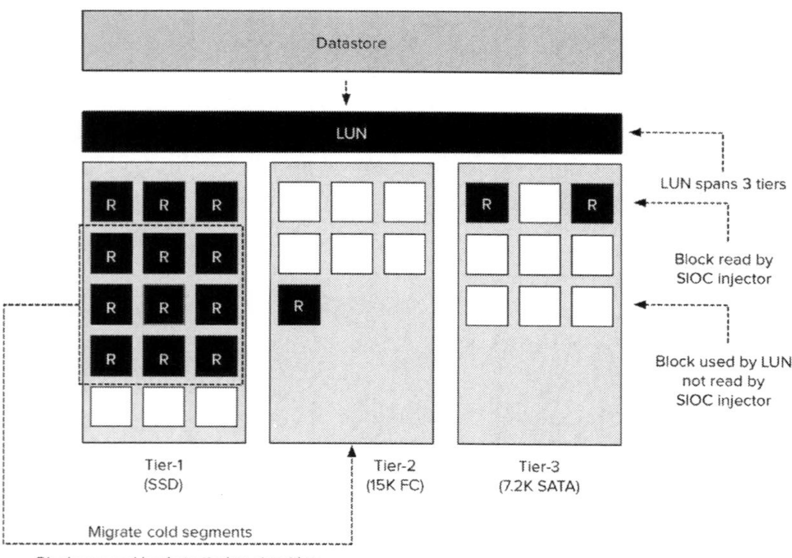

Figure 234: Migrate Cold Segments by Auto-Tiering

Auto-tiering solutions might change the underlying structure of the datastore based on its algorithms and timescales, possibly conflicting with SIOC computations.

> **Because of possible SIOC implications when using the I/O-injector with the automatic latency threshold computation in combination with auto-tiering storage solutions, we would recommend to configure the SIOC latency threshold to a manual value.**

Also, be sure to verify the recommendations with your storage vendor with regards to SIOC. Now that we discussed the I/O-injector mechanism, let's have a look at what queue depths are all about.

Queue Depth

When contention does occur, SIOC will throttle VM storage entitlement by controlling the storage device queue depths.

Depending on the storage backend solution, the ESXi VMkernel storage paths connect the workload inside in the VM to the physical storage device, that consists of either flash or disk devices.

Various VMkernel and storage components are touched along the way. Every step of the way impacts performance because each step hits a queue or buffer.

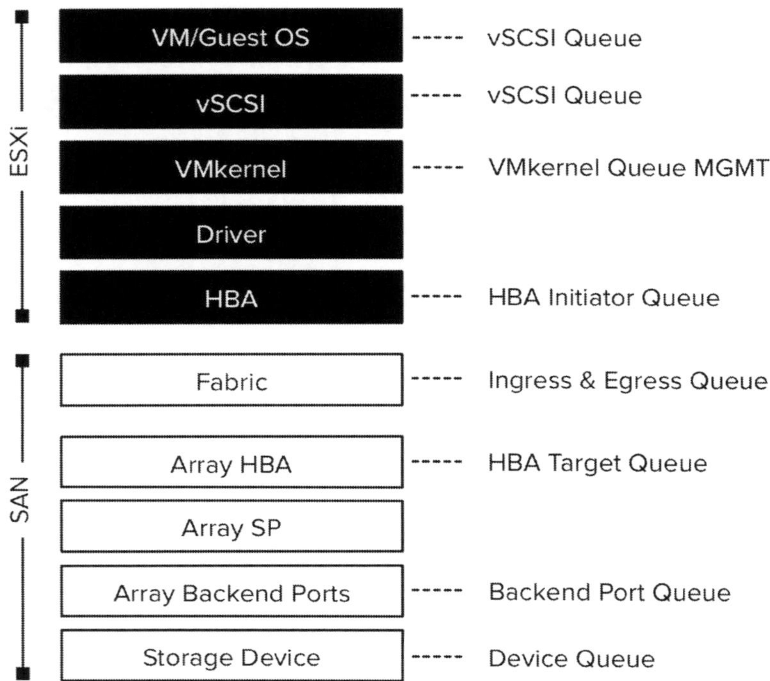

Figure 235: Storage Path SAN

This diagram shows the queues in the path from a guest OS to a storage device in a storage array. It traverses the ESXi stack and connects to the Storage Processors in the array over fabric. The fabric itself incorporates switch port buffers (ingress and egress) that have similar behaviour to queues.

It is possible for each queue to have a different queue depth. This phenomenon can lead to a possible saturation in storage I/O processing. For example, you have an ESXi host with six local storage devices with a queue depth of 32 each. That will make for a theoretical queue depth total of 192. If these storage devices are connected to a storage controller using a queue depth of 128, it could result in 64 I/O's that will be held back by the VMkernel.

When a VM is accessing data stored on server-side resources, like with VMware vSAN, the storage path is notable shorter in comparison to storage array resources. However, this chapter focuses on SIOC that is only applicable when using storage arrays.

The VMkernel storage framework consists of queues that correlate with some of the metrics that are seen in esxtop. These metrics provide insights on how your storage environment is setup in terms of queue depths.

QUEUE	DESCRIPTION
WQLEN	World Queue Length
AQLEN	Adapter Queue Length
DQLEN	Device Queue Length

Table 33: Storage I/O Queues

The *World Queue* (WQLEN) determines the maximum number of VMkernel active I/O's that the world is allowed to contain simultaneously. The storage *Adapter Queue* (AQLEN) determines the maximum of active I/O's in the VMkernel for the driver of a storage controller. The *Storage Device* (DQLEN) is the maximum number of active I/O for a specific storage device. Looking in esxtop, these metrics are seen in the disk adapter, disk device and disk VM views.

If we look at the storage device view in esxtop, we will examine the Device Queue (DQLEN) as this value is utilized by SIOC when operating in manual mode.

```
DEVICE                                       DQLEN
naa.600140506e5e1fed871dd418eda5c8d1           128
naa.60014058c025a22d0aedd4f56d97cfd9           128
naa.6001405ddc6ea44d187bd4d8cdb9c2d4           128
naa.6001405ff8b7cced690dd47cadaba4d7           128
t10.ATA_____INTEL_SSDSC2BA100G300000            31
t10.ATA_____KINGSTON_SE100S3200G____            31
```

Figure 236: Esxtop Disk Device View

Checking what device or LUN is behind the storage device queue may require some research. The esxcli storage core device list command will present detailed information and capabilities for the storage device. This allows you to map the device name to the used storage array.

```
naa.600140506e5elfed871dd418eda5c8d1
   Display Name: SYNOLOGY iSCSI Disk (naa.600140506e5elfed871dd418eda5c8d1)
   Has Settable Display Name: true
   Size: 696320
   Device Type: Direct-Access
   Multipath Plugin: NMP
   Devfs Path: /vmfs/devices/disks/naa.600140506e5elfed871dd418eda5c8d1
   Vendor: SYNOLOGY
   Model: iSCSI Storage
   Revision: 4.0
   SCSI Level: 5
   Is Pseudo: false
   Status: on
   Is RDM Capable: true
   Is Local: false
   Is Removable: false
   Is SSD: false
   Is VVOL PE: false
   Is Offline: false
   Is Perennially Reserved: false
   Queue Full Sample Size: 0
   Queue Full Threshold: 0
   Thin Provisioning Status: yes
   Attached Filters:
   VAAI Status: supported
   Other UIDs: vml.0200000000600140506e5elfed871dd418eda5c8d1695343534920
   Is Shared Clusterwide: true
   Is Local SAS Device: false
   Is SAS: false
   Is USB: false
   Is Boot USB Device: false
   Is Boot Device: false
   Device Max Queue Depth: 128
   No of outstanding IOs with competing worlds: 32
   Drive Type: unknown
   RAID Level: unknown
   Number of Physical Drives: unknown
   Protection Enabled: false
   PI Activated: false
   PI Type: 0
   PI Protection Mask: NO PROTECTION
   Supported Guard Types: NO GUARD SUPPORT
   DIX Enabled: false
   DIX Guard Type: NO GUARD SUPPORT
   Emulated DIX/DIF Enabled: false
```

Figure 237: Storage Device List

SIOC Logging

All logging regarding datastores, queue depth and workload shares are stored in the storagerm.log file. This file is located in the ESXi host local /logs directory in the scratch partition mount point.

Although it is not necessary to examine this file from an operational point of view, it can give some understanding on what's happening under the hood when SIOC is enabled. Typical output looks like this:

```
Storage I/O Control: ANOMALY - external workload detected on datastore 10G-AFA-01
<10G-AFA-01, 0> Default max Qdepth for datastore 10G-AFA-01 is 128
<10G-AFA-01, 0> naa.600140506e5elfed871dd418eda5c8d1 is not an SSD device
stat file /vmfs/volumes/10G-AFA-01/.iormstats.sf already exists.
<10G-AFA-01, 0> Successfully set shares for 67340 on naa.600140506e5elfed871dd418eda5c8d1 to 50000
<10G-AFA-01, 0> Default max Qdepth for datastore 10G-AFA-01 is 128
<10G-AFA-01, 0> naa.600140506e5elfed871dd418eda5c8d1 is not an SSD device
stat file /vmfs/volumes/10G-AFA-01/.iormstats.sf already exists.
<10G-AFA-01, 0> Successfully set shares for 67340 on naa.600140506e5elfed871dd418eda5c8d1 to 50000
Storage I/O Control: ANOMALY - external workload detected on datastore 10G-AFA-01
Storage I/O Control: ANOMALY - external workload detected on datastore 10G-AFA-01
<10G-AFA-01, 0> Default max Qdepth for datastore 10G-AFA-01 is 128
<10G-AFA-01, 0> naa.600140506e5elfed871dd418eda5c8d1 is not an SSD device
stat file /vmfs/volumes/10G-AFA-01/.iormstats.sf already exists.
<10G-AFA-01, 0> Successfully set shares for 67340 on naa.600140506e5elfed871dd418eda5c8d1 to 50000
<10G-AFA-01, 0> Number of hosts has changed to 4
<10G-AFA-02, 0> Default max Qdepth for datastore 10G-AFA-02 is 128
<10G-AFA-02, 0> naa.6001405ddc6ea44d187bd4d8cdb9c2d4 is not an SSD device
stat file /vmfs/volumes/10G-AFA-02/.iormstats.sf already exists.
<10G-AFA-02, 0> Successfully set shares for 67340 on naa.6001405ddc6ea44d187bd4d8cdb9c2d4 to 50000
```

Figure 238: Storagerm.log Output

Interestingly, you will spot several '*Storage I/O Control: ANOMALY – external workload detected on datastore*' log entries. That could relate to workloads outside of the SIOC scope that are also sending I/O towards the datastore in question. Several situations could lead to similar behavior:

- Not all ESXi hosts accessing the datastore are managed by vCenter or by the same vCenter instance
- The physical storage media (spindles or flash) on the storage device where this datastores is located are shared with other datastores that are not SIOC enabled
- The SIOC enabled datastore has multiple extents

When you make sure that none of the above situations are applicable to your configuration, you should not see the behavior of the stated SIOC anomalies.

Communication Mechanism

When SIOC is enabled, it will request the maximum device queue depth per device and set it to the maximum. SIOC also needs a way to know the datastore-wide latency and I/O load from all the ESXi hosts using the datastore. It does so by having a data-point (file) per datastore.

```
[root@ESXi01:/vmfs/volumes/5a2410c3-85315afe-f8d4-0cc47a6f23aa] ls -la
total 1839872
drwxr-xr-t    1 root     root        905216 Jun 24 11:10 .
drwxr-xr-x    1 root     root           512 Jun 24 13:41 ..
drwxr-xr-x    1 root     root         73728 May 14 20:15 .dvsData
-r--------    1 root     root      11927552 Dec  3  2017 .fbb.sf
-r--------    1 root     root     134807552 Dec  3  2017 .fdc.sf
-rwxr-xr-x    1 root     root       1048576 Jun 24 11:10 .iormstats.sf
-r--------    1 root     root     268632064 Dec  3  2017 .jbc.sf
```

Figure 239: Iormstats.sf Listing

Similar to vSphere HA, SIOC uses a shared file on each SIOC enabled datastore called: .iormstats.sf. This file can be accessed by multiple ESXi hosts simultaneously. Each host periodically writes its average latency and the number of I/O's for that datastore into the iormstats.sf file. Remember that datastore access is not cluster bound. ESXi hosts outside the cluster could access the datastore impacting SIOC calculations.

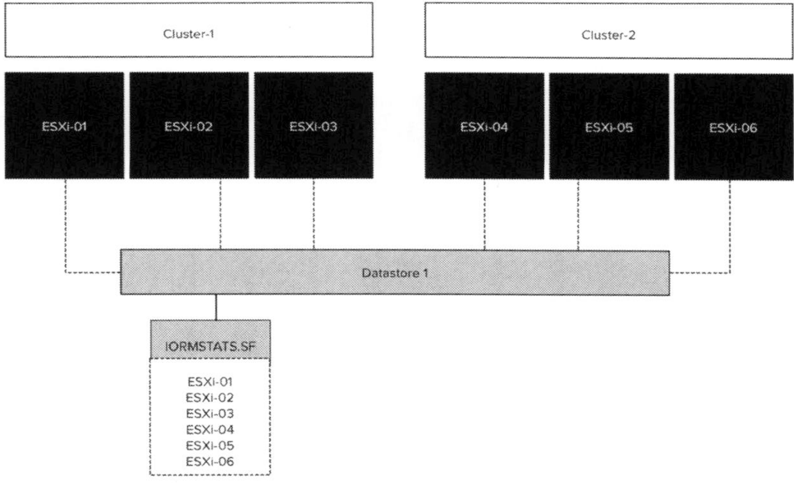

Figure 240: ESXi Host Accessing IORMSTATS.SF

This enables all ESXi hosts to read the file and compute the datastore-wide latency average, which in turn allows for the computation of the Queue Depth for each host based on the I/O slot entitlement.
This may sound complex, so let's have a look at some exemplary scenarios that visualize how SIOC works in the following sections.

Local Scheduler

Datastore-wide scheduling is done by SIOC, but the current local ESXi disk I/O scheduler is called mClock that was introduced in vSphere 5.5. It replaced the *Start-time Fair Queuing* (SFQ) local disk scheduler that was used up to vSphere 5.1.

The mClock scheduler is primarily developed to provide better disk I/O scheduling that allows for setting storage limits, shares and reservations on a VMDK level. Prior to mClock, it was only possible to configure IOPS limits and shares on a VMDK. Both SIOC and Storage DRS both honor IOPS reservations.

Local disk scheduling influences the ESXi host-level prioritization for all VMs running on the a ESXi host. This, by itself, could be of great value when high value workloads need a higher priority compared to low value workloads, but also when all VMs should be treated equally. mClock focuses on submitting I/O request from all VMs on the ESXi host.

The following diagram depicts a scenario where three VMs all have equal shares with an exemplary queue depth of 32. VM03 is the only running VM on ESXi-02. The other VMs (VM01 and VM02) receive less storage entitlement on the shared datastore because they are running on the same ESXi host.

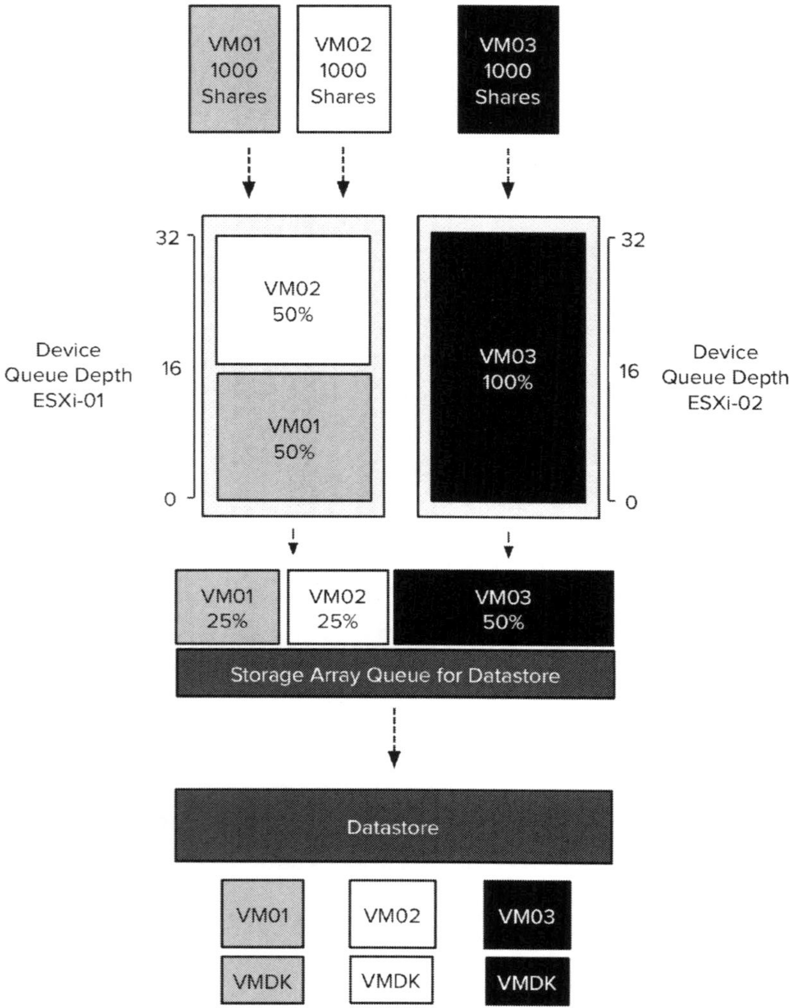

Figure 241: Local Disk Scheduler

The local disk scheduler is not able to see beyond the boundaries of the ESXi host and has no knowledge of what other workloads are consuming on the datastore.

Datastore-Wide Scheduler

SIOC keep tracks of a performance metric called normalized latency, compares it with the congestion latency threshold every four seconds, and only kicks in if the normalized latency is above the threshold.

SIOC calculates this normalized latency by factoring in latency values for all hosts (the iormstats.sf file we discussed earlier) and all VMs accessing the datastore, taking into account different I/O sizes. Larger I/O sizes means higher observed latency than with smaller I/O sizes.

An example would probably clarify how this works. The following diagram depicts the scenario where a host is throttled as the latency threshold has been exceeded.

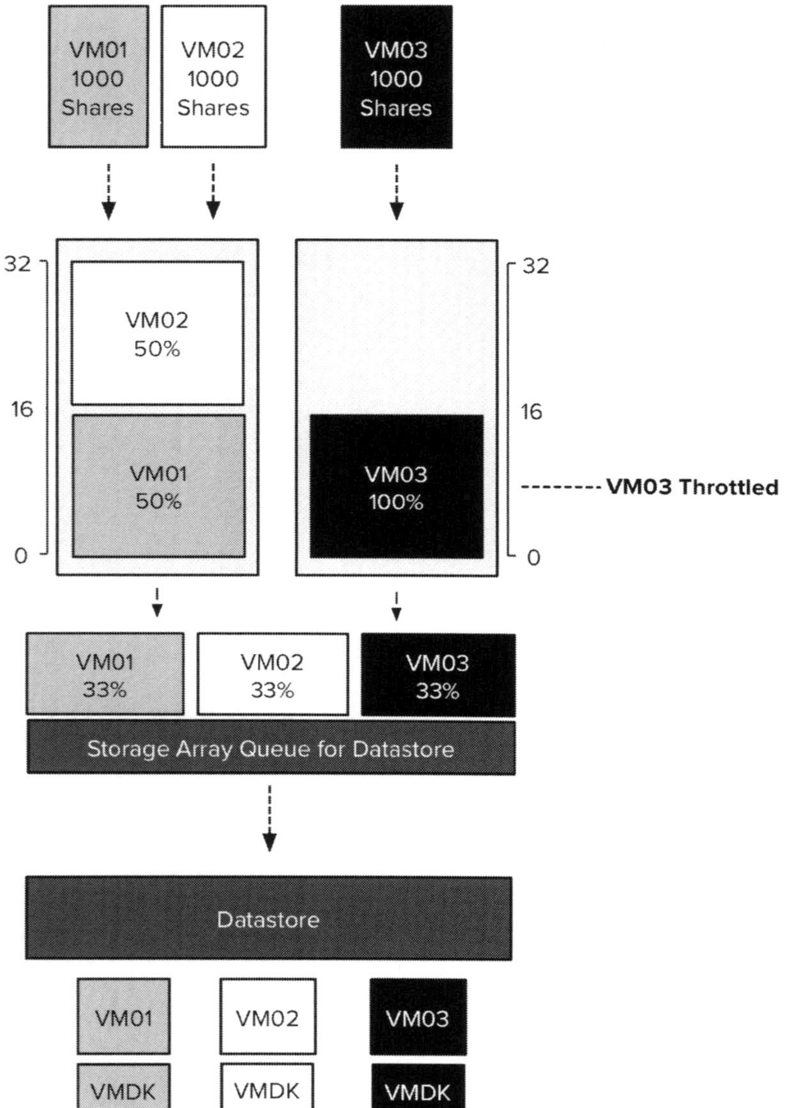

Figure 242: Datastore-wide Disk Scheduler (SIOC)

The datastore-wide disk scheduler resembles the local disk scheduler (mClock) in that it will prioritize VMs over others depending on the number of shares assigned to their respective disks.

It does so by calculating the I/O slot entitlement, but only when the configurable latency threshold is exceeded.

The datastore-wide disk scheduler sums up the disk shares for each of the VMDKs of the virtual machines on the datastore. In the case of ESXi-01, that is 2000, and in the case of ESXi-02, it is 1000. Next, the datastore-wide disk scheduler will calculate the I/O slot entitlement based on the host-level shares and it will throttle the queue. In the example, each of the virtual machines is entitled to 33% of the storage resources. Host ESXi-01 will receive 66% and ESXi-02 will receive 33%. If you compare this to the first scenario, you can understand why it is recommended to enable SIOC on all datastores, even if there is no need to prioritize.

> **Even when there is no need to prioritize VMs, there is a benefit to enabling Storage I/O Control as it helps prevent self-inflicted Denial of Service attacks.**

Let it be clear that SIOC does not make latency magically dissolve. By throttling the queue, latency moves up the stack from the device to the kernel. However, this does imply that only a subset of VMs on a datastore incurs higher latency instead of all VMs on that datastore. On top of that, it is based on the entitlement of the VM; a VM with a lower I/O slot entitlement will incur more latency, which is how it should be.

Share Variety

Using an example where all VMs have equal shared is fairly simple. It becomes more complex when we provide different share values to the VMs in the following scenario and diagram. We have three VMs residing on two ESXi hosts and on a SIOC enabled datastore.

Two VMs (VM02 and VM03) have been assigned 500 shares each where VM01 has 1500 shared assigned to it. VM01 is entitled to 60% of the available I/O slots. VM02 and VM03 both are entitled to 20% each. We can calculate this by adding up all the shared and dividing the number of shares per VM by the result. Looking at VM01, the following formula applies: 1500 / (1500 + 500 + 500) = 0,60 that translates to 60%.

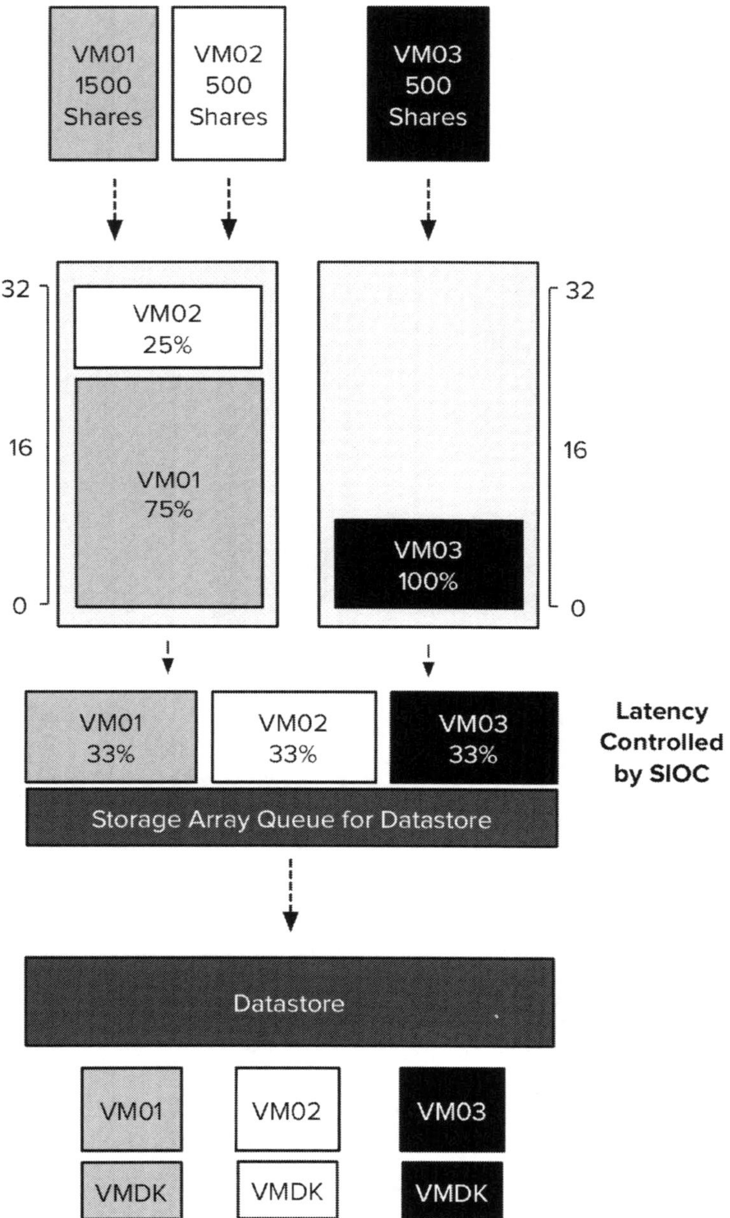

Figure 243: SIOC Share Variance Example

VAIO

With the release of vSphere 6.5, SIOC is refactored to use the *vSphere APIs for I/O Filtering* (VAIO) framework. The VAIO framework enables VMware and third-party plugins to tap into I/O flows, in this case between the VM and its VMDK.

> **I/O filters that are associated with virtual disks gain direct access to the virtual machine I/O path regardless of the underlying storage topology.** Source: *vsphere-esxi-vcenter-server-65-resource-management-guide.pdf*

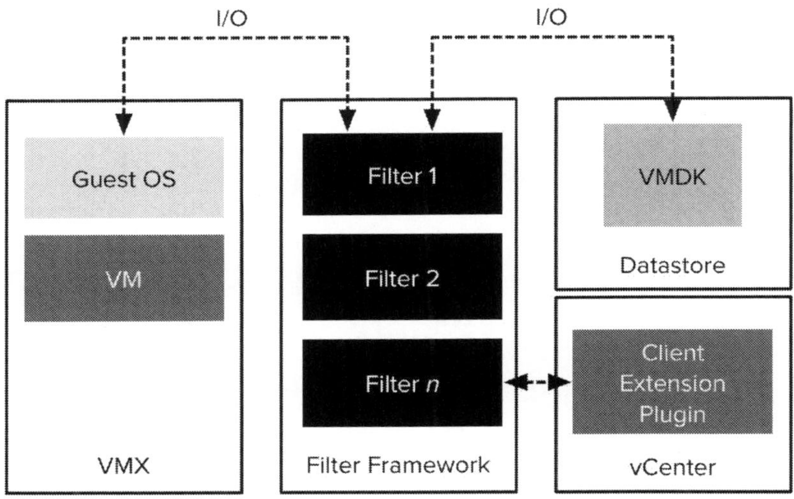

Figure 244: VAIO Framework for SIOC

The big benefit of SIOC utilizing the VAIO framework is that we now can enforce SIOC constructs to VMs using *Storage Policy Based Management* (SPBM).

Following the trend of being as efficient as possible from a manageability and configuration consistency point-of-view, applying storage shares, limits and reservations to VMs has never been easier. SPBM allows for common management across storage tier and quality control automation using a policy-driver control plane.

You simply assign the applicable storage policy to your VM and SPBM will make sure the SIOC settings are applied. That also makes it very easy to change share, limit or reservations values if you have new insights concerning storage quality control. When a policy is changed, the VMs connected to it will automatically be updated with the new SIOC values.

The SIOC filter provider is installed by default on an ESXi host version 6.5 or higher. It is listed as filter 'SPM' in the Storage I/O Filters.

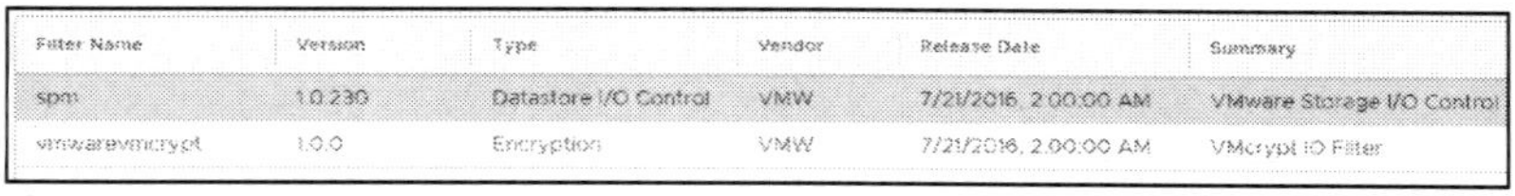

Filter Name	Version	Type	Vendor	Release Date	Summary
spm	1.0.230	Datastore I/O Control	VMW	7/21/2016, 2:00:00 AM	VMware Storage I/O Control
vmwarevmcrypt	1.0.0	Encryption	VMW	7/21/2016, 2:00:00 AM	VMcrypt IO Filter

Figure 245: SPM Filter Listing

vCenter 6.7 already includes three default SIOC policy components for low, normal and high I/O shares allocation.

Storage Policy Components

+ Create Storage Policy Component

Name	Description	Category
Default encryption properties	Storage policy component for VM and v...	Encryption
Low IO shares allocation	Storage policy component for Low SIO...	Storage I/O Control
High IO shares allocation	Storage policy component for High SIO...	Storage I/O Control
Normal IO shares allocation	Storage policy component for Medium ...	Storage I/O Control

Figure 246: Default SIOC Policy Components

When the default policies do not fit your requirements, it is easy to create additional policies. Log in to your vCenter instance, go to the Policies and Profiles view and choose to create a new Storage Policy Component. The provider 'VMware Storage I/O Control' is automatically selected once you choose the category 'Storage I/O Control'.

Just set the appropriate SIOC settings for the policy and pay extra attention to the IOPS limit value. Limits should be handled with care.

Typically, if there is no requirement for limits, a general recommendation is to leave it disabled. Looking at the policy, you can achieve this by setting the IOPS limit to value "-1" in the policy component.

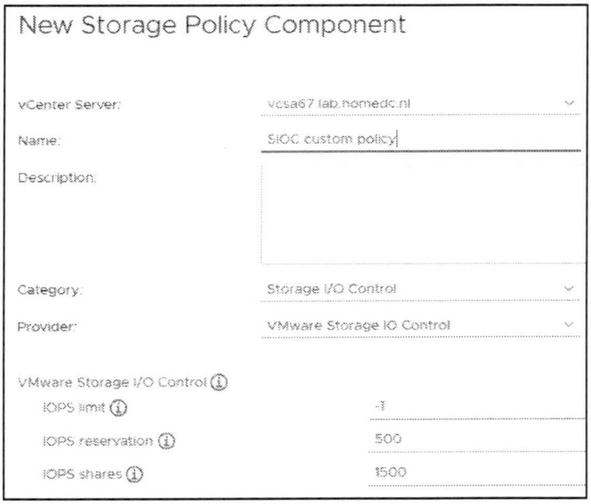

Figure 247: Custom SIOC Policy Component

The next step is to create a VM Storage Policy. That allows us to create a new policy structure that includes host based services based on SIOC.

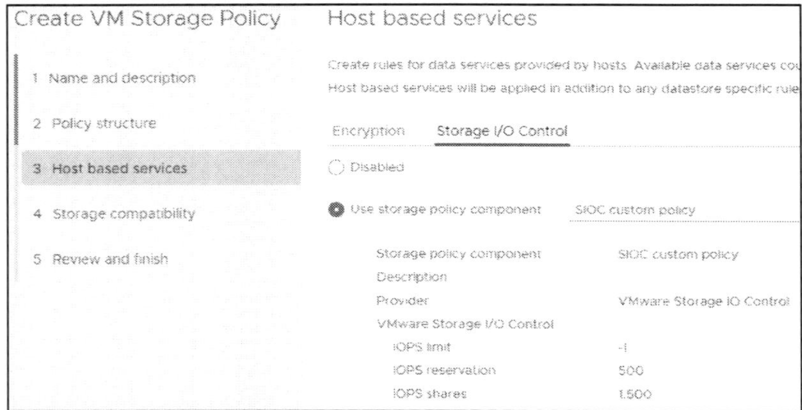

Figure 248: Host Based Services in VM Storage Policy

Once the VM Storage Policy is created, you will be able to assign it to current or new VMs by selecting the policy when defining the storage options.

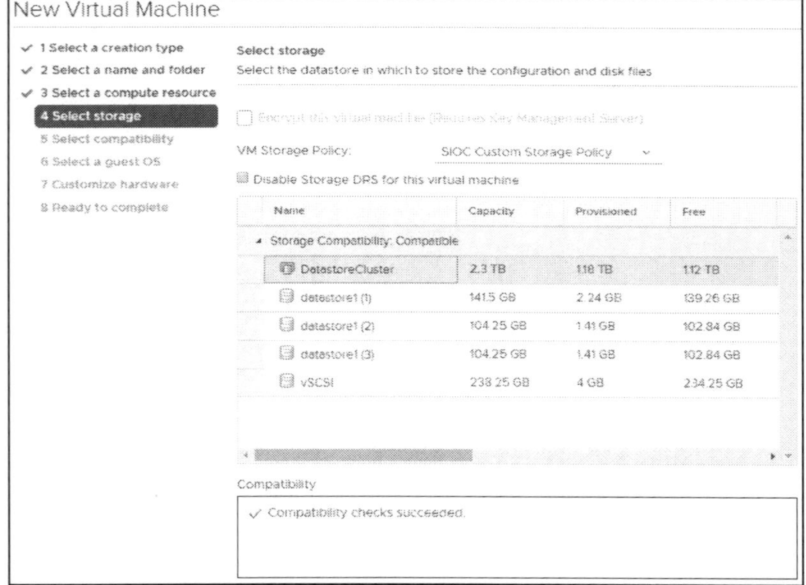

Figure 249: Assigning a VM Storage Policy

> **Adopting a policy-based control plane allows for programmability. Programmability enables automation. Without programmatic control, there's no foundation for effective, coordinated automation.**

Once the VM storage policy is applied to a VM, it is easily checked if the VM is still compliant to the policy by selecting the VM Compliance overview. You will get instant insight on what VMs are using the policy and together with their compliancy status.

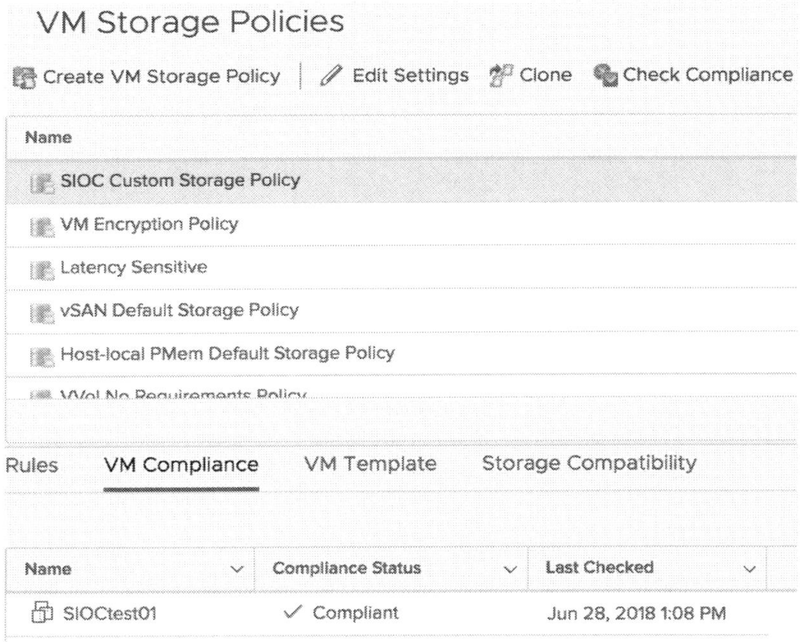

Figure 250: VM Storage Policy Compliancy

Statistics Collection Only

SIOC stats-only mode gathers statistics to provide you insights on the I/O utilization of the datastore. Please note that stats-only mode does not enable the datastore-wide scheduler and will not enforce throttling.

Beware that enabling stats-only mode increases the footprint of log data into the vCenter database. Then again, this is also the case when SIOC is used as that automatically enables the statistics collection.

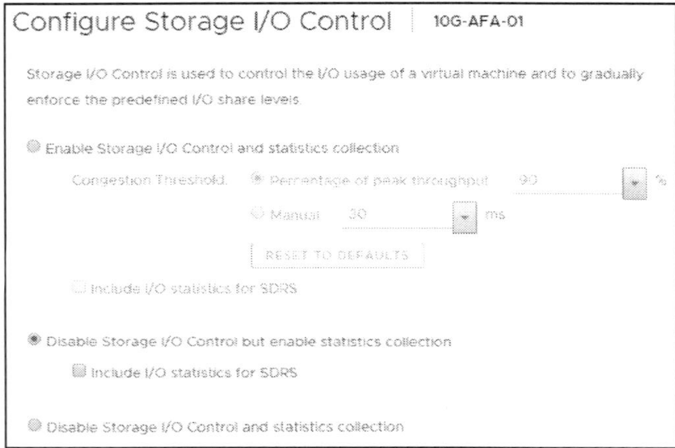

Figure 251: Enable Stats-Only Mode

Once SIOC statistics collection is enabled, you will find four additional performance views collecting data in vCenter.

> **Because of the additional load on the vCenter database, only use statistics mode if you really require the SIOC datastore insights. If not, it is not recommended to enable the stats only mode.**

Use this when you are prohibited from using SIOC but do benefit from having more knowledge about datastore-wide performance like normalized latency, aggregated IOPS or maximum queue depths.

☐	Storage I/O Control active time percentage	Average	%
☐	Storage I/O Control aggregated IOPS	Average	num
☐	Storage I/O Control datastore maximum queue depth	Latest	num
☐	Storage I/O Control normalized latency	Average	µs

Figure 252: SIOC Performance Views

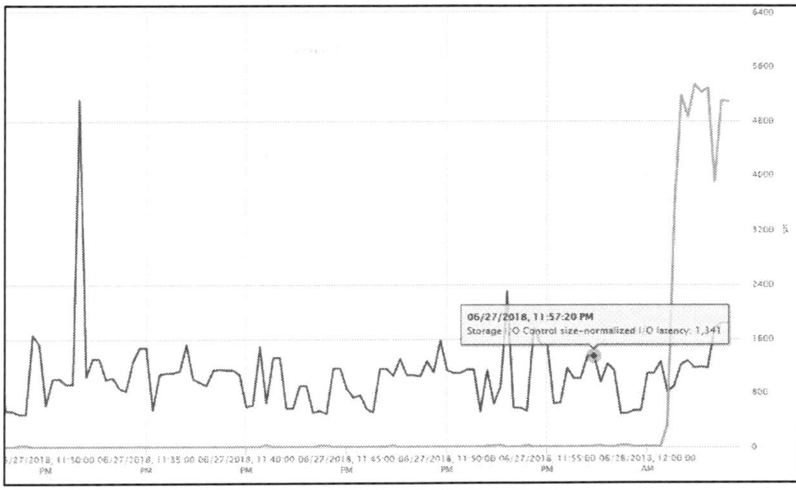

Figure 253: SIOC Stats-Only Exemplary Performance View

Sometimes it is necessary to troubleshoot your environment and having logs to review is helpful in determining what is happening. Like the SIOC feature itself, SIOC logging is disabled by default. You explicitly need to enable SIOC or the SIOC stats-only mode.

Storage I/O Allocation

The following chapters will elaborate on the various SIOC constructs that allow you to manage storage entitlement allocations. It is strongly recommended to apply shares, limits and reservations using the VM storage policies as explained in the VAIO chapter.

Shares

We already discussed how shares work in the datastore-wide scheduler chapter. Shares represent a relative priority of storage entitlement against the other VMs residing on the same datastore. The pre-set share levels are low (500), medium (1000) and high (2000). Even though these settings probably suitable most situations, you can configure custom values within the range of 200-4000 to fit your requirement.

Limits and Reservations

The limit construct with SIOC works as expected. Once configured, the VM is not able to consume more IOPS as stated in the limit value. Note that in previous releases I/O limits were normalized at 32KB, meaning that a 64KB I/O would count as two I/Os. In the current release I/Os are not normalized. One other big difference between the current release of vSphere and previous versions is that for instance SvMotion I/Os are not billed to the VM. This results in SvMotion no longer being limited to a certain IOPS value when the VM, or it's virtual disks are.

> **The big differentiator between memory or network and storage reservations is that the disk I/O scheduler will soft-claim the IOPS. It allows unused resources to be consumed by other VMs.**

As long as the VM IOPS reservations are satisfied, the disk I/O scheduler will look at the share value to determine the storage entitlement per ESXi host and VMs.

Even though VM02 is assigned to a VMware storage policy that includes an IOPS reservation of 1000 IOPS, VM01 and VM03 can use the vacant IOPS if VM02 does not consume that much I/O. When the VM02 starts to consume IOPS up to its reserved IOPS value, they will be re-assigned to VM02 adhering to the configured reservations almost instantly.

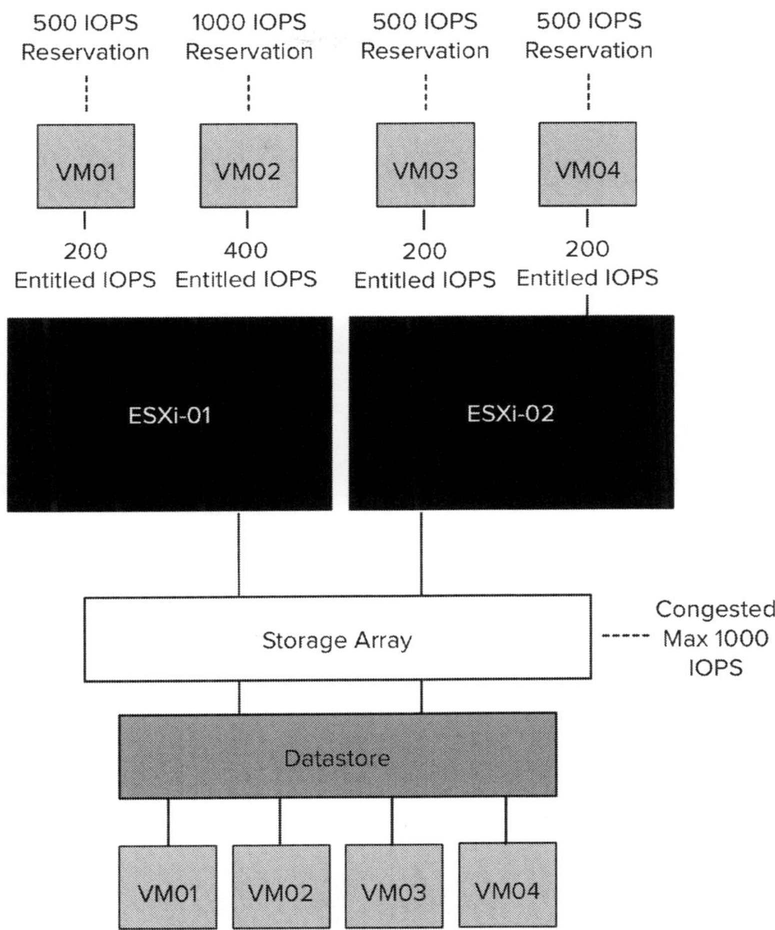

Figure 254: Storage Entitlement Based on Reservations

The exemplary scenario in the diagram above elaborates on how IOPS assignment works when a storage array is congested and VMs have IOPS reservations. In this scenario, because the storage array is congested, it is only able to deliver 1000 IOPS to the datastore. This situation will force the disk I/O scheduler to distribute the available IOPS based on the reservations rather than share values. When the full reservation demand cannot be met, a percentage is calculated based on the reserved IOPS per VM.

A total of 2500 IOPS are reserved in this scenario. The allocation formula is the *VM IOPS reservation / Total reserved IOPS*. Therefore, the allocation per VM would be as follows:

- VM01 : 500 / 2500 = 20%
- VM02 : 1000 / 2500 = 40%
- VM03 : 500 / 2500 = 20%
- VM04 : 500 / 2500 = 20%

Bringing that back to the relative IOPS per VM allocation, that results in:

- VM01 : 20% x 1000 = 200 IOPS
- VM02 : 40% x 1000 = 400 IOPS
- VM03 : 20% x 1000 = 200 IOPS
- VM04 : 20% x 1000 = 200 IOPS

This example helps to explain how the disk I/O scheduler is handling reservations in time of contention. Reality will probably paint a different picture when it comes to VM demand for storage I/O, but it is good to have an understanding of how the IOPS reservation construct works.

Interoperability

SIOC does have several limitations. We talked about SIOC when using auto-tiering mechanisms. That situation could lead to mismatching computations depending on the storage array or its configuration. Always check the *VMware Hardware Compatibility List* (HCL) and consult your storage vendor whether to enable or disable SIOC.

It is important to understand that SIOC is not supported when using:

- VMware vSAN or Virtual Volumes
- *Raw Device Mappings* (RDM)
- Multiple VMFS extents
- *vSphere Metro Storage Cluster* (vMSC) environment

Stretched storage solutions, or vMSC, are not supported to use SIOC as described in VMware KB article 2042596.

When your environment does allow you to utilize SIOC, it is generally a good idea to let it help you in maintaining storage fairness in your VMware infrastructures.

25

NETWORK I/O CONTROL

We are dealing with various network traffic streams within our virtual data centers. Ranging from VMware vSphere system traffic like HA, vMotion, and vSAN next to IP storage protocols like iSCSI or NFS. Equally or even more important is the network traffic generated by the virtualized workloads, your applications.

All these network traffic flows are directed to other ESXi hosts in your virtual environment and external applications, servers or devices.

The primary element these network flows have in coming is that they all utilize Ethernet-based networks. All the network flows are typically segmented using VLAN (dot1q) or VXLAN with VMware NSX.

Back when 1GbE connections were the de-facto standard in data centers, it was no exception to have more than six network interfaces per ESXi host. One of the reasons we used as much network interfaces as we could, was to mitigate the risk of experiencing network bandwidth contention. We needed to ensure all our processes and applications had adequate bandwidth available. It was not uncommon to saturate a 1GbE using vMotion or IP storage datastores.

Nowadays, we are moving towards fewer network interfaces per ESXi host. The 10GbE bandwidth pNICs are widely adopted, and we are on the verge of adopting 40GbE or higher pNICs.

> **Network I/O characteristics are changing, and we need to cater to that need by providing and ensuring network bandwidth.**

Two network interfaces per host is a new possible standard. Modern reference architectures like the *VMware Validated Design* (VVD) advocate the use of two 10GbE network interfaces for all network traffic. That includes ESXi management, vMotion, vSAN, vSphere Replication and production workload traffic.

There are multiple advantages when using as few network interfaces as possible. Think about decreasing complexity, less configuration to be done. More important, the positive impact on economics. Each network port on a physical switch is eating budget. Using fewer network interfaces per ESXi host allows for a more efficient switch port allocation.

The apparent disadvantage is that we have more network traffic types running parallel on the same network interfaces in our ESXi hosts with a re-introduced risk of network bandwidth contention. That is where VMware vSphere *Network I/O Control* (NIOC) comes into play.

Network I/O Control Constructs

NIOC is a feature that provides additional control over the usage of network bandwidth. The network resource management feature uses constructs of shares, reservations, and limits. It is very similar to the model like DRS does for compute resources.

> **Network I/O Control is only available on a Distributed vSwitch that is available in the vSphere Enterprise Plus Edition. It is also included in your vSAN licenses.**

NIOC enforces the share value specified for the different traffic types in the event of network contention. When contention occurs, NIOC applies the share values set to each traffic type. As a result, less important traffic, as defined by the share percentage, will be throttled. That allows more critical traffic types to gain access to more network resources. NIOC also allows for bandwidth reservation for system traffic, based on the capacity of the physical adapters on an ESXi host. All these configurable constructs enable you to have fine-grained network resource control at the virtual machine network adapter level.

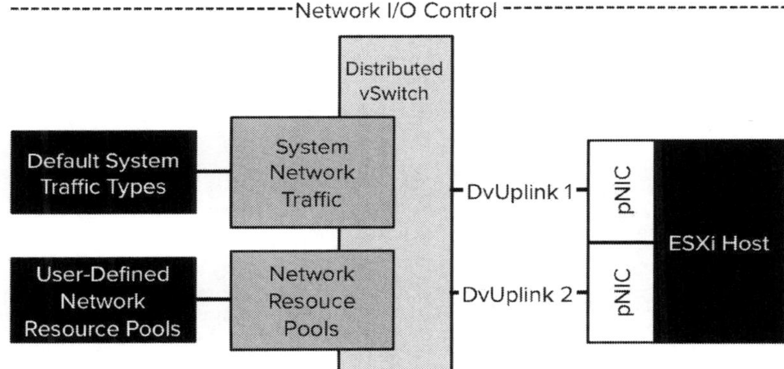

Figure 255: Basic Network I/O Control Constructs

Evolution of NIOC

NIOC was initially introduced in vSphere 4.1 and evolved with the releases of new vSphere and Distributed vSwitch versions over time.

NETWORK I/O CONTROL VERSION	DISTRIBUTED VSWITCH VERSION	VSPHERE VERSION
v1	4.1.0	4.1
	5.0.0	5.0
v2	5.1.0	5.1
		5.5
		6.0
	5.5.0	5.5
		6.0
v3	6.0.0	6.0
		6.5
	6.6.0	6.7

Table 34: Network I/O Control Releases

With NIOC version 3, that was introduced in vSphere 6.0, you had the option to operate either version. It was possible to stick to version 2 or to upgrade to version 3 if no unsupported features were used that could prevent a successful upgrade.

The principal difference between version 2 and 3 is the ability to setup *Class of Service* (CoS) tagging and physical adapter shares in user-defined resource pools in version 2.

It is not supported anymore to use user-defined resource pools and to assign QoS to system traffic. Network I/O Control Version 3 moved towards the usage of *Network Resource Pools* (NRP) at the level of the entire Distributed port groups and the ability to have per vNIC defined network shares. This approach allows for a more fine-grained network bandwidth guarantee across a cluster when using a Distributed vSwitch. We'll go further into detail how NIOC works under the hoods in the next chapters.

A newly created Distributed vSwitch, using one of the available versions, in vSphere 6.7 dictates the use of NIOC version 3. Even when you opt for the Distributed vSwitch version 6.0.0, NIOC version 3 is still the only option available. Version 2 is depreciated. It can differ when you upgraded your environment to vSphere 6.7 from an earlier release.

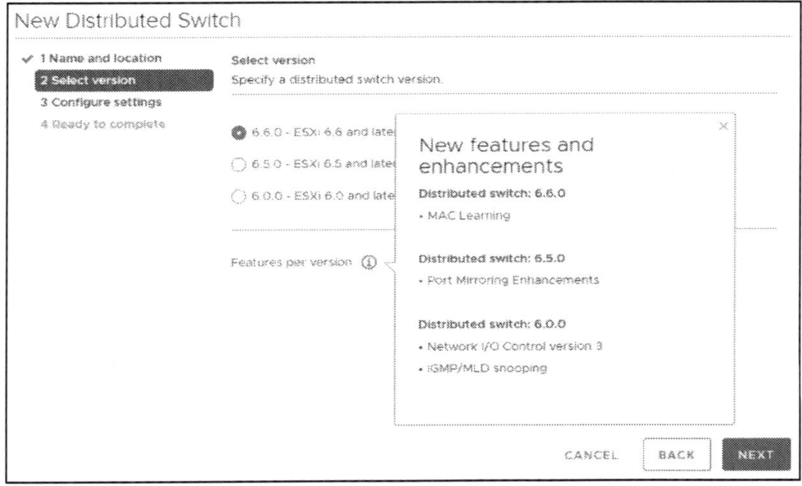

Figure 256: Distributed vSwitch Versions in vSphere 6.7

An existing Distributed vSwitch can be quickly checked on its Distributed vSwitch version. It will also allow you to determine the current NIOC version. You can do so by levering the GUI looking at the Distributed vSwitch settings.

Summary | Monitor | Configure | Permissions | VMs | Datastores | Networks

Networks | Distributed Switches

Name ↑	Version ↑	NIOC Version ↑	LACP Version ↑	VC
DSwitch	6.6.0	Network I/O Control ver. 3	Enhanced LACP	vcsa67.le

Figure 257: Verify NIOC Version in the GUI

NIOC Defaults

When you create a new Distributed vSwitch, the NIOC feature will be enabled automatically. If not desired for whatever reason, it must be explicitly set to disabled.

The following traffic types are defined by default:

- Management Traffic
- *Fault Tolerance* (FT) Traffic
- vMotion Traffic
- Virtual Machine Traffic
- iSCSI Traffic
- NFS Traffic
- *vSphere Replication* (VR) Traffic
- vSAN Traffic
- *vSphere Data Protection Backup* (VDP) Traffic

NIOC provides three predefined share levels and a custom share level. The pre-set share levels; low, normal and high, provide an easy method of assigning a number of shares to the network resource pool. Setting the share level to Low assigns 25 shares to the network resource pool, Normal assigns 50 shares and High 100 shares. The custom option allows you to assign the number of shares yourself within the supported range of 1 – 100. By default, each system network resource pool is assigned 50 shares except for the virtual machine traffic resource pool. This pool gets 100 shares.

By default, NIOC is set up to ensure that Virtual Machine network traffic is getting a higher priority (100) than vSphere system traffic. It does so solely to protect the most critical data flows, being your virtual workloads running on top of ESXi.

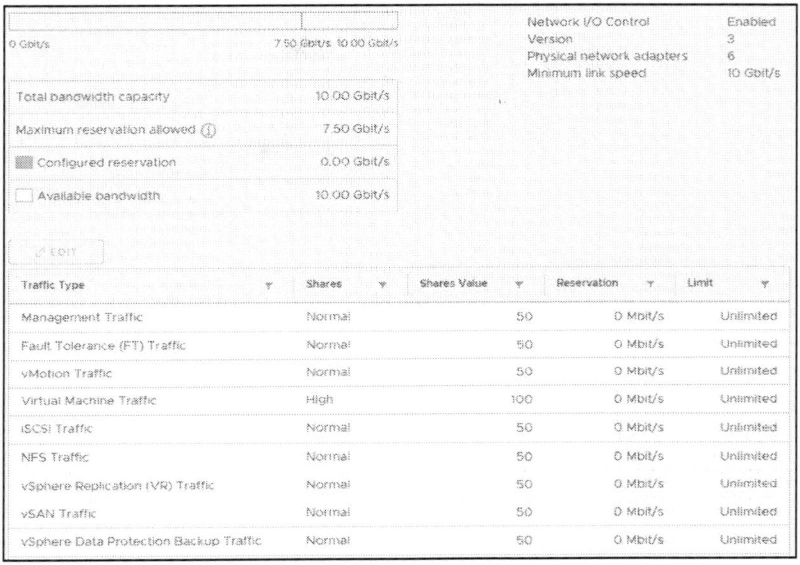

0 Gbit/s 7.50 Gbit/s 10.00 Gbit/s

Total bandwidth capacity	10.00 Gbit/s
Maximum reservation allowed	7.50 Gbit/s
Configured reservation	0.00 Gbit/s
Available bandwidth	10.00 Gbit/s

Network I/O Control	Enabled
Version	3
Physical network adapters	6
Minimum link speed	10 Gbit/s

EDIT

Traffic Type	Shares	Shares Value	Reservation	Limit
Management Traffic	Normal	50	0 Mbit/s	Unlimited
Fault Tolerance (FT) Traffic	Normal	50	0 Mbit/s	Unlimited
vMotion Traffic	Normal	50	0 Mbit/s	Unlimited
Virtual Machine Traffic	High	100	0 Mbit/s	Unlimited
iSCSI Traffic	Normal	50	0 Mbit/s	Unlimited
NFS Traffic	Normal	50	0 Mbit/s	Unlimited
vSphere Replication (VR) Traffic	Normal	50	0 Mbit/s	Unlimited
vSAN Traffic	Normal	50	0 Mbit/s	Unlimited
vSphere Data Protection Backup Traffic	Normal	50	0 Mbit/s	Unlimited

Figure 258: Default Configured NIOC Traffic Types in vSphere 6.7

All traffic type heuristics are configurable. It is up to you to decide that the default values match your requirements or if these need customisations to fit your workloads and architecture.

Re-configuring the default values can be done within the boundaries of the Distributed vSwitch uplink bandwidth. Working with 10GbE interfaces in an environment will allow you to reserve up to that value. NIOC calculates the minimum uplink speed that is available. Meaning an uplink setup of two 10GbE interfaces per ESXi host will result in 10GbE of bandwidth that is available to divide over your traffic profiles. It will state the minimum available bandwidth as 'Minimal link speed'. That means that is it not possible to overcommit network bandwidth.

NIOC Advanced Setting

A Distributed vSwitch is able to mix pNIC's with different bandwidth capabilities, for example, 1GbE and 10GbE. In such a scenario, it could prove useful to exclude the lower capacity pNICs from the bandwidth allocation model of NIOC.

You can do so by configuring the per-ESXi host advanced setting `Net.IOControlPnicOptOut`. The value should be a comma-separated list with the vmnic adapters that need to be opted out from NIOC. In the following example, vmnic2 and vmnic3 are excluded.

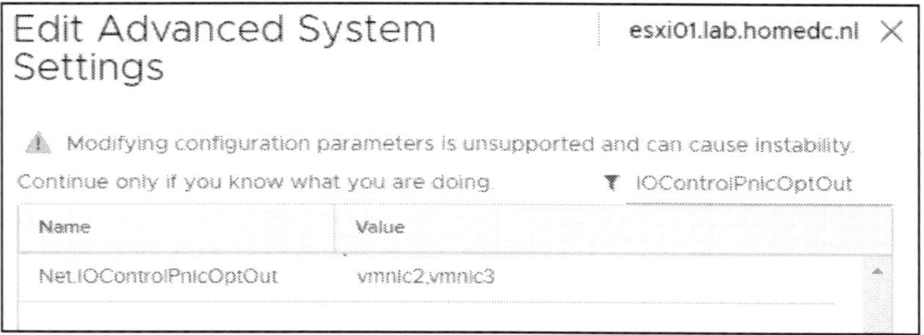

Figure 259: Example NIOC Exclude Configuration

Bursty Network Consumers

By having NIOC enabled and with all settings at their default value, it priorities virtual machine traffic by setting a higher share value. NIOC provides a quality control mechanism by allowing customers to weigh the nine pre-configured network traffic types.

> **The presence of potential bursty bandwidth consumers fuels the necessity for network bandwidth resource control.**

Talking about potential bursty network consumers, think about the behavior of vMotion operations. They introduce temporary network traffic that tries to consume as much bandwidth as possible. For instance, in a (hyper)converged network infrastructure using two pNICs as uplink interfaces, this may have a disruptive effect on other network traffic streams. Strongly depending on the running workloads and its I/O characteristics, storage-related network types could inflict a comparable impact.

Due to way NIOC operates shares, it provides control for predictable networking performance while different network traffic streams are contending for the same bandwidth.

Bandwidth Allocation

The following chapters will dig deeper into the various NIOC constructs that allow you to manage network bandwidth allocations.

Shares

We already discussed some parts of the default share values between the various system traffic types and the pre-set share levels. Shares represent a relative priority of a network traffic type against the other network types within the same ESXi host and physical adapter.
The available bandwidth per network traffic types is adaptive and calculated by its relative shared and by the amount of data that other network types are consuming. This situation comes into effect when a physical network adapter is saturated. NIOC will then assign the appropriate network bandwidth to each network traffic type based on the share configuration.

For example; your Distributed vSwitch is configured with a Management, vMotion, NFS and Virtual Machine port group. All network traffic types are using the default share value. The ESXi host is connected to the Distributed vSwitch using two 10Gbe uplinks in an active/active state.

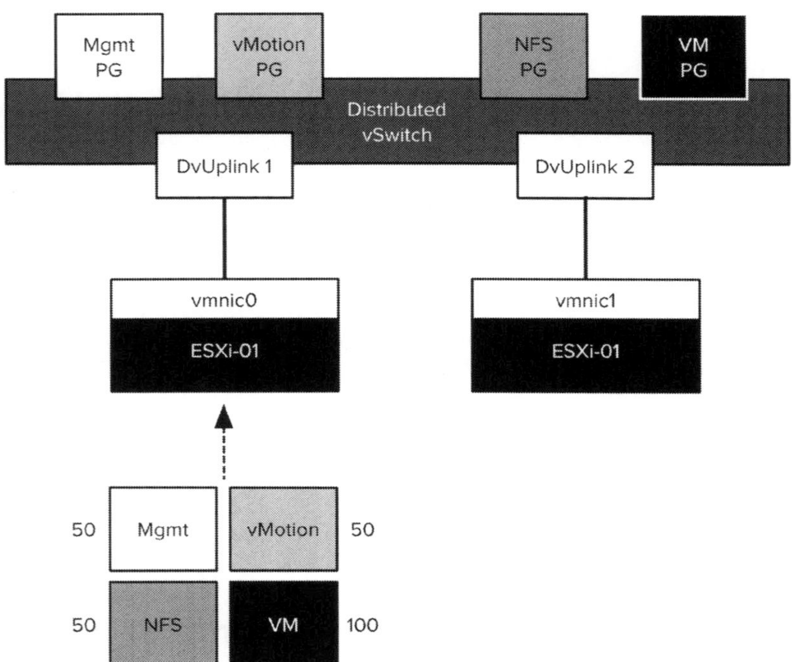

Figure 260: NIOC Shares Example

This means that 50+50+50+100=250 shares are active on vmnic0 connected to DvUplink1. In this situation, the Virtual Machine network traffic type gets to divide 40% (100/(50+50+50+100)) of the available physical adapter network bandwidth. Because we are using 10GbE pNICs, this translates to 4 Gbit/s bandwidth to distribute over the actively transmitting virtual machines on this ESXi host.

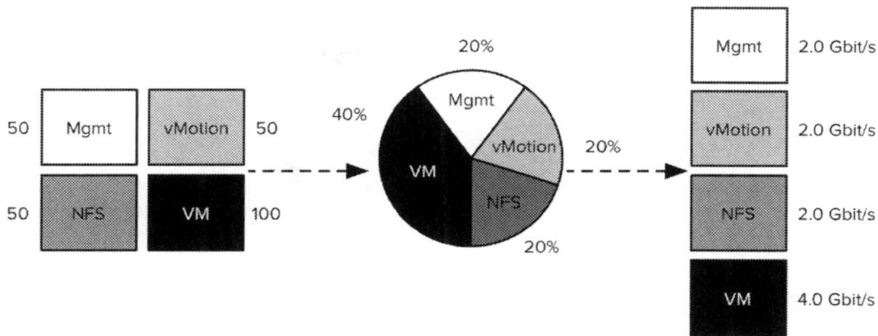

Figure 261: NIOC Shares Distribution

The stated example is a worst-case scenario because usually not all port groups are transmitting, as the shares are relative to other network pools actively using the physical adapter. Virtual Machine and vMotion traffic might be only active on this pNIC. In that case, only the shares of the vMotion and VM network traffic pools are compared against each other to determine the available bandwidth for both network resource pools.

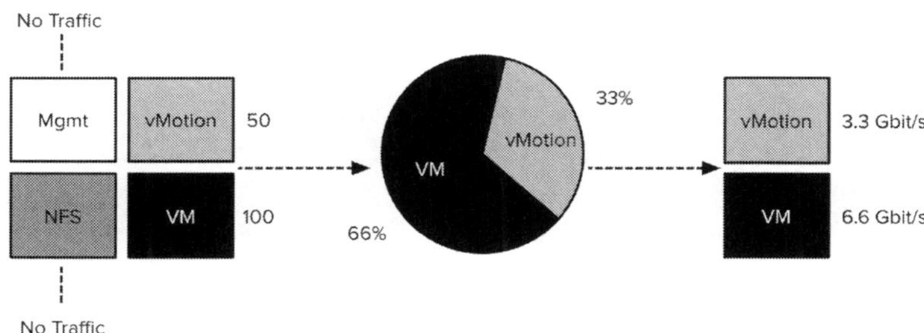

Figure 262: NIOC Shares Deviation with Fewer Traffic Sources

The moment another traffic source transmits to the Distributed vSwitch, a new calculation is made to determine the available bandwidth for the network traffic types.

It's a continuous process to determine the available network bandwidth per network traffic type to make sure each network traffic type gets its piece of the bandwidth pie.

Ingress and Egress Perspective

Important to note is that NIOC only applies to ingress traffic from the Distributed vSwitch its perspective. Incoming traffic from the VM or VMkernel interface to the Distributed vSwitch is seen as an ingress traffic flow. That means a limit only affects native traffic coming from an active VM running on the ESXi host or VMkernel interface traffic initiated on the ESXi host itself.

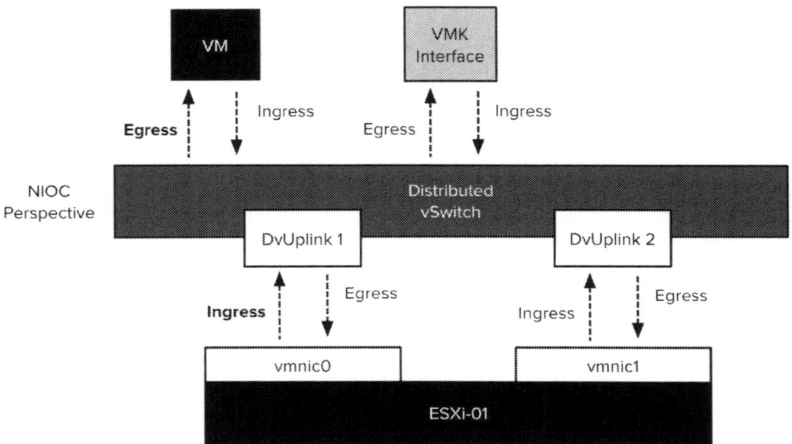

Figure 263: NIOC Ingress and Egress Perspective

Limits

Limits can be applied to restrict a particular network traffic type. A limit is a hard stop for network bandwidth consumption. Because it cannot consume outside its configured value, it introduces a risk of service impact. Generally, using limits is not recommended because it is sensitive to service interruption when misconfigured or set up too conservative.

The bandwidth limit applies to each individual interface in the ESXi host configured as DvUplink. For example, you configure a *vSphere Data Protection Backup* (VDP) network traffic type limit on a Distributed vSwitch that is using two uplinks per ESXi host. Both uplinks are configured to forward VDP traffic.

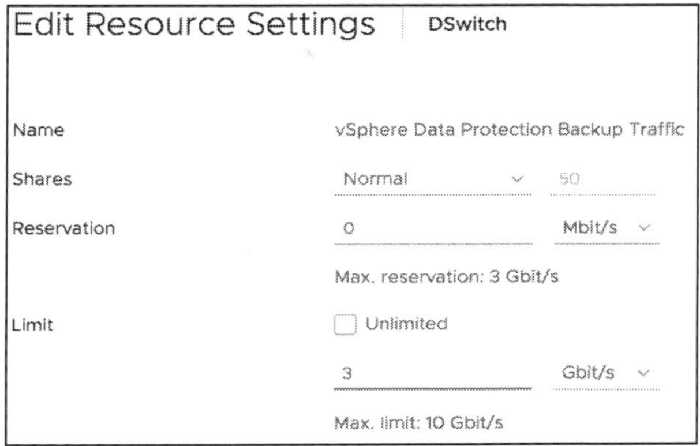

Figure 264: NIOC VDP Traffic Type Limit Configuration Example

Setting the network bandwidth limit to 3 Gbit/s results in an actual limitation of 6 Gbit/s per ESXi host.

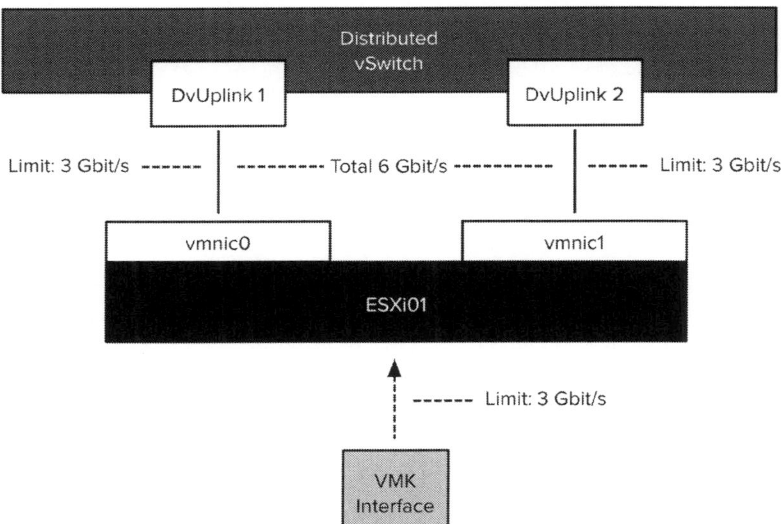

Figure 265: NIOC VDP Traffic Type Limit Example

Test Scenario

Let's have a look at how this scenario looks like in real-life. We are using a packet generator that will consume practically every bit of bandwidth it can lay its hands on within the boundaries of its CPU constraints (check the vSphere Host Resources Deep Dive book for more information). We configured the system traffic type with a limit at 3 Gbit/s.

PORT-ID	UPLINK	UP	SPEED	FDUPLX	TEAM-PNIC	DNAME	PKTTX/s	MbTX/s	MbRX/s
50331649	N	-	-	-	n/a	DvsPortset-0	0.00	0.00	0.00
50331650	N	-	-	-	vmnic1	DvsPortset-0	7.04	0.12	0.00
50331651	N	-	-	-	vmnic1	DvsPortset-0	0.00	0.00	0.00
50331652	Y	Y	10000	Y	-	DvsPortset-0	790017.18	2989.66	0.04
50331653	N	-	-	-	n/a	DvsPortset-0	0.00	0.00	0.00
50331654	Y	Y	10000	Y	-	DvsPortset-0	790097.78	2989.87	0.03
50331655	N	-	-	-	n/a	DvsPortset-0	0.00	0.00	0.00

Figure 266: NIOC Traffic Type 3 Gbit/s Limit Test

When examining the esxtop output in the screenshot above and zoom in on the MbTX/s metrics, we notice the network I/O scheduler enforces a limit to both uplink interfaces at the configured value. That leads to a total uplink capacity for the limited traffic type of 3+3=6 Gbit/s.

The network I/O scheduler reacts to changes in the NIOC settings quite promptly. That means if you have new insights that lead to changed values for shares, reservations or limits, the network I/O scheduler will adhere to these changes instantaneous.

During the test workload, we changed the limit for the system traffic type from 3 to 2 Gbit/s. In the following screenshot, you will notice that the uplink won't go beyond the updated limit value. There is no need to restart a network traffic flow or the VM.

PORT-ID	UPLINK	UP	SPEED	FDUPLX	TEAM-PNIC	DNAME	PKTTX/s	MbTX/s	MbRX/s
50331649	N	-	-	-	n/a	DvsPortset-0	0.00	0.00	0.00
50331650	N	-	-	-	vmnic1	DvsPortset-0	10.37	0.04	0.02
50331651	N	-	-	-	vmnic1	DvsPortset-0	0.00	0.00	0.00
50331652	Y	Y	10000	Y	-	DvsPortset-0	520632.25	1970.17	0.02
50331653	N	-	-	-	n/a	DvsPortset-0	0.00	0.00	0.00
50331654	Y	Y	10000	Y	-	DvsPortset-0	520775.84	1970.71	0.00
50331655	N	-	-	-	n/a	DvsPortset-0	0.00	0.00	0.00

Figure 267: NIOC Traffic Type 2 Gbit/s Limit Test

Scheduled Limit Values

When applying limits to vSphere replication or VDP system traffic network pools, you don't have the ability within vCenter today to have time-driven or scheduled, bandwidth limit values.

For example, if you need to limit the vSphere Replication traffic type during office hours because they consume too much bandwidth, but they should be able to absorb all the bandwidth they need during the night. To make this happen, you can consider implementing scripted limit schedules. That would allow you to schedule to limit the specific network traffic types to, let's say, 1 Gbit/s at 8.00 AM and change the limit to 4 Gbit/s at 19.00 PM each office day.

Chris Wahl (@ChrisWahl) included a PowerShell script on his GitHub repository that could prove useful to achieve scripted limit schedules. Make sure you check it out at *https://github.com/WahlNetwork.*

Destination Traffic Saturation

Even though the usage of NIOC bandwidth limits, another possible issue can be imposed. The issue at hand is related to NIOC and its nature to only be able to control ingress traffic flows.

For example, in the situation of bursty network consumers like vSphere vMotion operations, it is perfectly possible for vMotion network flows to consume a large or entire portion of the vMotion network traffic type on the vMotion destination VMkernel interface. That could happen when vMotion migrations are initiated on multiple ESXi hosts and are sent towards the same destination host. By doing so, the bandwidth of the destination host is at risk of being saturated, even though NIOC is active.

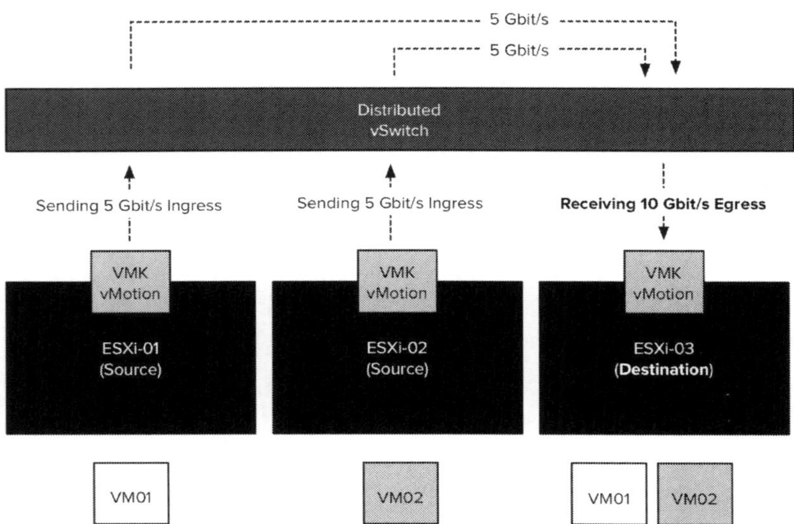

Figure 268: NIOC Limit Consumption by Other ESXi Hosts

In the example as shown in the diagram above, the two source ESXi hosts are already devouring all the destination host bandwidth. Both source ESXi hosts vMotion traffic flows are limited at 5 Gbit/s using NIOC limits, but NIOC does not control the egress traffic towards the destination ESXi host. The vMotion VMkernel interface on the destination host is saturated, impacting migration times.

> **Use NIOC to enforce source-based network bandwidth control. Use traffic shaping for destination-based bandwidth management.**

Traffic Shaping

To counter the risk of egress bandwidth exhaustion, we can control the egress vMotion traffic flows using traffic shaping. By doing so, the outgoing traffic is also limited to a fixed bandwidth value. Traffic shaping is configured on a Distributed port group. Because our example is about vMotion, we will set the vMotion port group with an egress traffic shape configuration.

When configuring traffics shaping, we have the following three parameters to be set for either ingress or egress traffic:

- Average bandwidth (kbit/s)
- Peak bandwidth (kbit/s)
- Burst size (KB)

The average bandwidth is the bits per second value flowing through the specific Distributed port group over time. The peak bandwidth is the absolute maximum bandwidth the port group is able to consume. The burst size is a safe-net as it allows the port group to burst. It is a multiplicative factor that defines how long the bandwidth can exceed the average bandwidth setting.

The configuration values for the peak and average bandwidth are in kbit/s meaning you need to calculate what specific numbers you need. So, if you have a 10 Gbit/s NIC interface for your Distributed vSwitch uplinks, it means you have a total of 10,485,760 kbit/s. When you enable Traffic Shaping by default, it is set to have an average bandwidth of 100,000 kbit/s, Peak Bandwidth of 100,000 kbit/s and a burst size of 102400 KB. That means that if you enable traffic shaping and leave it by its default configuration, it will result in the traffic limited to 100,000 Kbps. 100,000 Kbps is around 100 Mbit/s and not a lot to work with for vMotion operations. It is not even a support vMotion configuration.

With the specific use-case we have in this example, to limit the destination host vMotion traffic, we need to configure the egress traffic shaping for the vMotion port group to, for example, 7 Gbit/s.

vMotion - Edit Settings

General
Advanced
VLAN
Security
Teaming and failover
Traffic shaping
Monitoring
Miscellaneous

Ingress traffic shaping

Status	Disabled
Average bandwidth (kbit/s)	100000
Peak bandwidth (kbit/s)	100000
Burst size	102400

Egress traffic shaping

Status	Enabled
Average bandwidth (kbit/s)	7340032
Peak bandwidth (kbit/s)	7340032
Burst size (KB)	102400

Figure 269: Egress Traffic Shaping Configuration

Once configured correctly, traffic shaping will throttle down the bandwidth on the destination host and by doing so automatically tune down the bandwidth send from the source ESXi hosts.

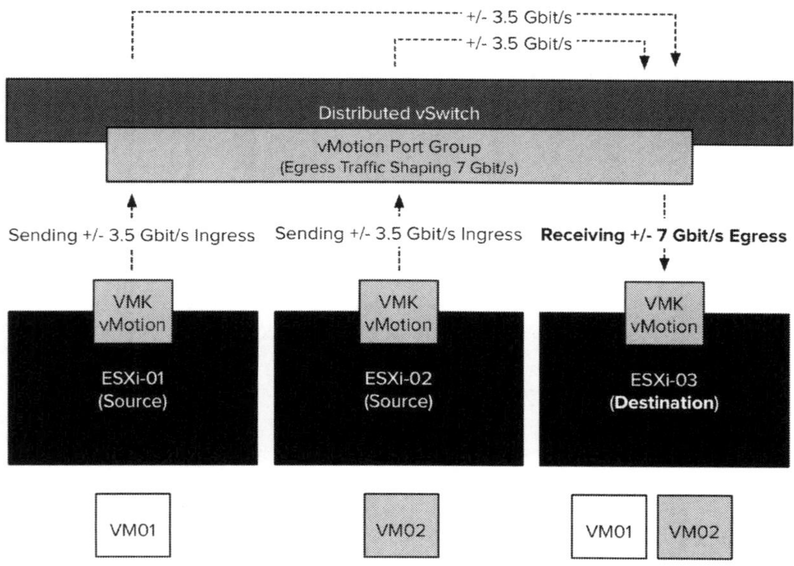

Figure 270: NIOC Limit Consumption Solved with Traffic-Shaping

We cannot stress enough to be very careful when configuring traffic-shaping values. With regards to the vMotion network traffic as described in this chapter, misconfiguration could lead to slower vMotion performance and possible vMotion failing because of time-outs.

Even though the stated scenario may be a corner-case, it is wise to think it through. Especially in larger clusters where multiple ESXi hosts are regularly simultaneously put in maintenance mode for patching.

Reservations

To enforce bandwidth availability, it is possible to reserve a portion of the available uplink bandwidth. It may be necessary to configure bandwidth reservations to meet business requirements with regards to network resources availability. In the system traffic overview, under the resource allocation option in the Distributed vSwitch settings, you can configure reservations. Reservations are set per system traffic type or per VM which we will cover in the upcoming chapters.

Strongly depending on your IT architecture, it could make sense to reserve bandwidth for specific business critical workloads or your vSAN network or IP storage network backend. However, be aware that network bandwidth allocated in a reservation cannot be consumed by other network traffic types. When a reservation is not used to the fullest, NIOC does not redistribute the capacity to the bandwidth pool that is accessible to different network traffic types or network resource pools. Since you cannot overcommit bandwidth reservations by default, it means you should be careful when applying reservations to ensure no bandwidth is gone to waste. Thoroughly think through the minimal amount of reservation that you are required to guarantee for network traffic types.

> **For NIOC to be able to guarantee bandwidth for all system traffic types, you can only reserve up to 75% of the bandwidth relative to the minimum link speed of the uplink interfaces.**

When configuring a reservation, it guarantees network bandwidth for that network traffic type or VM. It is the minimum amount of bandwidth that is accessible. Unlike limits, a network resource can burst beyond the configured value for its bandwidth reservation, as it doesn't state a maximum consumable amount of bandwidth.

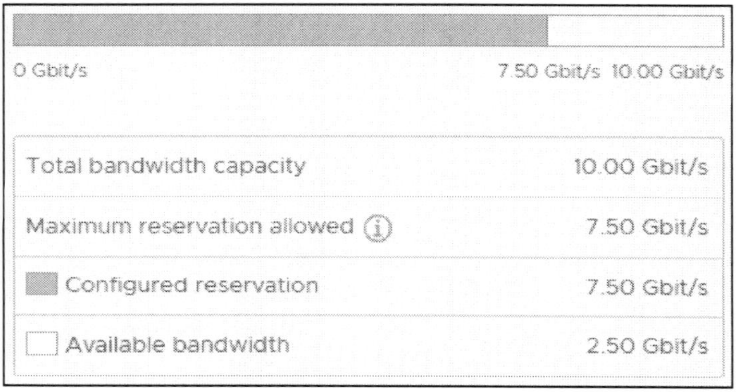

0 Gbit/s 7.50 Gbit/s 10.00 Gbit/s

Total bandwidth capacity	10.00 Gbit/s
Maximum reservation allowed ⓘ	7.50 Gbit/s
Configured reservation	7.50 Gbit/s
Available bandwidth	2.50 Gbit/s

Figure 271: NIOC Maximum Reservation Value

You cannot exceed the value of the maximum reservation allowed. It will always keep aside 25% bandwidth per physical uplink to ensure the basic ESXi network necessities like Management traffic. As seen in the screenshot above, a 10GbE network adapter can only be configured with reservations up to 7.5 Gbit/s.

> **As with bandwidth limits, the configured reservation value applies per physical adapter that is used as uplink in the Distributed vSwitch.**

A bandwidth reservation applies to each Distributed vSwitch uplink. For example, if you set a reservation of 2 Gbit/s for vSAN, a total of 4 Gbit/s is reserved when using two Distributed vSwitch uplinks per ESXi host.

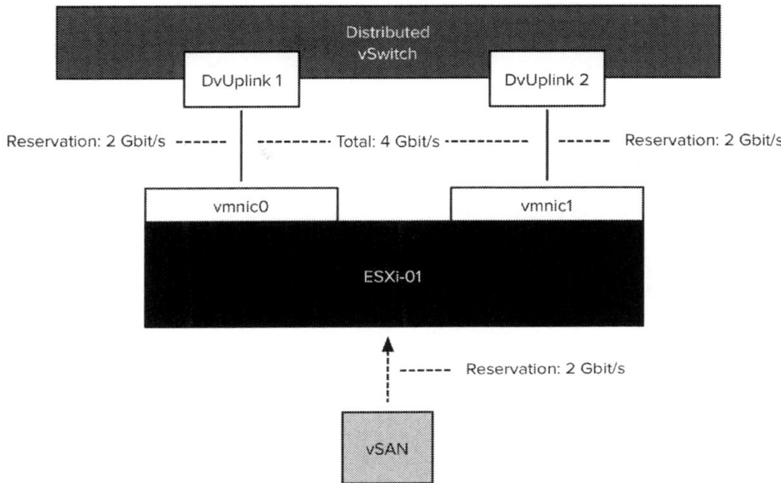

Figure 272: NIOC Reservation Example

Looking into this example, it means that if your cluster contains five ESXi hosts each with two uplinks, the total cluster reservation will be 5*(2+2)=20 Gbit/s.

Reservations could prove very useful to guarantee network bandwidth for multiple tenants running on the same Distributed vSwitch. By allocating a reservation on a Distributed port group level when each tenant is using its own port group.

Network Resource Pools

To create more individual network bandwidth reservations for specific workloads, you can configure more fine-grained reservations. These bandwidth reservations are configurable on port groups residing on a Distributed vSwitch. It allows you to create more detailed quality control between various workloads or tenants within your virtual data center.

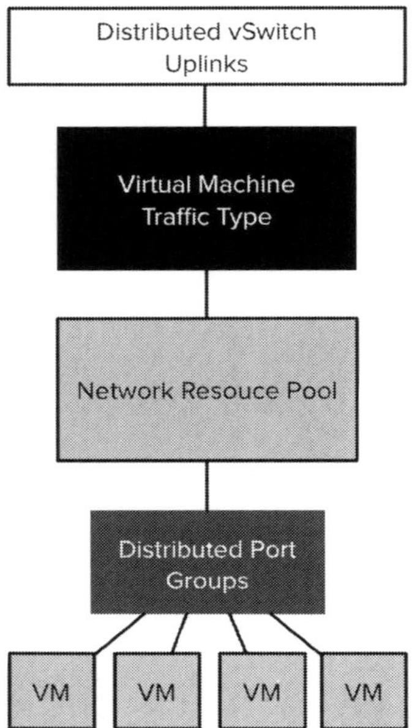

Figure 273: Network Resource Pool Constructs

To set network resource pools values, you first need to reserve bandwidth for the VM traffic type. Once an amount of bandwidth is allocated for VM traffic, networks resource pools can be defined.

0 Gbit/s 7.50 Gbit/s 10.00 Gbit/s

Network I/O Control	Enabled
Version	3
Physical network adapters	6
Minimum link speed	10 Gbit/s

Total bandwidth capacity	10.00 Gbit/s
Maximum reservation allowed	7.50 Gbit/s
Configured reservation	2.00 Gbit/s
Available bandwidth	8.00 Gbit/s

EDIT

Traffic Type	Shares	Shares Value	Reservation	Limit
Management Traffic	Normal	50	0 Mbit/s	Unlimited
Fault Tolerance (FT) Traffic	Normal	50	0 Mbit/s	Unlimited
vMotion Traffic	Normal	50	0 Mbit/s	Unlimited
Virtual Machine Traffic	High	100	2 Gbit/s	Unlimited
iSCSI Traffic	Normal	50	0 Mbit/s	Unlimited
NFS Traffic	Normal	50	0 Mbit/s	Unlimited
vSphere Replication (VR) Traffic	Normal	50	0 Mbit/s	Unlimited
vSAN Traffic	Normal	50	0 Mbit/s	Unlimited
vSphere Data Protection Backup Traffic	Normal	50	0 Mbit/s	Unlimited

Figure 274: Virtual Machine Traffic Reservation Example

All bandwidth available to the Virtual Machine traffic type can be sliced up over the network resource pools. That allows for an easy way to facilitate bandwidth reservations for Distributed port groups and all VMs connected to it. In this example, we reserved 2 Gbit/s for the Virtual Machine traffic type.

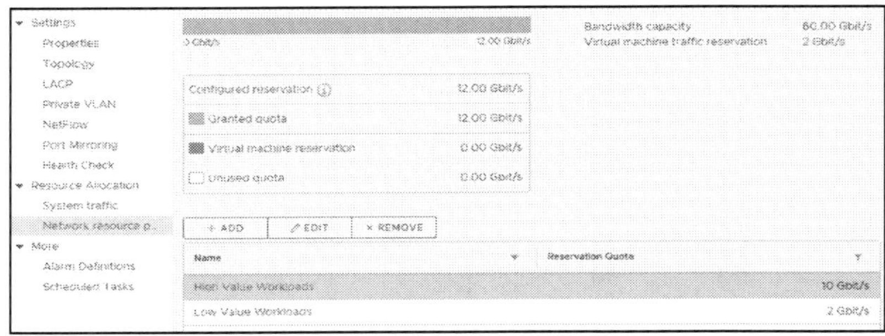

Figure 275: Network Resource Pools

Our lab cluster consists of three ESXi hosts each equipped with two pNICs resulting in a total of six Distributed vSwitch uplinks. The total amount of available bandwidth to be divided over the network resource pools will be 12 Gbit/s. The following calculations are applicable for NIOC to determine the maximum reservations allowed for a network resource pool.

*Configured reservation for VM system traffic * number of DvUplinks = Aggregated reservation for network resource pools*

In our test environment that translates to 2 Gbit/s * 6 = 12 Gbit/s. That is the cluster-wide maximum for network resource pool reservations. When you add more hosts to the cluster and the Distributed vSwitch, it will adjust the aggregated reservation accordingly.

Distributed port groups can be mapped to a network resource pool. In the following example, we can select both our created network resource pools for the 'Application X' port group.

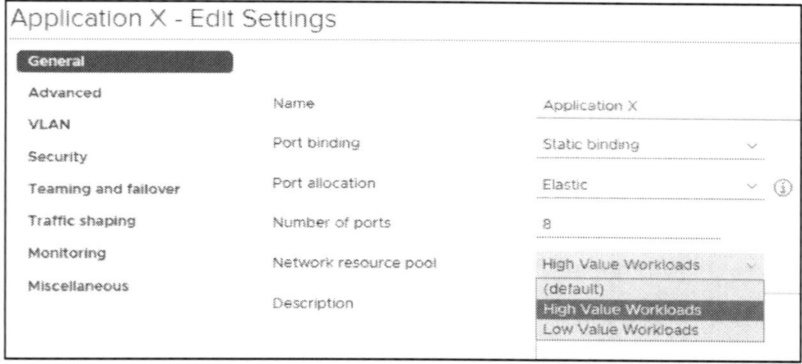

Figure 276: Network Resource Pool on a Distributed Port Group

VMs connected to this port group, that is mapped to a custom network resource pool, is now able to consume the reserved bandwidth. More insights on all Distributed port groups and VMs connected to a specific network resource pool is available in vCenter by clicking on the network resource pool.

High Value Workloads | ACTIONS

Distributed Port Groups | Virtual Machines

Name	Network Protocol Profile	Port Binding	VLAN ID	VMs	Ports
VM Network		Static binding (elastic)	VLAN access: 116	4	29
Application X		Static binding (elastic)	VLAN access: 120	0	8

Figure 277: Network Resource Pool Usage Overview

Individual VM Parameters

Adding port groups to a network resource pool helps you to manage the bandwidth allocation over all the VMs connected to it. However, if you are required to enforce a level of bandwidth prioritisation per VM, network resources pools won't help you as they only provide bandwidth reservations. You are able to configure individual NIOC setting at the *virtual NIC* (vNIC) level in each VM by selecting the appropriate network adapter and configure the NIOC settings.

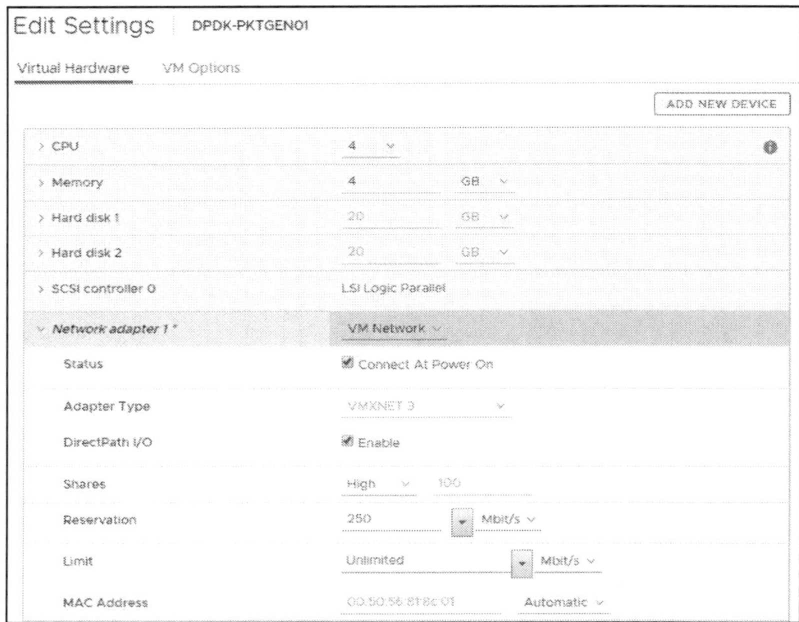

Figure 278: Per vNIC Reservation Example

You can also consult the VM overview within a network resource pool. It will give you a better understanding on what is configured across all VMs.

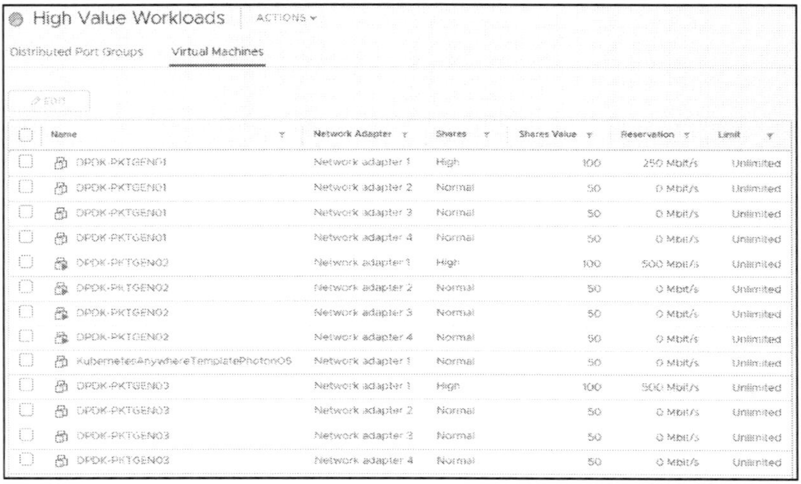

High Value Workloads | ACTIONS

Distributed Port Groups | Virtual Machines

EDIT

Name	Network Adapter	Shares	Shares Value	Reservation	Limit
DPDK-PKTGEN01	Network adapter 1	High	100	250 Mbit/s	Unlimited
DPDK-PKTGEN01	Network adapter 2	Normal	50	0 Mbit/s	Unlimited
DPDK-PKTGEN01	Network adapter 3	Normal	50	0 Mbit/s	Unlimited
DPDK-PKTGEN01	Network adapter 4	Normal	50	0 Mbit/s	Unlimited
DPDK-PKTGEN02	Network adapter 1	High	100	500 Mbit/s	Unlimited
DPDK-PKTGEN02	Network adapter 2	Normal	50	0 Mbit/s	Unlimited
DPDK-PKTGEN02	Network adapter 3	Normal	50	0 Mbit/s	Unlimited
DPDK-PKTGEN02	Network adapter 4	Normal	50	0 Mbit/s	Unlimited
KubernetesAnywhereTemplatePhotonOS	Network adapter 1	Normal	50	0 Mbit/s	Unlimited
DPDK-PKTGEN03	Network adapter 1	High	100	500 Mbit/s	Unlimited
DPDK-PKTGEN03	Network adapter 2	Normal	50	0 Mbit/s	Unlimited
DPDK-PKTGEN03	Network adapter 3	Normal	50	0 Mbit/s	Unlimited
DPDK-PKTGEN03	Network adapter 4	Normal	50	0 Mbit/s	Unlimited

Figure 279: Network Resource Pool VM Overview

You can use shares, reservations and limits for individual VMs and their vNICs that are connected to a Distributed port group.
Ensure that the reserved bandwidth for all vNICs do not exceed the bandwidth of the DvUplinks on the ESXi host the VM is registered on. With vSphere DRS enabled on the cluster, this will prevent the VM from booting.

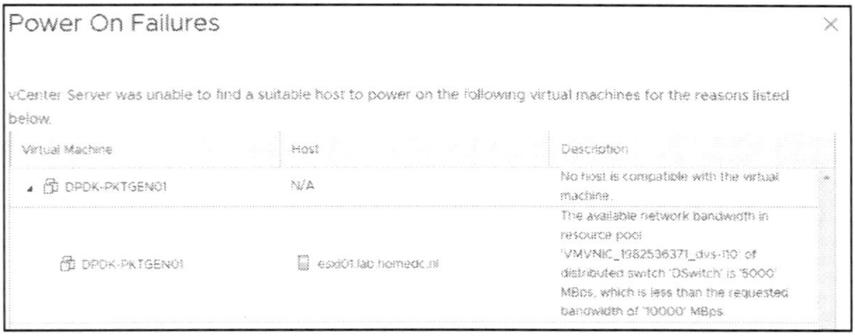

Power On Failures

vCenter Server was unable to find a suitable host to power on the following virtual machines for the reasons listed below.

Virtual Machine	Host	Description
DPDK-PKTGEN01	N/A	No host is compatible with the virtual machine.
DPDK-PKTGEN01	esxi01.lab.homedc.nl	The available network bandwidth in resource pool 'VMVNIC_1982536371_dvs-110' of distributed switch 'DSwitch' is '5000' MBps, which is less than the requested bandwidth of '10000' MBps.

Figure 280: Power On Failure by vSphere DRS

Bandwidth Management

We talked about the various constructs and possibilities to tune Network I/O Control to your need. Using NIOC can be beneficial and help you managing network bandwidth to comply to your SLA agreements and to mitigate the risk of pNIC saturation because of that one bandwidth-greedy network traffic type or VM.

However, advanced NIOC configurations come at the price of additional operational overhead and the associated risk of misconfiguration. When wrongfully applied, it can do more harm than good. Reservations or limits and the possible coherent traffic shaping configurations are by nature very sensitive to human error. Especially when you utilize them on multiple levels:

- Network traffic type
- Network resource pool
- Virtual Machine per vNIC

A general recommendation is to keep the NIOC layer as simple as possible. While there are use cases for reservations and perhaps even limits, it is recommended to utilise the shares for prioritisation of virtual network traffic.

Making sure each network traffic type can consume all its requested network bandwidth is essential. Use proper network bandwidth performance and capacity management to ensure all demands can be met with the available bandwidth per ESXi hosts. VMware vRealize Operations can help you with that.

Traffic Marking

NIOC is focused on the virtual networking layer within in VMware data center. But what about the physical layer?

In converged infrastructures or enterprise networking environments, it is not uncommon for *Quality of Service* (QoS) to be configured in the physical layers. QoS is the ability to provide different priorities to network flows, or to guarantee a certain level of performance to a network flow by using tags. In vSphere 6.7, you have the ability to create flow-based traffic marking policies to mark network flows for QoS.

Quality of Service

vSphere 6.7 supports *Class of Service* (CoS) and *Differentiated Services Code Point* (DSCP). Both are QoS mechanisms used to differentiate traffic types to allow for policing network traffic flows.

> **As related to network technology, CoS is a 3-bit field that is present in an Ethernet frame header when 802.1Q VLAN tagging is present. The field specifies a priority value between 0 and 7, more commonly known as CS0 through CS7, that can be used by quality of service (QoS) disciplines to differentiate and shape/police network traffic.**
> Source: *https://en.wikipedia.org/wiki/Class_of_service*

One of the main differentiators is that CoS operates at data link layer in an Ethernet based network (layer-2). DSCP operates at the IP network layer (layer-3).

> **Differentiated services or DiffServ is a computer networking architecture that specifies a simple and scalable mechanism for classifying and managing network traffic and providing quality of service (QoS) on modern IP networks. DiffServ uses a 6-bit differentiated services code point (DSCP) in the 8-bit differentiated services field (DS field) in the IP header for packet classification purposes.** Source: *https://en.wikipedia.org/wiki/Differentiated_services*

When a traffic marking policy is configured for CoS or DSCP, its value is advertised towards the physical layer to create an end-to-end QoS path.

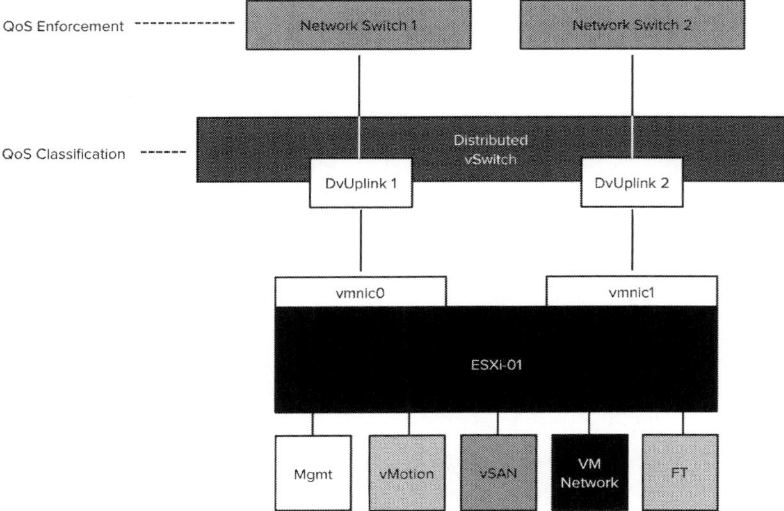

Figure 281: QoS Classification Advertised from Virtual to Physical Layer

Traffic marking policies are configurable on Distributed port groups or on the DvUplinks. To match certain traffic flows, a traffic qualifier needs to be set. This can be realized using very specific traffic flows with specific IP address and TCP/UDP ports or by using a selected traffic type. The qualifier options are extensive.

For example, you are required to tag iSCSI traffic from the ESXi hosts towards the physical network layer using CoS tag 4. using a CoS value to mark Management traffic, you could configure the Distributed uplink group with an egress Cos tag rule that matches system type traffic iSCSI.

CoS tag 4 - Edit Traffic Rule | DSwitch-DVUplinks-110

Name: CoS tag 4
Action: Tag | CoS tag 4 | DSCP tag 0 - 63
Traffic direction: Egress

Traffic Qualifiers
IP | MAC | System traffic

Enable qualifier
System traffic: is | iSCSI

Figure 282: CoS Tag Traffic iSCSI Rule Example

After configuring this traffic rule, you need to enable it by using the 'Enable and re-order' button. Now your outgoing iSCSI traffic is marked with CoS value 4. This is just a simple example of what is possible with traffic rules in vSphere 6.7. When you are required to implement QoS tags, be sure to think about where to apply the traffic rule, keeping the configuration as simple and manageable as possible.

The Distributed vSwitch applies rules on traffic at different places in the data stream. It is able to apply traffic filter rules between uplink interfaces and the pNIC or between the vNIC and the port on the Distributed vSwitch. Important to note is that vSphere does not shape traffic according to the QoS tagging, this is done appropriately in the physical layer.

P5

STRETCHED CLUSTERS

26

USE CASE: STRETCHED CLUSTERS

In this part we will be discussing a specific infrastructure architecture and how HA, DRS and Storage DRS can be leveraged and should be deployed to increase availability. Be it availability of your workload or the resources provided to your workload, we will guide you through some of the design considerations and decision points along the way. Of course, a full understanding of your environment will be required in order to make appropriate decisions regarding specific implementation details. Nevertheless, we hope that this section will provide a proper understanding of how certain features play together and how these can be used to meet the requirements of your environment and build the desired architecture.

Scenario

The scenario we have chosen is a stretched cluster also referred to as a VMware vSphere Metro Storage Cluster solution. We have chosen this specific scenario as it allows us to explain a multitude of design and architectural considerations. Although this scenario has been tested and validated in our lab, every environment is unique and our recommendations are based on our experience and your mileage may vary.

A VMware vSphere Metro Storage Cluster (vMSC) configuration is a VMware vSphere certified solution that combines synchronous replication with storage array-based clustering. These solutions are typically deployed in environments where the distance between datacenters is limited, often metropolitan or campus environments.

The primary benefit of a stretched cluster model is to enable fully active and workload-balanced datacenters to be used to their full potential. Many customers find this architecture attractive due to the capability of migrating VMs with vMotion and Storage vMotion between sites. This enables on-demand and non-intrusive cross-site mobility of workloads. The capability of a stretched cluster to provide this active balancing of resources should always be the primary design and implementation goal.

Stretched cluster solutions offer the benefit of:

- Workload mobility
- Cross-site automated load balancing
- Enhanced downtime avoidance
- Disaster avoidance
- Fast recovery

Technical Requirements and Constraints

Due to the technical constraints of an online migration of VMs, the following specific requirements must be met prior to consideration of a stretched cluster implementation:

- Storage connectivity using Fibre Channel, iSCSI, NFS, and FCoE is supported
- The maximum supported network latency between sites for the vSphere ESXi management networks is 10ms round-trip time (RTT)
- vMotion, and Storage vMotion, supports a maximum of 150ms latency as of vSphere 6.0, but this is not intended for stretched clustering usage (Requires Enterprise Plus license)
- The vMotion network has a 250 Mbps of dedicated bandwidth per concurrent vMotion session requirement
- The maximum supported latency for synchronous storage

replication links is 10ms RTT. Refer to documentation from the storage vendor because the maximum tolerated latency is lower in most cases. The most commonly supported maximum RTT is 5ms

- SMP FT is not supported
- Storage IO Control is not supported

The storage requirements are slightly more complex. A vSphere Metro Storage Cluster requires what is in effect a single storage subsystem that spans both sites. In this design, a given datastore must be accessible—that is, be able to be read and be written to—simultaneously from both sites. Further, when problems occur, the vSphere hosts must be able to continue to access datastores from either location transparently and with no impact to ongoing storage operations.

This precludes traditional synchronous replication solutions because they create a primary–secondary relationship between the active (primary) LUN where data is being accessed and the secondary LUN that is receiving replication. To access the secondary LUN, replication is stopped, or reversed, and the LUN is made visible to hosts. This "promoted" secondary LUN has a completely different LUN ID and is essentially a newly available copy of a former primary LUN. This type of solution works for traditional disaster recovery–type configurations because it is expected that VM's must be started up on the secondary site. The vMSC configuration requires simultaneous, uninterrupted access to enable live migration of running VMs between sites.

The storage subsystem for a vMSC must be able to be read from and write to both locations simultaneously. All disk writes are committed synchronously at both locations to ensure that data is always consistent regardless of the location from which it is being read. This storage architecture requires significant bandwidth and very low latency between the sites in the cluster. Increased distances or latencies cause delays in writing to disk and a dramatic decline in performance. They also preclude successful vMotion migration between cluster nodes that reside in different locations.

Note that initially vMSC storage configurations had to go through a mandatory certification program. As of vSphere 6.0 this is no longer needed. vMSC configurations are now fully partner supported and can be found on the vmware.com website under PVSP (Partner Verified and Supported Products). Before purchasing, designing or implementing please consult the PVSP listing to ensure the partner has filed for PVSP and has tested with the correct vSphere versions.

The vMSC listings typically also provide a link to the specifics of the implementation by the partner. As an example, the PVSP Listing for Dell/EMC VPLEX provides the following link: https://kb.vmware.com/kb/2007545. This link provides all tested scenarios and supported components with Dell/EMC VPLEX.

> **Verify the PVSP list before acquiring hardware. Being able to receive proper support is crucial for any business or mission critical environment!**

Uniform Versus Non-Uniform vMSC Configurations

vMSC solutions are classified into two distinct types. These categories are based on a fundamental difference in how hosts access storage. It is important to understand the different types of stretched storage solutions because this influences design considerations. The two types are:

- Uniform host access configuration – vSphere hosts from both sites are all connected to a storage node in the storage cluster across all sites. Paths presented to vSphere hosts are stretched across a distance
- Non-uniform host access configuration – vSphere hosts at each site are connected only to storage node(s) at the same site. Paths presented to vSphere hosts from storage nodes are limited to the local site

The following in-depth descriptions of both types clearly define them from architectural and implementation perspectives.

With **uniform** host access configuration, hosts in data center A and data center B have access to the storage systems in both data centers. In effect, the storage area network is stretched between the sites, and all hosts can access all LUNs. NetApp MetroCluster is an example of uniform storage. In this configuration, read/write access to a LUN takes place on one of the two arrays, and a synchronous mirror is maintained in a hidden, read-only state on the second array. For example, if a LUN containing a datastore is read/write on the array in data center A, all vSphere hosts access that datastore via the array in data center A. For vSphere hosts in data center A, this is local access. vSphere hosts in data center B that are running VMs hosted on this datastore send read/write traffic across the network between data centers. In case of an outage or an operator-controlled shift of control of the LUN to data center B, all vSphere hosts continue to detect the identical LUN being presented, but it is now being accessed via the array in data center B.

The ideal situation is one in which VMs access a datastore that is controlled (read/write) by the array in the same data center. This minimizes traffic between data centers to avoid the performance impact of reads' traversing the interconnect.

The notion of "site affinity" for a VM is dictated by the read/write copy of the datastore. "Site affinity" is also sometimes referred to as "site bias" or "LUN locality." This means that when a VM has site affinity with data center A, its read/write copy of the datastore is located in data center A. This is explained in more detail in the "DRS" subsection of this paper.

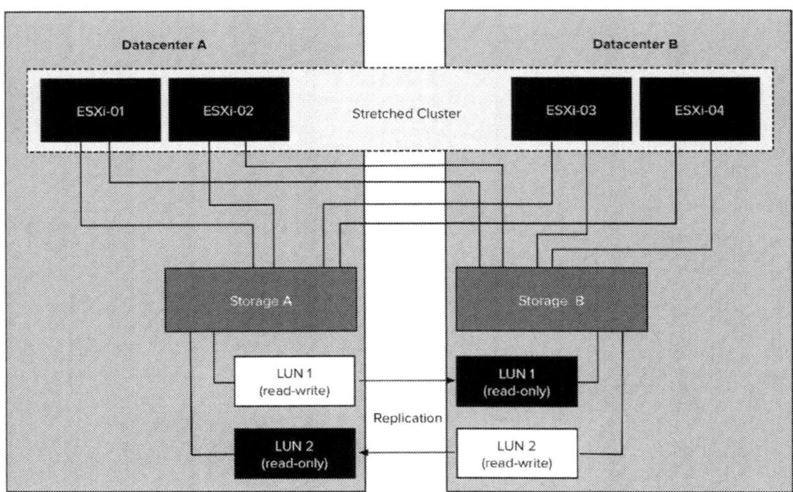

Figure 283: Uniform Access

With **non-uniform** host access configuration, hosts in data center A have access only to the array within the local data center. The array, as well as its peer array in the opposite data center, is responsible for providing access to datastores in one data center. Dell EMC® VPLEX® is an example of a storage system that can be deployed as a non-uniform storage cluster, although it can also be configured in a uniform manner. VPLEX provides the concept of a “virtual LUN,” which enables vSphere hosts in each data center to read and write to the same datastore or LUN. VPLEX technology maintains the cache state on each array so vSphere hosts in either data center detect the LUN as local. EMC calls this solution “write anywhere.” Even when two VMs reside on the same datastore but are located in different data centers, they write locally without any performance impact on either VM. A key point with this configuration is that each LUN or datastore has “site affinity,” also sometimes referred to as “site bias” or “LUN locality.” In other words, if anything happens to the link between the sites, the storage system on the preferred site for a given datastore will be the only one remaining with read/write access to it. This prevents any data corruption in case of a failure scenario. If VMs by any chance are not running within the location that has read/write access to the datastore they will end up being killed and restarted by HA. We will discuss this in-depth in the upcoming sections.

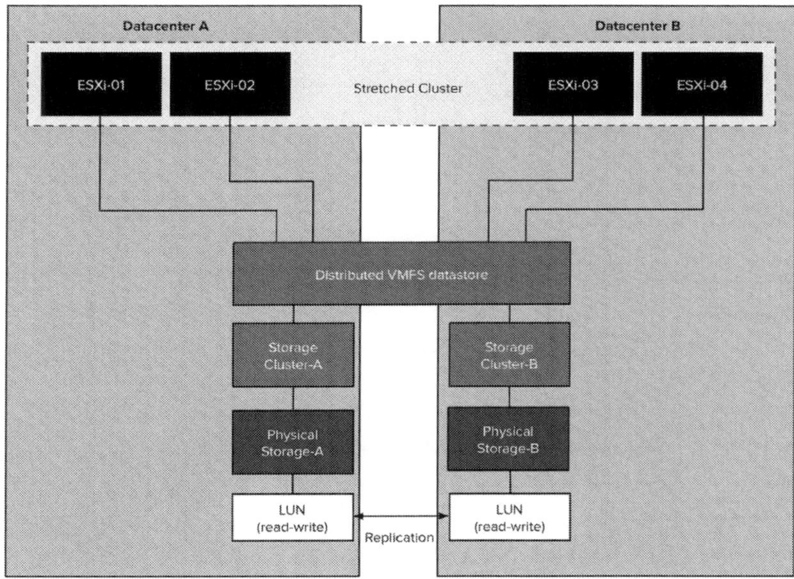

Figure 284: Non-Uniform Access

Our examples use uniform storage because these configurations are currently the most commonly deployed. Many of the design considerations, however, also apply to non-uniform configurations. We point out exceptions when this is not the case.

> **Understand the difference between Uniform and Non-uniform access. There are advantages to either and specific design considerations for each configuration.**

Infrastructure Architecture

In this section, we describe the basic architecture referenced in this document. We also discuss basic configuration and performance of the various vSphere features. For an in-depth explanation of each feature, refer to the *vSphere 6.7 Availability Guide* and the *vSphere 6.7 Resource*

Management Guide. We make specific recommendations based on VMware best practices and provide operational guidance where applicable. We also like to refer to the official vSphere Metro Storage Cluster white paper hosted on storagehub.vmware.com. This paper was written by Duncan based on the use case in this book, it may however contain more recent recommendations as it is updated more frequent.

Infrastructure

The described infrastructure consists of a single vSphere 6.7 cluster with four vSphere 6.7 hosts. These hosts are managed by a VMware vCenter Server Appliance™ 6.7 instance. When we originally wrote this section for the book our lab environment was located in our data center's in Amsterdam and London. Due to Brexit, and the potential data compliancy impact, we decide to move our data centers to The Netherlands. The first site is now located (and called) in Amsterdam; the second site is located (and called) in Rotterdam. The network between Amsterdam data center and Rotterdam data center is a stretched layer 2 network. There is a minimal distance between the sites, as is typical in campus cluster scenarios.

Each site has two vSphere hosts, and the vCenter Server instance is configured with vSphere VM-Host affinity to the hosts in Rotterdam data center. In a stretched cluster environment, only a single vCenter Server instance is used. This is different from a traditional Site Recovery Manager configuration in which a dual vCenter Server configuration is required. The configuration of VM-Host affinity rules is discussed in more detail in the "DRS" subsection of this document.

Eight LUNs are depicted in the diagram below. Four of these are accessed through the virtual IP address active on the iSCSI storage system in the Amsterdam data center; four are accessed through the virtual IP address active on the iSCSI storage system in the Rotterdam data center.

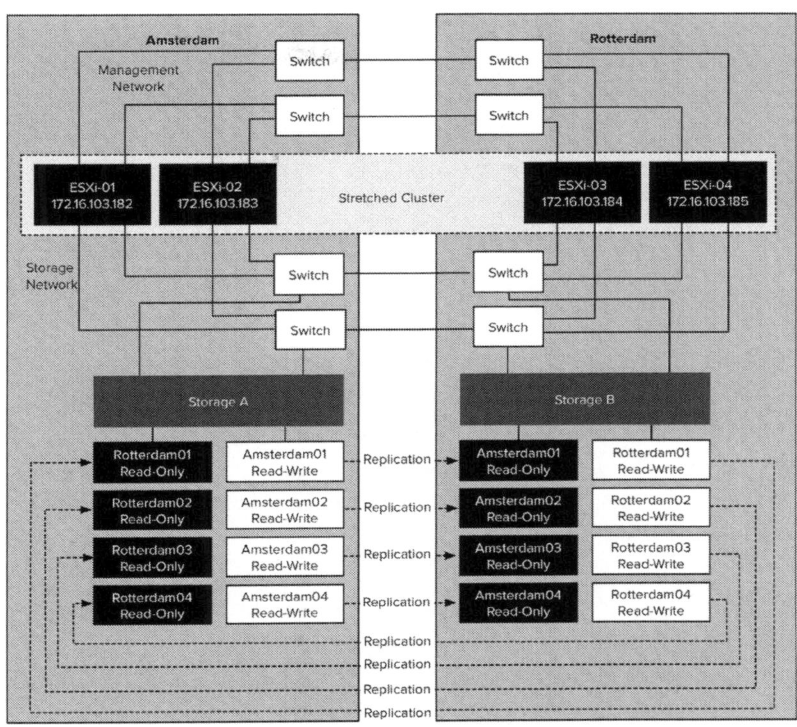

Figure 285: Our Lab Infrastructure

LOCATION	HOST IP	DATASTORES	LOCAL ISOLATION ADDRESS
Amsterdam	172.16.103.182	Amsterdam01	172.16.103.10
	172.16.103.183	Amsterdam02	
		Amsterdam03	
		Amsterdam04	
Rotterdam	172.16.103.184	Rotterdam01	172.16.103.10
	172.16.103.185	Rotterdam02	
		Rotterdam03	
		Rotterdam04	

Table 35: Infrastructure Details

The vSphere cluster is connected to a stretched storage system in a fabric configuration with a uniform device access model. This means that every host in the cluster is connected to both storage heads. Each of the heads is connected to two switches, which are connected to two similar switches in the secondary location. For any given LUN, one of the two storage heads present the LUN as read/write via iSCSI. The other storage head maintains the replicated, read-only copy that is effectively hidden from the vSphere hosts.

vSphere Configuration

Our focus in this document is on HA, DRS, and Storage DRS in relation to stretched cluster environments. Design and operational considerations regarding vSphere are commonly overlooked and underestimated. Much emphasis has traditionally been placed on the storage layer, but little attention has been applied to how workloads are provisioned and managed.

One of the key drivers for using a stretched cluster is workload balance and disaster avoidance. How do we ensure that our environment is properly balanced without impacting availability or severely increasing the operational expenditure? How do we build the requirements into our provisioning process and validate periodically that we still meet them? Ignoring these requirements makes the environment confusing to administrate and less predictable during the various failure scenarios for which it should be of help.

Each of these three vSphere features has very specific configuration requirements and can enhance environment resiliency and workload availability. Architectural recommendations based on our findings during the testing of the various failure scenarios, and our understanding of vSphere, are given throughout this section.

vSphere HA

Our environment has four hosts and a uniform stretched storage solution. A full site failure is one scenario that must be taken into account in a resilient architecture, alongside host failures, network failures and different types of storage failures. HA is crucial in any environment to provide a certain level of availability, but even more so in a vMSC configuration. We recommend enabling HA and recommend thoroughly reading the following guidelines for an optimal HA configuration for vMSC based infrastructures.

Admission Control

We recommend enabling **HA Admission Control**. Workload availability is the primary driver for most stretched cluster environments, so providing sufficient capacity for a full site failure is recommended. Such hosts are equally divided across both sites. To ensure that all workloads can be restarted by HA on just one site, configuring the admission control policy to 50 percent for both memory and CPU is recommended.

We recommend using a **percentage-based** policy because it offers the most flexibility and reduces operational overhead. Even when new hosts are introduced to the environment, there is no need to change the percentage and no risk of a skewed consolidation ratio due to possible use of VM level reservations. For more details about admission control policies and the associated algorithms, refer to the vSphere 6.7 Availability Guide.

Additionally, as of vSphere 6.5 it is also possible to specify how much **Performance Degradation (VMs Tolerate)** you are willing to tolerate for your workloads. By default, this setting is configured to 100%. You can change this to your liking and should be based on your SLA with the business. As this setting is new, we will briefly explain how it works by looking at an example.

An environment has 75 GB of memory available in a three-node cluster. One host failure to tolerate is specified and 60 GB of memory is actively used by VMs. In the UI, it is also specified that 0% resource reduction is tolerated.

HA will now take a single host failure in to account for this cluster. This results in 75 GB – 25 GB (1 host worth of memory) = 50 GB of memory available to run workloads. There is 60 GB of memory used. This implies that with 0% resource reduction to tolerate, 60 GB of memory is required. However, after a failure there is only 50 GB available and as such vSphere issues a warning. Note that this does not stop the provisioning of new VMs or the power-on of VMs. That is what Admission Control is for.

The following screenshot a HA cluster configured with Admission Control enabled. Note that as of vSphere 6.5 specific settings around admission control need to be set after creating the cluster.

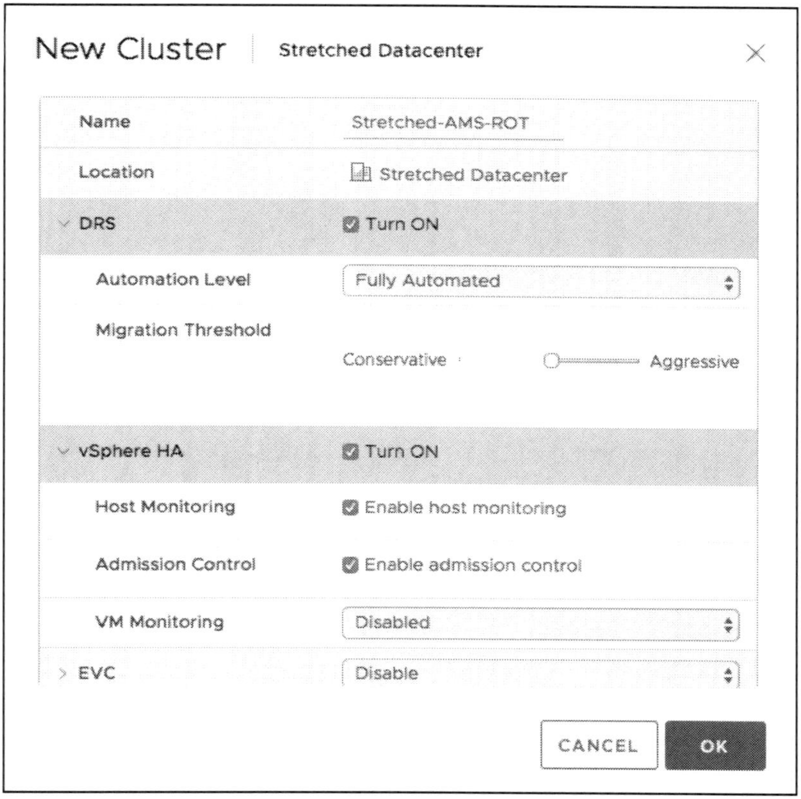

Figure 286: Cluster Creation

First recommendation is to ensure that admission control is configured to reserve 50% of both CPU and Memory resources for HA. This is to ensure, that in the case of a full site failure, all VMs can be restarted. Starting vSphere 6.5 the UI for Admission Control has slightly changed. In the interface, you now specify the number of hosts failures to tolerate which is then, converted to a percentage, or you can alternatively override the calculations and manually specify the percentage. We recommend using the **Cluster Resource Percentage admission control policy** algorithm as it is the most flexible policy. As we always want to protect against a full site failure we will manually set the percentage to 50% for both memory and CPU capacity. For more details please read the chapter describing admission control.

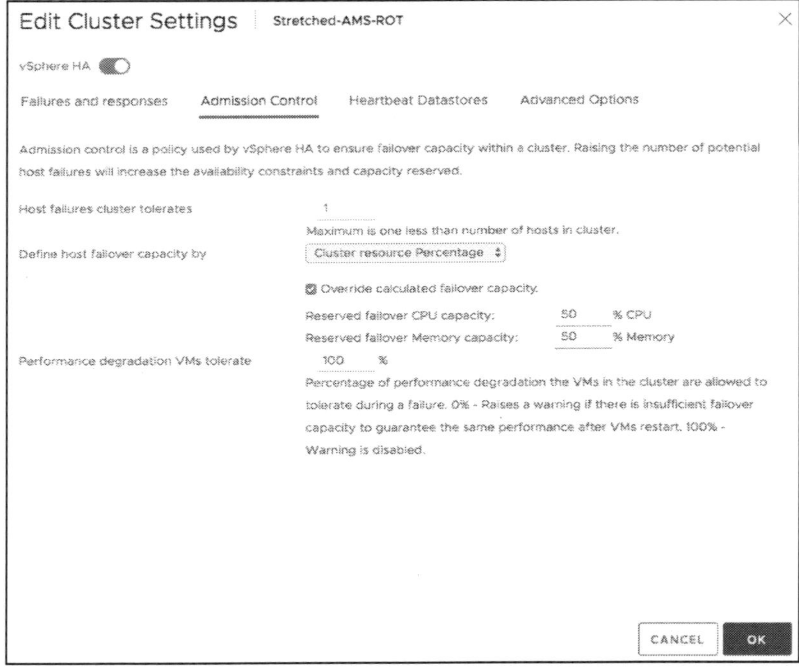

Figure 287: Admission Control

HA Heartbeats

HA uses heartbeat mechanisms to validate the state of a host. There are two such mechanisms: network heartbeating and datastore heartbeating. Network heartbeating is the primary mechanism for HA to validate availability of the hosts. Datastore heartbeating is the secondary mechanism used by HA; it determines the exact state of the host after network heartbeating has failed.

If a host is not receiving any heartbeats, it uses a fail-safe mechanism to detect if it is merely isolated from its master node or completely isolated from the network. It does this by pinging the default gateway. In addition to this mechanism, one or more isolation addresses can be specified manually to enhance reliability of isolation validation. We recommend specifying a minimum of two additional isolation addresses, with each address being local to a particular site.

In our scenario, one of these addresses physically resides in the Amsterdam data center; the other physically resides in the Rotterdam data center. This enables HA validation for complete network isolation, even in case of a connection failure between sites. The next figure shows an example of how to configure multiple isolation addresses. The HA advanced setting used is `das.isolationAddress`. More details on how to configure this can be found in VMware KB article 1002117.

> **Use a minimum of two isolation addresses, each being local to either location. This will allow validating site local host isolation even during a partition.**

The minimum number of heartbeat datastores is two and the maximum is five. For HA datastore heartbeating to function correctly in any type of failure scenario, We recommend increasing the number of heartbeat datastores from two to four in a stretched cluster environment. This provides full redundancy for both data center locations. Defining four specific datastores as preferred heartbeat datastores is also recommended, selecting two from one site and two from the other. This enables HA to heartbeat to a datastore even in the case of a connection failure between sites. Subsequently, it enables HA to determine the state of a host in any scenario.

Adding an advanced setting called `das.heartbeatDsPerHost` can increase the number of heartbeat datastores. This is shown below:

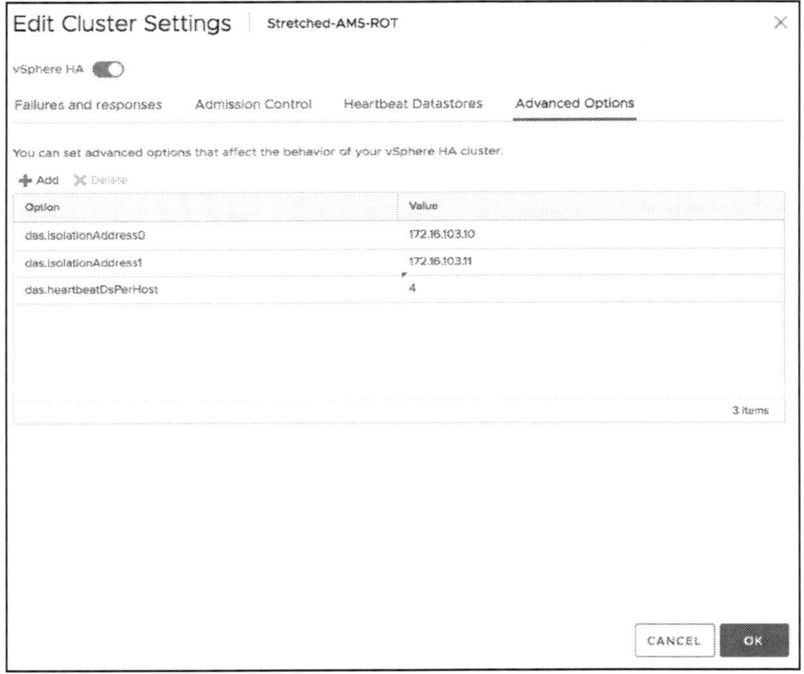

Figure 288: Heartbeat Datastores

To designate specific datastores as heartbeat devices, we recommend using Use datastores from the specified list and complement automatically if needed. This enables HA to select any other datastore if the four designated datastores that have been manually selected become unavailable. We recommend selecting two datastores local to each location to ensure that datastores are available at each site in the case of a site partition.

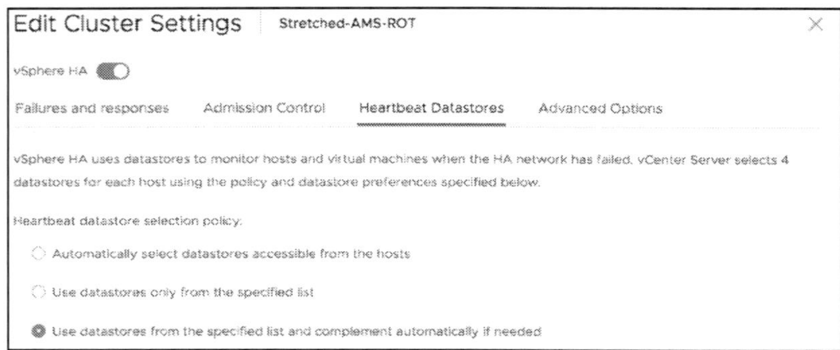

Figure 289: Configuration of Heartbeat Datastores

> **Increase the number of heartbeat datastores and select specific site local heartbeat datastores to allow the use even during double failure scenarios.**

Permanent Device Loss and All Paths Down Scenarios

As of vSphere 6.0, enhancements have been introduced to enable an automated failover of VMs residing on a datastore that has either an *all paths down* (APD) or a *permanent device loss* (PDL) condition. PDL is applicable only to block storage devices.

A PDL condition, as is discussed in one of our failure scenarios, is a condition that is communicated by the array controller to the vSphere host via a SCSI sense code. This condition indicates that a device (LUN) has become unavailable and is likely permanently unavailable. An example scenario in which this condition is communicated by the array is when a LUN is set offline. This condition is used in non-uniform models during a failure scenario to ensure that the vSphere host takes appropriate action when access to a LUN is revoked. When a full storage failure occurs, it is impossible to generate the PDL condition because there is no communication possible between the array and the vSphere host. This state is identified by the vSphere host as an APD condition. Another example of an APD condition is where the storage network has failed completely. In this scenario, the vSphere host also does not detect what has happened with the storage and declares an APD.

To enable HA to respond to both an APD and a PDL condition, HA must be configured in a specific way. We recommend enabling *VM Component Protection* (VMCP). Note that in the current UI this feature is not labeled as “VM Component Protection” or “VMCP”. Within the UI you simply specify the response to a Datastore with PDL and a Datastore with APD under Failures and Responses as shown below:

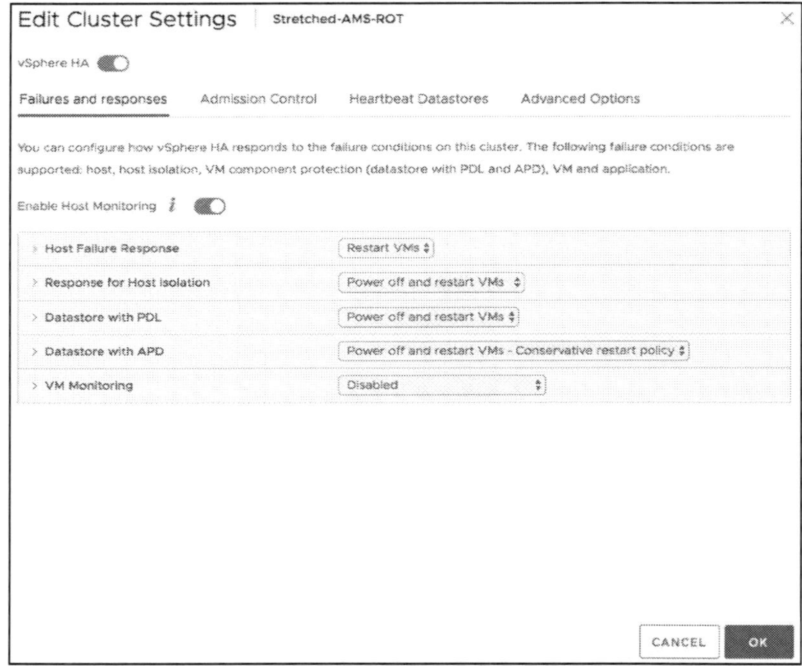

Figure 290: Failure Condition and Responses Configuration

The configuration screen can be found as follows:

- Log in to VMware vSphere Web Client
- Click Hosts and Clusters
- Click the cluster object

- Click the Manage tab
- Click HA and then Edit
- Select Failures and Responses
- Select individual functionality, as displayed in figure 8

The configuration for PDL is basic. In the Failures and Responses section, the response following detection of a PDL condition can be configured. We recommend setting this to Power off and restart VMs. When this condition is detected, a VM is restarted instantly on a healthy host within the HA cluster.

For an APD scenario, configuration must occur in the same section, as is shown in Figure 8. Besides defining the response to an APD condition, it is also possible to alter the timing and to configure the behavior when the failure is restored before the APD timeout has passed as shown below.

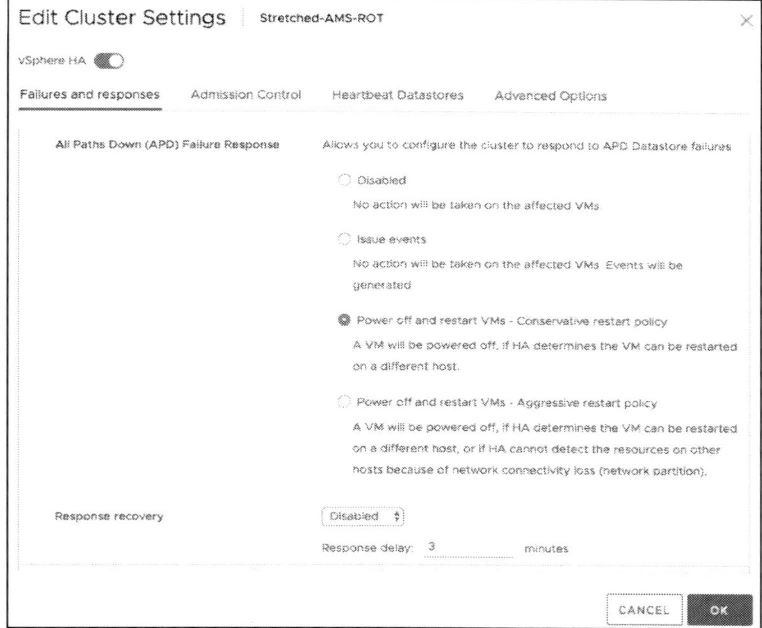

Figure 291: APD Response Delay

When an APD condition is detected, a timer is started. After 140 seconds, the APD condition is officially declared and the device is marked as APD timeout. When 140 seconds have passed, HA starts counting. The default HA timeout is 3 minutes. When the 3 minutes have passed, HA restarts the impacted VMs, but VMCP can be configured to respond differently if preferred. We recommend configuring it to Power off and restart VMs, with an Aggressive or Conservative restart policy.

What do you select? Aggressive or Conservative? *Conservative* refers to the likelihood that HA will be able to restart VMs. When set to conservative, HA restarts only the VM that is impacted by the APD if it detects that a host in the cluster can access the datastore on which the VM resides, additionally HA also verifies whether there are enough resources to start a VM. In the case of *aggressive*, HA attempts to restart the VM even if it doesn't detect the state of the other hosts. This can lead to a situation in which a VM is not restarted because there is no host that has access to the datastore on which the VM is located. So when can you find yourself in the situation where HA does not know if it can or cannot restart a VM, well for instance in the case of a site partition. If the likelihood of getting in to an APD scenario where it is impossible to detect if other hosts have access is high, then the *aggressive restart policy* should be used. If this is very unlikely then *conservative restart policy* should be used. It is impossible for us to provide guidance in this matter, as the network implementation and type of stretched storage system implemented determines the likelihood.

If the APD is lifted and access to the storage is restored before the timeout has passed, HA does not unnecessarily reset the VM unless explicitly configured to do so. If a response is chosen even when the environment has recovered from the APD condition, Response recovery can be configured to Reset VMs. We recommend leaving this setting disabled. Note that if Reset VMs is selected, any configured Restart Priority and / or dependency will not be taken in to account during the reset phase. Restart priority and / or dependency is only applied when VMs are restarted. (A restart is substantially different then a reset!)

Starting with vSphere 5.5, an advanced setting called `Disk.AutoremoveOnPDL` was introduced, and is implemented by default. This functionality enables vSphere to remove devices marked as PDL and helps prevent reaching, for example, the 512-device limit for a vSphere host. However, if the PDL scenario is resolved and the device returns, the vSphere host's storage system must be rescanned before the device will appear. We recommend disabling `Disk.AutoremoveOnPDL` for vSphere 5.5 hosts by setting the host advanced settings value to 0. From vSphere 6.0 and higher, this advanced setting is no longer required to be changed from the default configuration to properly recover the devices marked as PDL, it should be set to 1. Please ensure to change the setting from 0 to 1 when upgrading from vSphere 5.5 to a vSphere 6 version.

> **Enable automatic response to APD and PDL scenarios. Ensure tests are conducted after every change to validate VMs are restarted accordingly.**

Restart Ordering and Priority

Starting with vSphere 6.5 it is now possible to provide additional granularity and control in terms of restart sequence and dependencies for VMs in the VM Overrides section. Pre-vSphere 6.5 it was already possible to set a restart priority, but as each host in a cluster could power-on 32 VMs at a time and there was no option to specify a delay or a dependency of any kind, it would usually lead to all VM s being powered-on simultaneously. Per vSphere 6.5 it is now possible to specify to which priority group each VM belongs (VM Restart Priority: Lowest, low, medium, high, highest)

We recommend configuring VM Restart Priority for important infrastructure components like vCenter Server, DNS or Active Directory, and for applications which are formed out of multiple tiers. For example, a VM may have an application, web and database tier where, in most cases, the database tier would need to be started first. First select all the VMs for which you want to change the restart priority as shown in the screenshot below. By default, all VMs have a restart priority of Medium.

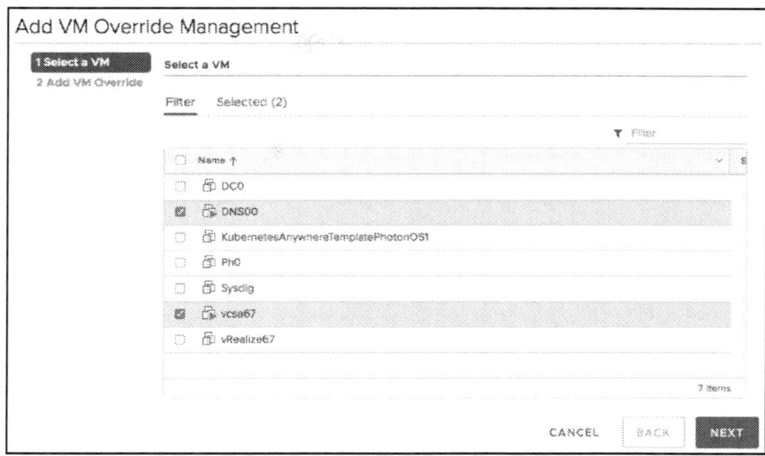

Figure 292: VM Group – Select a VM

Next select the desired restart priority. As the selected VMs in our case are important for the application layer we give them the restart priority of Highest.

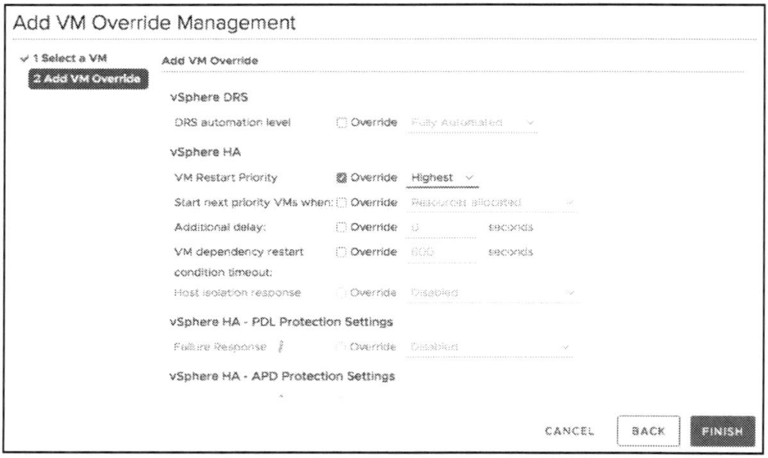

Add VM Override Management

1 Select a VM

2 Add VM Override

Add VM Override

vSphere DRS

DRS automation level — Override

vSphere HA

VM Restart Priority — Override — Highest

Start next priority VMs when: — Override

Additional delay: — Override — seconds

VM dependency restart condition timeout: — Override — seconds

Host isolation response — Override

vSphere HA - PDL Protection Settings

Failure Response — Override

vSphere HA - APD Protection Settings

CANCEL BACK FINISH

Figure 293: Restart Priority

On top of that, it is possible to specify when to start powering-on the VMs which belong to the next group. This is specified by the "Start next priority VMs when" drop down. You can set this to "guest heartbeats detected" for instance, which means HA will wait for VMware Tools to report a "liveness" heartbeat. If, however, a heartbeat is not received then by default after 600 seconds the next group is started. This can be increased, or decreased, by specifying the "or after timeout occurs at" value. We recommend leaving this set to the default of 600.

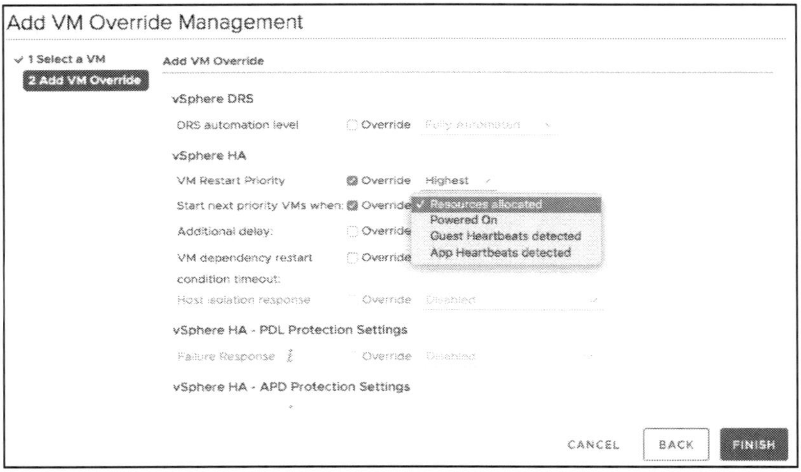

Figure 294: Start Next Priority VMs

Starting in vSphere 6.5 there is a second option to specify restart order, but in this case, it is a restart dependency between VMs. This is leveraging the HA and DRS cluster rules. A dependency can simply be created by creating two VM groups and then defining a VM to VM rule in which the dependency is specified. Here the next group is only started when the configured VM Dependency Restart Condition is met. If the cluster wide condition is set to the default Resources Allocated, then the second group of VMs is powered-on a split second after the first group as this is purely a restart scheduling exercise. Powered-on or even Guest Heartbeats detected are more appropriate in most cases.

Note that the specified rules are considered mandatory rules and these rules will not be violated as a result. In other words, if the power-on of the first group is unsuccessful and the specified condition is “powered on” then the second group will never be powered on.

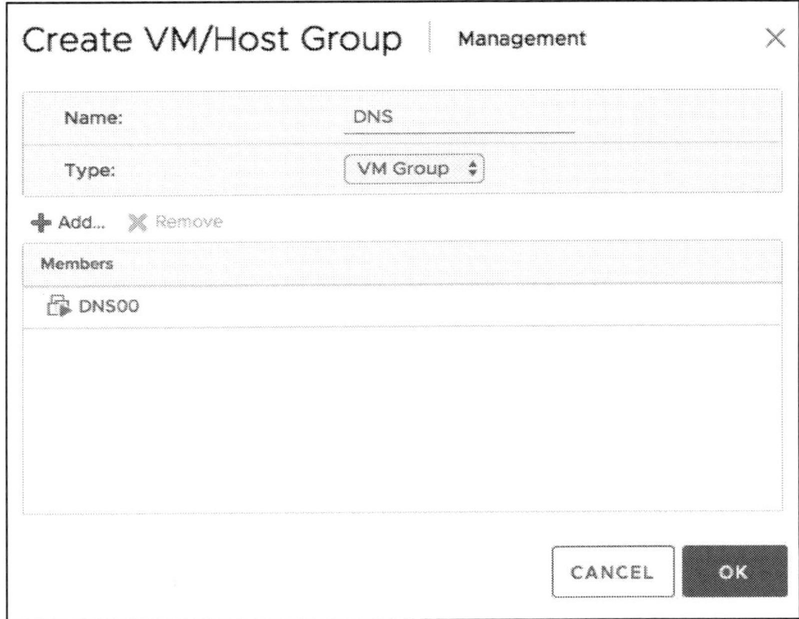

Figure 295: VM Group

We have gone through the UI various times, and still find it difficult to read. The second group will be powered on only when the first group is powered on, as depicted in the next screenshot.

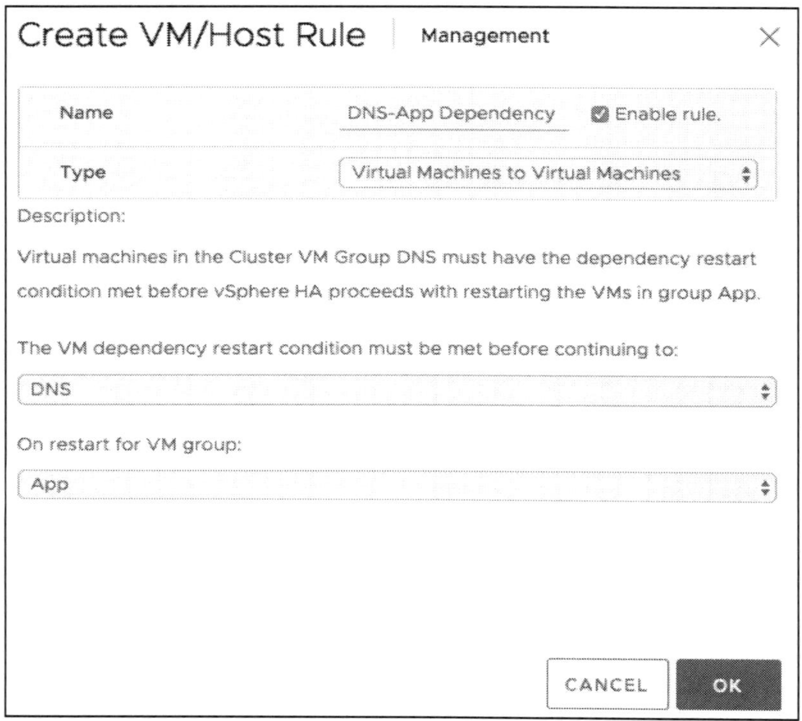

Figure 296: Restart Dependency

> **Restart order and dependency can be complex to configure. Document the restart order and dependency to ensure environments can be restarted correctly even when HA does not respond correctly to a failure.**

ProActive HA

ProActive HA was introduced in vSphere 6.5 and is found in the UI under Availability but technically it is a function of DRS. ProActive HA enables you to configure actions for events that may lead to VM downtime. Downtime avoidance is the key reason typically for deploying a vMSC configuration, therefore we recommend enabling ProActive HA.

In order to enable ProActive HA, a health provider (vSphere Web Client Plugin) needs to be installed first. At the time of writing only the following server vendors provide a health provider: HPE, Dell and Cisco.

After the installation of the health provider, Proactive HA can be enabled. We recommend setting the Proactive HA automation level to Automated so that action is immediately taken when a potential issue arises.

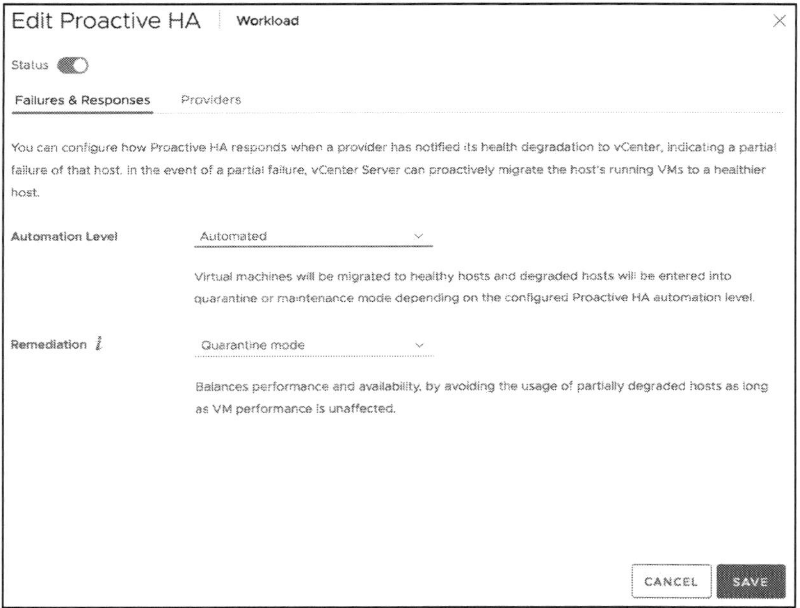

Figure 297: Proactive HA Automated Remediation

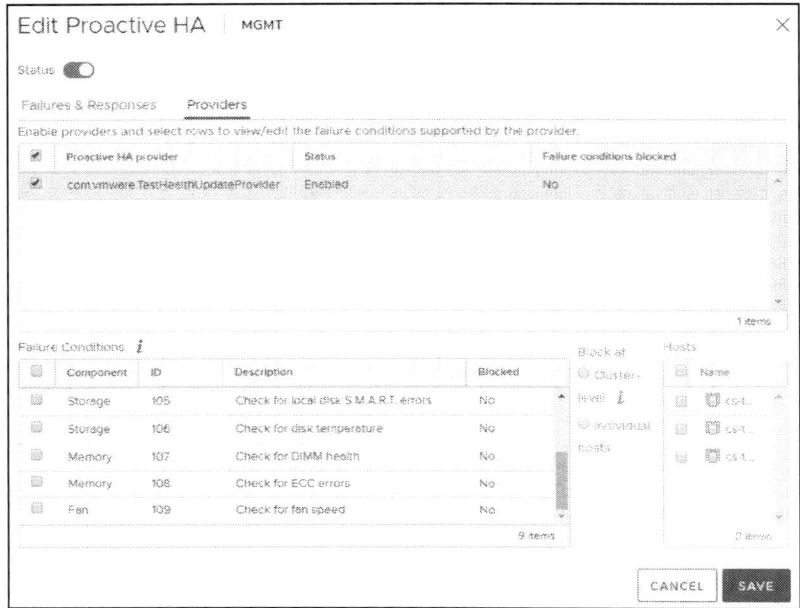

Figure 298: Proactive HA Provider

Next, the Remediation needs to be configured. We recommend configuring this with Quarantine mode for moderate and Maintenance mode for severe failure(Mixed). The other options are Maintenance Mode and Quarantine Mode. Before selecting either, it is useful to understand the difference.

- Quarantine Mode – Only places the host in quarantine mode. DRS will try to migrate VMs from this host to others. However, if there is some level of over commitment or HA/DRS Cluster rules are defined VM VMs may not be migrated
- Maintenance Mode – All VMs will be migrated
- Quarantine for Moderate / Maintenance for severe – Depending on the type of failure, the host will either be placed in to Quarantine Mode or Maintenance Mode. This is best described as conservative (should) and aggressive (must) host evacuation

ProActive HA can respond to different types of failures, depending on the version of the health provider plugin and the different types of vendor components that are being monitored. For example, Dell OpenManage (OMIVV) 4.0.x only supports monitoring of Power Supplies, Fans and Storage (SD Cards). The ProActive HA framework however also additionally supports Memory and Network monitoring. However, responses to Memory and Network failures can only be configured when the health provider supports this.

When an issue arises, the severity of the issue determines the ProActive HA response. These severities are color coded, where Yellow and Red are the states in which ProActive HA takes action. Some plugins will allow you to specify the severity of an issue manually, like Dell OpenManage. We recommend however to leave severity as pre-defined by the server vendor.

STATE	COLOR
Unknown	Gray
Ok	Green
Moderately degraded	Yellow
Severely degraded	Red

Table 36: Status ProActive HA

For more details on configuring the health provider and health provider specific settings we would like to refer to the server vendor documentation.

> **Enable Pro-Active HA to prevent outages. Note however that additional server vendor plugins are required, test these and validate they are supported for the vSphere version you will be running.**

DRS

DRS is used in many environments to distribute load within a cluster. It offers many other features that can be very helpful in stretched cluster environments. We recommend enabling DRS to facilitate load balancing across hosts in the cluster. The DRS load-balancing calculation is based on CPU and memory use. Care should be taken with regard to both storage and networking resources as well as to traffic flow. To avoid storage and network traffic overhead in a stretched cluster environment, we recommend implementing DRS affinity rules to enable a logical separation of VMs. This subsequently helps improve availability. For VMs that are responsible for infrastructure services, such as Microsoft Active Directory and DNS, it assists in ensuring separation of these services across sites.

Site Affinity

DRS affinity rules also help prevent unnecessary downtime, and storage and network traffic flow overhead, by enforcing preferred site affinity. We recommend aligning vSphere VM-to-host affinity rules with the storage configuration—that is, setting VM-to-host affinity rules with a preference that a VM run on a host at the same site as the array that is configured as the primary read/write node for a given datastore. For example, in our test configuration, VMs stored on the Amsterdam01 datastore are set with VM-to-host affinity with a preference for hosts in the Amsterdam data center. This ensures that in the case of a network connection failure between sites, VMs do not lose connection with the storage system that is primary for their datastore. VM-to-host affinity rules aim to ensure that VMs stay local to the storage primary for that datastore. This coincidentally also results in all read I/O's staying local.

> **Different storage vendors use different terminology to describe the relationship of a LUN to a particular array or controller. For the purposes of this document, we use the generic term "storage site affinity," which refers to the preferred location for access to a given LUN.**

We recommend implementing "should rules" because these are violated by HA in the case of a full site failure. Availability of services should always prevail. In the case of "must rules," HA does not violate the rule set, and this can potentially lead to service outages. In the scenario where a full data center fails, "must rules" do not allow HA to restart the

VMs, because they do not have the required affinity to start on the hosts in the other data center. This necessitates the recommendation to implement "should rules." DRS communicates these rules to HA, and these are stored in a "compatibility list" governing allowed start-up. If a single host fails, VM-to-host "should rules" are respected by default. Pre-vSphere 6.5 we recommended configuring the HA rule settings to respect VM-to-host affinity rules where possible, as by default HA used to ignore these should rules during a restart event.

With a full site failure, HA can restart the VMs on hosts that violate the rules. Availability takes preference in this scenario. Below it can be seen what this looked like with vSphere 6.0. In vSphere 6.5 this option disappeared completely, by default HA respects the rules going forward.

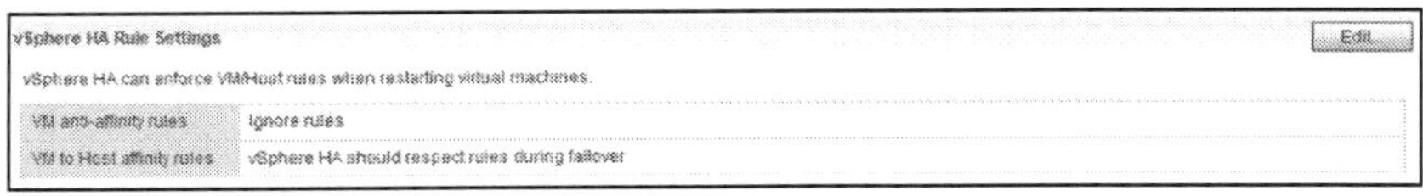

Figure 299: Former Required HA Rule Settings

Under certain circumstances, such as massive host saturation coupled with aggressive recommendation settings, DRS can also violate "should rules." Although this is very rare, we recommend monitoring for violation of these rules because a violation might impact availability and workload performance. If there is a desire to change the default behavior the following advanced settings can be configured:

- `das.respectVmVmAntiAffinityRules` – set to "true" by default, set to "false" if you want to disable HA respecting VM-VM affinity and anti-affinity rules
- `das.respectVmHostSoftAffinityRules` – set to "true" by default, set to "false" if you want to disable HA respecting VM-Host affinity rules

We recommend manually defining "sites" by creating a group of hosts that belong to a site and then adding VMs to these sites based on the affinity of the datastore on which they are provisioned. In our scenario, only a limited number of VMs were provisioned. We recommend automating the process of defining site affinity by using tools such as PowerCLI. If automating the process is not an option, use of a generic naming convention is recommended to simplify the creation of these groups. We recommend that these groups be validated on a regular basis to ensure that all VMs belong to the group with the correct site affinity.

The next series of screenshots depicts the configuration used for this chapter. In the first screenshot, all VMs that should remain local to the Amsterdam data center are added to the Amsterdam VM group, of course we have done the same for the Rotterdam data center, this however is not depicted. We also have to create a VM/Host Group.

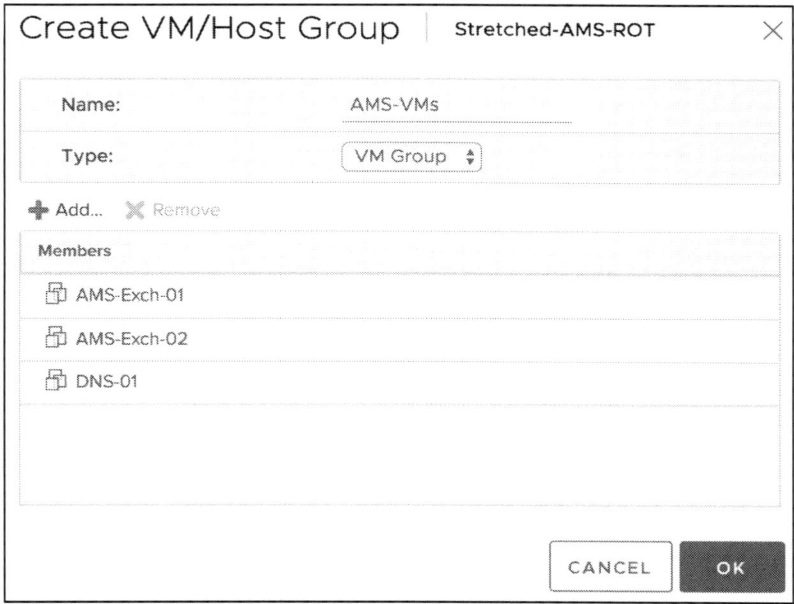

Figure 300: VM/Host Group Creation Part 1

Next, an Amsterdam host group is created that contains all hosts residing in this location.

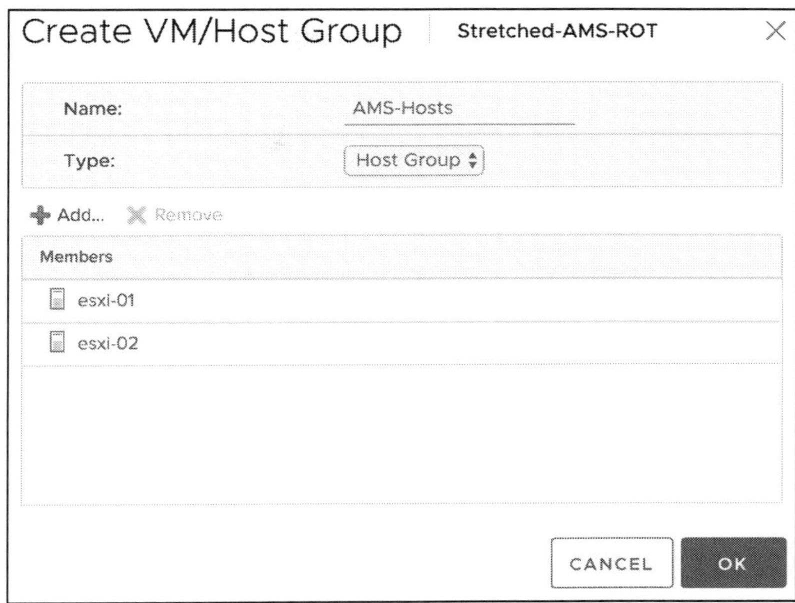

Figure 301: VM/Host Group Creation Part 2

Next, a new rule is created that is defined as a "should run on rule." It links the host group and the VM group for the Amsterdam location.

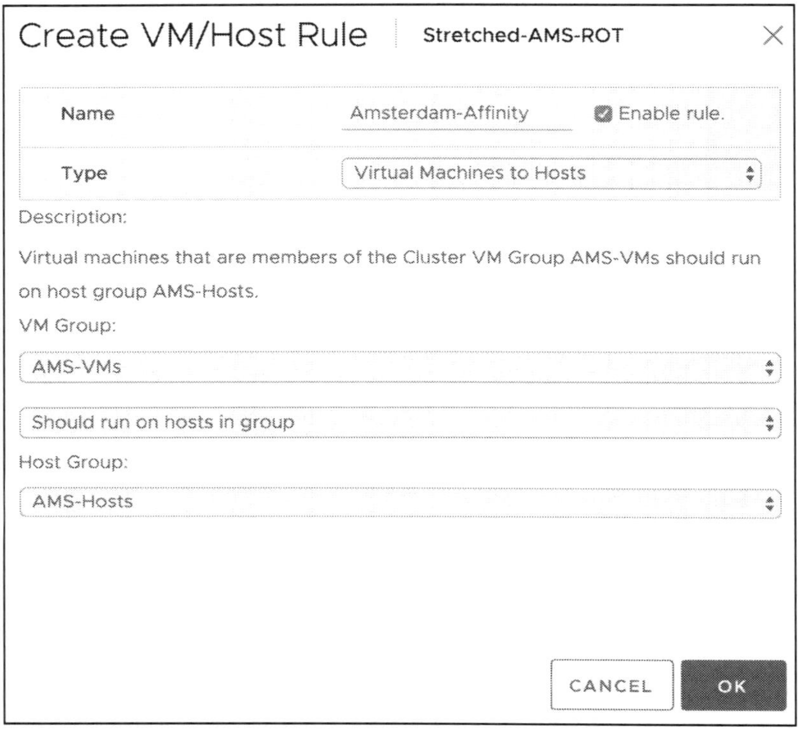

Create VM/Host Rule | Stretched-AMS-ROT

Name: Amsterdam-Affinity — Enable rule.

Type: Virtual Machines to Hosts

Description:

Virtual machines that are members of the Cluster VM Group AMS-VMs should run on host group AMS-Hosts.

VM Group:

AMS-VMs

Should run on hosts in group

Host Group:

AMS-Hosts

CANCEL OK

Figure 302: VM/Host Group Creation Part 3

This should be done for both locations, which should result in two rules at a minimum. Note that we have in this particular case configured should rules as we prefer the VMs to be restarted in our Rotterdam data center when an outage has occurred. However, if these VMs are not replicated, you should define a "must run on hosts in group" rule instead.

> **Limit the use of rules as they decrease the number of placement options DRS has. Subsequently incorrect use of rules can also result in VMs not being restarted by HA after a failure.**

Advanced Settings

Starting vSphere 6.5 the UI for DRS has also changed. In the past many configurations required advanced settings to be entered in the DRS configuration screen. Now that these settings are easier to find, the chances are that you will also want to try these. Note that we do not describe all advanced configuration options here, or any functionality, which has no specific impact on vMSC configurations. As an example, the option VM Distribution allows you to distribute the number of VMs more evenly across hosts. However, this is based on the number of VMs per host, and not on resources. In order to ensure distribution, it can (and will) ignore any configured non-mandatory (should) "VM-to-Host" rules. In other words, it could force VMs to be placed in a location where you do not expect them to be placed. Before using any of these new options, ensure that after configuring you re-test the different failures scenarios and validate the outcome with the expected outcome.

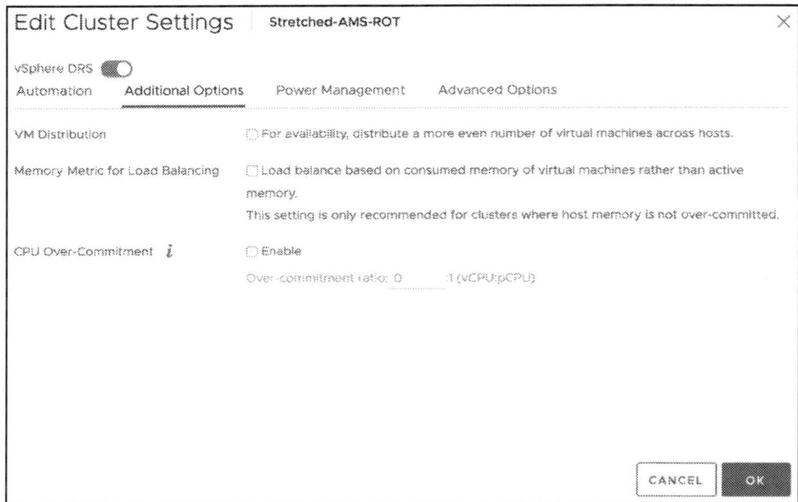

Figure 303: DRS Additional Options

Correcting Affinity Rule Violation

DRS assigns a high priority to correcting affinity rule violations. During invocation, the primary goal of DRS is to correct any violations and generate recommendations to migrate VMs to the hosts listed in the host group. These migrations have a higher priority than load-balancing moves and are started before them.

DRS is invoked every 5 minutes by default, but it is also triggered if the cluster detects changes. For instance, when a host reconnects to the cluster, DRS is invoked and generates recommendations to correct the violation. Our testing has shown that DRS generates recommendations to correct affinity rules violations within 30 seconds after a host reconnects to the cluster. DRS is limited by the overall capacity of the vMotion network, so it might take multiple invocations before all affinity rule violations are corrected.

Storage DRS

Storage DRS enables aggregation of datastores to a single unit of consumption from an administrative perspective, and it balances VM disks when defined thresholds are exceeded. It ensures that sufficient disk resources are available to a workload. We recommend enabling Storage DRS in Manual Mode with I/O Metric disabled. The use of I/O Metric or VMware vSphere Storage I/O Control is not supported in a vMSC configuration, as is described in VMware KB article 2042596.

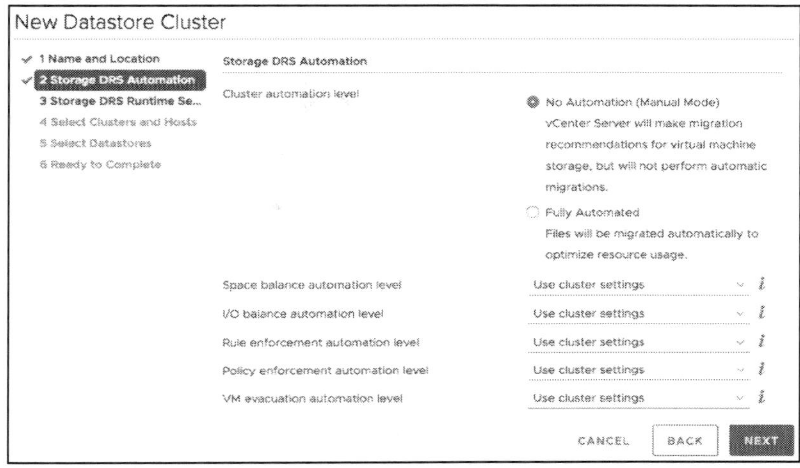

Figure 304: Storage DRS Configuration

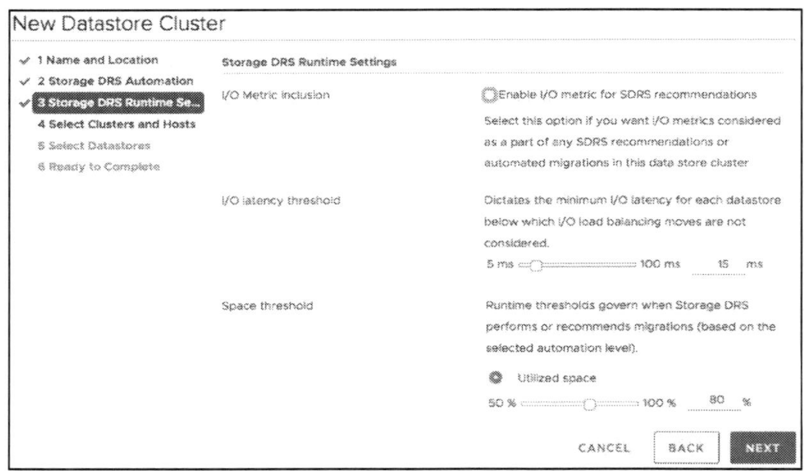

Figure 305: Storage DRS Runtime Settings

Migrations

Storage DRS uses Storage vMotion to migrate VM disks between datastores within a datastore cluster. Because the underlying stretched storage systems use synchronous replication, a migration or series of migrations have an impact on replication traffic and might cause the VMs to become temporarily unavailable due to contention for network resources during the movement of disks. Migration to random datastores can also potentially lead to additional I/O latency in uniform host access configurations if VMs are not migrated along with their virtual disks. For example, if a VM residing on a host at site A has its disk migrated to a datastore at site B, it continues operating but with potentially degraded performance. The VM's disk reads now are subject to the increased latency associated with reading from the array at site B. Reads are subject to inter-site latency rather than being satisfied by a local target.

To control if and when migrations occur, we recommend configuring Storage DRS in manual mode. This enables human validation per recommendation as well as recommendations to be applied during off-peak hours, while gaining the operational benefit and efficiency of the initial placement functionality.
We recommend creating datastore clusters based on the storage configuration with respect to storage site affinity. Datastores with a site affinity for site A should not be mixed in datastore clusters with datastores with a site affinity for site B. This enables operational consistency and eases the creation and ongoing management of DRS VM-to-host affinity rules. Ensure that all DRS VM-to-host affinity rules are updated accordingly when VMs are migrated via Storage vMotion between datastore clusters and when crossing defined storage site affinity boundaries. To simplify the provisioning process, we recommend aligning naming conventions for datastore clusters and VM-to-host affinity rules.

The naming convention used in our testing gives both datastores and datastore clusters a site-specific name to provide ease of alignment of DRS host affinity with VM deployment in the correlate site.

Failure Scenarios

There are many failures that can be introduced in clustered systems. But in a properly architected environment, HA, DRS, and the storage subsystem do not detect many of these. We do not address the zero-impact failures, such as the failure of a single network cable, because they are explained in depth in the documentation provided by the storage vendor of the various solutions. We discuss the following "common" failure scenarios:

- Single-host failure in Amsterdam data center
- Single-host isolation in Amsterdam data center
- Storage partition
- Data center partition
- Disk shelf failure in Amsterdam data center
- Full storage failure in Amsterdam data center
- Full compute failure in Amsterdam data center
- Full compute failure in Amsterdam data center and full storage failure in Rotterdam data center
- Loss of complete Amsterdam data center

We also examine scenarios in which specific settings are incorrectly configured. These settings determine the availability and recoverability of VMs in a failure scenario. It is important to understand the impact of misconfigurations such as the following:

- Incorrectly configured VM-to-host affinity rules
- Incorrectly configured heartbeat datastores
- Incorrectly configured isolation address
- Incorrectly configured PDL handling
- vCenter Server split-brain scenario

Single-Host Failure in Amsterdam Data Center

In this scenario, we describe the complete failure of a host (ESXi-01) in Amsterdam data center. This scenario is depicted below.

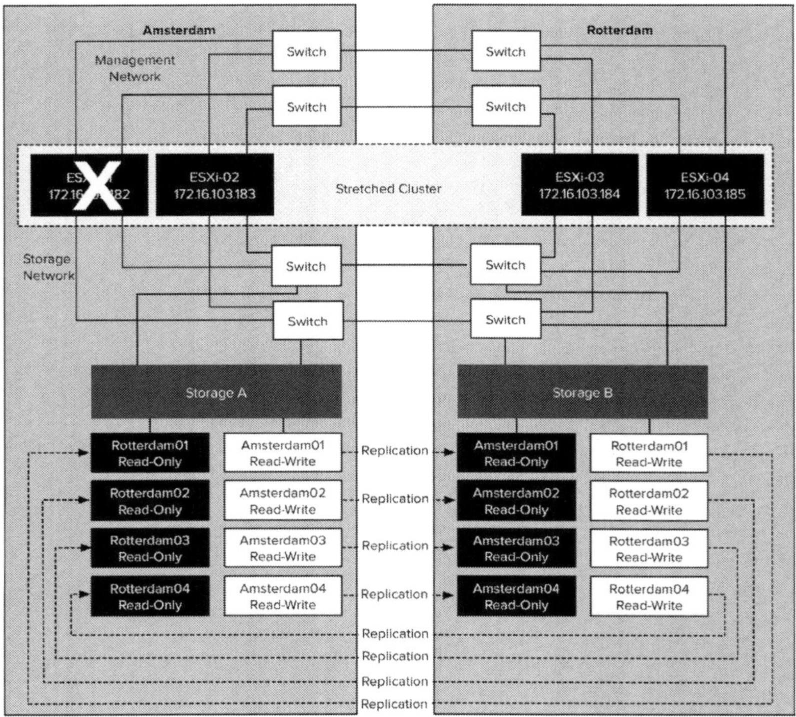

Figure 306: Single Host Failure

Result

HA successfully restarted all VMs in accordance with VM-to-host affinity rules.

Explanation

If a host fails, the cluster's HA master node detects the failure because it no longer is receiving network heartbeats from the host. Then the master starts monitoring for datastore heartbeats. Because the host has failed completely, it cannot generate datastore heartbeats; these too are detected as missing by the HA master node. During this time, a third availability check—pinging the management addresses of the failed hosts—is conducted.

If all of these checks return as unsuccessful, the master declares the missing host as dead and attempts to restart all the protected VMs that had been running on the host before the master lost contact with the host.

The vSphere VM-to-host affinity rules defined on a cluster level are "should rules." HA VM-to-host affinity rules will be respected so all VMs are restarted within the correct site.

However, if the host elements of the VM-to-host group are temporarily without resources, or if they are unavailable for restarts for any other reason, HA can disregard the rules and restart the remaining VMs on any of the remaining hosts in the cluster, regardless of location and rules. If this occurs, DRS attempts to correct any violated affinity rules at the first invocation and automatically migrates VMs in accordance with their affinity rules to bring VM placement in alignment. We recommend manually invoking DRS after the cause for the failure has been identified and resolved. This ensures that all VMs are placed on hosts in the correct location to avoid possible performance degradation due to misplacement.

Single-Host Isolation in Amsterdam Data Center

In this scenario, we describe the response to isolation of a single host in Amsterdam data center from the rest of the network.

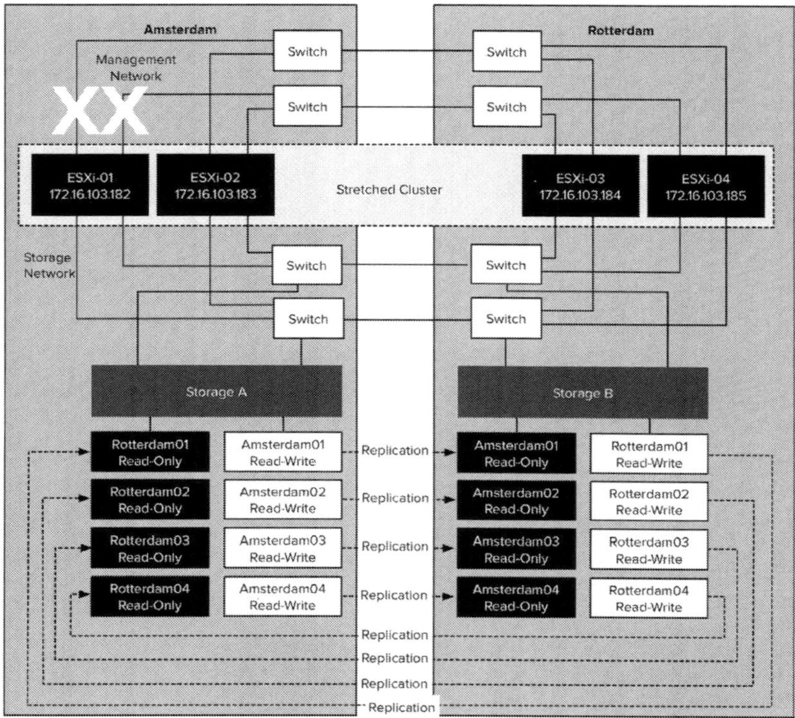

Figure 307: Single Host Isolation

Result

VMs remain running because isolation response is configured to leave powered on.

Explanation

When a host is isolated, the HA master node detects the isolation because it no longer is receiving network heartbeats from the host. Then the master starts monitoring for datastore heartbeats. Because the host is isolated, it generates datastore heartbeats for the secondary HA detection mechanism. Detection of valid host heartbeats enables the HA master node to determine that the host is running but is isolated from the network. Depending on the isolation response configured, the impacted host can power off or shut down VMs or can leave them powered on. The isolation response is triggered 30 seconds after the host has detected that it is isolated.

We recommend aligning the isolation response to business requirements and physical constraints. From a best practices perspective, leave powered on is the recommended isolation response setting for the majority of environments. Isolated hosts are rare in a properly architected environment, given the built-in redundancy of most modern designs. In environments that use network-based storage protocols, such as iSCSI and NFS, and where networks are converged, the recommended isolation response is power off. In these environments, it is more likely that a network outage that causes a host to become isolated also affects the host's ability to communicate to the datastores.

If an isolation response different from the recommended leave powered on is selected and a power off or shut down response is triggered, the HA master restarts VMs on the remaining nodes in the cluster. The vSphere VM-to-host affinity rules defined on a cluster level are "should rules." However, because HA respects VM-to-host affinity rules by all VMs are restarted within the correct site under "normal" circumstances.

Storage Partition

In this scenario, a failure has occurred on the storage network between data centers, as is depicted below.

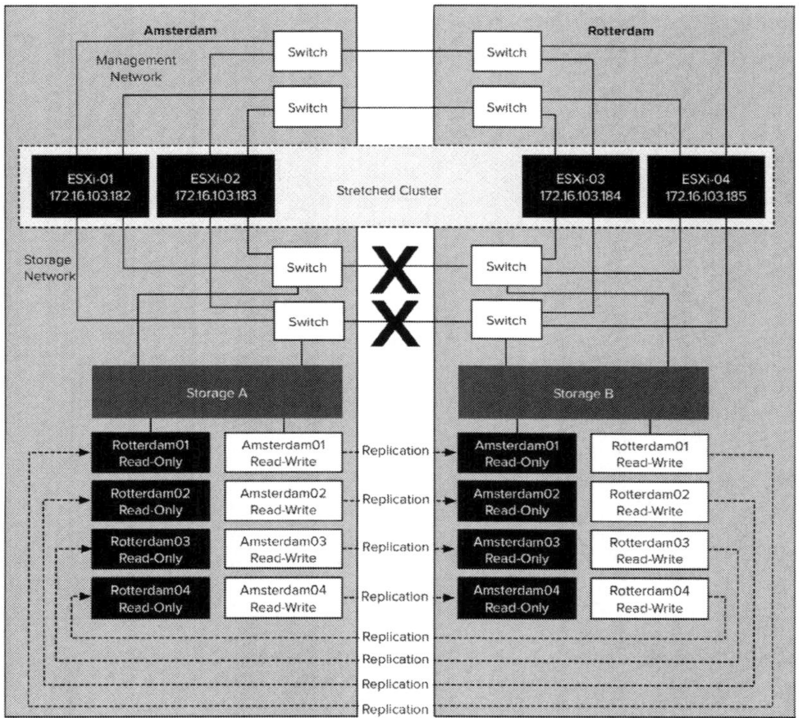

Figure 308: Storage Partition

Result

VMs remain running with no impact.

Explanation

Storage site affinity is defined for each LUN, and DRS rules align with this affinity. Therefore, because storage remains available within the site, no VM is impacted.

If for any reason the affinity rule for a VM has been violated and the VM is running on a host in Amsterdam data center while its disk resides on a datastore that has affinity with Rotterdam data center, it cannot successfully issue I/O following an inter-site storage partition. This is because the datastore is in an APD condition. In this scenario, the VM can be restarted because HA is configured to respond to APD conditions. The response occurs after the 3-minute grace period has passed. This 3-minute period starts after the APD timeout of 140 seconds has passed and the APD condition has been declared.

Note that it is possible to define what should happen when the APD is lifted before the 3-minute grace period has passed. One of the options is to reset the VM. If resetting the VM is configured then when the APD is lifted the VM will be reset. Note that any restart ordering will not take effect. Restart Order and dependency only applies to VMs, which are restarted.

To avoid unnecessary downtime in an APD scenario, we recommend monitoring compliance of DRS rules. Although DRS is invoked every 5 minutes, this does not guarantee resolution of all affinity rule violations. Therefore, to prevent unnecessary downtime, rigid monitoring is recommended that enables quick identification of anomalies such as a VM's compute's residing in one site while its storage resides in the other site.

Data Center Partition

In this scenario, the Amsterdam data center is isolated from the Rotterdam data center, as is depicted below:

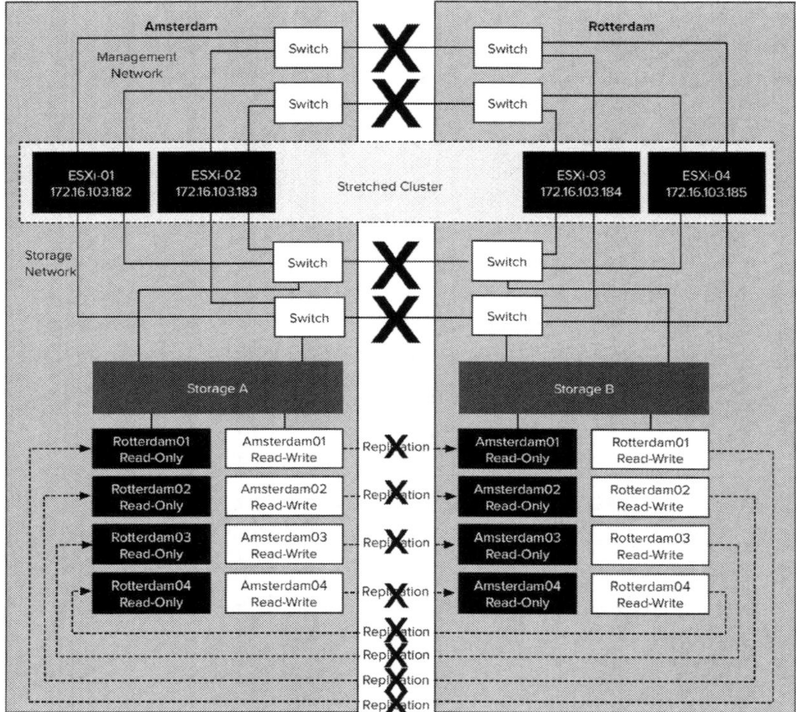

Figure 309: Data Center Partition

Result

VMs remain running with no impact.

Explanation

In this scenario, the two data centers are fully isolated from each other. This scenario is similar to both the storage partition and the host isolation scenario. VMs are not impacted by this failure because DRS rules were correctly implemented, and no rules were violated. HA follows this logical process to determine which VMs require restarting during a cluster partition:

The HA master node running in Amsterdam data center detects that all hosts in Rotterdam data center are unreachable. It first detects that no network heartbeats are being received. It then determines whether any storage heartbeats are being generated. This check does not detect storage heartbeats because the storage connection between sites also has failed, and the heartbeat datastores are updated only "locally." Because the VMs with affinity to the remaining hosts are still running, no action is needed for them. Next, HA determines whether a restart can be attempted. However, the read/write version of the datastores located in Rotterdam data center are not accessible by the hosts in Amsterdam data center. Therefore, no attempt is made to start the missing VMs.

Similarly, the vSphere hosts in Rotterdam data center detect that there is no master available, and they initiate a master election process. After the master has been elected, it tries to determine which VMs had been running before the failure and it attempts to restart them. Because all VMs with affinity to Rotterdam data center are still running there, there is no need for a restart. Only the VMs with affinity to Amsterdam data center are unavailable, and HA cannot restart them because the datastores on which they are stored have affinity with Amsterdam data center and are unavailable in Rotterdam data center.

If VM-to-host affinity rules have been violated—that is, VMs have been running at a location where their storage is not defined as read/write by default—the behavior changes. The following sequence describes what would happen in that case:

1. The VM with affinity to Amsterdam data center but residing in Rotterdam data center is unable to reach its datastore. This results in the VM's being unable to write to or read from disk.
2. In Amsterdam data center, this VM is restarted by HA because the hosts in Amsterdam data center do not detect the instance's running in Rotterdam data center.
3. Because the datastore is available only to Amsterdam data center, one of the hosts in Amsterdam data center acquires a lock on the VMDK and is able to power on this VM.

4. This can result in a scenario in which the same VM is powered on and running in both data centers.

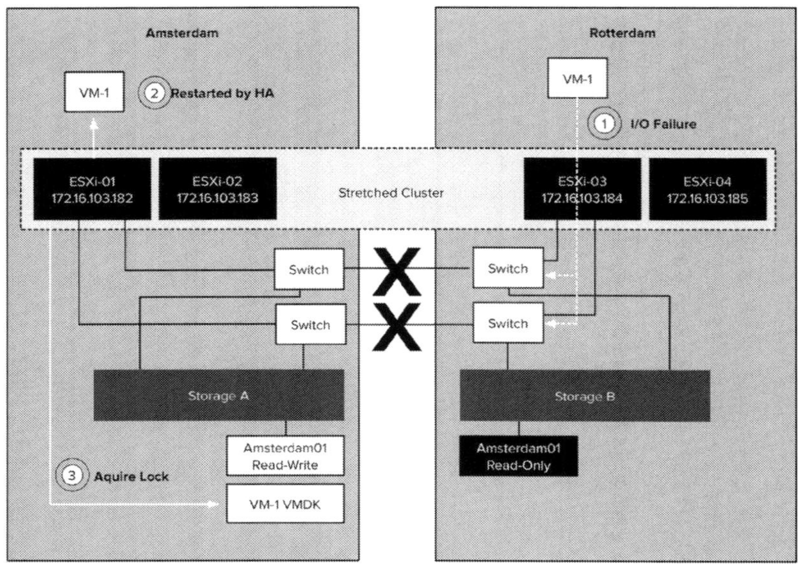

Figure 310: Lock on VMDK

5. If the APD response is configured to Power off and restart VMs (aggressive), the VM is powered off after the APD timeout and the grace period have passed. This behavior is new starting vSphere 6.0. Note that if the restart policy is set to conservative, depending on the type of partition, and HA's ability to talk to the hosts in the second location, VMs may or may not be automatically killed.

If the APD response is not correctly configured, two VMs will be running, for the following possible reasons:

- The network heartbeat from the host that is running this VM is missing because there is no connection to that site
- The datastore heartbeat is missing because there is no connection to that site

- A ping to the management address of the host that is running the VM fails because there is no connection to that site
- The master located in Amsterdam data center detects that the VM had been powered on before the failure. Because it is unable to communicate with the VM's host in Rotterdam data center after the failure, it attempts to restart the VM because it cannot detect the actual state

If the connection between sites is restored, a classic "VM split-brain scenario" will exist. For a short period of time, two copies of the VM will be active on the network, with both having the same MAC address. Only one copy, however, will have access to the VM files, and HA will detect this. As soon as this is detected, all processes belonging to the VM copy that has no access to the VM files will be killed, as is depicted below.

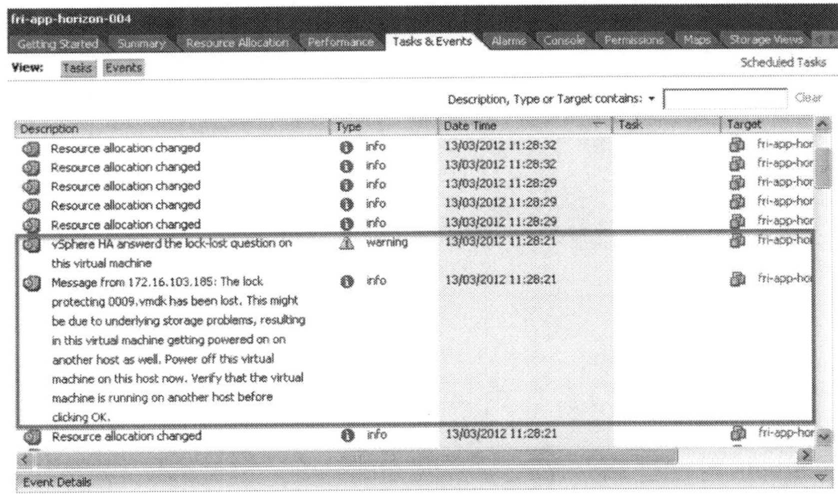

Figure 311: Lock Lost Message

In this example, the downtime equates to a VM's having to be restarted. Proper maintenance of site affinity can prevent this. To avoid unnecessary downtime, we recommend close monitoring to ensure that HA and DRS cluster rules align with datastore site affinity.

Disk Shelf Failure in Amsterdam Data Center

In this scenario, one of the disk shelves in Amsterdam data center has failed. Both Amsterdam01 and Amsterdam02 on storage A are impacted.

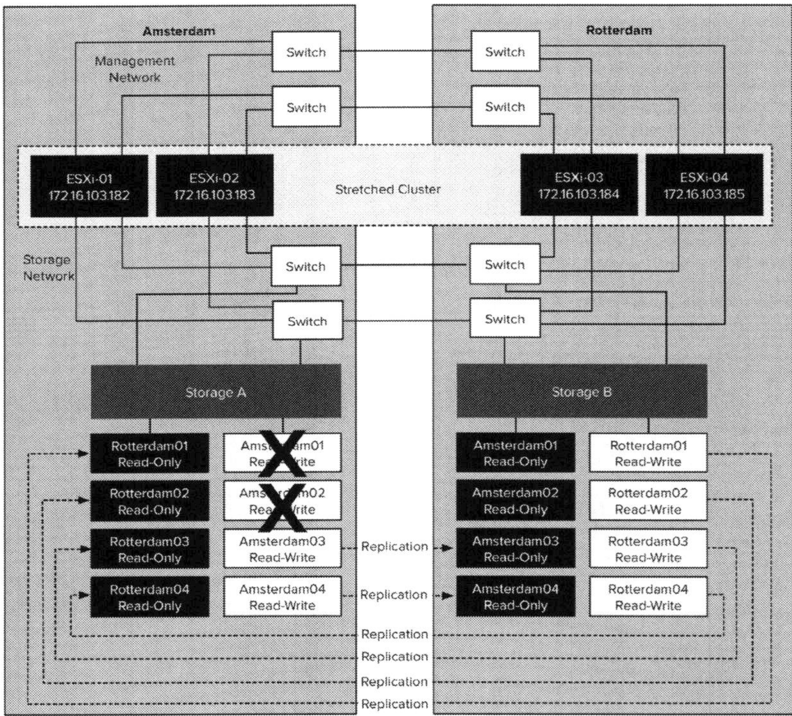

Figure 312: Disk Shelf Failure

Result

VMs remain running with no impact.

Explanation

In this scenario, only a disk shelf in Amsterdam data center has failed. The storage processor has detected the failure and has instantly switched from the primary disk shelf in Amsterdam data center to the mirror copy in Rotterdam data center. There is no noticeable impact to any of the VMs except for a typical short spike in I/O response time. The storage solution fully detects and handles this scenario. There is no need for a rescan of the datastores or the HBAs because the switchover is seamless, and the LUNs are identical from the vSphere host perspective.

Full Storage Failure in Amsterdam Data Center

In this scenario, a full storage system failure has occurred in Amsterdam data center.

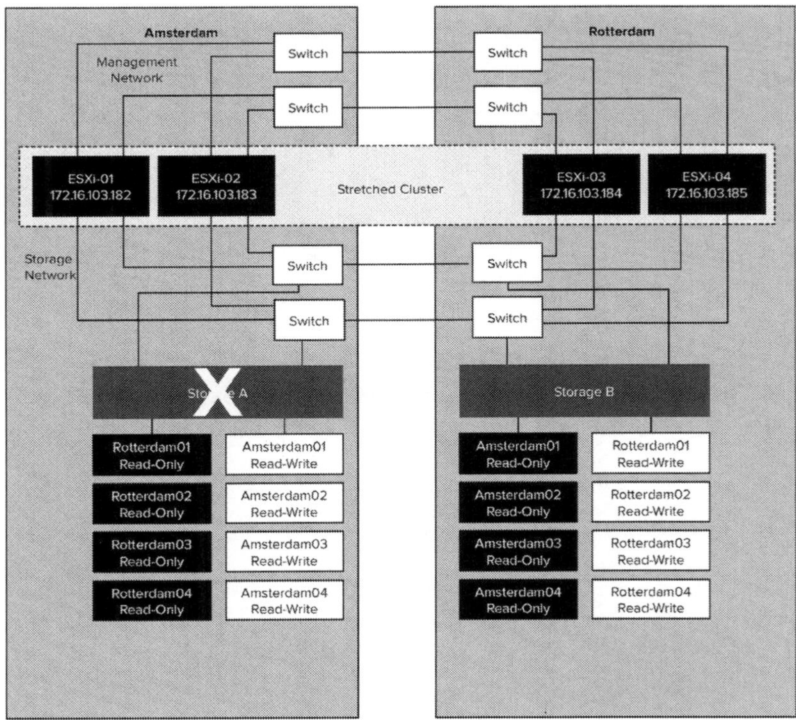

Figure 313: Full Storage Failure Site Amsterdam

Result

VMs remain running with no impact.

Explanation

When the full storage system fails in Amsterdam data center, a take over command must be initiated manually. As described previously, we used a NetApp MetroCluster configuration to describe this behavior. This take over command is particular to NetApp environments; depending on the implemented storage system, the required procedure can differ. After the command has been initiated, the mirrored, read-only copy of each of the failed datastores is set to read/write and is instantly accessible. We have described this process on an extremely high level. For more details, refer to the storage vendor's documentation.

From the VM perspective, this failover is seamless: The storage controllers handle this, and no action is required from either the vSphere or storage administrator. All I/O now passes across the intra-site connection to the other data center because VMs remain running in Amsterdam data center while their datastores are accessible only in Rotterdam data center.

HA does not detect this type of failure. Although the datastore heartbeat might be lost briefly, HA does not take action because the HA master agent checks for the datastore heartbeat only when the network heartbeat is not received for 3 seconds. Because the network heartbeat remains available throughout the storage failure, HA is not required to initiate any restarts.

Permanent Device Loss

In the scenario shown the next figure, a permanent device loss (PDL) condition occurs because datastore Amsterdam01 has been taken offline for ESXi-01 and ESXi-02. PDL scenarios are uncommon in uniform configurations and are more likely to occur in a non-uniform vMSC configuration. However, a PDL scenario can, for instance, occur when the configuration of a storage group changes as in the case of this described scenario.

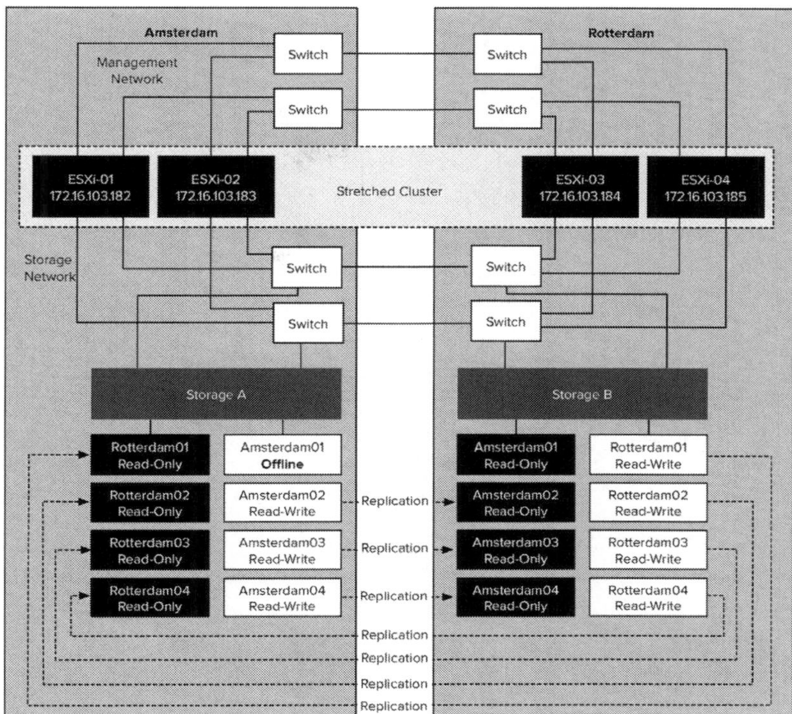

Figure 314: Permanent Device Loss

Result

VMs from ESXi-01 and ESXi-02 are restarted by HA on ESXi-03 and ESXi-04.

Explanation

When the PDL condition occurs, VMs running on datastore Amsterdam01 on hosts ESXi-01 and ESXi-02 are killed instantly. They then are restarted by HA on hosts within the cluster that have access to the datastore, ESXi-03 and ESXi-04 in this scenario. The PDL and killing of the VM world group leader can be witnessed by following the entries in the vmkernel.log file located in /var/log/ on the vSphere hosts. The following is an outtake of the vmkernel.log file where a PDL is recognized and appropriate action is taken.

```
2017-03-14T13:39:25.085Z cpu7:4499)WARNING: VSCSI: 4055: handle
8198(vscsi4:0):opened by wid 4499 (vmm0:fri-iscsi-02) has Permanent
Device Loss. Killing world group leader 4491
```

We recommend configuring Response for Datastore with Permanent Device Loss (PDL) to Power off and restart VMs. This setting ensures that appropriate action is taken when a PDL condition exists. The correct configuration is shown below.

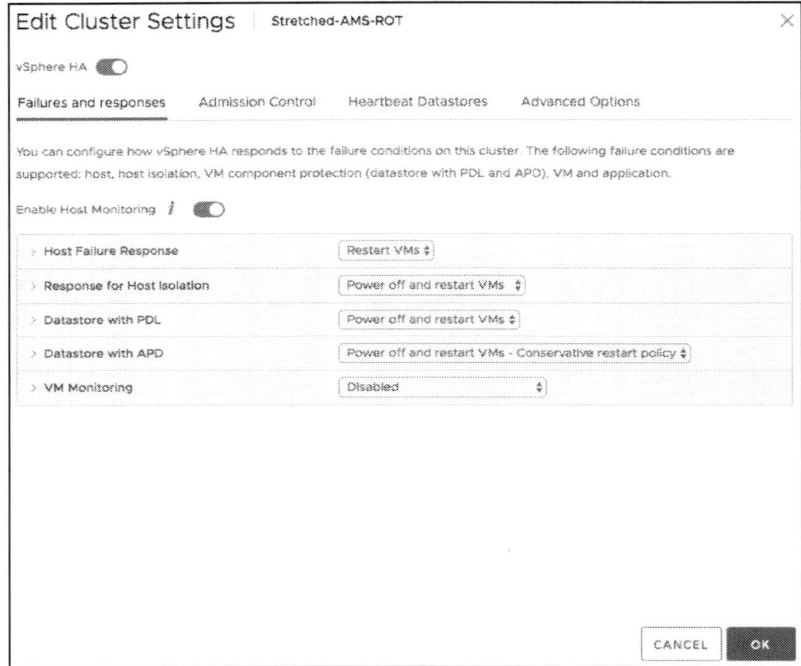

Figure 315: HA PDL Response Configuration

Full Compute Failure in Amsterdam Data Center

In this scenario, a full compute failure has occurred in Amsterdam data center.

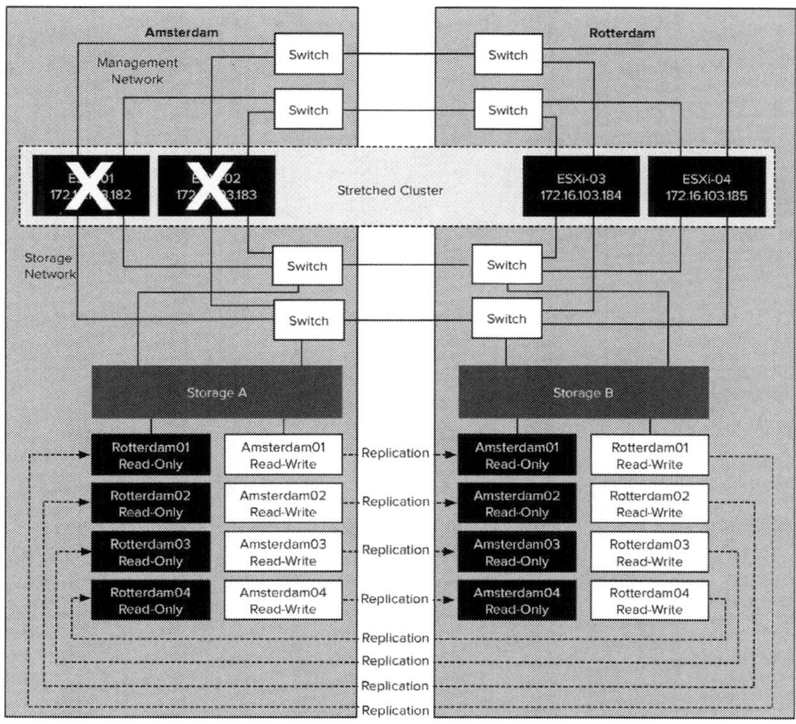

Figure 316: Full Compute Failure

Result

All VMs are successfully restarted in Rotterdam data center.

Explanation

The HA master was located in Amsterdam data center at the time of the full compute failure at that location. After the hosts in Rotterdam data center detected that no network heartbeats had been received, an election process was started. Within approximately 20 seconds, a new

HA master was elected from the remaining hosts. Then the new master determined which hosts had failed and which VMs had been impacted by this failure. Because all hosts at the other site had failed and all VMs residing on them had been impacted, HA initiated the restart of all of these VMs. HA first schedules the restart, which only can only succeed when sufficient unreserved resources are available. In order to ensure this we had HA admission control enabled and set to reserve 50% (2 host failures) of CPU and memory capacity.

HA can initiate 32 concurrent restarts on a single host, providing a low restart latency for most environments. As described in the HA section of this paper, there is the ability to sequence the order of restart for VMs leveraging the VM Overrides feature (there are 5 options: lowest, low, medium, high, highest). This policy must be set on a per-VM basis. These policies were determined to have been adhered to; highest-priority VMs started first, followed by high-, medium-, low- and lowest-priority VMs.

As part of the test, the hosts at the Amsterdam data center were again powered on. As soon as DRS detected that these hosts were available, a DRS run was invoked. Because the initial DRS run corrects only the DRS affinity rule violations, resource imbalance was not corrected until the next full invocation of DRS. DRS is invoked by default every 5 minutes or when VMs are powered off or on through the use of vSphere Web Client.

Loss of Amsterdam Data Center

In this scenario, a full failure of Amsterdam data center is simulated.

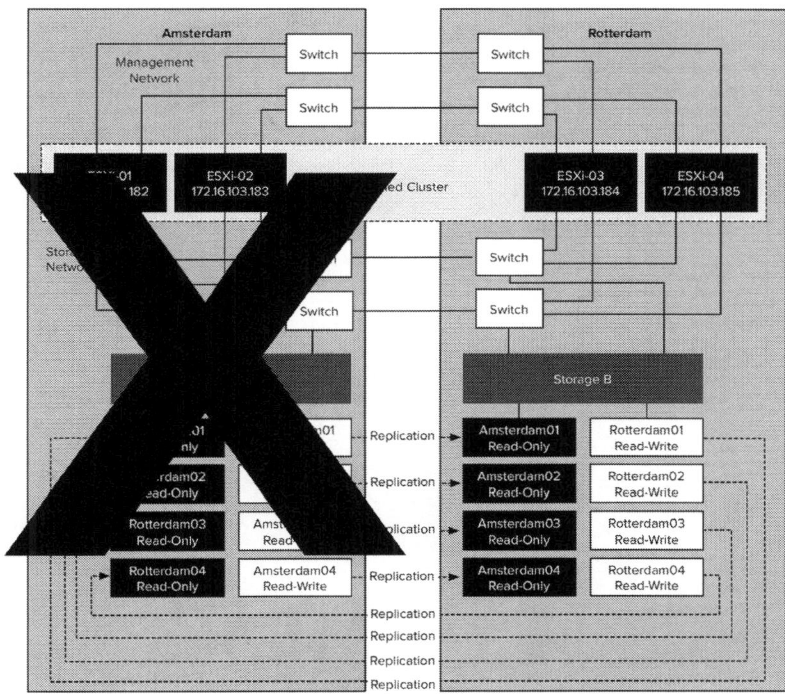

Figure 317: Full Loss of Data Center

Result

All VMs were successfully restarted in Rotterdam data center.

Explanation

In this scenario, the hosts in Rotterdam data center lost contact with the HA master and elected a new HA master. As the storage system had failed, a take over command had to be initiated on the surviving site, again due to the NetApp-specific process. After the take over command had been initiated, the new HA master accessed the per-datastore files that HA uses to record the set of protected VMs. The HA master then attempted to restart the VMs that were not running on the surviving hosts in Rotterdam data center. In our scenario, all VMs were restarted within 2 minutes after failure and were fully accessible and functional again.

> **By default, HA stops attempting to start a VM after 30 minutes. If the storage team does not issue a takeover command within that time frame, the vSphere administrator may need to manually start up VMs after the storage becomes available.**

Summary

When properly operated and architected, stretched clusters are an excellent solution to increase resiliency and offer inter-site workload mobility. There has always been, however, confusion regarding failure scenarios and the various types of responses from both the vSphere layer and the storage layer. In this white paper, we have tried to explain how HA and DRS respond to certain failures in a stretched cluster environment and to offer recommendations for configuration of a vSphere cluster in this type of environment. This paper highlights the importance of site affinity, the role played by HA and DRS Cluster rules and groups, how HA interacts with those rules and groups, and how users must ensure that the logic enforced by those rules and groups is maintained over time to provide the reliability and predictability of the cluster.

INDEX

W

17573289R00302

Printed in Great Britain
by Amazon